REGENTS/P

TOEFL® PREP BOOK

Lin Lougheed
Instructional Design International, Inc.

TOEFL® is a registered trademark of Educational Testing Service (ETS).
No affiliation between ETS and Regents/Prentice Hall is implied.

REGENTS/PRENTICE HALL
Englewood Cliffs, New Jersey 07632

Library of Congress Cataloging-in-Publishing Data

Lougheed, Lin
    Regents/Prentice Hall TOEFL prep book / Lin Lougheed.
      p.   cm.
    Rev. ed. of: Prentice-Hall TOEFL prep book, ©1986.
    ISBN 0-13-714072-X (paper)
    1. English language—Textbooks for foreign speakers. 2. English language—Examinations—Study guides. I. Lougheed, Lin, (date) Prentice-Hall TOEFL prep book. II. Title.
PE1128.L65 1992
428'.0076—dc20   92-15216
                                                          CIP

Production Editor: Shirley Hinkamp
Interior Design: Shirley Hinkamp
Cover Design: Bruce Kenselaar
Cover Artist: Slide Graphics
Prepress Buyer: Ray Keating
Manufacturing Buyer: Lori Bulwin
Scheduler: Leslie Coward

TOEFL test directions are reprinted by permission of Educational Testing Service, the copyright owner of the directions. All additional test questions (other than the sample questions provided with the directions) and other testing information are provided by Regents/Prentice Hall.

©1992 by REGENTS/PRENTICE HALL
A Division of Simon & Schuster
Englewood Cliffs, New Jersey 07632

All rights reserved. No part of this book may be
reproduced, in any form or by any means,
without permission in writing from the publisher.

Printed in the United States of America
10 9 8 7 6 5 4 3 2 1

ISBN 0-13-714072-X

Prentice-Hall International (UK) Limited, *London*
Prentice-Hall of Australia Pty. Limited, *Sydney*
Prentice-Hall Canada Inc., *Toronto*
Prentice-Hall Hispanoamericana, S.A., *Mexico*
Prentice-Hall of India Private Limited, *New Delhi*
Prentice-Hall of Japan, Inc., *Tokyo*
Simon & Schuster Asia Pte. Ltd., *Singapore*
Editora Prentice-Hall do Brasil, Ltda., *Rio de Janeiro*

CONTENTS

PREFACE v

TO THE SELF-STUDY STUDENT vii

TO THE TEACHER viii

1 REGENTS/PRENTICE HALL TOEFL PREP BOOK 1
    The TOEFL: What is it?   1
    The TOEFL: Who needs it?   2
    The TOEFL: Who takes it?   2
    TOEFL Information   3

2 PRACTICE TESTS 6
    How to Take the Practice Tests   6
    How to Score the Practice Tests   8
    Practice Test 1   10
    Practice Test 2   33
    Practice Test 3   55
    Practice Test 4   78
    Practice Test 5   100
    Practice Test 6   124

3 LISTENING TARGETS 147
    Statements   147
    Short Dialogs   158
    Mini-Talks and Dialogs   163

4 STRUCTURE AND WRITTEN EXPRESSION TARGETS 168
    Incomplete Sentence   168
    Incorrect Sentence Part   169
        Subject   170
        Verbs   174
        Subject-Verb Agreement   188
        Articles   198
        Word Order   204
        Pronouns   208
        Prepositions and Two-Three-Letter Word Verbs   214
        Subordinate Clauses   221
        Adjective Clauses   223
        Adverb Clauses   227
        Reduced Adjective Clauses   231
        Reduced Adverb Clauses   234
        Parallel Structures and Conjunctions   237
        Gerunds and Infinitives   241
        Participles   246
        Conditionals   248

Comparisons   253
Subjunctive   260
Word Families   264
Active/Passive Verbs   267
Grammar Review   273

5 VOCABULARY TARGETS   278
Vocabulary Questions   278
Synonyms   280
Common Prefixes   286
Negative Prefixes   288

6 READING TARGETS   293
Reading Questions   293
Humanities   303
History   306
Education   309
Science   313
Applied Science   316
General Readings   320

7 ESSAY TARGETS   324
Test of Written English   324
Sample Student Essays   327
Strategy-Building Activity   338
Essay Questions   341

APPENDIX   345
Practice Test Tapescripts   345
Listening Targets Tapescripts   355
Explanatory Answers   360
    Listening Targets Answer Key   373
    Structure Answer Key   375
    Vocabulary Answer Key   382
    Reading Targets Answer Key   383

ANSWER SHEETS   385

PERSONAL STUDY PLAN   409

PREFACE

The *Regents/Prentice Hall TOEFL Prep Book* is designed to help self-study students and busy teachers determine priorities in preparing for the TOEFL. There is never enough time to do a complete review of every grammar rule and vocabulary item in English. If students try to review all of English grammar and vocabulary, they will not use their time efficiently. The *Regents/Prentice Hall TOEFL Prep Book*, with its diagnostic tests and explanatory answers, helps students focus on their particular weaknesses. By studying only those areas where the students have proved weak, their study time can be made more efficient and more effective.

As students study a Target exercise, they will encounter and be able to review structures and vocabulary that are not necessarily the target of the exercise. English is not made up of isolated grammar points. When one grammar exercise is studied, other grammar points in the same exercise should be reviewed. These Target exercises (whether in Listening, Structure, or Reading) should alert the student to the interdependence of grammar items.

Every exercise in the *Regents/Prentice Hall TOEFL Prep Book* is designed to help students improve their general knowledge of English and, as a result, to improve their scores on the TOEFL.

■ TO OBTAIN THE ACCOMPANYING TAPES

IN THE UNITED STATES

The audio cassette tapes for the *Regents/Prentice Hall TOEFL Prep Book* are available from your local Regents/Prentice Hall representative, or by writing to Regents/Prentice Hall.

By mail or phone from institutional customers:
Please forward your purchase order on official letterhead and mail to:
Regents/Prentice Hall
Order Department
200 Old Tappan Road
Old Tappan, NJ 07675
1-800-223-1360

All orders from individuals must be sent to:
Regents/Prentice Hall
Mail Order Processing
200 Old Tappan Road
Old Tappan, NJ 07675

Individuals without accounts who wish to place order may call Mail Order Billing at (201) 767-5937

OUTSIDE THE UNITED STATES

Contact your nearest Prentice Hall International representative.

Canada
Please forward your purchase order, offical letterhead, and mail to:
Jerry Smith
Prentice Hall Canada
ESL/Cambridge Adult Education Division
1870 Birchmount Road
Scarborough, Ontario M1P 2J7
(416) 293-3621

Mexico, Central America & South America
Simon & Schuster International
Regents/Prentice Hall
International Customer Service Group
200 Old Tappan Road
Old Tappan, New Jersey 07675 U.S.A.
Tel: (201) 767-4990
Telex: 990348
FAX: (201) 767-5625

United Kingdom, Europe, Africa & Middle East
Norman Harris
Prentice Hall International (UK) Limited
Campus 400
Maylands Avenue
Hemel Hempstead
Herts., HP2 7EZ England
Tel: (442) 881-900
Telex: 82445
FAX: (442) 882-099

Japan
Harry Jennings
Prentice Hall of Japan
Jochi Kojimachi Bldg. 3F
1-25, Kojimachi 6-chome
Chiyoda-ku
Tokyo 102, Japan
Tel: (03) 238-1050
Telex: 650-295-8590
FAX: (03) 237-1460

For All Other Asian Orders
Karen Chiang
Simon & Schuster (Asia) Pte. Ltd.
24 Pasir Panjang Road
#04-31 PSA Multi-Storey Complex
Singapore 0511
Tel: 2789611
Telex: RS 37270
FAX: 2734400

Australia & New Zealand
Simon & Schuster (Australia) Pty. Ltd.
P.O. Box 151
7 Grosvenor Place
Brookvale, N.S.W. 2100
Australia
Tel: (02) 939-1333
Telex: PHASYD AA 74010
FAX: (02) 938-6826

TO THE SELF-STUDY STUDENT

Here is a suggested study plan if you are studying without a teacher. You will probably spend many more hours than the time suggested. The more time you spend studying, the higher your score will be. Before you begin to study, you must spend at least 45 minutes becoming acquainted with the organization of the *Regents/Prentice Hall TOEFL Prep Book* and with the organization of the TOEFL exam.

SELF-STUDY SCHEDULE

1. Survey this book to learn its organization. (15 minutes)
2. Read the introduction to the practice tests. (30 minutes)
3. Take a practice test. (120 minutes)
4. Review your answers and prepare your Personal Study Plan.
5. Read the introduction to the Listening Targets.
6. Read the introduction to the Structure Targets.
7. Read the introduction to the Vocabulary Targets.
8. Read the introduction to the Reading Targets.
9. Read the introduction to the Essay Targets.
10. Determine your available study time.
11. Study the most difficult items from your Personal Study Plan.
    For each Listening and Structure exercise, allow 20 minutes.
    For each Reading passage, allow 15 minutes.
    For each Essay exercise, allow 30 minutes.
12. After you have done about 20 Target exercises, or when you feel you are ready, take another practice test.
13. Prepare a new Personal Study Plan; repeat steps 10 through 13.

PERSONAL STUDY PLAN

The Personal Study Plan (PSP) is the record of your strengths and weaknesses in English. Each question on a practice test is keyed to a Target exercise. If you miss a test question, you are referred to the Target exercise that gives you extra practice on that particular problem.

When you finish a practice test, look at the Practice Tests Answer Key in the Appendix. The answers are coded according to the type of structure and listening questions. The code refers you to a particular Target exercise to study. These Target exercises are listed on the Personal Study Plan: Listening Targets and the Personal Study Plan: Structure Targets. If you missed a question on a practice test, note the corresponding Target on your Personal Study Plan. For example, if the explanatory answer code indicates

23. (C) Word Order: Subject-Verb,

put a circle next to the Structure Target, *Word Order: Subject-Verb,* in the appropriate Practice Test column.

STRUCTURE	1	2	3	4	5	6
Word Order: Subject-Verb	O					

You should put a circle next to every Target you missed on the practice test. When you begin to study for the TOEFL, first study those targets where you put a circle. After you have finished a particular Target exercise, put an X in the circle:

STRUCTURE	1	2	3	4	5	6
Word Order: Subject-Verb	⊗					

Then go on to the next Target.

In the Personal Study Plan, there are six columns in which to record the results of six different practice tests. After you have studied the Target exercises for a period of time, take another practice test to see how much you have improved.

ANSWER SHEETS

The *Regents/Prentice Hall TOEFL Prep Book* uses answer sheets similar to those used on the TOEFL exam. Using these answer sheets for both the practice tests and the Target exercises will help you develop the coordination necessary to move your eyes quickly from the test booklet to the proper slot on the answer sheet. The answer sheets are located at the back of the book.

■ TO THE TEACHER

The *Regents/Prentice Hall TOEFL Prep Book* contains more material than could ever be taught in an average course. This extra material will give you the flexibility to develop an appropriae TOEFL preparatory course for the special needs of your class. Here are some suggestions to assist you in preparing your lessons and to use the exercises in the book effectively.

TIME SCHEDULE

The *Regents/Prentice Hall TOEFL Prep Book* may be used in a variety of learning situations: a short four-hour workshop, an all-day session, or a 15-week course. The following timetables are guides for lesson planning. They are approximate and do not account for administrative considerations like holidays or school breaks.

Four-Hour Class

- 30 min.: Explain TOEFL question types.
- 120 min.: Administer a practice test.
- 30 min.: Correct the practice test.
- 15 min.: Discuss the use of the Personal Study Plan.
- 15 min.: Explain the self-study Vocabulary Strategies and Skills.
- 15 min.: Explain the Essay Strategies and Skills.

Eight-Hour Class

- 30 min.: Explain TOEFL question types.
- 120 min.: Administer a practice test.
- 30 min.: Correct the practice test.

30 min.: Discuss the use of the Personal Study Plan.
Compute the Class Study Plan (CSP).
50 min.: Do the top two Listening Targets from CSP.
50 min.: Do the top two Structure Targets from CSP.
50 min.: Do the Reading Targets introduction. Discuss the reading theories outlined.
30 min.: Explain how to organize an essay. Discuss the discourse styles outlined.
30 min.: Discuss the self-study Vocabulary Strategies and Skills.

Eight- to Forty-five-Hour Class

30 min.: Explain TOEFL question types.
120 min.: Administer a practice test.
30 min.: Correct practice test.
30 min.: Discuss the use of the Personal Study Plan. Compute the Class Study Plan (CSP).
60 min.: Do Reading Targets introduction. Discuss the Reading Comprehension Strategies and Skills.
30 min.: Discuss the self-study Vocabulary Strategies and Skills.

Listening Target
For every 30 minutes of available class time, do one LT exercise group. (i.e., 6 hours for Listening = 12 LT exercises)

Structure Target
For every 30 minutes of available class time, do one ST exercise group. (i.e., 6 hours for Structure = 12 ST exercises)

Reading Target
For every 30 minutes of available class time, do one RT exercise group. (i.e., 6 hours for Reading = 12 RT exercises)

Vocabulary Target
For every 15 minutes of available class time, do one VT exercise group. (i.e., 1 hour for Vocabulary = 4 VT exercises)
Review Word Notebooks.

Essay Target
For every 15 minutes of available class time, discuss one outline/essay done as homework. (i.e., 1 hour for essay discussion = 4 essays)

120 min.: Administer a practice test.
90 min.: Correct and discuss the test.

Personal Study Plan

The Personal Study Plan (PSP) is a personal record of a student's strengths and weaknesses in English. Each question on a practice test is keyed to an exercise. If a question is answered incorrectly, a student is referred to a particular exercise for extra practice. Each student should take a practice test and complete the PSP. Directions for completing the PSP are given in the Personal Study Plan section of To the Self-Study Student.

Class Study Plan

A Class Study Plan (CSP) is a compilation of the PSPs of the individual class members. To prepare a Class Study Plan, the teacher should read aloud the list of PSP items and ask the students to raise their hands if they missed that item on the practice test and marked that item on their PSP. The teacher then tabulates the class results and plans which exercises to assign for the class as a whole and which to assign as homework to individual students.

For example, the CSP for a class of 20 students may look like this:

Class Study Plan

Pronouns: Form	3
Pronouns: Agreement	0
Prepositions	10
Articles	18
Noun Clauses	15
Adjective Clauses	2

The teacher will definitely cover articles and noun clauses, which were indicated as problem areas by 18 and 15 class members, respectively. If time permits, prepositions will be covered.

Pronouns: Form and Adjective Clauses will be done individually by the students who had difficulty with those particular structures.

The Personal Study Plan is located with the answer sheets at the back of the book.

HOW TO TEACH THE LISTENING TARGETS

Overview

The Listening Target exercises are divided into discrete problem areas that the students may encounter in the answer choices (distractors) of the test questions. These might be problems with similar sounds, number discrimination, conditionals, and so forth. Each answer choice is attractive to the student in a particular way. One choice may use some of the same words from the stimulus (the oral statement, conversation, question, or mini-talk), but in a different context. Another answer choice may use words that sound similar to words used in the stimulus. Still another choice may use a negative form of the verb used in the stimulus.

The students must be made aware of the various potential types of distractors and develop strategies to deal with them. By focusing the student's attention on one specific problem area and providing exercises that, in many instances, are more difficult than the TOEFL, the Listening Targets alert the students to potential problems and help them develop appropriate strategies.

The Listening Target exercises may be more difficult than those found on the TOEFL or in the practice tests because they are more narrow in purpose. The Listening Target exercises emphasize *one* aspect of the listening process so that students may practice the parts to better understand the whole. Examples of the global approach to listening comprehension, which incorporates all parts of the Listening Target exercises, may be found in the practice tests.

In the Classroom

After the students have taken a practice test, you should do a Class Study Plan (CSP) to determine the Listening Target priorities.

One procedure that might be followed to teach the Listening Target section is illustrated below. The Listening Target Statements: Similar Sounds is used as an example. This is, of course, only one technique. There are as many techniques to teach listening as there are teachers.

Sample Lesson
Identify the Potential Distractor

1. Define the Listening Target: Similar Sounds. A minimal pair is a pair of words that are different in meaning but sound alike except for one vowel or consonant change.

Examples: bit=bat; bit=pit

Use the Answer Choices

2. Turn to the practice test, Part A, Listening Comprehension. Look at the example. Have the students examine the first four answer choices in the example and try to guess which word or words might be the focus of the statement they are to match.

    Example
    (A) He will not eat beets.
    (B) The candidate did not bet.
    (C) They thought the dates sweet.
    (D) His rival cannot beat him.

    Similar Sounds: beets   beat   bet   sweet   candidate   the date

    The students should learn to use the answer choices to *predict* the type of statement they are to match.

3. Read the first example in the practice test and discuss the problems caused by similar sounds.

4. Turn to the Listening Target Section: Similar Sounds. Have the students examine the first four answer choices in question 1 and try to guess what word or words might be the focus of the statement. Then read the question and discuss the answer.

5. Give the students 60 seconds to read the answer choices for questions 2, 3, 4, and 5. They should circle the words they feel might have similar sounds. It is important that these exercises be timed so that students get used to working under pressure.

6. After the students have read the answer choices for questions 2 through 5, read the questions to them one at a time. Allow the student 20 seconds to answer. (The TOEFL allows the student 12 seconds.)

7. When you have finished questions 2 through 5, discuss the correct answers with the class.

Encourage Development of Speed

8. Now tell your students you want them to study the answer choices and write down the potential problems in questions 6, 7, 8, 9, and 10. You will give them 10 seconds per question. At the end of 10 seconds you will say "Next!" and the students must move to the next question.

Note:

You are not testing the students in the Target sections. You are preparing the students for a test. It is more important at this stage that the students understand the target problems and have quick reactions. You may want to increase the number of seconds allowed for searching for similar sounds and increase the time allowed for answering the questions as well. The times given are only a guide. You must determine the length of time appropriate for your class.

9. Read the questions to the class, allowing 12 seconds for them to answer.

10. Discuss the answers with the class.

Put the Students On Their Own

11. Tell the students you will read a question. Give them 12 seconds to answer, then say "Next!" When you say "Next!" they will have 5 seconds to preview the next set of answer choices before you read the next question. This will train them to look ahead.

12. Read the answers and discuss the problems. Have the students compare the number of correct answers in the first section, where they had more time to think, with the number of correct answers in the last sections. Refer the students to the Listening Target Tapescripts at the end of the book for further study.

HOW TO TEACH THE STRUCTURE TARGETS

Overview

The Structure Target section was not written as a grammar course or as a complete grammar review. It provides a selected review of grammar items that have proved difficult to many students of English. It also alerts students to the problems they are likely to encounter in either the answer choices or in the stimulus. These problems are identified in the introductions to the individual structure targets.

Each Structure Target is defined using standard terminology found in most textbooks. This will help students locate grammar items easily for further review.

In the Classroom

The technique suggested below is only one of many possible ways to teach the structure section.

1. After the students have taken a practice test, do a Class Study Plan (CSP) to determine the target priorities.

2. During the first class, discuss the introductions to the Structure Target exercises being assigned. These will be the first few Structure Targets identified by the majority of the students. Point out the potential problems. Do two or three examples in class for each Structure Target and then assign the Target exercise(s) as homework.

3. During the next class, have the students pair up and compare and correct their answers. While they correct their exercises, walk around the room and note general problem areas. When the students have finished, ask them if they need any particular item explained in more detail. Discuss why something was wrong. Which of the common problems was the difficulty? What other structure items in the exercise may have caused a problem?

4. After their homework has been corrected and discussed, assign the next Structure Target exercise from the CSP and begin again as suggested in steps 2 and 3 above.

HOW TO TEACH THE VOCABULARY TARGETS

Overview

The vocabulary items included in the exercises are representative of the words found on the TOEFL.

Outside the Classroom

1. Encourage the students to read as much as possible. Discuss with them where and how they can find print materials in English. Discuss when and how often they should read. Have them keep a daily list of the articles or books they read—even if they read only a few paragraphs.

2. Encourage the students to keep a Word Notebook as suggested in the Vocabulary Target introduction. Establish a minimum number of words per day for them to study.

In the Classroom

1. Discuss the words the students have collected in their Word Notebooks. Have the students quiz one another on the words they collected. Every other week use their words as part of a vocabulary quiz.

2. Have the students tell one another about the passages they read. Have them discuss the specific areas (science, arts, humanities, etc.) that they read about. This will turn their passive vocabulary into an active one.

3. Discuss contextual clues. Choose a reading passage and have them scan the passage and circle all noun markers or other contextual clue markers. Have them compare their passages with one another. Then have them scan the passage again and circle all verb markers. Once more, ask them to scan the same passage or another passage, circling adjective and adverb markers. Each time they finish scanning a passage, have them compare their findings with their classmates.

4. In discussing adjective and adverb markers, refer the students to the Structure Target section on adverbs and adjectives.

5. To illustrate the prefix clues, write a prefix (or a root) on the board. Have the students use the prefix or root and try to provide a new vocabulary word from their notebooks.

6. Show them how to use the dictionary to find a root and a prefix. Have them do some dictionary work at home by researching word roots.

Vocabulary Exercises

7. The students should do the vocabulary exercises at home on their own time and at their own pace. Have them circle every word they do not know and add it to their Word Notebook or flash cards. You need not spend class time discussing the answers since the students should be able to look up the answers in the answer key and find further clarification in a dictionary.

HOW TO TEACH THE READING TARGETS

Overview

The Reading Targets explain the types of reading comprehension questions found on the TOEFL. The students will get practice with the TOEFL format and will learn the skills necessary to be a good reader. Then they must read, read, and read some more.

Outside the Classroom

1. Tell the students that reading is a very private activity; they can improve only by reading, reading some more, and then reading even more.

2. The students must develop a conscientious reading plan. Have the students keep a record of *when* and *why* they read. Have them notice what they read (magazines versus texts) and when they read most frequently. They should set aside definite times (after lunch, before dinner, before bed) to read, even if only for five to ten minutes per session.

3. They should try to use SQ3R every time they read. (SQ3R is a reading technique that is summarized below and explained in detail in the Reading Target introduction.) The students should never read anything without first trying to guess *who? what? when? where?* and *why?*

In the Classroom

1. You can help your students read more efficiently by using the following techniques.

    A. **SQ3R**
    Survey: Have the students survey the *Regents/Prentice Hall TOEFL Prep Book*, a newspaper, or a textbook and let them try to form the five *wh* questions: *who? what? when? where?* and *why?*

Questions: The five *wh* questions are only a begining. Teach the students to develop their own questions about a passage. The more personally involved in a reading passage they become, the more they will learn from it.

    B. **Skimming and Scanning**

Have the students skim for the general idea; have them scan for specific details. These specific details could include various contextual markers, such as transition words. Point out how these transition words might change the meaning of a reading passage and thereby influence the answer choice.

    C. **Speed Reading**

Most people have lazy eyes; you must train the students' eyes and minds to move faster. To train the students to move their eyes quickly, give them 5 minutes to skim a passage; then give them another 2 minutes to skim the same passage from the beginning; finally, give them only 1 minute to skim the same passage. This technique will not be easy for them; they will try to read every word. Pushing them faster forces them to read in phrases and groups of words. Another speed technique is to give the students 1 minute to read as far as they can. After 1 minute, say "Stop!" Have them put their fingers on the words they were reading when you said "Stop!" Then tell them to start again at the beginning and give them 1 minute to see if they can read beyond where they stopped previously. Again, say "Stop!" after 1 minute and ask them to put their fingers on the words they were reading when you told them to stop.

Do the drill one more time. They will see how they can read faster and faster and, since they are reading the same passage, understand more of what they read. They will discover that it may be better for them to read the passage several times in 2 minutes than only once in 2 minutes.

2. Analyze the comprehension questions. What kind of information do the questions that follow the reading passage want from the students?

    an inference?   a specific detail?
    an opinion?   the main idea?
    a definition?   a general piece of information?

The reading test items are coded in the Practice Test Answer Keys according to what the question required the student to do. However, there is no Personal Study Plan (PSP) for the Reading Target section. The target areas (facts, inferences, main idea, and definitions) are specific enough that a student can learn to recognize these questions by carefully studying the examples in the practice tests and by doing the additional readings in the Reading Targets section.

3. Guess at the answers. Occasionally, let the students try to answer the questions *before* they read the passage. Then let them read the passage and correct their guesses.

4. Vary your teaching activities. Each hour, you might do three passages focusing on a particular skill. Here are some examples:

    A. In one passage, help the students identify referents. Have them scan the passage and circle all pronouns. Then have them, in pairs, identify the referents for the pronouns.

    B. In one passage, help the students identify the discourse markers they find. Have them compare their results with a classmate and then with the whole class.

    C. In one passage, have the students scan and circle all transition markers. As a class, have them discuss the particular markers and the kinds of transitions they found.

HOW TO TEACH THE ESSAY TARGETS

Overview

The Essay Target section should be studied by those students taking the Test of Written English (TWE). There are no essay exams on the practice tests in the *Regents/Prentice Hall TOEFL Prep Book*. The students should use the essay questions in the Essay Targets section for practice.

The Essay Target exercises stress the importance of organization. Students should be encouraged to develop their own styles of introduction and conclusions but within the accepted rhetorical framework of American English.

Outside the Classroom

There is no need for the students to take precious class time to compose a 250- to 300-word essay. This work should be done at home. Homework should consist of using the Reading Target passages to practice outlining and using the Essay Target exercises to write their essays.

The students should be encouraged to edit their own essays and those of their classmates. This can also be done at home. The teacher should read only one of every four essays a student writes (depending on available class time and teacher preparation time).

In the Classroom

1. Explain the format of the Essay Targets section.
2. Discuss the structure of an essay.
3. Discuss the linear style of essay organization.
4. Explain the organization of a paragraph.
5. Discuss the four rhetorical styles.
6. Develop sentences using the vocabulary of the four styles.
7. Explain the outline.
8. Outline a reading passage with the class.
9. Discuss the concept of general statements and facts.
10. Locate general and specific statements in the reading passages.
11. Assign Reading Target passages to be outlined every night.
12. Discuss in class the first few outlines done as homework.
13. Assign one essay to be written every two days.
14. Discuss in class the first few essays done as homework.

1

REGENTS/PRENTICE HALL TOEFL PREP BOOK

■ THE TOEFL: WHAT IS IT?

The TOEFL, the Test of English as a Foreign Language, measures the English proficiency of non-native English speakers. It tests their ability to understand spoken English, recognize correct grammatical constructions, identify synonyms, and comprehend reading passages.

The test is divided into three sections. Each section is timed. The chart below gives a general outline of the exam. The exact format of the exam may vary; the number of questions and the time given occasionally differ from test to test. The TOEFL uses several different forms, some of which may include 50 experimental questions. These questions look like the other test questions but will not be counted in your score. The experimental questions and the time allotted for them are in parentheses in the chart.

Section	Questions	Minutes
Section One **Listening Comprehension** Part A: Short Statements Part B: Short Conversations Part C: Mini-Talks	50 20 15 15	40
Section Two **Structure and Written Expression** Part A: Choose a correct word or phrase Part B: Identify an incorrect word or phrase	40 (60) 15 25	25 (35)
Section Three **Vocabulary and Reading Comprehension** Part A: Synonyms Part B: Reading Comprehension	60 (90) 30 30	45 (65)
Section Four Essay	1	30
Total	150 (200) + Essay	140 (170)

THE TOEFL: WHO NEEDS IT?

Most American colleges and universities require evidence of a student's English language proficiency for admission. The TOEFL is one of the tests given for this purpose. The TOEFL, however, is only one of the criteria for admission. A satisfactory score on the TOEFL does not guarantee admission to a university.

The following chart is a guide to admission requirements at various educational institutions. It is only a guide. Admission requirements vary from institution to institution and from year to year.

Admissions Policy	Graduate Humanities	Graduate Sciences	Undergraduate	Technical School or 2-year College
Acceptable	550–600	500–600	500–600	450–600
Acceptable, with supplementary language training and reduced course load	500–550	450–500	400–500	400–450
Further English training required	Below 500	Below 450	Below 400	Below 400

THE TOEFL: WHO TAKES IT?

Different language groups score differently on the TOEFL. You should recognize those areas that have statistically proved difficult for others in your language group and then focus on these areas during your preparation.

Source: Information is based on data from the TOEFL Test and Score Manual, 1987-88 Edition. Princeton, New Jersey: Educational Testing Service, p. 24.

TOEFL INFORMATION

TOEFL BULLETIN

All candidates for the TOEFL will need the *TOEFL Bulletin of Information and Application Form*. This bulletin lists the TOEFL test centers around the world, provides information regarding the cost of the TOEFL, and includes an application form.

To receive a copy of the *Bulletin* outside the United States, contact the Cultural Affairs Officer of the local U.S. Information Service or an AMIDEAST or IIE regional office. You may also write directly to the TOEFL office:

TOEFL
P.O. Box 6151
Princeton, NJ 08541-6151
U.S.A.

Letter of Request

The letter you write may be similar to this:

Dear TOEFL Administrators:

Please send the latest edition of the *TOEFL Bulletin of Information and Application Form* to:

Print your name
Print your street address
Print your city, state/province
Print your postal code
Print your country

Sincerely,

Sign your name

TEST CENTERS

International, Special Center, and Institutional TOEFL

The International TOEFL and Special Center TOEFL are identical in question format, length and difficulty. New exams are given on each test date.

Test	Frequency/yr	Countries	Day
International TOEFL	6 times/yr	135	Saturday
Special Center TOEFL	6 times/yr	50	Friday

The Institutional TOEFL is used by local institutions and businesses to measure their students' language proficiency. The exam is scheduled at the convenience of the testing institution. Old exams are used for the Institutional TOEFL; consequently, the scores are not considered valid by university admissions officers.

REGISTRATION

International and Special Center TOEFL

You should complete the application in the *TOEFL Bulletin of Information and Application Form*. After the Educational Testing Service (ETS) receives your completed application and money, it will process a Confirmation Ticket for you. You will receive this Confirmation Ticket approximately one month before the test date.

Institutional TOEFL

Registration for the Institutional TOEFL is handled by the particular institutions administering these tests. You should contact them for more information.

SCORES

Current TOEFL Scores

On the day of the exam, you will be asked to list on your answer sheet four institutions, colleges, or universities that you wish to receive your scores. The institutions, colleges, or universities that you designate will receive the scores approximately one month after the test date. You also will receive your score approximately one month after you take the test.

If you listed fewer than four institutions, the remaining score reports will be sent to you. You may send them yourself to other colleges; however, the college may require an official score report received directly from ETS in Princeton.

Previous TOEFL Scores

The TOEFL scores are kept for only two years. If you took the test more than two years ago, you will have to take the TOEFL again to receive a new score.

If you took the test more than once, it is possible to have only your highest score sent to the institution or college. You will have to complete the *Request Form for Official Score Reports* and note the test date on which you scored higher.

GENERAL TEST-TAKING STRATEGIES

Before the Test

- Take a practice test in this book.
- Prepare your Personal Study Plan (PSP).
- Study the Targets indicated on your PSP.
- Read as much English as you can.
- Listen to as much English as you can.
- Relax the day before the exam.

On the Day of the Test

- Arrive on time.
- Bring only:
  (a) 3 or 4 No. 2 pencils with erasers
  (b) your Confirmation Ticket from ETS
  (c) your passport or photo identification
  (d) a watch
- Sit near the speakers.
- Make sure you are comfortable and can hear well.

During the Test

- Work rapidly but carefully.
- Do NOT read the directions.
- Read all choices carefully.
- Answer all the questions on your answer sheet. Do not leave blanks.
- Guess: if you have no idea which choice is correct, choose A (or your favorite letter). Leave no question unanswered.
- Keep your mind and eyes on your own test.
- Check to make sure that you have answered every question.
- Match the question number with the number on the answer sheet.
- Do the questions that seem easy first.
- Do NOT go back to previous sections.

GUESSING

There is no penalty for guessing. If you don't know an answer, make a guess. If you guess, it is better statistically always to guess using the same letter (always A, always B, always C, or always D—choose your favorite).

THE ANSWER SHEET

Your answer sheet is divided into columns with numbers followed by letters enclosed in ovals.

Sample Answer
Ⓐ Ⓑ Ⓒ Ⓓ

Each number stands for one question. There is only one answer per question. To mark an answer, completely fill in the corresponding oval. A soft lead (no. 2) pencil is best.

The day after Monday is

(A) Wednesday
(B) Sunday
(C) Tuesday
(D) Thursday

Sample Answer
Ⓐ Ⓑ ● Ⓓ

DO NOT mark two answers. Both will be counted wrong.

Sample Answer
● ● Ⓒ Ⓓ

A mark like this will NOT be counted.

This one →
Ⓐ ● ⊗ Ⓓ

DO NOT make any pencil marks elsewhere on the page. YOU MAY erase, but do it *completely*.

DO NOT DRAW arrows or make other marks. The test is scored by a machine that cannot read your messages. If it reads more than one answer per question, it marks the answers wrong.

Regents/Prentice Hall TOEFL Prep Book 5

2

PRACTICE TESTS

■ HOW TO TAKE THE PRACTICE TESTS

The practice tests, when used with the Personal Study Plan, will give you an idea of your strengths and weaknesses in English. The results of the practice tests will guide you in studying for the TOEFL. Before you begin to study any of the Target exercises in this book, you should take a practice test. Take the test as if you were taking the real TOEFL. Find a room where you will be undisturbed and allow yourself three hours to take the exam.

The answer sheets for the practice tests are found in the back of the book. You should tear one out before you begin. Mark the answers on the answer sheet just as if you were taking the TOEFL.

You will need the tapes that accompany the Prentice Hall *TOEFL Prep Book* and a tape recorder to do the listening comprehension sections. If you do not have the tapes or a tape recorder, the tapescripts are in the back of the book. You can have someone read the tapescripts to you.

PERSONAL STUDY PLAN

When you finish a practice test, look at the Practice Test Explanatory Answer Key in the Appendix. The answers are coded according to the type of structure and listening questions being tested. The code refers you to a particular Target exercise to study. These Target exercises are listed on the Personal Study Plan: Listening Targets and the Personal Study Plan: Structure Targets. If you missed a question on a practice test, note the corresponding Target on your Personal Study Plan. For example, if the explanatory answer code says

        23. (C) Word order: subject/verb

you should put a circle next to the Structure Target, Word order: subject/verb, in the appropriate practice test column.

PRACTICE TESTS

Structure	1	2	3	4	5	6
Word order: subject/verb	O					

You should put a circle next to every Target you missed on the practice test. When you begin to study for the TOEFL, you should first study those Targets where you put a circle. This will make your study time more efficient.

After you have finished a particular Target exercise, put an X in the circle and go on to the next Target.

PRACTICE TESTS

Structure	1	2	3	4	5	6
Word order: subject/verb	⊗					

In the Personal Study Plan, there are six columns to record the results of six different practice tests. After you study the Target exercises for a period of time, take another practice test to see how much you have improved.

HOW TO SCORE THE PRACTICE TESTS

After you finish a practice test, you can tally your scores on each section. The chart below will help you determine your approximate total score. Add the three sections together and divide by 3 for your total score.

Number Correct	Score Section 1 *Listening Comprehension*	Score Section 2 *Structure and Written Expression*	Score Section 3 *Vocabulary and Reading Comprehension*
0	200	200	200
1	220	210	210
2	250	230	220
3	270	240	230
4	280	250	240
5	290	260	240
6	300	280	250
7	310	300	260
8	320	310	260
9	330	330	270
10	350	340	280
11	360	340	290
12	370	350	300
13	380	360	310
14	390	370	320
15	400	380	330
16	410	390	340
17	420	400	350
18	420	410	360
19	430	420	370
20	430	430	380
21	440	440	390
22	450	450	400
23	450	460	400
24	460	470	410
25	470	480	420
26	470	490	430
27	480	500	430
28	480	510	440
29	490	520	450
30	490	530	450
31	500	540	460
32	510	560	470
33	510	570	470
34	520	580	480
35	530	590	480
36	530	610	490
37	540	630	500
38	550	640	500

Number Correct	Score Section 1 *Listening Comprehension*	Score Section 2 *Structure and Written Expression*	Score Section 3 *Vocabulary and Reading Comprehension*
39	560	650	510
40	570	680	520
41	570	—	520
42	580	—	530
43	590	—	540
44	600	—	540
45	610	—	550
46	620	—	560
47	630	—	560
48	640	—	570
49	660	—	580
50	680	—	580
51	—	—	590
52	—	—	600
53	—	—	610
54	—	—	610
55	—	—	620
56	—	—	630
57	—	—	640
58	—	—	650
59	—	—	660
60	—	—	670

Practice Test	Score Section 1	Score Section 2	Score Section 3	Total Score	÷3	Approximate Score
1					÷3	
2					÷3	
3					÷3	
4					÷3	
5					÷3	
6					÷3	

PRACTICE TEST 1

SECTION 1

LISTENING COMPREHENSION

The questions in Section 1 of the test are on a recording.

In this section of the test, you will have an opportunity to demonstrate your ability to understand spoken English. There are three parts to this section, with special directions for each part.

Part A

Directions: For each question in Part A, you will hear a short sentence. Each sentence will be spoken just one time. The sentences you hear will not be written out for you. Therefore, you must listen carefully to understand what the speaker says.

After you hear a sentence, read the four choices in your test book, marked (A), (B), (C), and (D), and decide which *one* is closest in meaning to the sentence you heard. Then, on your answer sheet, find the number of the question and fill in the space that matches the letter of the answer you have chosen. Fill in the space so that the letter inside the oval cannot be seen.

Example I
    You will hear: *Mary swam out to the island with her friends.*
    You will read: (A) Mary outswam the others.
                       (B) Mary ought to swim with them.
                       (C) Mary and her friends swam to the island.
                       (D) Mary's friends owned the island.

Sample Answer
Ⓐ Ⓑ ● Ⓓ

The speaker said, "Mary swam out to the island with her friends." Sentence (C), "Mary and her friends swam to the island," is closest in meaning to the sentence you heard. Therefore, you should choose answer (C).

Example II
    You will hear: *Would you mind helping me with this load of books?*
    You will read: (A) Please remind me to read this book.
                       (B) Could you help me carry these books?
                       (C) I don't mind if you help me.
                     (D) Do you have a heavy course load this term?

Sample Answer
Ⓐ ● Ⓒ Ⓓ

The speaker said, "Would you mind helping me with this load of books?" Sentence (B), "Could you help me carry these books?" is closest in meaning to the sentence you heard. Therefore, you should choose answer (B).

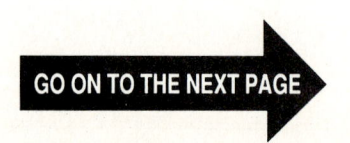

GO ON TO THE NEXT PAGE ➤

1 • 1 • 1 • 1 • 1 • 1 • 1

1. (A) Joan will take a plane.
   (B) Joan's father will drive.
   (C) Joan and I will come by car.
   (D) Joan likes to drive.

2. (A) Walking is the best exercise.
   (B) Walking is not as good an exercise as swimming.
   (C) Swimming is good for you.
   (D) Swimming and walking are both good exercises.

3. (A) Don't stand in the sun.
   (B) Put your hands in the air now.
   (C) Let me know if you want an explanation.
   (D) You never understand anything.

4. (A) It may rain this morning.
   (B) The local weather is always the same.
   (C) The news comes before the weather report.
   (D) I never follow the weather report.

5. (A) Someone is following Margaret.
   (B) Margaret gives easy directions.
   (C) Only Margaret can follow directions.
   (D) People should follow Margaret.

6. (A) The two of us went to the movies.
   (B) Mary saw one movie after the other.
   (C) Both movies started at noon.
   (D) Mary wanted to go to the movies on Tuesday.

7. (A) Mark got off first.
   (B) Mark took the last bus.
   (C) Everyone got off before Mark.
   (D) Mark missed the last bus.

8. (A) You shouldn't do so much work.
   (B) There is too much work for you.
   (C) You usually don't do so much.
   (D) There's not enough work to do.

9. (A) Are you free to have lunch together soon?
   (B) Why don't you eat lunch every day?
   (C) Why do we always have lunch at the same place?
   (D) Are we having lunch today?

10. (A) Our friends moved to the city recently.
    (B) We moved to be closer to our friends.
    (C) We developed new friendships when we moved.
    (D) We moved to the city with our friends.

11. (A) We did not wait inside.
    (B) If it were warmer, I'd stay outside.
    (C) It was too hot to wait outside.
    (D) We waited for warmer weather.

12. (A) Buy me some stamps if you go near the post office.
    (B) You bought some stamps at the post office.
    (C) I'll buy some stamps at the post office.
    (D) I passed the post office this morning.

13. (A) I won't be late tomorrow.
    (B) I won't be on time tomorrow.
    (C) I won't eat until tomorrow.
    (D) I'm sorry I can't be there tomorrow.

14. (A) The gym is above the Athletic Office.
    (B) Jim signed up in the locker room.
    (C) To get to the Athletic Office, you have to go upstairs.
    (D) You must apply for a locker in the Athletic Office.

GO ON TO THE NEXT PAGE ➤

Practice Tests 11

15. (A) Are you learning to play any music?
    (B) Do you like classical music better than rock?
    (C) Do you listen to rock music?
    (D) Are you taking a music class this semester?

16. (A) The afternoon mail has already come.
    (B) The letter will arrive on Monday if it's mailed today.
    (C) They should receive your letters this afternoon.
    (D) You shouldn't mail the letter until next Monday.

17. (A) The library closes at 6:00 this evening and is not open tomorrow.
    (B) The library is closed tonight.
    (C) Tomorrow the library closes at 6:00.
    (D) The library closes at 6:00 tonight and tomorrow.

18. (A) The room is very bright.
    (B) Please turn on another lamp.
    (C) The light is better in the other room.
    (D) The other light is much better.

19. (A) The class started before I arrived.
    (B) I didn't do the experiment.
    (C) It was difficult to follow the directions.
    (D) Don't start the experiment without reading the directions.

20. (A) I always read on the weekends.
    (B) I finished the book last week.
    (C) I have to read all of the book by Saturday.
    (D) I'll make a bookcase this weekend.

GO ON TO THE NEXT PAGE

Part B

Directions: In Part B you will hear short conversations between two speakers. At the end of each conversation, a third person will ask a question about what was said. You will hear each conversation and question about it just one time. The sentences you hear will not be written out for you. Therefore, you must listen carefully to understand what each speaker says. After you hear a conversation and the question about it, read the four possible answers in your test book and decide which *one* is the best answer to the question you heard. Then, on your answer sheet, find the number of the question and fill in the space that corresponds to the letter of the answer you have chosen.

Example
   You will hear:
      (first man) *Professor Smith is going to retire soon. What kind of gift shall we give her?*
      (woman) *I think she'd like to have a photograph of our class.*
      (second man) *What does the woman think the class should do?*
   You will read: (A) Present Professor Smith with a picture.
                   (B) Photograph Professor Smith.
                   (C) Put glass over the photograph.
                   (D) Replace the broken headlight.

Sample Answer
● Ⓑ Ⓒ Ⓓ

From the conversation you learn that the woman thinks Professor Smith would like a photograph of the class. The best answer to the question "What does the woman think the class should do?" is (A), "Present Professor Smith with a picture." Therefore, you should choose answer (A).

21. (A) At a police station.
    (B) At a military post.
    (C) At an employment agency.
    (D) At a bank.

22. (A) She missed her appointment.
    (B) She's sick.
    (C) She's a busy doctor.
    (D) She's cold.

23. (A) At a movie theater.
    (B) At a bus stop.
    (C) In a train station.
    (D) On a football field.

24. (A) Go shopping.
    (B) Brew tea.
    (C) Make a cake.
    (D) Serve coffee.

25. (A) Once a week.
    (B) Twice a week.
    (C) Three times a week.
    (D) Every day.

26. (A) Phone later.
    (B) Try harder.
    (C) Get busy.
    (D) Look up the number again.

27. (A) Go to a movie.
    (B) Go home.
    (C) Eat dinner.
    (D) Meet their friends.

28. (A) He can't eat in the restaurant.
    (B) He can't smoke.
    (C) He's in the wrong restaurant.
    (D) He doesn't like people who smoke.

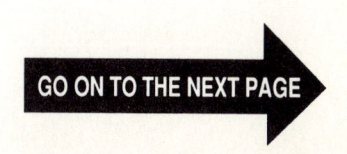

GO ON TO THE NEXT PAGE

29. (A) He's afraid of flying.
    (B) He's nervous.
    (C) He wants more coffee.
    (D) He lost his watch.

30. (A) The man doesn't know how to read.
    (B) He can't see without his glasses.
    (C) He lost his vision.
    (D) He forgot his car.

31. (A) Start school.
    (B) Park her car.
    (C) Go to the park.
    (D) Open an office.

32. (A) Stop working.
    (B) Buy new tires.
    (C) Fix the door.
    (D) Take a walk.

33. (A) At a supermarket.
    (B) At a power plant.
    (C) At a gas station.
    (D) At a tennis match.

34. (A) She can't come to lunch tomorrow.
    (B) She has to take a train.
    (C) She doesn't join clubs.
    (D) She'd like to meet his friend.

35. (A) In a restaurant.
    (B) At a library.
    (C) At a hotel.
    (D) In a classroom.

GO ON TO THE NEXT PAGE

Part C

Directions: In this part of the test, you will hear several short talks and conversations. After each of them, you will be asked some questions. You will hear the talks and conversations and the questions about them just one time. They will not be written out for you. Therefore, you must listen carefully in order to understand what each speaker says.

After you hear a question, read the four possible answers in your test book and decide which *one* is the best answer to the question you heard. Then, on your answer sheet, find the number of the question and fill in the space that corresponds to the letter of the answer you have chosen.

Answer all questions on the basis of what is *stated* or *implied* in the talk or conversation.

Listen to this sample talk.
   You will hear:
      (first man) *Balloons have been used for about a hundred years. There are two kinds of sport balloons, gas and hot air. Hot-air balloons are safer than gas balloons, which may catch fire. Hot-air balloons are preferred by most balloonists in the United States because of their safety. They are also cheaper and easier to manage than gas balloons. Despite the ease of operating a balloon, pilots must watch the weather carefully. Sport balloon flights are best early in the morning or late in the afternoon, when the wind is light.*

Sample Answer
Ⓐ ● Ⓒ Ⓓ

Now look at the following example.
   You will hear:
      (second man) *Why are gas balloons considered dangerous?*
   You will read: (A) They are impossible to guide.
                   (B) They may go up in flames.
                   (C) They tend to leak gas.
                   (D) They are cheaply made.

The best answer to the question "Why are gas balloons considered dangerous?" is (B). "They may go up in flames." Therefore, you should choose answer (B).

Sample Answer
● Ⓑ Ⓒ Ⓓ

Now look at the next example.
   You will hear:
      (second man) *According to the speaker, what must balloon pilots be careful to do?*
   You will read: (A) Watch for changes in weather.
                   (B) Watch their altitude.
                   (C) Check for weak spots in their balloons.
                   (D) Test the strength of the ropes.

The best answer to the question "According to the speaker, what must balloon pilots be careful to do?" is (A), "Watch for changes in weather." Therefore, you should choose answer (A).

GO ON TO THE NEXT PAGE ➡

36. (A) Dreams.
    (B) Scientific investigations.
    (C) Happiness.
    (D) Crowds.

37. (A) Only since this year.
    (B) At the turn of the century.
    (C) Since a long time ago.
    (D) Within the last ten years.

38. (A) One.
    (B) Four.
    (C) Five.
    (D) Six.

39. (A) Relaxed.
    (B) Resting.
    (C) Rapid.
    (D) Romantic.

40. (A) Dreams.
    (B) Wakefulness.
    (C) Friendship.
    (D) Loneliness.

41. (A) Frustration.
    (B) Happiness.
    (C) Anger.
    (D) Restfulness.

42. (A) Whether or not the girl will become deaf.
    (B) How loudly her daughter plays the music.
    (C) That high noise levels are harmful to them.
    (D) That she's talking too loud.

43. (A) One.
    (B) Two.
    (C) One hundred.
    (D) One hundred thirty.

44. (A) People in their 20s.
    (B) Senior citizens.
    (C) Airline pilots.
    (D) Music librarians.

45. (A) 95.
    (B) 130.
    (C) 150.
    (D) 200.

46. (A) The first week of class.
    (B) The end of the semester.
    (C) During the first exam.
    (D) The middle of the term.

47. (A) Home economics.
    (B) Anthropology.
    (C) Social welfare.
    (D) Archaeology.

48. (A) They are thrifty.
    (B) They are wasteful.
    (C) They are quality-oriented.
    (D) They are usually poor.

49. (A) Choice cuts of meat.
    (B) Educational toys.
    (C) Low-quality produce.
    (D) Expensive kitchen materials.

50. (A) To gather information from it.
    (B) To clean up their neighborhoods.
    (C) To become better consumers.
    (D) To avoid poor eating habits.

THIS IS THE END OF THE LISTENING COMPREHENSION SECTION OF THE TEST

THE NEXT PART OF THE TEST IS SECTION 2. TURN TO THE DIRECTIONS FOR SECTION 2 IN YOUR TEST BOOK. READ THEM, AND BEGIN WORK. DO NOT READ OR WORK ON ANY OTHER SECTION OF THE TEST.

SECTION 2
STRUCTURE AND WRITTEN EXPRESSION

Time: 25 minutes

This section tests your ability to recognize language that is appropriate for standard written English. There are two types of questions in this section, with special directions for each type.

Directions: Questions 1–15 are incomplete sentences. Beneath each sentence you will see four words or phrases, marked (A), (B), (C), and (D). Choose the *one* word or phrase that best completes the sentence. Then, on your answer sheet, find the number of the question and fill in the space that corresponds to the letter of the answer you have chosen. Fill in the space so that the letter inside the oval cannot be seen.

Example I

Vegetables are an excellent source _____ vitamins.
(A) of
(B) has
(C) where
(D) that

Sample Answer
● Ⓑ Ⓒ Ⓓ

The sentence should read, "Vegetables are an excellent source of vitamins." Therefore, you should choose answer (A).

Example II

_____ in history when remarkable progress was made within a relatively short span of time.
(A) Periods
(B) Throughout periods
(C) There have been periods
(D) Periods have been

Sample Answer
Ⓐ Ⓑ ● Ⓓ

The sentence should read, "There have been periods in history when remarkable progress was made within a relatively short span of time." Therefore, you should choose answer (C).

Now begin work on the questions.

1. _____, the world's economic leaders have been the dominant political and military powers.
   (A) Traditional
   (B) Traditionally
   (C) The tradition
   (D) A tradition

2. Corporations of the future will be _____ those that flourished in recent years.
   (A) differ from
   (B) different from
   (C) different
   (D) difference

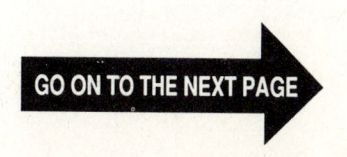

GO ON TO THE NEXT PAGE

3. Occupations in _____ current participants have the most education are projected to have the most rapid growth rate.
   (A) that
   (B) which
   (C) who
   (D) these

4. Because counterfeit products are often of substandard quality, _____ a potential for safety risks.
   (A) there are
   (B) it is
   (C) they are
   (D) there is

5. The worldwide warming of _____ threatens to raise the earth's average temperature by 1.5–4.5 degrees Celsius by the year 2050.
   (A) atmosphere
   (B) an atmosphere
   (C) the atmosphere
   (D) any atmosphere

6. Over a billion people live in countries that are already _____ firewood shortages.
   (A) experienced
   (B) experiencing
   (C) experience
   (D) have experienced

7. As society grows increasingly dependent on technology, computer skills are not just desirable, _____ essential.
   (A) and
   (B) but
   (C) for
   (D) not

8. At the turn of the century, scientists wondered whether the atoms of chemical elements were _____ of smaller particles.
   (A) been composed
   (B) composing
   (C) to compose
   (D) composed

9. The Census Bureau for years used the completion of the fourth grade as _____ standard of literacy.
   (A) its
   (B) it's
   (C) their
   (D) there is

10. For every ton of grain _____, American farmers were losing six tons of their top soil.
    (A) they produced
    (B) which produced
    (C) that were producing
    (D) they are producing

11. From about 1910–1930, most physicists believed _____ atomic energy would be of no practical value.
    (A) in
    (B) that
    (C) for
    (D) which

12. Over 2,100 valley residents and visitors lost _____ lives in the Johnstown Flood.
    (A) their
    (B) they're
    (C) there
    (D) themselves

13. If our future is to be environmentally and _____ sustainable, many adjustments will have to be made.
    (A) economic
    (B) economy
    (C) economically
    (D) economical

GO ON TO THE NEXT PAGE

18 Practice Tests

2 • 2 • 2 • 2 • 2 • 2 • 2

14. The first zoological garden in the United States _____ in Philadelphia in 1874.
    (A) was establishing
    (B) being established
    (C) establishing
    (D) was established

15. Jet lag is more pronounced in older adults _____ motion sickness is a problem for the young.
    (A) for
    (B) or
    (C) by
    (D) while

Directions: In questions 16–40, each sentence has four underlined words or phrases. The four underlined parts of the sentence are marked (A), (B), (C), and (D). Identify the *one* underlined word or phrase that must be changed in order for the sentence to be correct. Then, on your answer sheet, find the number of the question and fill in the space that corresponds to the letter of the answer you have chosen.

Example I

A ray of light passing <u>through</u> <u>the center</u> of a thin lens <u>keep</u> its
                       A   B   C

<u>original</u> direction.
   D

Sample Answer
Ⓐ Ⓑ ● Ⓓ

The sentence should read, "A ray of light passing through the center of a thin lens keeps its original direction." Therefore, you should choose answer (C).

Example II

The mandolin, a musical <u>instrument</u> <u>that has</u> strings, was proba-
                            A   B

bly copied <u>from</u> the lute, a <u>many</u> older instrument.
          C   D

Sample Answer
Ⓐ Ⓑ Ⓒ ●

The sentence should read, "The mandolin, a musical instrument that has strings, was probably copied from the lute, a much older instrument." Therefore, you should choose answer (D).

Now begin work on the questions.

16. <u>A</u> writer of biographies <u>are</u> heavily influenced <u>by</u> the <u>dominant</u> literary theory.
     A   B   C   D

17. Birds have a <u>relatively</u> large brain, keen sight, and acute <u>hearing</u>, but <u>they</u> little <u>sense of</u>
                A   B   C   D

    smell.

18. Bonds, which were <u>sold</u> by the U.S. government <u>to finance</u> both world wars, <u>and are still</u>
                        A   B   C

    an important money-<u>raising</u> device.
                              D

GO ON TO THE NEXT PAGE ➡

19. Unlikely sound, light can travel through a vacuum.
        A   B   C   D

20. Vegetarians who drinking no alcohol and do not smoke live longer than the
                 A B   C   D

    general population.

21. Consumer protection groups like the Consumer Guardian checks the safety and reliability
        A   B   C   D

    of products and services.

22. Citizens can become affiliated with a political party by check the appropriate box when
                 A   B

    they register to vote.
      C   D

23. The psychologist B.F. Skinner is know for his studies of conditions that affect the learning
      A   B   C   D

    of behavior.

24. Scientists have proof that groups of songbirds have its own distinct dialects.
        A   B   C D

25. The growing number of old people in America means there is a need growing for service
                                            A   B   C

    workers in the health care field.
         D

26. Conditions like being too fat or too thinner are both associated with increased health risks.
        A   B   C   D

27. Socialist governments provide many social welfare programs such as healthy care and aid
      A   B   C

    to the poor.
     D

28. Cells can exist independently of other cells and which are capable of reproducing
          A   B   C

    themselves.
      D

GO ON TO THE NEXT PAGE

20 Practice Tests

29. Leaves that seemingly turn yellow or orange in autumn has actually contained that color
    　　　　A　　　　　　　　　　　　　　　　　　　　　B　　　　　　C

    throughout the summer.
    　　　　　　D

30. Most small mammals live only two or three years, while an elephant may life for as long
    　　　　　　　　　　　　　　　A　　　　　　　B　　　　　　　　　　　C　D

    as sixty years.

31. Recent experiments conducted on laboratory animals have shown that exposing to ozone
    　　　　　　　　　A　　　　　　　　　　　　　　　B　　　　　　C

    gas in great quantities may cause cancer.
    　　　D

32. When hot and cold water they are mixed together, the hot water will give up heat to the
    　　　　　　　　　A　　　B　　　　　　　　　　　　　　　　　C　　　　D

    cold water.

33. The Amazon River flows largely through the sparsely inhabited jungles of Brazil on their
    　　　　　　　　　A　　　　　　　　　　　　　　　　　　　　　　B　　　　　C

    way to the Atlantic Ocean.
    　　　D

34. Consumers who spend more money on automobiles than on furniture and
    　　　　　　A　　　B　　　　　　　　　　　C

    household equipment.
    　　　D

35. The first elevator electric was installed in New York City in 1889.
    　　　A　　　　　B　　　　C　　　　　　　　　　　D

36. Honey, a food found in the tombs of ancient Egypt, is the only food that not spoil.
    　　　　　A　　　　　　　　　　　　　　　　　　　　B　　　　　　　C　　D

37. The federal government can increase taxes or decrease spending to reducing the size of
    　　　A　　　　　　　　　　　　　　　B　　　　　　　　　　C

    its debt.
    　D

38. On a hot day, the land heats up faster than ocean.
    　　　A　　　　　B　　　C　　　D

GO ON TO THE NEXT PAGE

Practice Tests   21

2 ● 2 ● 2 ● 2 ● 2 ● 2 ● 2

39. <u>Contrarily</u> to what we would <u>expect</u>, scientists <u>measure</u> distance, not time, <u>by using</u>
       A   B   C   D

    "light years."

40. The Mississippi River is <u>the long</u> river <u>in the United States</u>, and <u>is the</u> nation's
                                  A   B   C

    <u>most important</u> inland waterway.
          D

THIS IS THE END OF SECTION 2

IF YOU FINISH BEFORE TIME IS CALLED, CHECK YOUR WORK ON SECTION 2
ONLY.
DO NOT READ OR WORK ON ANY OTHER SECTION OF THE TEST.
THE SUPERVISOR WILL TELL YOU WHEN TO BEGIN WORK ON SECTION 3.

STOP STOP STOP STOP STOP STOP STOP

22 Practice Tests

SECTION 3
VOCABULARY AND READING COMPREHENSION

Time: 45 minutes

This section tests your comprehension of standard written English. There are two types of questions in this section, with special directions for each type.

Directions: In questions 1–30, each sentence has an underlined word or phrase. Below each sentence are four other words or phrases, marked (A), (B), (C), and (D). You are to choose the *one* word or phrase that *best keeps the meaning* of the original sentence if it is substituted for the underlined word or phrase. Then, on your answer sheet, find the number of the question and fill in the space that matches the letter you have chosen. Fill in the space so that the letter inside the oval cannot be seen.

Example

Passenger ships and aircraft are often equipped with ship-to-shore or air-to-land radio telephones.
(A) highways
(B) railroads
(C) planes
(D) sailboats

Sample Answer
(A) (B) ● (D)

The best answer is (C), because "Passenger ships and planes are often equipped with ship-to-shore or air-to-land radio telephones" is closest in meaning to the original sentence. Therefore, you should choose answer (C).

Now begin work on the questions.

1. Countries export their excess resources and products.
   (A) valuable
   (B) inferior
   (C) surplus
   (D) expensive

2. No one may copy an invention without the permission of the patent holder.
   (A) signature
   (B) consent
   (C) intervention
   (D) persistence

3. Religious practices are often dependent on a culture's environment.
   (A) history
   (B) government
   (C) beliefs
   (D) surroundings

4. When the United States entered World War I, some people thought women should cease their attempts to get the vote.
   (A) stop
   (B) prolong
   (C) increase
   (D) postpone

5. Platinum is an unusually dense metal, twice as heavy as silver and one-third heavier than gold.
   (A) expensive
   (B) concentrated
   (C) dark
   (D) common

GO ON TO THE NEXT PAGE

6. Throughout history, settlements have grown where one kind of transportation ended and another began.
   (A) stations
   (B) communities
   (C) tenements
   (D) crops

7. Satellite photos help a cartographer draw accurate maps.
   (A) colorful
   (B) circular
   (C) weather
   (D) precise

8. The first permanent English colony in North America was Jamestown, Virginia.
   (A) period
   (B) enduring
   (C) successful
   (D) established

9. Stings of bees, wasps, and ants can have life-threatening, even fatal results in minutes.
   (A) inconvenient
   (B) annoying
   (C) deadly
   (D) unbelievable

10. Social indicators depict the standard of living more accurately than do economic statistics.
    (A) predict
    (B) illustrate
    (C) determine
    (D) stimulate

11. Concern for protecting a country's workers motivates popular support for trade tariffs.
    (A) determines
    (B) hastens
    (C) prevents
    (D) encourages

12. One barrier to world peace is the nuclear arms buildup.
    (A) obstacle
    (B) threat
    (C) end
    (D) contribution

13. Florence Nightingale, who reformed the British Army, was the founder of modern nursing.
    (A) led
    (B) improved
    (C) established
    (D) challenged

14. Irrigation is required to grow crops in arid areas.
    (A) urban
    (B) fertile
    (C) dry
    (D) mountainous

15. Scientific experiments with animal subjects that proliferated in the 1950s are on the decline.
    (A) increased
    (B) started
    (C) disappeared
    (D) improved

16. The American sculptor Isamu Noguchi is a celebrated designer of furniture and costumes.
    (A) fanciful
    (B) celibate
    (C) famous
    (D) creative

17. The phenomenal growth of the suburbs has increased the demand for better roads.
    (A) recent
    (B) extraordinary
    (C) predicted
    (D) gradual

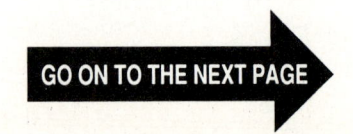

GO ON TO THE NEXT PAGE

18. Differences in climate mean differences in temperature, precipitation, and the length of the growing season.
    (A) rainfall
    (B) altitude
    (C) topography
    (D) winds

19. By 1900, the United States had shifted from being a country of farmers to a country of factory workers.
    (A) drifted
    (B) changed
    (C) improved
    (D) geared itself

20. The Dawes Act of 1887 encouraged Native Americans to become farmers and give up their tribal practices.
    (A) religions
    (B) leaders
    (C) lands
    (D) customs

21. Infectious diseases have increased as a major cause of death.
    (A) Adolescent
    (B) Insidious
    (C) Fatal
    (D) Contagious

22. Technology has provided a way to recycle water but not purify it.
    (A) pump
    (B) freeze
    (C) reuse
    (D) deliver

23. Compulsory education was established to improve the lot of the working classes.
    (A) Vocational
    (B) Secondary
    (C) Obligatory
    (D) Universal

24. When World War I broke out in Europe in 1914, the United States remained neutral at first.
    (A) nonaligned
    (B) belligerent
    (C) prepared
    (D) isolated

25. Most parents are unaware of how ineffectively they react when their children misbehave.
    (A) naturally
    (B) futilely
    (C) emotionally
    (D) reasonably

26. After World War II, the United States and Russia emerged as world powers.
    (A) remained
    (B) became
    (C) competed as
    (D) functioned as

27. Iceland is a remote, romantic island in the Atlantic Ocean.
    (A) changeable
    (B) lovely
    (C) turbulent
    (D) distant

28. The Civil Rights Act of 1964 prohibited discrimination in voting.
    (A) encouraged
    (B) forbade
    (C) proposed
    (D) reduced

29. The *Iliad* and the *Odyssey* are both popularly attributed to Homer.
    (A) infamously
    (B) knowingly
    (C) usually
    (D) generously

GO ON TO THE NEXT PAGE

30. <u>Instructive</u> pictures are taken of the planet earth from satellites hovering above.
    (A) Informative
    (B) Detailed
    (C) Delayed
    (D) Frequent

Directions: In the rest of this section you will read several passages. Each one is followed by several questions about it. For questions 31–60, you are to choose the *one* best answer, (A), (B), (C), or (D), to each question. Then, on your answer sheet, find the number of the question and fill in the space that matches the letter of the answer you have chosen.

Answer all questions following a passage on the basis of what is *stated* or *implied* in the reading passage.

Example passage and questions
The rattles with which a rattlesnake warns of its presence are formed by loosely interlocking hollow rings of hard skin, which make a buzzing sound when its tail is shaken. As a baby, the snake begins to form its rattles from the button at the very tip of its tail. Thereafter, each time it sheds its skin, a new ring is formed. Popular belief holds that a snake's age can be told by counting the rings, but this idea is fallacious. In fact, a snake may lose its old skin as often as four times a year. Also, rattles tend to wear or break off with time.

Example   **Sample Answer**
A rattlesnake's rattles are made of   ● Ⓑ Ⓒ Ⓓ
(A) skin
(B) bone
(C) wood
(D) muscle

According to the passage, a rattlesnake's rattles are made of rings of hard skin. Therefore, you should choose answer (A).

Example   **Sample Answer**
How often does a rattlesnake shed its skin?   Ⓐ Ⓑ ● Ⓓ
(A) Once every four years
(B) Once every four months
(C) Up to four times every year
(D) Four times more often than other snakes

The passage states that "a snake may lose its old skin as often as four times a year." Therefore, you should choose answer (C).

Now begin work on the questions.

GO ON TO THE NEXT PAGE

Questions 31–36

The sun's radiation striking the earth supplies the energy to heat the ocean surface and to warm the lower atmosphere. Energy from the sun is filtered as it passes through the atmosphere and is filtered again in surface ocean waters. Within the first 10 centimeters of even pure water, virtually all the infrared portion of the light spectrum is absorbed and changed into heat. Within the first meter of seawater, about 60 percent of the entering radiation is absorbed, and about 80 percent is absorbed in the first 10 meters. Only about 1 percent remains at 140 meters in the clearest subtropical ocean waters.

In coastal waters, abundant marine organisms, suspended sediment particles, and dissolved organic substances absorb light at even shallower depths. Near Cape Cod, Massachusetts, for instance, only 1 percent of the surface light commonly penetrates to 16 meters. In such waters the maximum transparency shifts from the bluish region typical of clear oceanic waters to longer wavelengths. In turbid coastal waters, absorption of all light takes place within a few centimeters of the water surface.

Far from the coast, ocean water often has a deep luminous blue color quite unlike the greenish or brownish colors common to coastal waters. The deep blue color indicates an absence of particles, i.e., clean water. In these areas, the color of the water is thought to result from a scattering of light rays within the water. A similar type of scattering is responsible for the blue color of the clean atmosphere.

31. How is the ocean surface heated?
    (A) By the radiation hitting the earth
    (B) By warming the atmosphere
    (C) By warm water rising to the surface
    (D) By the movement of the ocean's waters

32. The sun's energy is first filtered by
    (A) the ocean
    (B) the atmosphere
    (C) suspended sediment
    (D) tropical currents

33. The greatest percentage of radiation entering seawater is absorbed within the first
    (A) meter
    (B) 10 meters
    (C) 16 meters
    (D) 140 meters

34. Where are the clearest waters likely to be found?
    (A) In coastal waters
    (B) In subtropical areas
    (C) Around Cape Cod
    (D) Around marine organisms

35. In which of the following would you most likely find the color deep blue?
    (A) In shallow waters
    (B) In clean waters
    (C) In turbid waters
    (D) In coastal harbors

36. What is the cause of the deep blue color of the ocean?
    (A) Scattering of light rays
    (B) Abundant marine organisms
    (C) Absorption of all light
    (D) Proliferation of particles

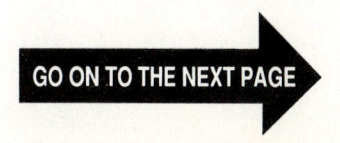

GO ON TO THE NEXT PAGE

Questions 37–43

Design, although we can usually recognize it, is, like art, hard to define. It has been described as intention—the alternative to chance—which indicates that anything that is designed is thought about and conclusions are reached that result in a particular arrangement of the elements and a specific relationship of the parts. The design of buildings involves consideration of construction materials, setting, function, etc.

There is a further element in design, which is expressed by Professor Pevsner's distinction between building and architecture. "A bicycle shed is a building; Lincoln Cathedral is a piece of architecture." Nearly everything that encloses space on a scale sufficient for human beings to move in is a building; the term architecture applies only to a building designed with a view to aesthetic appeal.

Pevsner suggests that in architecture the design also must incorporate "aesthetic appeal." This certainly is the study of beauty and ugliness, the philosophy of taste. From this we may conclude that amid all his practical decisions, the architect must also consider the beauty or ugliness of his structure. Simply taking beauty into consideration will result in architecture, but whether it is good or bad architecture will depend on the architect's sensitivity, his "taste" and as the reader will now suppose, his success or failure will lie in the individual judgment of the observer.

The same considerations, of course, also apply to the other visual arts. Aesthetics, notions of beauty and ugliness, truth and falsehood, the pseudo and the real, are the constant preoccupations of aestheticians and all other students of the arts. Value judgments are what appreciation and understanding are all about.

37. The author of the passage believes that design, like art, is
    (A) easily recognizable, but difficult to define
    (B) very easy to define
    (C) hard to recognize
    (D) unintentional

38. Which of the following was NOT included in the list of design considerations?
    (A) Equipment
    (B) Cost
    (C) Location
    (D) Purpose

39. Professor Pevsner makes a distinction between architecture and
    (A) aesthetic appeal
    (B) art
    (C) building
    (D) function

40. In the second paragraph, how does the author define architecture?
    (A) As a tasteful building
    (B) As a bicycle shed
    (C) As a scaled space
    (D) As moveable

41. What determines whether the architect was successful?
    (A) The opinion of the observers
    (B) The functionality of the building
    (C) The endurance of the structure
    (D) The architect's sensitivity

42. Which of the following characteristics would the author think most important?
    (A) Practicality
    (B) Consistency
    (C) Sensitivity
    (D) Honesty

43. What do aestheticians share with other students of the arts?
    (A) Longing for success
    (B) Disregard for functionality
    (C) Considerations of aesthetic appeal
    (D) Observant critics

Questions 44–48

Value judgments cannot be made in science in the way that such judgments are made in philosophy, religion, and the arts, and indeed in our daily lives. Whether or not something is good or beautiful or right in a moral sense, for example, cannot be determined by scientific methods. Such judgments, even though they may be supported by a broad consensus, are not subject to scientific testing.

At one time, the sciences, like the arts, were pursued for their own sake. They were pursued for pleasure and satisfaction of the insatiable curiosity with which we are both cursed and blessed. In the twentieth century, however, the sciences have spawned a host of giant technological achievements—the hydrogen bomb, the polio vaccine, pesticides, indestructible plastics, nuclear energy plants, perhaps even ways to manipulate our genetic heritage—but have not given us any clues about how to use them wisely. Moreover, science, as a result of these very achievements, appears enormously powerful. It is thus little wonder that there are many people who are angry at science, as one would be angry at an omnipotent authority who apparently has the power to grant one's wishes but who refuses to do so.

The reason that science cannot and does not solve the problems we want it to is inherent in its nature. Most of the problems we now confront can be solved only by value judgments. For example, science gave us nuclear power and can give us predictions as to the extent of the biological damage that might result from accidents that allowed varying levels of radioactivity to escape into the environment. Yet it cannot help us, as citizens, in weighing the risk of damage from conceivable accidents against our energy needs. It can give us data to weigh our judgments on, but it cannot make those judgments for us.

44. Why does the author feel that science and the arts were similar?
    (A) Both were intensely sought after
    (B) Both had enormous power
    (C) Both made people angry
    (D) Both helped solve many problems

45. Which of the following is the best title for the passage?
    (A) Technological Achievements of the Twentieth Century
    (B) Science versus Art
    (C) Art for Art's Sake
    (D) Scientific Investigation and Value Judgments

46. With which of the following statements would the author of the passage LEAST agree?
    (A) Science creates more problems than it solves.
    (B) Science is enormously powerful.
    (C) Science can measure right and wrong.
    (D) Science can make predictions about nuclear damage.

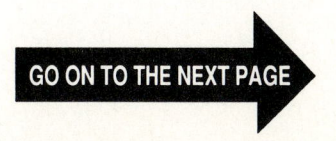

GO ON TO THE NEXT PAGE

47. What is the author's attitude toward science?
    (A) Objective
    (B) Pessimistic
    (C) Awed
    (D) Disgusted

48. Which of the following would NOT be a subject of scientific inquiry?
    (A) Manipulating genetic heritage
    (B) Being right in a moral sense
    (C) Measuring levels of radioactivity
    (D) Developing indestructible plastics

Questions 49–52

Since art forgery is a very big business, enormous sums of money are involved, and the successful passing off of a fake will be very rewarding. In consequence, a great deal of ingenuity is devoted to establishing the authenticity of a work of art. In many instances its provenance (place of origin) and its successive owners, in the case of an historical work, are known, and its authenticity,
5 if not its quality, is unchallengeable. Many works in public galleries and private collections are of this order.

Frequently, however, there are gaps in the histories of many works—sometimes covering many centuries. In these circumstances the internal evidence in the work itself—its material, its finish, its condition, its similarity to other works by the same artist from the same period—has to
10 be considered and specialist expertise consulted.

49. In line 2, the word *fake* refers to which of the following?
    (A) Counterfeit money
    (B) A phony artist
    (C) A piece of art
    (D) Big collectors

50. The provenance of a work of art refers to
    (A) how well it's crafted
    (B) how beautiful it is
    (C) its success
    (D) where it's from

51. To prove the authenticity of a work of art whose past is only partly known, one usually
    (A) considers the internal evidence
    (B) considers the external evidence
    (C) consults successive owners
    (D) consults public galleries and private collections

52. Which of the following is the best title for the passage?
    (A) How to Make Enormous Sums of Money from Art
    (B) How to Establish the Authenticity of a Work of Art
    (C) The Business of Forging Art
    (D) Ordering Art from Public Galleries

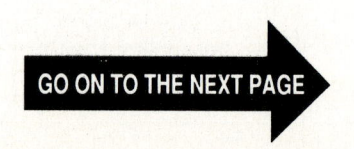

GO ON TO THE NEXT PAGE

Questions 53–56

The Food and Drug Administration (FDA) was created by Congress in 1906, primarily to address unsanitary conditions in the nation's food industries and to control the sale of dangerous and ineffective medicines. Its legislation essentially required the correct labeling of food and drugs and the inspection and certification of food industries by this agency in the U.S. Department of Agriculture. A "pure food" certification from the federal government protected domestic markets and export sales to Europe. Government certification remains a critical factor in the successful marketing of food products and protects the public from contaminated food.

The 1906 act reflected the willingness of individuals and firms to accept the restriction of certain liberties in exchange for the protection of other rights. Thus, consumers cannot buy and firms cannot sell tainted or adulterated food products. In return for the limitation on their "freedom" to buy or sell, individuals receive greater personal health security, and firms benefit from consumer confidence in their products.

The speculative risks of drug companies are especially high. The pharmaceutical industry develops an estimated 30,000 chemical compounds for each one approved for prescription use. As one research institute has noted, "many new drugs are discovered or developed, but few are cleared for marketing." Research, testing, and FDA approval frequently require a decade before a new product enters the market; thus, returns on investment are extremely delayed, and once on the market, drugs may have only seven or eight years of the seventeen-year patent life remaining. And, even more likely, they may be replaced on the shelf by a new product from a competitor. Nevertheless, such delays in market approval serve the purpose of providing greater assurances of the safety and effectiveness of drugs. Ironically, early release to the markets of other countries can provide evidence of problems if any develop. On the other hand, delayed release increases costs, can contribute to the perpetuation of suffering or illness, and can also indirectly create real economic loss. Current debates over FDA regulations generally concern methods of expediting or improving testing and release rather than the question of whether the agency should or should not regulate.

53. What is the main idea of the passage?
    (A) Thousands of drugs are constantly being developed.
    (B) The FDA plays a critical role in approving new drugs.
    (C) Many individuals desire greater freedom in buying and selling food and drug products.
    (D) The FDA should be abolished.

54. It can be inferred that the FDA was most likely created because
    (A) only the government can prevent unsanitary food conditions
    (B) some industries were operating under unsanitary conditions
    (C) many industries were opposed to sanitation measures
    (D) death from food poisoning was rampant prior to 1906

55. Discussions about FDA regulations are generally concerned with which of the following?
    (A) Whether the agency should regulate drugs
    (B) Improved testing and release of drugs
    (C) Competition from other countries
    (D) Extending the current patent agreement

56. According to the passage, approximately how many years does it take to bring a new drug to market?
    (A) 1
    (B) 7 to 8
    (C) 10
    (D) 17

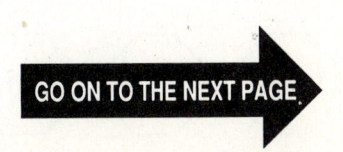

GO ON TO THE NEXT PAGE

Questions 57–60

The principal choice in typewriters today is between the electric and the electronic models. The electronic typewriter appears to be the direction of the future. By 1984 sales of electronic machines had already surpassed those of electric models. The fundamental difference between electric and electronic models is that electric typewriters use numerous mechanically driven parts, whereas electronic models have fewer parts (hence less breakage) and function by means of microprocessor controls. In addition, electric typewriters have no memory, display, or automated functions. As the cost of electronic models declines and their superior capabilities become more widely known, they will become even more popular and more widely used.

Electronic typewriters were introduced in 1978 and since then have advanced technologically to compete successfully not only with electric typewriters but, in many cases, with more expensive word processors and computers. The features of electronic typewriters vary from one model to another, but most have a memory feature that enables users to store a certain amount of text that can be recalled later.

This and other features (such as memory protection, pitch selection, right-margin justification, and automatic hyphenation) amount to less work for the user, faster and easier production (up to 50-percent increase in performance), more accurate and attractive results, and generally more efficient office operations. Business analysts predict that in the coming decade electronic typewriters will be used primarily in secretarial-administrative work stations in large companies, but will also be widely used throughout small and medium-size firms.

57. According to the passage, what is the fundamental difference between electric and electronic typewriters?
  (A) Cost
  (B) Number of parts
  (C) Number of models available
  (D) Size

58. According to the passage, features on electronic typewriters are
  (A) likely to be modified within a short period of time
  (B) similar to those on an electric typewriter
  (C) difficult to learn
  (D) likely to increase a user's performance

59. The author predicts that electronic typewriters will become more widely used when
  (A) their price comes down
  (B) they have more features
  (C) their memory capacity is increased
  (D) most electric typewriters have broken down

60. The author would most likely agree with which of the following statements?
  (A) The electronic typewriter is superior to the electric typewriter.
  (B) The electric typewriter is superior to the electronic typewriter.
  (C) Both typewriters are equal.
  (D) The two typewriters cannot be compared.

THIS IS THE END OF SECTION 3

IF YOU FINISH BEFORE TIME IS CALLED, CHECK YOUR WORK ON SECTION 3 ONLY.
DO NOT READ OR WORK ON ANY OTHER SECTION OF THE TEST.

1●1●1●1●1●1●1

PRACTICE TEST 2

SECTION 1

LISTENING COMPREHENSION

The questions in Section 1 of the test are on a recording.

In this section of the test, you will have an opportunity to demonstrate your ability to understand spoken English. There are three parts to this section, with special directions for each part.

Part A

Directions: For each question in Part A, you will hear a short sentence. Each sentence will be spoken just one time. The sentences you hear will not be written out for you. Therefore, you must listen carefully to understand what the speaker says.

After you hear a sentence, read the four choices in your test book, marked (A), (B), (C), and (D), and decide with *one* is closest in meaning to the sentence you heard. Then, on your answer sheet, find the number of the question and fill in the space that matches the letter of the answer you have chosen. Fill in the space so that the letter inside the oval cannot be seen.

Example I
You will hear: *Mary swam out to the island with her friends.*
You will read: (A) Mary outswam the others.
              (B) Mary ought to swim with them.
              (C) Mary and her friends swam to the island.
              (D) Mary's friends owned the island.

Sample Answer
Ⓐ Ⓑ ● Ⓓ

The speaker said, "Mary swam out to the island with her friends." Sentence (C), "Mary and her friends swam to the island," is closest in meaning to the sentence you heard. Therefore, you should choose answer (C).

Example II
You will hear: *Would you mind helping me with this load of books?*
You will read: (A) Please remind me to read this book.
              (B) Could you help me carry these books?
              (C) I don't mind if you help me.
              (D) Do you have a heavy course load this term?

Sample Answer
Ⓐ ● Ⓒ Ⓓ

The speaker said, "Would you mind helping me with this load of books?" Sentence (B), "Could you help me carry these books?" is closest in meaning to the sentence you heard. Therefore, you should choose answer (B).

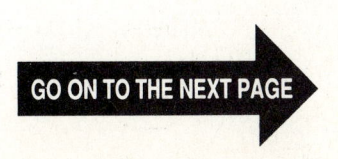

GO ON TO THE NEXT PAGE

1. (A) Where are you?
    (B) What road did you take?
    (C) How long did it take?
    (D) What took you so long?

2. (A) The newspaper comes every two days.
    (B) I need a receipt for the paper.
    (C) I have two newspapers.
    (D) The paper hasn't been delivered for two days.

3. (A) There are only four chapters in the book.
    (B) The examination is on top of the book.
    (C) First, I'll read all four chapters.
    (D) The test will cover Chapters 1–4.

4. (A) Eat a little something if you feel hungry.
    (B) Don't eat before dinner time.
    (C) If you don't eat, you'll be hungry.
    (D) Why don't you wait until dinner?

5. (A) Ten of us went by taxi.
    (B) The airport is ten miles from town.
    (C) We spent ten dollars to take the taxi to the airport.
    (D) The taxi from the airport cost ten dollars.

6. (A) How often do you go riding?
    (B) How long is the ride?
    (C) Would you like to go in the car this afternoon?
    (D) Are you leaving at noon?

7. (A) I have to do housework this weekend.
    (B) I have to stay home and study.
    (C) I always go out on Saturdays.
    (D) I didn't have to work this weekend.

8. (A) The train is ten minutes late.
    (B) The plane will be here in ten minutes.
    (C) It will rain before we go.
    (D) The grain was loaded long ago.

9. (A) I'll phone you after I wake up.
    (B) I walked to the phone booth.
    (C) I was asleep before the phone rang.
    (D) I didn't hear the phone ring.

10. (A) The park was preserved by the faculty.
    (B) The facility was planned for visitors.
    (C) Visitors must have a reservation.
    (D) Only staff members and visitors may park in these spaces.

11. (A) Did the books belong to Richard?
    (B) Is Richard going to the library?
    (C) Did Richard take the books back to the library?
    (D) Are these the books Richard returned to the library?

12. (A) The statue is two blocks on the right.
    (B) Walk until you see the statue.
    (C) Make two right turns and you'll see the statue.
    (D) At the statue, turn right and go two more blocks.

13. (A) Approximately 2,000 people will attend the conference.
    (B) We counted a thousand people at the conference.
    (C) We expect you will attend the conference.
    (D) The conference was last weekend.

14. (A) The news is over at 6 every evening.
    (B) I never miss the newscast at 6.
    (C) I usually watch the news between 4 and 6.
    (D) Channel Six shows the news at 4.

GO ON TO THE NEXT PAGE

15. (A) I ordered a telephone last week.
    (B) The phone's been broken for a week.
    (C) My loan was due last week.
    (D) I asked for a loan last week.

16. (A) They're building a three-story office.
    (B) A fire began on the third floor.
    (C) They broke the door on the third floor.
    (D) The fire spread throughout the building.

17. (A) Mr. Johnson fell asleep at 10.
    (B) Mr. Johnson went to bed after midnight.
    (C) Mr. Johnson slept until midnight.
    (D) Mr. Johnson was in bed by 10.

18. (A) The restaurant is next to the movie.
    (B) We'll watch a movie after we eat.
    (C) Before moving, we must get something to eat.
    (D) Let's buy some food before we leave.

19. (A) All schools require good grades.
    (B) The best schools won't admit me.
    (C) I get good grades in school.
    (D) I got my best grades in high school.

20. (A) The rain killed the grass.
    (B) We need less rain.
    (C) Rain water filled the glass.
    (D) The lawn needs water.

GO ON TO THE NEXT PAGE

Part B

Directions: In Part B you will hear short conversations between two speakers. At the end of each conversation, a third person will ask a question about what was said. You will hear each conversation and question about it just one time. The sentences you hear will not be written out for you. Therefore, you must listen carefully to understand what each speaker says. After you hear a conversation and the question about it, read the four possible answers in your test book and decide which *one* is the best answer to the question you heard. Then, on your answer sheet, find the number of the question and fill in the space that corresponds to the letter of the answer you have chosen.

Example

You will hear:

    (first man) *Professor Smith is going to retire soon. What kind of gift shall we give her?*
    (woman) *I think she'd like to have a photograph of our class.*
    (second man) *What does the woman think the class should do?*

You will read: (A) Present Professor Smith with a picture.
                    (B) Photograph Professor Smith.
                    (C) Put glass over the photograph.
                    (D) Replace the broken headlight.

Sample Answer
● Ⓑ Ⓒ Ⓓ

From the conversation you learn that the woman thinks Professor Smith would like a photograph of the class. The best answer to the question "What does the woman think the class should do?" is (A), "Present Professor Smith with a picture." Therefore, you should choose answer (A).

21. (A) Mrs. Smith is always on time.
    (B) They need to turn on the furnace.
    (C) It's hot in the building.
    (D) He was expecting Mrs. Smith this morning.

22. (A) Math.
    (B) Reading.
    (C) English.
    (D) History.

23. (A) His keys.
    (B) His glasses.
    (C) His book.
    (D) His briefcase.

24. (A) She doesn't like to read.
    (B) She already finished it.
    (C) She doesn't have a watch.
    (D) She's very busy.

25. (A) In a department store.
    (B) In a post office.
    (C) In a lamp store.
    (D) In a supermarket.

26. (A) Schools won't accept him.
    (B) He wants to travel more.
    (C) He gets too much mail.
    (D) His school isn't good enough.

27. (A) At a bus stop.
    (B) At a cinema.
    (C) At a bank.
    (D) At a clothing store.

28. (A) He prefers milk and sugar.
    (B) He's sorry he caused so much trouble.
    (C) He doesn't want too much sugar.
    (D) He doesn't want coffee.

GO ON TO THE NEXT PAGE

29. (A) To a gas station.
    (B) To an air conditioning repair shop.
    (C) To a stationery store.
    (D) To a sporting goods store.

30. (A) She did well on the test.
    (B) The test was easy.
    (C) She earned a lot of money.
    (D) She's going away for awhile.

31. (A) He doesn't plan to write the paper.
    (B) He doesn't like to sleep.
    (C) The book is overdue.
    (D) He'll finish the paper tonight.

32. (A) She's rearranging furniture.
    (B) She has a bad back.
    (C) She can't open the window.
    (D) She's buying a new desk.

33. (A) Cancel a trip.
    (B) Buy a car.
    (C) Return a car.
    (D) Purchase a ticket.

34. (A) One night.
    (B) A week.
    (C) Four weeks.
    (D) Four months.

35. (A) She prefers taxis.
    (B) She doesn't have enough money.
    (C) She doesn't have exact change.
    (D) She thinks the cab will be faster.

GO ON TO THE NEXT PAGE

Part C

Directions: In this part of the test, you will hear several short talks and conversations. After each of them, you will be asked some questions. You will hear the talks and conversations and the questions about them just one time. They will not be written out for you. Therefore, you must listen carefully in order to understand what each speaker says.

After you hear a question, read the four possible answers in your test book and decide which *one* is the best answer to the question you heard. Then, on the your answer sheet, find the number of the question and fill in the space that corresponds to the letter of the answer you have chosen.

Answer all questions on the basis of what is *stated* or *implied* in the talk or conversation.

Listen to this sample talk.
   You will hear:
   (first man) *Balloons have been used for about a hundred years. There are two kinds of sport balloons, gas and hot air. Hot-air balloons are safer than gas balloons, which may catch fire. Hot-air balloons are preferred by most balloonists in the United States because of their safety. They are also cheaper and easier to manage than gas balloons. Despite the ease of operating a balloon, pilots must watch the weather carefully. Sport balloon flights are best early in the morning or late in the afternoon, when the wind is light.*

Sample Answer
Ⓐ ● Ⓒ Ⓓ

Now look at the following example.
   You will hear:
   (second man) *Why are gas balloons considered dangerous?*
   You will read: (A) They are impossible to guide.
   (B) They may go up in flames.
   (C) They tend to leak gas.
   (D) They are cheaply made.

The best answer to the question "Why are gas balloons considered dangerous?" is (B), "They may go up in flames." Therefore, you should choose answer (B).

Now look at the next example.

Sample Answer
● Ⓑ Ⓒ Ⓓ

   You will hear:
   (second man) *According to the speaker, what must balloon pilots be careful to do?*
   You will read: (A) Watch for changes in weather.
   (B) Watch their altitude.
   (C) Check for weak spots in their balloons.
   (D) Test the strength of the ropes.

The best answer to the question "According to the speaker, what must balloon pilots be careful to do?" is (A), "Watch for changes in weather." Therefore, you should choose answer (A).

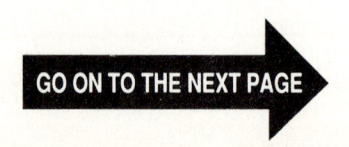

GO ON TO THE NEXT PAGE

36. (A) Their lack of water.
    (B) Their extra helium.
    (C) Their density.
    (D) Their lack of oxygen.

37. (A) It is denser.
    (B) It is not as light.
    (C) It can be released by heating.
    (D) It cannot be extracted.

38. (A) In Colorado.
    (B) In lowland areas.
    (C) Below the lunar surface.
    (D) On highland plateaus.

39. (A) Meteorites.
    (B) Low levels of oxygen.
    (C) Lava.
    (D) Fusion of the rocks.

40. (A) In Hawaii.
    (B) In Iowa.
    (C) In Swaziland.
    (D) In the eastern United States.

41. (A) Travel agents.
    (B) Common people.
    (C) The government.
    (D) The industrial sector.

42. (A) Red is a prettier color.
    (B) More people want red ones.
    (C) Red is cheaper to produce.
    (D) Red is very elegant.

43. (A) Children.
    (B) Civic groups.
    (C) Our changing income.
    (D) Working parents.

44. (A) The introduction of the jet plane.
    (B) The inconvenient schedule.
    (C) The lack of comfort.
    (D) The quality of advertisements.

45. (A) Demand for train service.
    (B) Government support.
    (C) Better workers.
    (D) Elegant service.

46. (A) Like a snapshot.
    (B) A good investment.
    (C) A popular art form.
    (D) An established fashion.

47. (A) More interesting.
    (B) More expensive.
    (C) Better quality.
    (D) More in demand.

48. (A) Museum collections.
    (B) Price.
    (C) Fashion.
    (D) Artist's reputation.

49. (A) Informal.
    (B) Inexpensive.
    (C) Stylized.
    (D) Fashionable.

50. (A) By price.
    (B) By resale value.
    (C) By fad.
    (D) By size.

THIS IS THE END OF THE LISTENING COMPREHENSION SECTION OF THE TEST

THE NEXT PART OF THE TEST IS SECTION 2. TURN TO THE DIRECTIONS FOR SECTION 2 IN YOUR TEST BOOK. READ THEM, AND BEGIN WORK. DO NOT READ OR WORK ON ANY OTHER SECTION OF THE TEST.

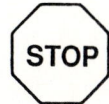

SECTION 2

STRUCTURE AND WRITTEN EXPRESSION

Time: 25 minutes

This section tests your ability to recognize language that is appropriate for standard written English. There are two types of questions in this section, with special directions for each type.

Directions: Questions 1–15 are incomplete sentences. Beneath each sentence you will see four words or phrases, marked (A), (B), (C), and (D). Choose the *one* word or phrase that best completes the sentence. Then, on your answer sheet, find the number of the question and fill in the space that corresponds to the letter of the answer you have chosen. Fill in the space so that the letter inside the oval cannot be seen.

Example I

Vegetables are an excellent source _____ vitamins.
(A) of
(B) has
(C) where
(D) that

Sample Answer
● Ⓑ Ⓒ Ⓓ

The sentence should read, "Vegetables are an excellent source of vitamins." Therefore, you should choose answer (A).

Example II

_____ in history when remarkable progress was made within a relatively short span of time.
(A) Periods
(B) Throughout periods
(C) There have been periods
(D) Periods have been

Sample Answer
Ⓐ Ⓑ ● Ⓓ

The sentence should read, "There have been periods in history when remarkable progress was made within a relatively short span of time." Therefore, you should choose answer (C).

Now begin work on the questions.

1. With a few exceptions, a passport is required _____ all U.S. citizens who depart and enter the United States.
   (A) to
   (B) with
   (C) of
   (D) at

2. The first large-scale migration from the Old World to the New _____ during the last ice age, around 11,500 years ago.
   (A) have been happening
   (B) happened
   (C) was happened
   (D) happening

GO ON TO THE NEXT PAGE

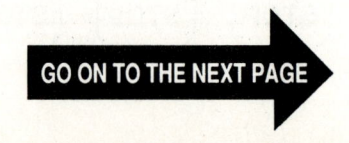

3. To early man, the distinction _____ animate and inanimate objects was not always obvious.
   (A) from
   (B) among
   (C) with
   (D) between

4. In order to win a plurality, a candidate must receive _____ votes than anyone running against him or her.
   (A) a greater number of
   (B) of greater number
   (C) greater number of
   (D) of a greater number

5. Few major advances in science have been the work of only _____ person.
   (A) some
   (B) any
   (C) the
   (D) one

6. Most foods have more than one nutrient, but _____ provides all the essential nutrients.
   (A) single no food
   (B) no single food
   (C) food no single
   (D) no food single

7. During the meeting, the leaders agreed _____ ambassadors and renew cultural contacts.
   (A) exchanging
   (B) exchange
   (C) to exchange
   (D) for exchanging

8. Robert Goddard is generally acknowledged _____ the father of modern rocketry.
   (A) being
   (B) to be
   (C) who is
   (D) is

9. Rhode Island, _____ of the 50 states, is densely populated and highly industrialized.
   (A) small
   (B) the small
   (C) smaller
   (D) the smallest

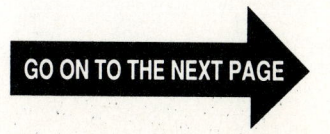

10. After a one-year cruise, an unmanned spacecraft will arrive at and _____ orbiting Mars.
    (A) begin to
    (B) to begin
    (C) has began
    (D) begin

11. About 500 volcanoes have had recorded eruptions within _____ times.
    (A) history
    (B) historically
    (C) historian
    (D) historical

12. The _____ geological history of the Earth since the beginning of the Cambrian Period is subdivided into three eras.
    (A) knowing
    (B) knew
    (C) known
    (D) know

13. _____ provides more income and jobs than any other segment of the economy.
    (A) To manufacture
    (B) Manufacturing
    (C) Manufactured
    (D) Being manufactured

14. Since 1958, the United States has consumed more energy than it _____.
    (A) producing
    (B) has produced
    (C) produced
    (D) production

15. The seasons _____ by the tilt of the Earth's axis.
    (A) cause
    (B) are causing
    (C) are caused
    (D) caused

GO ON TO THE NEXT PAGE

Directions: In questions 16–40, each sentence has four underlined words or phrases. The four underlined parts of the sentence are marked (A), (B), (C), and (D). Identify the *one* underlined word or phrase that must be changed in order for the sentence to be correct. Then, on your answer sheet, find the number of the question and fill in the space that corresponds to the letter of the answer you have chosen.

Example I

A ray of light passing through the center of a thin lens keep its
                             A   B   C

original direction.
   D

Sample Answer
Ⓐ Ⓑ ● Ⓓ

The sentence should read, "A ray of light passing through the center of a thin lens keeps its original direction." Therefore, you should choose answer (C).

Example II

The mandolin, a musical instrument that has strings, was proba-
                        A   B

bly copied from the lute, a many older instrument.
         C   D

Sample Answer
Ⓐ Ⓑ Ⓒ ●

The sentence should read, "The mandolin, a musical instrument that has strings, was probably copied from the lute, a much older instrument." Therefore, you should choose answer (D).

Now begin work on the questions.

16. Highly prices for food result from middlemen who make a profit from the farmer's crops.
    A   B   C   D

17. Since little rain falls in the desert, plants need to be conserve whatever water they can.
                    A   B   C   D

18. The Boy Scout organization stresses outdoor knowledge and training citizenship.
    A   B   C   D

19. Broadway, the famous thoroughfare of New York City, is the most long street in the world.
             A   B   C   D

20. The President annual submits a budget to Congress in January.
          A   B   C   D

21. Butter should contain at least 80 percents fat and no more than 15 percent water.
          A   B   C   D

22. Buttons, originally made of bronze or bone, are now usual made of plastic.
    A   B   C   D

GO ON TO THE NEXT PAGE

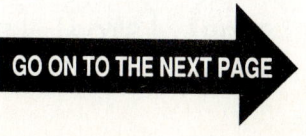

23. California's pleasant climate and beauty natural have attracted great numbers of retired
    _____A_____B_____C_____D
    persons.

24. Financial contributions to politicians by individuals and corporations restricted by law.
    _____A_____B_____C_____D

25. In 1901, the Library of Congress began the practice of printing their catalog entries on
    _____A_____B
    small cards and to sell them to other libraries.
    _____C__D

26. Cattle were first brought to the Western Hemisphere by Columbus on his twice voyage.
    _____A_____B_____C___D

27. American films which were first made in New York City, but by 1913 Hollywood,
    _____A_____B_____C
    California became the movie capital.
    _____D

28. Although geologists studying earthquakes have refined his predictions in recent years, they
    _____A_____B_____C
    still cannot determine the exact date of a quake.
    _____D

29. The establishment of large national parks in the early 1900s provide an additional source
    _____A_____B_____C
    of revenue through the tourist trade.
    _____D

30. The sudden melting of snow or ice are a primary cause of flooding.
    _____A_____B___C_____D

31. The invented of the telegraph made possible almost instantaneous communication.
    _____A_____B_____C_____D

32. The computer that developed from the calculating machine it could perform only one
    _____A_____B_____C
    operation at a time.
    _____D

GO ON TO THE NEXT PAGE

Practice Tests   43

33. Grain is easy handle and, because of its low water content, it can be stored for long
          A   B   C   D

    periods.

34. Babies, on the average, double their weight at six months of age, and triple it by her first
              A   B   C   D

    birthday.

35. Fossil records indicate that many insect species exist today in much the same form as they
                         A   B   C

    do 200 million years ago.
    D

36. Some physicians practice medicine as a group so that specialized treatment will be
             A   B

    availability at a lower cost.
    C   D

37. For many industrial uses, the melting points of metal is important when selecting alloys for
              A   B   C   D

    a compound.

38. Pottery, the oldest and most widespread art form, was one of the most enduring materials
            A   B   C

    to know to man.
    D

39. Private mail companies have begun to replace the long establishing public postal system.
            A   B   C   D

40. Most color blind people finds it difficult to identify red or green.
         A   B   C   D

THIS IS THE END OF SECTION 2

IF YOU FINISH BEFORE TIME IS CALLED, CHECK YOUR WORK ON SECTION 2 ONLY.
DO NOT READ OR WORK ON ANY OTHER SECTION OF THE TEST. THE SUPERVISOR WILL TELL YOU WHEN TO BEGIN WORK ON SECTION 3.

SECTION 3

VOCABULARY AND READING COMPREHENSION

Time: 45 minutes

This section tests your comprehension of standard written English. There are two types of questions in this section, with special directions for each type.

Directions: In questions 1–30, each sentence has an underlined word or phrase. Below each sentence are four other words or phrases, marked (A), (B), (C), and (D). You are to choose the *one* word or phrase that *best keeps the meaning* of the original sentence if it is substituted for the underlined word or phrase. Then, on your answer sheet, find the number of the question and fill in the space that matches the letter you have chosen. Fill in the space so that the letter inside the oval cannot be seen.

Example

Passenger ships and aircraft are often equipped with ship-to-shore or air-to-land radio telephones.
(A) highways
(B) railroads
(C) planes
(D) sailboats

Sample Answer
(A) (B) ● (D)

The best answer is (C), because "Passenger ships and planes are often equipped with ship-to-shore or air-to-land radio telephones" is closest in meaning to the original sentence. Therefore, you should choose answer (C).

Now begin work on the questions.

1. Rivers provide a link between inland areas and the sea.
   (A) force
   (B) portal
   (C) connection
   (D) canal

2. Rival companies compete to produce a better product at a lower price.
   (A) battle
   (B) endeavor
   (C) work
   (D) continue

3. The quality and scope of hospital care vary in different parts of the world.
   (A) value
   (B) form
   (C) expense
   (D) range

4. It is the job of the labor unions to negotiate contracts for their members.
   (A) written agreements
   (B) vacation time
   (C) health benefits
   (D) new jobs

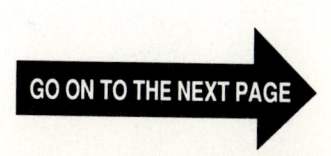

GO ON TO THE NEXT PAGE

Practice Tests 45

5. The 1920s have generally been considered a decade of growth and prosperity.
   (A) happiness
   (B) reform
   (C) success
   (D) stabilization

6. Heavy grazing by cattle reduces the amount of rainwater that soil can absorb.
   (A) tolerate
   (B) release
   (C) extract
   (D) take in

7. Considerable amounts of the Earth's fresh water are frozen in polar ice caps and glaciers.
   (A) Large
   (B) Increasing
   (C) Negligible
   (D) Sufficient

8. Many common household materials can produce toxic fumes.
   (A) poisonous
   (B) sweet
   (C) cleansing
   (D) odorous

9. Artificial reefs are successful in hiding small fish from predators.
   (A) Underwater
   (B) Dense
   (C) Shallow
   (D) Synthetic

10. Amateur athletes of many nations compete in the Olympic Games.
    (A) Qualified
    (B) Exceptional
    (C) Youthful
    (D) Nonprofessional

11. The United States has 25 percent of the world's available coal reserves.
    (A) hidden
    (B) mined
    (C) valuable
    (D) accessible

12. Studies have shown that diets high in fat increase the risk of heart disease.
    (A) incidence
    (B) danger
    (C) damage
    (D) rate

13. Forestry researchers speculate that trees communicate in some fashion.
    (A) prove
    (B) guess
    (C) predict
    (D) deny

14. Volcanoes are formed when molten rock erupts from the ground.
    (A) bursts
    (B) seeps
    (C) oozes
    (D) leaks

15. Experiments are often conducted in a laboratory under controlled conditions.
    (A) discussed
    (B) performed
    (C) debated
    (D) started

16. A plant's protective tissue forms an outer layer in order to reduce water loss.
    (A) promote
    (B) contain
    (C) diminish
    (D) delay

17. As water vapor rises, it cools.
    (A) temperature
    (B) level
    (C) mist
    (D) density

GO ON TO THE NEXT PAGE

18. The Atmosphere is 350 miles thick and is held to Earth by gravity.
    (A) high
    (B) dense
    (C) long
    (D) away

19. Climate is affected by a region's altitude.
    (A) determined
    (B) measured
    (C) regulated
    (D) influenced

20. The main source of energy in the United States today is oil.
    (A) principal
    (B) original
    (C) most abundant
    (D) most expensive

21. At the current rate of consumption, fossil fuels will probably run out within the next few hundred years.
    (A) use
    (B) contamination
    (C) isolation
    (D) waste

22. Nuclear engineers find it difficult to dispose of radioactive wastes in a safe manner.
    (A) produce
    (B) dissolve
    (C) discard
    (D) purchase

23. Body language conveys shades of meaning that words alone cannot express.
    (A) convenes
    (B) determines
    (C) transmits
    (D) hides

24. In office buildings, artificial light provides more uniform illumination than natural light.
    (A) consistent
    (B) bright
    (C) diffused
    (D) ambient

25. The diversity of New York's population creates an exciting environment.
    (A) strength
    (B) quality
    (C) population
    (D) variety

26. Technology has provided a way to recycle water and purify it.
    (A) chill
    (B) sell
    (C) clean
    (D) store

27. The diet of more than one-tenth of the world's population cannot sustain a person's health.
    (A) damage
    (B) improve
    (C) maintain
    (D) alter

28. Scientific dating techniques cannot reveal the age of molten rocks.
    (A) methods
    (B) equipment
    (C) experiments
    (D) data

29. Industrial growth was spurred by the use of electricity.
    (A) caused
    (B) guaranteed
    (C) stimulated
    (D) created

30. Acid rain presently threatens many major forests of the northeastern United States.
    (A) currently
    (B) usually
    (C) continually
    (D) accidently

GO ON TO THE NEXT PAGE

Directions: In the rest of this section you will read several passages. Each one is followed by several questions about it. For questions 31–60, you are to choose the *one* best answer, (A), (B), (C), or (D), to each question. Then, on your answer sheet, find the number of the question and fill in the space that matches the letter of the answer you have chosen.

Answer all questions following a passage on the basis of what is *stated* or *implied* in the reading passage.

Example passage and questions

The rattles with which a rattlesnake warns of its presence are formed by loosely interlocking hollow rings of hard skin, which make a buzzing sound when its tail is shaken. As a baby, the snake begins to form its rattles from the button at the very tip of its tail. Thereafter, each time it sheds its skin, a new ring is formed. Popular belief holds that a snake's age can be told by counting the rings, but this idea is fallacious. In fact, a snake may lose its old skin as often as four times a year. Also, rattles tend to wear or break off with time.

Example I   **Sample Answer**
   A rattlesnake's rattles are made of   ● Ⓑ Ⓒ Ⓓ
   (A) skin
   (B) bone
   (C) wood
   (D) muscle

According to the passage, a rattlesnake's rattles are made of rings of hard skin. Therefore, you should choose answer (A).

Example II   **Sample Answer**
   How often does a rattlesnake shed its skin?   Ⓐ Ⓑ ● Ⓓ
   (A) Once every four years
   (B) Once every four months
   (C) Up to four times every year
   (D) Four times more often than other snakes

The passage states that "a snake may lose its old skin as often as four times a year." Therefore, you should choose answer (C).

Now begin work on the questions.

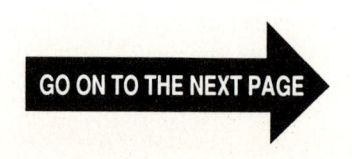

Questions 31–35

Many Americans aspire to "be their own boss." These aspirations became realities after 1945 with the boom in franchising. A franchise allows an individual to do business under the name and corporate image of a national firm. One of the world's best-known examples of a franchise is McDonald's Restaurants.

In return for the use of the corporate name and products, small-business entrepreneurs agree to operate in a prescribed manner. They can sell only the specified products. They have to pay an initial fee for the franchise, and they have to return to the franchiser a percentage of the sales. The franchise holders often obtain capital to start the business from the national corporation. Thus, the risk of entering a new business is somewhat reduced. Initially the capital required for most franchises was relatively small. However, in the 1980s, some large franchises required an investment of over half a million dollars.

When fast-food franchises became popular, franchises also emerged in electronics, bookstores, handicrafts, toys, clothing, and many other product lines and services. The spread of these small franchised businesses dramatically altered the marketing of some products. In the case of the fast-food industry, franchises also altered American dietary patterns.

31. What is the main subject of the passage?
 (A) American businesspeople are independent.
 (B) Franchises are an easy way to success.
 (C) Franchises have helped many Americans to start businesses.
 (D) Eating habits changed in 1945.

32. Which of the following can be inferred as the primary reason that franchising was successful?
 (A) People preferred to be their own boss.
 (B) The heads of large corporations wanted greater profits.
 (C) Franchising was more profitable than independent business.
 (D) Consumers wanted consistency.

33. The franchising of the fast-food business altered which of the following?
 (A) Corporate salaries
 (B) The nature of franchising
 (C) Many companies' corporate images
 (D) People's eating habits

34. According to the passage, which franchise promoted the growth of other franchises?
 (A) Fast food
 (B) Electronics
 (C) Bookstores
 (D) Toys

35. According to the passage, what is the main difference between the early and more recent days of franchising?
 (A) It cost nothing to use the corporate name in the early days.
 (B) Most of the early franchises made modest profits in the early days.
 (C) The initial investment is much higher in recent days.
 (D) The American public is more aware of franchises in recent days.

GO ON TO THE NEXT PAGE

Questions 36–41

The foreign policy of the United States in the 1920s and 1930s could be called isolationism. After World War I, war had lost its glamour. The invention of the movie camera in the 1930s made the horrors of war vividly real to millions of Americans.

For generations, a peace movement had existed in the United States. It had always been
5 relatively ineffectual, but now it grew to heights of unexampled influence. One wing argued strongly for the Untied States to prevent war by acting on the principle of collective security; that is, by banding together with other nations to present a common front to the aggressors. Other more radical groups—like the War Resister's League—preached isolationism. The League of Nations, they said, was weak; militarism was taking over everywhere, and the only answer was to refuse to
10 build armaments and follow totally noninterventionist policies.

36. According to the passage, the early peace movement had been
    (A) isolated
    (B) very influential
    (C) fairly ineffectual
    (D) conservative

37. According to the passage, it can be inferred that the War Resister's League did NOT support which of the following?
    (A) Isolationism
    (B) Militarism
    (C) The peace movement
    (D) The principle of collective security

38. With which of the following is the passage mainly concerned?
    (A) Glamour
    (B) First World War
    (C) Isolationism
    (D) War Resister's League

39. The author uses the expression "unexampled influence" (line 5) to imply that
    (A) the cause was not influential
    (B) no one could succeed
    (C) there was no precedent
    (D) peace was unattainable

40. The groups referred to in the last paragraph were against which of the following?
    (A) Intervention
    (B) War
    (C) Collective security
    (D) Isolationism

41. Which of the following argued that military armaments should not be built?
    (A) The British press
    (B) The War Resister's League
    (C) The League of Nations
    (D) The aggressors

GO ON TO THE NEXT PAGE

Questions 42–46

A number of artists in the past have practiced architecture, sculpture, and painting. For instance, in 16th-century Italy there was no feeling that it was improper to work in all three areas, and in the case of Michelangelo it would be difficult to determine in which discipline he was preeminent.

Today such a thing would be almost impossible. It has become common practice to specialize in painting or sculpture, occasionally to engage in both, but never to encompass all three disciplines. One of the obvious reasons is that training in architecture now involves so much technical instruction that demands of time exclude other studies. Thus, a historical link between the three arts has been broken. At least one unfortunate effect of this break is that the architect, who is frequently the purchaser of painting and sculpture for an architectural setting, may have an undeveloped pictorial and sculptural sensitivity, which may make his or her choices less than appropriate.

The most significant effect of the separation perhaps has been that painting and sculpture have come to be regarded as different from architecture, and when the fine arts are considered, it is these areas that are usually referred to. But painting and sculpture are as different in kind from each other as both are from architecture.

Sculpture has a long history of close connection with architectural structures. The integration of the building with the external sculptures on, say, an Indian temple or the north door of Chartres Cathedral is immediately evident. Because sculpture, like architecture, is generally three-dimensional, their relationship is easily compared.

42. The author of the passage would probably agree with which of the following statements?
    (A) Michelangelo would not be popular today.
    (B) An artist could specialize in more than two disciplines.
    (C) An artist could equal Michelangelo in sculpture.
    (D) Architects often desire to become painters.

43. The author mentions Michelangelo for which of the following reasons?
    (A) Michelangelo lived in Italy, where a lot of sculpture was made.
    (B) Michelangelo was a great patron of the arts.
    (C) Michelangelo was proficient in all three art forms.
    (D) Michelangelo worked only in three-dimensional objects.

44. The author of the passage suggests that
    (A) the art of 16th-century Italy is superior to anything being done today.
    (B) Michelangelo was the greatest artist that ever lived.
    (C) painting and sculpture are unrelated.
    (D) modern architects may not be as well-rounded as earlier architects.

45. According to the passage, modern architects do not study painting because they
    (A) do not have enough time
    (B) are insensitive
    (C) prefer sculpture
    (D) do not require technical instruction

GO ON TO THE NEXT PAGE

46. A modern architect's choices of paintings and sculptures might be less than appropriate because the architect
    (A) thinks mainly of profit
    (B) does not have time to study works of art
    (C) may lack sensitivity outside his or her area of expertise
    (D) doesn't have enough money to buy quality works of art

Questions 47–52

Two hundred thousand years after the appearance of man, an embryonic language began to develop, replacing a communication based mainly on touch. Regardless of whether this language developed from learning or instinct, genetic evolution had now been joined by language evolution. By about 7,000 B.C., *Homo sapiens* had evolved genetically to its present form, and the
5 ability to communicate had gained another medium: pictographics. These wall etchings inside cave walls and temples remain picture messages that depict life and religious beliefs of these first humans. In the first period from 3,000 to 2,000 B.C. these etchings became highly stylized, and the first symbols came into existence. Primitive alphabets, sometimes consisting of more than 600 characters, marked the beginning of recorded
10 history.

Humans were now able to record sociocultural events, attitudes, values, and habits and to trace the development of moral codes. Many of these techniques continued into modern cultures, such as those of the Native Americans, who recorded famous battles,
15 songs, and the lives of chiefs for posterity. Cultures learned about and studied other cultures. Historical perspectives developed so that when plotting our futures, we could examine our past.

47. The passage mainly discusses which of the following?
    (A) Communication theory
    (B) Styles of writing
    (C) Styles of language
    (D) The early development of language

48. According to the passage, before language was developed, humans communicated by doing which of the following?
    (A) Smoking
    (B) Touching
    (C) Dancing
    (D) Grunting

49. According to the passage, when did the first symbols come into existence?
    (A) 7,000 B.C.
    (B) 2,000 B.C.
    (C) 2,000 years ago
    (D) 600 years ago

50. The word "pictographics" in line 5 refers to which of the following?
    (A) Wall etchings
    (B) Cave walls
    (C) Temple remains
    (D) *Homo sapiens*

GO ON TO THE NEXT PAGE

52 Practice Tests

51. Recorded history was marked by the existence of which of the following?
    (A) New alphabets
    (B) Cave dwellers
    (C) Moral codes
    (D) Sociocultural events

52. According to the passage, what is the value of historical perspectives?
    (A) To live in the past
    (B) To learn about other cultures
    (C) To develop new moral codes
    (D) To trace our origins

Questions 53–56

Although the earliest scientific ideas date back to early recorded history, physics as we know it today began with Galileo Galilei (1564–1642). Indeed, Galileo and his successor Isaac Newton (1642–1727) created a revolution in scientific thought. The physics that developed over the next three centuries, reaching its culmination with the electromagnetic theory of light in the latter half of the 19th century, is now referred to as classical physics. By the turn of the century, it seemed that the physical world was very well understood. But in the early years of the century, new ideas and new experiments in physics indicated that some aspects of classical physics did not work for the tiny world of the atom or for objects traveling at very high speed. This brought on a second great revolution in physics, which gave birth to what is now called modern physics.

The principle aim of all sciences, including physics, is generally considered to be the ordering of the complex appearances detected by our senses—that is, an ordering of what we often refer to as the "world around us." Many people think of science as a mechanical process of collecting facts and devising theories. This is not the case. Science is a creative activity that in many respects resembles other creative activities of the human mind.

53. According to the passage, physics did not begin until
    (A) early recorded history
    (B) the time of Galileo
    (C) the 20th century
    (D) the formulation of the electromagnetic theory

54. Which of the following could classical theories of physics NOT explain?
    (A) Recorded history
    (B) Newton's experiments
    (C) The world of the atom
    (D) Electromagnetic theory

55. The age of classical physics dated from about
    (A) 1564 to 1642
    (B) 1564 to 1900
    (C) 1850 to 1900
    (D) 1642 to 1727

56. The author of the passage defines the "complex appearances detected by our senses" (line 11) as our
    (A) eye, ear, and nose
    (B) visions of the future
    (C) knowledge of physics
    (D) environment

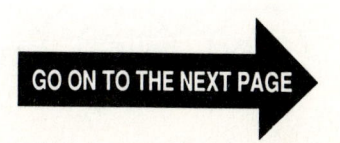

GO ON TO THE NEXT PAGE

Questions 57–60

Mass communication does not operate in a social vacuum as a machine does. When a computer receives a message, for instance, it will provide an answer based on that original message. If the computer is functioning properly, the same answer will appear every time we send it the identical message. Now contrast this process with what occurs in mass communication. Imagine that you, a consumer of mass media, read the newspaper story about a politician's speech. After you talked with your family, friends, and co-workers about it, you decided to write a letter to the politician. It is thus possible that three social groups, your family, friends, and co-workers, affected your reaction to the speech.

Now imagine that you are the newspaper reporter responsible for writing about the politician's speech. Social groups will affect your reporting of the story to the public. Perhaps you are a member of a union that goes on strike just as you return to your office to write the story. Or perhaps you belong to a journalism association with a code of reporting ethics to which you personally adhere. The code states that you cannot accept gifts as part of your job as a reporter, and your morning mail brings an invitation from a major oil company to be their guest on a flight to Alaska for an on-the-spot story about oil exploration. You are faced with accepting the free trip and doing the story or rejecting the free trip and permitting other media in your city to obtain the story. You obviously are faced with a dilemma attributable at least in part to the influence various social groups have on you.

57. According to the passage, a human language is unlike an artificial language because it
(A) has a social element
(B) is precise
(C) is more useful
(D) is complicated

58. What is the main idea of the passage?
(A) Our reactions are influenced by social groups.
(B) Alaska is an oil-producing state.
(C) Communication comes in many forms.
(D) Reporters should not accept gifts.

59. The author of the passage answers which of the following questions?
(A) How are political speeches received?
(B) How are your opinions influenced?
(C) How do you become a newspaper reporter?
(D) What is the value of a computer?

60. The paragraph following the passage most probably discusses which of the following?
(A) A code of ethics in journalism
(B) The role of a computer in society
(C) The impact of Alaskan oil exploration
(D) The effect of social influence on mass communication

THIS IS THE END OF SECTION 3

IF YOU FINISH BEFORE TIME IS CALLED, CHECK YOUR WORK ON SECTION 3 ONLY.
DO NOT READ OR WORK ON ANY OTHER SECTION OF THE TEST.

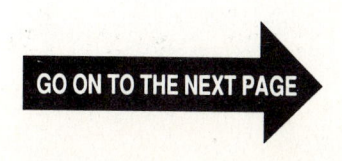

PRACTICE TEST 3

SECTION 1

LISTENING COMPREHENSION

The questions in Section 1 of the test are on a recording.

In this section of the test, you will have an opportunity to demonstrate your ability to understand spoken English. There are three parts to this section, with special directions for each part.

Part A

Directions: For each question in Part A, you will hear a short sentence. Each sentence will be spoken just one time. The sentences you hear will not be written out for you. Therefore, you must listen carefully to understand what the speaker says.

After you hear a sentence, read the four choices in your test book, marked (A), (B), (C), and (D), and decide which *one* is closest in meaning to the sentence you heard. Then, on your answer sheet, find the number of the question and fill in the space that matches the letter of the answer you have chosen. Fill in the space so that the letter inside the oval cannot be seen.

Example I
You will hear: *Mary swam out to the island with her friends.*
You will read: (A) Mary outswam the others.
    (B) Mary ought to swim with them.
    (C) Mary and her friends swam to the island.
    (D) Mary's friends owned the island.

Sample Answer
(A) (B) ● (D)

The speaker said, "Mary swam out to the island with her friends." Sentence (C), "Mary and her friends swam to the island," is closest in meaning to the sentence you heard. Therefore, you should choose answer (C).

Example II
You will hear: *Would you mind helping me with this load of books?*
You will read: (A) Please remind me to read this book.
    (B) Could you help me carry these books?
    (C) I don't mind if you help me.
    (D) Do you have a heavy course load this term?

Sample Answer
(A) ● (C) (D)

The speaker said, "Would you mind helping me with this load of books?" Sentence (B), "Could you help me carry these books?" is closest in meaning to the sentence you heard. Therefore, you should choose answer (B).

GO ON TO THE NEXT PAGE

1 • 1 • 1 • 1 • 1 • 1 • 1

1. (A) The train went through the mountains.
   (B) The birds travelled west.
   (C) The plane flew to Utah.
   (D) Denver is in the mountains.

2. (A) It's been an hour since we first tried.
   (B) Let's try every 30 minutes.
   (C) We've tried for half an hour.
   (D) We'll try again at 12:00.

3. (A) In distress she sat down.
   (B) Her dress was torn.
   (C) She gave her address downtown.
   (D) The store was close to town.

4. (A) The exam wasn't difficult.
   (B) I didn't study.
   (C) It was exactly the same.
   (D) I hadn't studied.

5. (A) The flight was late.
   (B) The flight never arrived.
   (C) Ten Brazilians arrived early at 6:00.
   (D) The flight finally arrived at 7:00.

6. (A) The editor saw it first.
   (B) The printer sent it to the editor.
   (C) The editor didn't approve the magazine.
   (D) The little girl was praised for her printing.

7. (A) It was cold.
   (B) We threw them a blanket.
   (C) We didn't need a blanket.
   (D) It was raining.

8. (A) He offered me some raisins.
   (B) He was too angry for a rational discussion.
   (C) He showed me his new play.
   (D) He showed me his list of reasons.

9. (A) I never heard the phone.
   (B) They'll sweep the top story.
   (C) I always cry at stories about orphans.
   (D) I never listen to sad children.

10. (A) All employees were given five prizes.
    (B) The five-year-old won a prize.
    (C) The company was five years old.
    (D) Prizes were given to employees with five years' tenure.

11. (A) Farmers sent bills to the senator's attention.
    (B) Bill lived in the top-floor apartment.
    (C) The rain was only one reason not to go.
    (D) There was a great deal of legislation.

12. (A) The lecture notes were almost blown away by the wind.
    (B) The guests asked for some paper.
    (C) The newspaper reported the speech.
    (D) Strong opinions should not be repeated.

13. (A) I arrived at 9:15.
    (B) I got there at 8:45.
    (C) I made my class on time.
    (D) I got up after 9:00.

14. (A) Three power generators will be installed next year.
    (B) People must not use electricity for cooking.
    (C) Demand for power will exceed supply.
    (D) This generation must eat less and reduce.

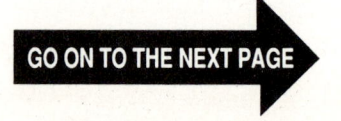

GO ON TO THE NEXT PAGE

15. (A) Buildings in earthquake zones need strong support.
    (B) The proof could not have been greater.
    (C) The motion was defeated.
    (D) The motion of the boat made it hard to stand on our feet.

16. (A) The men stood in a row.
    (B) Two soldiers received a promotion.
    (C) The commander stood higher than the others.
    (D) The men's names were on a list.

17. (A) The car ran out of gas during a long race.
    (B) This long sofa is not very functional.
    (C) A problem with the pump shortened the mission.
    (D) They jumped at the chance to stay longer.

18. (A) Mistakes are frequently displayed.
    (B) It was a mistake to advertise.
    (C) They purchased a new monitor.
    (D) Something was typed incorrectly.

19. (A) The gas for the new car is cheaper.
    (B) There is less gas in the new car's tank.
    (C) The gas for my old car was more expensive.
    (D) My new tank is bigger.

20. (A) We wanted to get up early.
    (B) We should have slept more.
    (C) The alarm didn't work.
    (D) We set the alarm for 12:00.

GO ON TO THE NEXT PAGE

Part B

Directions: In Part B you will hear short conversations between two speakers. At the end of each conversation, a third person will ask a question about what was said. You will hear each conversation and question about it just one time. The sentences you hear will not be written out for you. Therefore, you must listen carefully to understand what each speaker says. After you hear a conversation and the question about it, read the four possible answers in your test book and decide which *one* is the best answer to the question you heard. Then, on your answer sheet, find the number of the question and fill in the space that corresponds to the letter of the answer you have chosen.

Example

Sample Answer
● Ⓑ Ⓒ Ⓓ

You will hear:
    (first man) *Professor Smith is going to retire soon. What kind of gift shall we give her?*
    (woman) *I think she'd like to have a photograph of our class.*
    (second man) *What does the woman think the class should do?*
You will read: (A) Present Professor Smith with a picture.
               (B) Photograph Professor Smith.
               (C) Put glass over the photograph.
               (D) Replace the broken headlight.

From the conversation you learn that the woman thinks Professor Smith would like a photograph of the class. The best answer to the question "What does the woman think the class should do?" is (A), "Present Professor Smith with a picture." Therefore, you should choose answer (A).

21. (A) "Sorry to hear that."
    (B) "You've done something wrong."
    (C) "Contacts are no good."
    (D) "Nothing will help."

22. (A) 5 hours.
    (B) 7 hours.
    (C) 9 hours.
    (D) 10 hours.

23. (A) The 4:40 bus.
    (B) The 5:00 bus.
    (C) The 5:20 bus.
    (D) The 5:40 bus.

24. (A) Retired.
    (B) Withdrawn.
    (C) Fatigued.
    (D) Talkative.

25. (A) Avoid them.
    (B) Go home.
    (C) Repeat himself.
    (D) Attend a party.

26. (A) Mrs. Smith.
    (B) Her father's family.
    (C) Her husband's family.
    (D) Mr. Smith.

27. (A) The trash taken outside.
    (B) Something for her rash.
    (C) The man to fill the sack.
    (D) For him to get ready.

28. (A) They didn't like the other restaurant.
    (B) He generally eats more than she.
    (C) She eats more than he.
    (D) This is the most they've ever eaten.

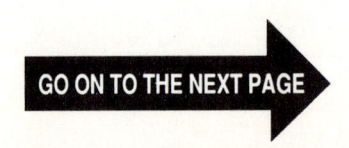

29. (A) Go to the mechanic.
    (B) Go to the office.
    (C) Go home.
    (D) Stop for groceries.

30. (A) Thin socks.
    (B) Thick socks.
    (C) New shoes.
    (D) Not enough exercise.

31. (A) The woman.
    (B) Too little sleep.
    (C) A hat.
    (D) The sun.

32. (A) The man's.
    (B) Annie's.
    (C) Bill's.
    (D) Joe's.

33. (A) Tall.
    (B) Short.
    (C) Bald.
    (D) Thin.

34. (A) With a funny story.
    (B) Promptly.
    (C) With a lecture.
    (D) Easily.

35. (A) It's the dullest.
    (B) It's ridiculous.
    (C) It's long.
    (D) It's plain.

GO ON TO THE NEXT PAGE

1 ● 1 ● 1 ● 1 ● 1 ● 1 ● 1

Part C

Directions: In this part of the test, you will hear several short talks and conversations. After each of them, you will be asked some questions. You will hear the talks and conversations and the questions about them just one time. They will not be written out for you. Therefore, you must listen carefully in order to understand what each speaker says.

After you hear a question, read the four possible answers in your test book and decide which *one* is the best answer to the question you heard. Then, on the your answer sheet, find the number of the question and fill in the space that corresponds to the letter of the answer you have chosen.

Answer all questions on the basis of what is *stated* or *implied* in the talk or conversation.

Listen to this sample talk.
    You will hear:
        (first man) *Balloons have been used for about a hundred years. There are two kinds of sport balloons, gas and hot air. Hot-air balloons are safer than gas balloons, which may catch fire. Hot-air balloons are preferred by most balloonists in the United States because of their safety. They are also cheaper and easier to manage than gas balloons. Despite the ease of operating a balloon, pilots must watch the weather carefully. Sport balloon flights are best early in the morning or late in the afternoon, when the wind is light.*

Sample Answer
Ⓐ ● Ⓒ Ⓓ

Now look at the following example.
    You will hear:
  (second man) *Why are gas balloons considered dangerous?*
    You will read: (A) They are impossible to guide.
                   (B) They may go up in flames.
                   (C) They tend to leak gas.
                   (D) They are cheaply made.

The best answer to the question "Why are gas balloons considered dangerous?" is (B), "They may go up in flames." Therefore, you should choose answer (B).

Now look at the next example.
    You will hear:
  (second man) *According to the speaker, what must balloon pilots be careful to do?*
    You will read: (A) Watch for changes in weather.
                   (B) Watch their altitude.
                   (C) Check for weak spots in their balloons.
                   (D) Test the strength of the ropes.

Sample Answer
● Ⓑ Ⓒ Ⓓ

The best answer to the question "According to the speaker, what must balloon pilots be careful to do?" is (A), "Watch for changes in weather." Therefore, you should choose answer (A).

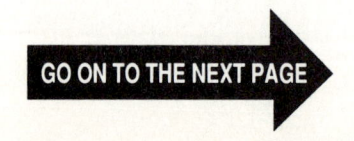

GO ON TO THE NEXT PAGE ➡

60 Practice Tests

36. (A) As popular.
    (B) As valuable.
    (C) As evil.
    (D) As suspicious.

37. (A) Their size.
    (B) Their wingspan.
    (C) Their echo.
    (D) Their eating habits.

38. (A) By sight.
    (B) By touch.
    (C) By echo.
    (D) By instinct.

39. (A) Other bats.
    (B) Weather.
    (C) Man.
    (D) Large mammals.

40. (A) They are very good to eat.
    (B) They are valuable mammals.
    (C) They live in caves.
    (D) They are evil creatures.

41. (A) Ships.
    (B) Cars.
    (C) Trucks.
    (D) Railroads.

42. (A) They're too long.
    (B) They have to be maintained.
    (C) They are too expensive to build.
    (D) There are too few of them.

43. (A) Those with strong navies.
    (B) Those with wooden ships.
    (C) Those with good roads.
    (D) Those with long coastlines.

44. (A) Wide rivers.
    (B) High cost of labor.
    (C) Availability of forests.
    (D) Easy access to China.

45. (A) Lack of good harbors.
    (B) High cost of shipping construction.
    (C) Too many shipping regulations.
    (D) Increased use of planes.

46. (A) Art techniques were introduced in Africa.
    (B) Benin sculptures were discovered.
    (C) The Cuban revolution began.
    (D) African art was widely recognized.

47. (A) The British expedition of 1897.
    (B) Cubism.
    (C) Benin carvings.
    (D) Ethnologists.

48. (A) For fifty years.
    (B) Since 1897.
    (C) Since the Cubist period.
    (D) For hundreds of years.

49. (A) As lacking in aesthetic theory.
    (B) As a great art tradition.
    (C) As a shocking discovery.
    (D) As no longer necessary.

50. (A) Bronze castings.
    (B) Benin carvings.
    (C) African masks.
    (D) Cubist works.

THIS IS THE END OF THE LISTENING COMPREHENSION SECTION OF THE TEST

THE NEXT PART OF THE TEST IS SECTION 2. TURN TO THE DIRECTIONS FOR SECTION 2 IN YOUR TEST BOOK. READ THEM, AND BEGIN WORK. DO NOT READ OR WORK ON ANY OTHER SECTION OF THE TEST.

STOP STOP STOP STOP STOP STOP STOP

SECTION 2

STRUCTURE AND WRITTEN EXPRESSION

Time: 25 minutes

This section tests your ability to recognize language that is appropriate for standard written English. There are two types of questions in this section, with special directions for each type.

Directions: Questions 1–15 are incomplete sentences. Beneath each sentence you will see four words or phrases, marked (A), (B), (C), and (D). Choose the *one* word or phrase that best completes the sentence. Then, on your answer sheet, find the number of the question and fill in the space that corresponds to the letter of the answer you have chosen. Fill in the space so that the letter inside the oval cannot be seen.

Example I

Vegetables are an excellent source _____ vitamins.
(A) of
(B) has
(C) where
(D) that

Sample Answer
● Ⓑ Ⓒ Ⓓ

The sentence should read, "Vegetables are an excellent source of vitamins." Therefore, you should choose answer (A).

Example II

_____ in history when remarkable progress was made within a relatively short span of time.
(A) Periods
(B) Throughout periods
(C) There have been periods
(D) Periods have been

Sample Answer
Ⓐ Ⓑ ● Ⓓ

The sentence should read, "There have been periods in history when remarkable progress was made within a relatively short span of time." Therefore, you should choose answer (C).

Now begin work on the questions.

1. Although we sent out invitations, we have no idea _____ coming to the party.
   (A) who are
   (B) whom are
   (C) who is
   (D) whom is

2. The mayor felt that the police, in spite of the reports, had done _____ best in a difficult situation.
   (A) its
   (B) their
   (C) his
   (D) our

GO ON TO THE NEXT PAGE

3. The pioneers _____ the frontier had a difficult life with few comforts.
   (A) on
   (B) in
   (C) inside
   (D) over

4. _____ there is a snowstorm or some other bad weather, the mail always comes on time.
   (A) Because
   (B) If
   (C) So
   (D) Unless

5. The typist was fast _____, and was hired immediately.
   (A) but efficient
   (B) and efficiently
   (C) so efficient
   (D) and efficient

6. Since calculators were introduced, they _____ to be useful tools for people weak in math.
   (A) proving
   (B) will prove
   (C) have proved
   (D) are proving

7. The _____ economy at the turn of the century was due in large part to the influx of thousands of immigrants.
   (A) rapid expanding
   (B) rapid expand
   (C) expand rapidly
   (D) rapidly expanding

8. Not being able to determine what _____ is the biggest obstacle for new managers.
   (A) the priority should be
   (B) it should be the priority
   (C) should the priority be
   (D) should be it the priority

9. Mr. Kwok cooks continental cuisine _____ as the best cooks in Europe.
   (A) as good
   (B) as better
   (C) better
   (D) as well

10. The nation was founded on the principle that all men are created _____.
    (A) equitable
    (B) equality
    (C) equal
    (D) equilibrium

11. Some doctors involved in brain research _____ that violence has its roots in certain sections of the brain.
    (A) are believing
    (B) believe
    (C) believing
    (D) believes

12. That woman _____ speaking softly can barely be understood.
    (A) whose
    (B) whom is
    (C) who is
    (D) who

13. Even _____ to believe otherwise, the central Arctic is not a solid sheet of ice.
    (A) though many do not want
    (B) many do want not
    (C) though not many do want
    (D) many do not want

14. The language of the Sumerians, _____, is unrelated to any known language.
    (A) which remains obscure origin
    (B) whose origin remains obscure
    (C) whose remains obscure origin
    (D) who is origin obscure remain

GO ON TO THE NEXT PAGE

Practice Tests 63

15. After _____ the angry mob shouting for his resignation, the President summoned his loyal aides to his office.
    (A) their hearing
    (B) they hearing
    (C) heard
    (D) hearing

Directions: In questions 16–40, each sentence has four underlined words or phrases. The four underlined parts of the sentence are marked (A), (B), (C), and (D). Identify the *one* underlined word or phrase that must be changed in order for the sentence to be correct. Then, on your answer sheet, find the number of the question and fill in the space that corresponds to the letter of the answer you have chosen.

Example I

A ray of light passing through the center of a thin lens keep its
                      A   B   C

original direction.
      D

Sample Answer
(A) (B) ● (D)

The sentence should read, "A ray of light passing through the center of a thin lens keeps its original direction." Therefore, you should choose answer (C).

Example II

The mandolin, a musical instrument that has strings, was proba-
                       A   B

bly copied from the lute, a many older instrument.
          C   D

Sample Answer
(A) (B) (C) ●

The sentence should read, "The mandolin, a musical instrument that has strings, was probably copied from the lute, a much older instrument." Therefore, you should choose answer (D).

Now begin work on the questions.

16. Physics is probably being the most highly organized branch of science today.
                   A   B   C   D

17. Psychologists who study sleep habits believes daydreaming is essential.
                A   B   C   D

18. People who always on time cannot understand the seemingly intentional tardiness of people
                  A   B   C

    who are always late.
     D

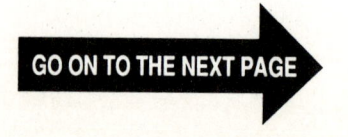

GO ON TO THE NEXT PAGE →

19. Elizabeth I of England had more wigs in her wardrobe than hairs on their head.
              A   B   C   D

20. Man can control changes in nature by imitating them, by using them, and
                    A   B   C

    also man can inhibit them, too.
              D

21. Greek science preserved for posterity by the Arabs, who also introduced the Arabic system
              A   B   C

    of numbers.
       D

22. If a hydrogen-filled balloon is brought near a flame, it exploded.
       A   B   C   D

23. Hormones are chemical substances are produced in the body by structures known
                                  A   B

    as glands, such as sweat glands and salivary glands.
       C   D

24. Outside of Japan seldom potters are regarded as anything more than craftsmen.
          A   B   C   D

25. Tourists like to travel to the eastern shore so the food is good, the people are friendly, and
                  A   B   C   D

    the prices are reasonable.

26. Getting used to eating fast food and traffic jams are problems newcomers have to face
       A   B   C

    after arriving in Los Angeles.
       D

27. Today it is almost impossible to imagination the boredom and constrictions of the average
       A   B   C

    middle-class woman's life before World War II.
                     D

GO ON TO THE NEXT PAGE

2 ● 2 ● 2 ● 2 ● 2 ● 2 ● 2

28. A World Health Organization survey showed that the incidence of eye disease along
       A   B   C

    the Nile three times that along the Amazon.
            D

29. In a recent ranking of American cities, Rand McNally rated Pittsburgh, Pennsylvania, as
           A

    the most livable city and Yuba City, California, as the less.
          B   C   D

30. The hippopotamus kills more men each year than lion and the elephant combined.
        A   B   C   D

31. The Federal Art Project of 1935 supported some 5,000 artists, enabling their to work all
                                                   A   B

    over America rather than come to New York in search of a market.
               C   D

32. Six times a day the bell in the tower in the center at the school tolls.
        A   B   C   D

33. Sophisticated communications have taken the challenge out of traveled in remote places.
       A   B   C   D

34. Since first it being performed on a bare stage in the fifties, Wagner's Ring Cycle
           A   B   C

    has usually been done in minimalist conceptual decor.
         D

35. Because the African tsetse is a serious threat to human health, it helps maintain
        A   B   C

    the delicate balance of nature.
      D

36. Serious bird watchers must know not only the appearance nor the sounds of the 840-odd
          A   B

    species that can be counted in North America.
       C   D

GO ON TO THE NEXT PAGE ▶

37. Rhodes Tavern, a quaint building over 200 years old which it will be torn down soon,
                                                        A   B
was considered a historical monument until investors wanted it.
     C   D

38. Many sociologists believe that sports organized serve both a recreational and a social
                      A   B   C
function by reflecting the values of society.
         D

39. Critics of television commercials would prefer that advertisers conform to a stricter code of
                         A   B
ethics than was currently in effect.
      C   D

40. Education on environmental issues it should include not only physical
    A   B
problems like pollution but also social problems caused by pollution.
         C   D

THIS IS THE END OF SECTION 2

IF YOU FINISH BEFORE TIME IS CALLED, CHECK YOUR WORK
ON SECTION 2 ONLY.
DO NOT READ OR WORK ON ANY OTHER SECTION OF THE TEST. THE SUPERVISOR
WILL TELL YOU WHEN TO BEGIN WORK ON SECTION 3.

Practice Tests 67

SECTION 3

READING COMPREHENSION AND VOCABULARY

Time: 45 minutes

This section tests your comprehension of standard written English. There are two types of questions in this section, with special directions for each type.

Directions: In questions 1–30, each sentence has an underlined word or phrase. Below each sentence are four other words or phrases, marked (A), (B), (C), and (D). You are to choose the *one* word or phrase that *best keeps the meaning* of the original sentence if it is substituted for the underlined word or phrase. Then, on your answer sheet, find the number of the question and fill in the space that matches the letter you have chosen. Fill in the space so that the letter inside the oval cannot be seen.

Example

Passenger ships and aircraft are often equipped with ship-to-shore or air-to-land radio telephones.
(A) highways
(B) railroads
(C) planes
(D) sailboats

Sample Answer
(A) (B) (C) ●

The best answer is (C), because "Passenger ships and planes are often equipped with ship-to-shore or air-to-land radio telephones" is closest in meaning to the original sentence. Therefore, you should choose answer (C).

Now begin work on the questions.

1. The icy roads made driving very hazardous.
   (A) challenging
   (B) dangerous
   (C) slippery
   (D) exciting

2. After watching the sunset, I was left with a very tranquil feeling.
   (A) queasy
   (B) sad
   (C) peaceful
   (D) sleepy

3. People with introverted personalities find it difficult to make friends.
   (A) obnoxious
   (B) forward
   (C) reserved
   (D) outgoing

4. The last mayor was assassinated when he was fifty years old.
   (A) honored
   (B) murdered
   (C) elected
   (D) impeached

GO ON TO THE NEXT PAGE

5. As a result of the expansion of the public transit system, the university will disband its shuttle bus service.
   (A) problems
   (B) painting
   (C) decrease
   (D) enlargement

6. The child charged down the steps.
   (A) ran
   (B) fell
   (C) tiptoed
   (D) slid

7. The speech was barely audible.
   (A) able to be heard
   (B) able to be read
   (C) able to be understood
   (D) able to be ignored

8. Self-confidence is an essential factor for a successful person.
   (A) a possible
   (B) an integral
   (C) a minor
   (D) a negative

9. The theater critics thought the movie was horrendous, and the audience agreed with them.
   (A) delightful
   (B) dreadful
   (C) spectacular
   (D) obscene

10. The politician's manner was blatantly dishonest, so the election results were not a surprise.
    (A) openly
    (B) hardly
    (C) offensively
    (D) extremely

11. The dog's furtive actions made me worry about him.
    (A) unusual
    (B) sleepy
    (C) secretive
    (D) sickly

12. His audacious behavior shocked his parents.
    (A) daring
    (B) brilliant
    (C) courageous
    (D) quiet

13. The popular singer was as ludicrous in his dress as he was in his speech.
    (A) comical
    (B) loud
    (C) somber
    (D) common

14. The teacher explained the nuances in Frost's poetry to the class.
    (A) images
    (B) subtleties
    (C) rhythm
    (D) rhymes

15. The opportune moment had arrived, but few took advantage of it.
    (A) awaited
    (B) lucky
    (C) appropriate
    (D) anticipated

16. The travel agent tried to tantalize me with details of a proposed trip to the islands.
    (A) tempt
    (B) dissuade
    (C) inform
    (D) fool

GO ON TO THE NEXT PAGE

17. The natural elements obliterated the writing from the walls of the monument.
    (A) outlined
    (B) erased
    (C) covered
    (D) produced

18. The sealed chambers of the ancient pharaohs were the goal of the expedition.
    (A) hidden
    (B) unreachable
    (C) ancient
    (D) closed

19. Many of the pictures were reproduced and enlarged.
    (A) taken again
    (B) printed again
    (C) renewed
    (D) restored

20. The valley, wild and inaccessible, had been the haunt of bandits.
    (A) unreachable
    (B) desolate
    (C) high
    (D) dry

21. Children often imitate their parents.
    (A) copy
    (B) criticize
    (C) admire
    (D) remember

22. The administration took for granted that we would agree.
    (A) hoped
    (B) assumed
    (C) guaranteed
    (D) were convinced

23. The tenor's singing captivated the audience.
    (A) frightened
    (B) bored
    (C) disgusted
    (D) enchanted

24. A review of the history of economics shows a recession may precede a depression.
    (A) point to
    (B) come before
    (C) indicate
    (D) cause

25. The punishment should reflect the severity of the crime.
    (A) seriousness
    (B) purpose
    (C) location
    (D) perpetrator

26. Many animals collect a supply of food for the winter.
    (A) bury
    (B) desire
    (C) accumulate
    (D) require

27. The robot, although reliable, has limited use.
    (A) dependable
    (B) automatic
    (C) versatile
    (D) fast

28. In the United States, a typical work day is eight hours long.
    (A) characteristic
    (B) complete
    (C) total
    (D) hard

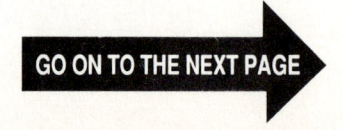

GO ON TO THE NEXT PAGE

29. If you are visiting a foreign country, you may be unaccustomed to eating unfamiliar foods.
    (A) surprised at
    (B) unused to
    (C) disappointed in
    (D) afraid of

30. Because the teenager was ashamed that she failed her driving test, she would not come home.
    (A) disappointed
    (B) unhappy
    (C) humiliated
    (D) disgusted

Directions: In the rest of this section you will read several passages. Each one is followed by several questions about it. For questions 31–60, you are to choose the *one* best answer, (A), (B), (C), or (D), to each question. Then, on your answer sheet, find the number of the question and fill in the space that matches the letter of the answer you have chosen.

Answer all questions following a passage on the basis of what is *stated* or *implied* in the reading passage.

Example passage and questions

The rattles with which a rattlesnake warns of its presence are formed by loosely interlocking hollow rings of hard skin, which make a buzzing sound when its tail is shaken. As a baby, the snake begins to form its rattles from the button at the very tip of its tail. Thereafter, each time it sheds its skin, a new ring is formed. Popular belief holds that a snake's age can be told by counting the rings, but this idea is fallacious. In fact, a snake may lose its old skin as often as four times a year. Also, rattles tend to wear or break off with time.

Example I
A rattlesnake's rattles are made of
(A) skin
(B) bone
(C) wood
(D) muscle

Sample Answer
● Ⓑ Ⓒ Ⓓ

According to the passage, a rattlesnake's rattles are made of rings of hard skin. Therefore, you should choose answer (A).

Example II
How often does a rattlesnake shed its skin?
(A) Once every four years
(B) Once every four months
(C) Up to four times every year
(D) Four times more often than other snakes

Sample Answer
Ⓐ Ⓑ ● Ⓓ

The passage states that "a snake may lose its old skin as often as four times a year." Therefore, you should choose answer (C).

Now begin work on the questions.

Questions 31–35

Some of the properties of magnets were known from very early times. For example, it was known over 2,000 years ago that the mineral magnetite, an oxide of iron, possesses the property of attracting iron. The Chinese, earlier than 2,500 B.C., knew that if a piece of magnetite is suspended so that it can turn freely in a horizontal plane it will set in a definite direction and can therefore be used as a primitive compass. Later it was found that if a bar of iron is rubbed with a piece of magnetite, or lodestone, the magnetic properties of the lodestone are transferred to the iron. The lodestone is called a natural magnet, as distinct from other types of magnet, which are made by various artificial processes.

Magnets today are usually made of special alloys of steel. A steel magnet differs from ordinary steel and from all other substances in three important respects: It attracts iron filings, it sets in a definite direction when freely suspended, and it converts iron and steel bars in its neighborhood into magnets. If we place a bar magnet in iron filings it will emerge with a cluster of filings attached to each end, showing that there is a center of magnetic force at each end of the bar. These centers are called the poles of the magnet. A bar magnet suspended horizontally in a paper stirrup will always set with the line joining its poles along a north and south line; in other words, the magnet has a north-seeking pole and a south-seeking pole. A bar magnet floating on a cork will set roughly north and south but it will not move either to the north or to the south, showing that the two poles are equal in strength. If we bring the north pole of one magnet close to the south pole of another magnet, the unlike poles attract one another, but if we bring two north poles or two south poles into proximity we find that like poles repel one another.

31. In what way are most modern magnets different from ancient ones?
    (A) They attract iron filings.
    (B) They set in a definite direction.
    (C) They are artificial.
    (D) They convert iron into magnets.

32. The ancient Chinese are known to have used magnets to
    (A) attract iron filings
    (B) make steel alloys
    (C) float corks
    (D) indicate direction

33. According to the passage, how many magnetic centers are there in each bar magnet?
    (A) 1
    (B) 2
    (C) 3
    (D) 4

34. Which one of the following is the best title for the passage?
    (A) Varieties of Magnets
    (B) How Magnets Work
    (C) The History of the Magnet
    (D) The Many Uses of Magnets

35. In this passage, the writer makes repeated use of
    (A) argumentative language
    (B) examples
    (C) technical terminology
    (D) hypothesis

GO ON TO THE NEXT PAGE

Questions 36–41

The study of business planning has a long history. For example, in 1916 in one of the earliest efforts to develop a science of management, Henri Fayol discussed the importance of planning to successful management and described the development of one-year and five-year budget plans. In his book he gives the following definition of business planning:

"The maxim 'managing means looking ahead' gives some idea of the importance attached to planning in the business world, and it is true that if foresight is not the whole of management, at least it is an essential part of it. To foresee, in this context, means both to assess the future and make provision for it. . . . The plan of action is, at one and the same time, the result envisaged, the line of action to be followed, the stages to go through and methods to use."

Subsequent studies of general management written during the next fifty years echo Fayol's thinking and reveal both a continuing interest in the subject and an ever-increasing awareness of how important planning is to successful business management. In their definitions of the planning process, the authors of these studies all stress two important aspects of planning: assessing the future and making plans to deal with the future.

36. Which of the following statements expresses the main idea of the passage?
(A) Foresight is critical in business planning.
(B) Know your methods.
(C) A science of management needs to be developed.
(D) The results of management studies from the past fifty years have changed dramatically.

37. It can be inferred from the passage that
(A) Henri Fayol was not looking ahead when he wrote his book
(B) five-year budget plans are preferable to one-year plans
(C) interest in assessing the future has only recently been considered important in business planning
(D) few studies regarding business planning were done prior to 1916

38. In line 7, the phrase "an essential part of it" refers to
(A) foresight
(B) management
(C) the future
(D) study

39. In line 7, the phrase "in this context" means
(A) according to the dictionary
(B) as usual
(C) as is used here
(D) in the future

40. Writers on management working after Fayol have generally
(A) reinforced Fayol's ideas
(B) emphasized budgets instead of time
(C) evolved away from Fayol's future orientation
(D) questioned the value of long-term planning

41. This passage covers management studies for the years
(A) 1900–1966
(B) 1916–1950
(C) 1916–1966
(D) 1916–present

Questions 42–47

When early versions of the typewriter first appeared on the market 100 years ago, salesmen loved the arrangement of letters on the keyboard because they could write TYPEWRITER without leaving the top row. At the time, it impressed customers. It ha~ . since.

After a century of typos, back strain and repetitive motion injuries, the standard QWERTY keyboard—so named for the first six letters of the third row—is considered one of the true abominations of modern design. Of the ten letters, ADEHINORST, for example, which make up about 70 percent of English words, just three are on the middle keys where the fingers normally rest. One of the ten requires the right index finger to jump to the left, six require the hands to hurdle a row either up or down, and one of the alphabet's most commonly used letters, A, is struck by the pinky, the weakest finger.

In recent years, customer complaints about QWERTY have led to a number of suggestions for improving the keyboard. Instead of rearranging the keys to minimize hand movement, as proposed unsuccessfully in the past, a number of researchers would junk the conventional keyboard in favor of much smaller arrays in which the typist would play combinations or chords of keys, much like a piano.

One of the most recent and ambitious chording arrangements, developed by Virginia engineer Larry Langley with the help of the Navy, has just eight keys, one for each finger. Each key has two active positions, front and back, which gives the typist a total of 64 combinations, corresponding to all letters of the alphabet and other necessary keyboard functions.

42. Which of the following statements best expresses the author's opinion of the standard typewriter keyboard?
    (A) It is the optimal arrangement for speed typing.
    (B) It is an exemplary example of modern design.
    (C) It was not designed well.
    (D) The keys need to be rearranged to minimize hand movement.

43. Which of the following does the author mention as a cause for changing the keyboard?
    (A) the suggestions of researchers
    (B) the advice of typewriter salespeople
    (C) customer complaints
    (D) new technology

44. The passage suggests an answer to which of the following questions?
    (A) Why do only ten letters make up about 70 percent of English words?
    (B) Has anyone designed a successful keyboard arrangement?
    (C) How can typists avoid typographical errors?
    (D) When will new chording arrangements be available to the public?

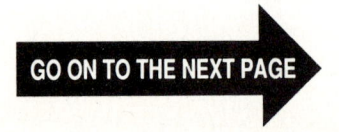

GO ON TO THE NEXT PAGE

45. How does the author organize the discussion of typewriter keyboards?
    (A) The author gives the background and outlines a number of suggestions.
    (B) The author states the problem, and supports his opinion with numerous examples.
    (C) The author gives the history, the subsequent problems, and one solution.
    (D) The author offers a rationale for his suggestions.

46. What is the author's attitude toward revised keyboard arrangements?
    (A) guarded
    (B) enthusiastic
    (C) hopeful
    (D) critical

47. In the first paragraph, the word "it" refers to
    (A) the arrangement of letters
    (B) early versions of the typewriter
    (C) typewriter salesmen
    (D) the first typewriter

Questions 48–53

The idea for the founding of Tucson was brought forth on a hot day in August 1775, when a colonel in the Spanish army, Don Hugo Oconor, and one of the greatest missionaries in the history of the Spanish expansion in the New World, Father Francisco Garces, decided that a military outpost was needed at a small settlement along the Santa Cruz River.

The outpost was to be a part of the Spanish system of presidios, or garrisons, of which there were seventeen along a 2,000-mile frontier stretching through what is now Texas, New Mexico, northern Mexico, Arizona, and California. The existence of the presidios served a dual purpose for the Spanish—to protect their interests from marauding Indians and, later, to form the genesis of new communities. The place along the river the men chose had been settled much earlier by ancestors of the local Pima Indians. The name *Tucson* is a Spanish corruption of the Pima word meaning "the place at the foot of the black mountain."

In June of 1777, a new commander, Captain Don Pedro Allande, was assigned to the fledgling presidio. When Spanish government funds were not available to build fortifications at the renamed San Augustin del Tucson, the money came from Captain Allande. On May Day 1782, the presidio was attacked by a force of 600 Apaches. The garrison survived, but Captain Allande was convinced that further protection was needed. He pushed for the completion of a three-foot-thick adobe wall ten to twelve feet high to enclose San Augustin del Tucson.

48. What does the passage mainly discuss?
    (A) The military strategy of Captain Don Pedro Allande
    (B) The history of the origin of Tucson
    (C) The beginnings of presidios
    (D) The importance of Indians in the founding of Tucson

49. It can be concluded from the passage that
    (A) Tucson is located at the base of a mountain.
    (B) Spanish is the most common language in the area.
    (C) the communities are very religious.
    (D) Tucson was originally settled by the Mexicans.

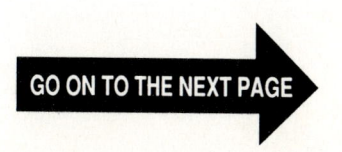

50. The author implies that Don Pedro Allande was
    (A) a Pima Indian
    (B) a poor commander
    (C) a missionary
    (D) a rich man

51. According to the passage, Tucson was founded as
    (A) a mission
    (B) a military outpost
    (C) an Indian reservation
    (D) the seat of the government

52. The paragraph following the passage most probably discusses
    (A) the layout of the city
    (B) instances of Indian attacks
    (C) a description of how the wall was built
    (D) the remaining six presidios

53. In line 10, the word "corruption" most probably means
    (A) destruction
    (B) breakage
    (C) translation
    (D) implication

Questions 54–60

How vividly most people remember the experience of being read to as children! They can tell you exactly whether it was mother or dad who read at bedtime. They know it was Aunt Louise who specialized in Kipling, and Mrs. Rossi in third grade who read *Charlotte's Web* the last thing every afternoon.

A loved adult's voice conjures up a colorful story-world. The memory evokes such warm and contented feelings as recollections of infant nursing might hold, if we could remember back that far. Indeed, the two experiences have common elements: the physical and emotional closeness of adult and child, the adult's attentiveness to the child, and the aim of satisfying a hunger. Clearly, both activities are nurturing ones.

But is the disappearance of communal reading something to mourn? Perhaps it's just a case of having replaced one pleasant pastime with others—gathering around the television set for "Monday Night Football," for instance. Maybe it balances out.

But no. We all recognize that the loss is a real loss, not just a change, and that the shared pleasure of reading aloud is not the only casualty. Many children today grow up with negative attitudes toward books and reading in any form. The media call it "a literacy crisis." The schools try new methods of teaching reading and test children more often, but nothing seems to cure the problems. Publishers bring out attractive books geared to poor readers; teachers report that these students are so turned off by books that the new formats don't entice them at all. Worried parents invest in expensive "teach your child to read" kits and high-powered electronic learning games, only to see their children growing up reading nothing on their own but an occasional comic book.

Meanwhile, research data have slowly been accumulating that suggest how we might resolve this crisis. Several studies of children from widely varied backgrounds who learned to read easily and remained good readers throughout their school years have revealed that they had something in common. They all had been read to regularly from early childhood and had as models adults or older children who read for pleasure.

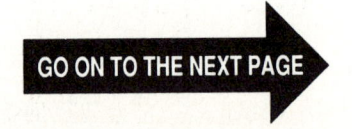

GO ON TO THE NEXT PAGE

54. What does the passage mainly discuss?
    (A) Recollections of communal reading
    (B) The value of reading aloud
    (C) New methods of teaching reading
    (D) Resolving negative attitudes about reading

55. Which of the following does the author mention as a possible cause for the decrease in communal reading?
    (A) Computer games
    (B) Television
    (C) Overscheduled children
    (D) Exhausted parents

56. According to the passage, what do good readers have in common?
    (A) They had library cards and were able to find high-interest books.
    (B) They were read to often as children and saw others reading for pleasure.
    (C) Their parents guided them through "teach your child to read" kits and computer games.
    (D) They attended schools with new methods of teaching reading.

57. The passage supports which of the following conclusions?
    (A) Parents play a critical role in their children's education.
    (B) Television viewing should be banned during the school year.
    (C) The benefits of communal TV watching can be comparable to communal reading.
    (D) The literacy crisis will worsen in the near future.

58. To which of the following activities does the author compare being read to?
    (A) Watching television
    (B) Nursing as an infant
    (C) Playing video games
    (D) Modeling reading opportunities

59. What does the paragraph following the passage most probably discuss?
    (A) Types of books that lend themselves to reading aloud
    (B) Additional explanations of the results of the research
    (C) Warnings about limiting communal reading
    (D) Reasons why children have negative attitudes toward reading

60. Which of the following best describes the tone of the passage?
    (A) Comical and realistic
    (B) Neutral but serious
    (C) Relaxed but persuasive
    (D) Arrogant and scathing

THIS IS THE END OF SECTION 3

IF YOU FINISH BEFORE TIME IS CALLED, CHECK YOUR WORK
ON SECTION 3 ONLY.
DO NOT READ OR WORK ON ANY OTHER SECTION OF THE TEST.

PRACTICE TEST 4

SECTION 1

LISTENING COMPREHENSION

The questions in Section 1 of the test are on a recording.

In this section of the test, you will have an opportunity to demonstrate your ability to understand spoken English. There are three parts to this section, with special directions for each part.

Part A

Directions: For each question in Part A, you will hear a short sentence. Each sentence will be spoken just one time. The sentences you hear will not be written out for you. Therefore, you must listen carefully to understand what the speaker says.

After you hear a sentence, read the four choices in your test book, marked (A), (B), (C), and (D), and decide which *one* is closest in meaning to the sentence you heard. Then, on your answer sheet, find the number of the question and fill in the space that matches the letter of the answer you have chosen. Fill in the space so that the letter inside the oval cannot be seen.

Example I
   You will hear: *Mary swam out to the island with her friends.*
   You will read: (A) Mary outswam the others.
              (B) Mary ought to swim with them.
              (C) Mary and her friends swam to the island.
              (D) Mary's friends owned the island.

Sample Answer
Ⓐ Ⓑ ● Ⓓ

The speaker said, "Mary swam out to the island with her friends." Sentence (C), "Mary and her friends swam to the island," is closest in meaning to the sentence you heard. Therefore, you should choose answer (C).

Example II
   You will hear: *Would you mind helping me with this load of books?*
   You will read: (A) Please remind me to read this book.
              (B) Could you help me carry these books?
              (C) I don't mind if you help me.
              (D) Do you have a heavy course load this term?

Sample Answer
Ⓐ ● Ⓒ Ⓓ

The speaker said, "Would you mind helping me with this load of books?" Sentence (B), "Could you help me carry these books?" is closest in meaning to the sentence you heard. Therefore, you should choose answer (B).

GO ON TO THE NEXT PAGE

78 Practice Tests

1. (A) I couldn't hear well.
   (B) The bugs ran through the dust.
   (C) I got dusty beating the rug.
   (D) My hair is clean.

2. (A) Two boys completed the course.
   (B) Nine boys took the entire course.
   (C) Eleven boys didn't want to finish.
   (D) Thirteen boys wouldn't take the course.

3. (A) There were 17 reservations.
   (B) There were 17 of us.
   (C) Thirty-two people came to the party.
   (D) The party was on the 15th.

4. (A) Many people know who he was.
   (B) Nobody paid any attention.
   (C) He became infamous.
   (D) He had no good intentions.

5. (A) He has never studied geology.
   (B) The geologist had never seen a cannon.
   (C) The canyon was not unique.
   (D) The geologist was impressed.

6. (A) The trainer must return all sports equipment.
   (B) The school no longer is in session.
   (C) All school equipment is used for sports.
   (D) The trainer is in charge of the school's equipment.

7. (A) Nobody could find paper clips.
   (B) We could clip the hedges.
   (C) The eclipse was invisible.
   (D) People went outside to get a good view.

8. (A) The fireman yelled, "Fire!"
   (B) We called them to put out the fire.
   (C) You put out the fire when you were called.
   (D) The fire burned because no one was there to put it out.

9. (A) Jim saw the movie before I did.
   (B) I saw the movie before Jim.
   (C) I saw the movie, then ate.
   (D) Jim ate, then saw the movie.

10. (A) Plan C is the most comprehensive.
    (B) Plan A is better than Plan C.
    (C) Plan B is less complete than Plan A.
    (D) Plan A is less comprehensive than Plan C.

11. (A) The further the distance, the narrower the river.
    (B) Her wide smile is contagious.
    (C) You can see her smile from here.
    (D) The river gets wider a few miles away.

12. (A) The bus started after the bags were loaded.
    (B) Two of us pulled the candy away from the boys.
    (C) The suitcases were left on the curb.
    (D) Those attending brought a bag lunch.

13. (A) She always stays away from hospitals.
    (B) The county erected a memorial to the wounded.
    (C) Many people don't value their vote.
    (D) Some ballots were not counted.

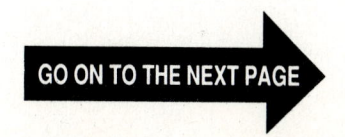

GO ON TO THE NEXT PAGE

14. (A) The beds are in a long row in the room.
    (B) The batteries are dead.
    (C) Photographers work long hours.
    (D) The film was overexposed.

15. (A) The technicians were reluctant to work.
    (B) The technicians deserve more responsibility.
    (C) The technician did not earn our trust.
    (D) The technician worked without pay.

16. (A) They avoided the problem by obeying the rules.
    (B) The rules were not followed.
    (C) Ignoring the rules caused no problem.
    (D) They were unaware of the rules.

17. (A) The program finished sooner than expected.
    (B) The series of programs was very long.
    (C) The issue grew worse over time.
    (D) These problems are hardly serious.

18. (A) The Board reviewed 13 committees.
    (B) The committee recommended 30 items.
    (C) The review took half an hour.
    (D) The Board refused to consider the recommendations.

19. (A) We were not on time.
    (B) The ceremony began 30 minutes ago.
    (C) We'll leave within the next 30 minutes.
    (D) We're going to be tardy.

20. (A) The sun shone after the rain.
    (B) Rye is a shiny grain.
    (C) I would have polished it.
    (D) The wood had a gray color.

GO ON TO THE NEXT PAGE

Part B

Directions: In Part B you will hear short conversations between two speakers. At the end of each conversation, a third person will ask a question about what was said. You will hear each conversation and question about it just one time. The sentences you hear will not be written out for you. Therefore, you must listen carefully to understand what each speaker says. After you hear a conversation and the question about it, read the four possible answers in your test book and decide which *one* is the best answer to the question you heard. Then, on your answer sheet, find the number of the question and fill in the space that corresponds to the letter of the answer you have chosen.

Example
  You will hear:

(first man) *Professor Smith is going to retire soon. What kind of gift shall we give her?*
(woman) *I think she'd like to have a photograph of our class.*
(second man) *What does the woman think the class should do?*

You will read: (A) Present Professor Smith with a picture.
  (B) Photograph Professor Smith.
  (C) Put glass over the photograph.
  (D) Replace the broken headlight.

Sample Answer
● Ⓑ Ⓒ Ⓓ

From the conversation you learn that the woman thinks Professor Smith would like a photograph of the class. The best answer to the question "What does the woman think the class should do?" is (A), "Present Professor Smith with a picture." Therefore, you should choose answer (A).

21. (A) The woman should walk faster.
    (B) The woman is a fast walker.
    (C) The woman can't walk.
    (D) The woman walks too quickly.

22. (A) Met friends.
    (B) Saw a movie.
    (C) Went for a walk.
    (D) Made a phone call.

23. (A) The man can't drive.
    (B) The party is over.
    (C) They can't turn around.
    (D) They're lost.

24. (A) A librarian.
    (B) A laborer.
    (C) A banker.
    (D) A thief.

25. (A) Her grandfather's.
    (B) Her mother's.
    (C) Her brother's.
    (D) Her father's.

26. (A) A hand.
    (B) His briefcase.
    (C) A typewriter.
    (D) His papers.

27. (A) Look for work.
    (B) Take a lonely cruise.
    (C) Buy a horse.
    (D) Cut the grass.

28. (A) 7
    (B) 8
    (C) 18
    (D) 80

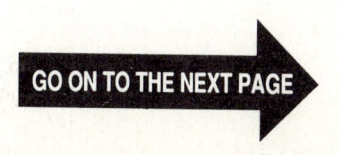

GO ON TO THE NEXT PAGE

29. (A) 50 cents.
    (B) $1.00.
    (C) $1.50.
    (D) $2.00.

30. (A) The shirts.
    (B) The color.
    (C) The size.
    (D) The suits.

31. (A) Look for his friends.
    (B) Go outside.
    (C) Stay inside.
    (D) Take a train.

32. (A) She started swimming.
    (B) She stopped reading.
    (C) She baked some bread.
    (D) She lost weight.

33. (A) At a park.
    (B) In a classroom.
    (C) At an office.
    (D) At church.

34. (A) She's not hungry.
    (B) She'd prefer to cook.
    (C) She wants to go out.
    (D) She only wants to sleep.

35. (A) There will be inflation.
    (B) Prices should increase.
    (C) She shouldn't have to diet.
    (D) She should lose weight.

Part C

Directions: In this part of the test, you will hear several short talks and conversations. After each of them, you will be asked some questions. You will hear the talks and conversations and the questions about them just one time. They will not be written out for you. Therefore, you must listen carefully in order to understand what each speaker says.

After you hear a question, read the four possible answers in your test book and decide which *one* is the best answer to the question you heard. Then, on your answer sheet, find the number of the question and fill in the space that corresponds to the letter of the answer you have chosen.

Answer all questions on the basis of what is *stated* or *implied* in the talk or conversation.

Listen to this sample talk.
  You will hear:
   (first man) *Balloons have been used for about a hundred years. There are two kinds of sport balloons, gas and hot air. Hot-air balloons are safer than gas balloons, which may catch fire. Hot-air balloons are preferred by most balloonists in the United States because of their safety. They are also cheaper and easier to manage than gas balloons. Despite the ease of operating a balloon, pilots must watch the weather carefully. Sport balloon flights are best early in the morning or late in the afternoon, when the wind is light.*

Sample Answer
Ⓐ ● Ⓒ Ⓓ

Now look at the following example.
  You will hear:
   (second man) *Why are gas balloons considered dangerous?*
  You will read: (A) They are impossible to guide.
   (B) They may go up in flames.
   (C) They tend to leak gas.
   (D) They are cheaply made.

The best answer to the question "Why are gas balloons considered dangerous?" is (B), "They may go up in flames." Therefore, you should choose answer (B).

Now look at the next example.

Sample Answer
● Ⓑ Ⓒ Ⓓ

  You will hear:
   (second man) *According to the speaker, what must balloon pilots be careful to do?*
  You will read: (A) Watch for changes in weather.
   (B) Watch their altitude.
   (C) Check for weak spots in their balloons.
   (D) Test the strength of the ropes.

The best answer to the question "According to the speaker, what must balloon pilots be careful to do?" is (A), "Watch for changes in weather." Therefore, you should choose answer (A).

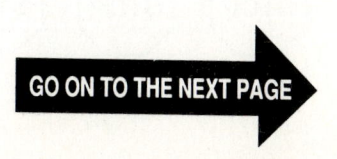

GO ON TO THE NEXT PAGE ➡

36. (A) People are either intelligent or not.
    (B) Humans have multiple intelligences.
    (C) IQs are not indicative of intelligence.
    (D) People are born without intelligence.

37. (A) IQs are extremely important.
    (B) Secrets must be uncovered.
    (C) All people are smart.
    (D) People can be both smart and stupid.

38. (A) Superior cultures.
    (B) Different abilities.
    (C) Intelligence quotients.
    (D) Intelligent races.

39. (A) Minimal.
    (B) None whatsoever.
    (C) Essential.
    (D) Inexplicable.

40. (A) We're smart in different ways.
    (B) Some are smarter than others.
    (C) They are discovered.
    (D) Their IQs reflect their intelligences.

41. (A) Undesirable.
    (B) Necessary.
    (C) Fattening.
    (D) Damaging.

42. (A) Calories.
    (B) Proteins.
    (C) Cereal.
    (D) Energy.

43. (A) Hamburgers.
    (B) Fruit salad.
    (C) Ice cream.
    (D) Purified water.

44. (A) Cereal grains.
    (B) Animals.
    (C) Plants.
    (D) Vegetables.

45. (A) Oxygen.
    (B) Plant tissue.
    (C) Proteins.
    (D) Carbon.

46. (A) California.
    (B) New York.
    (C) Pennsylvania.
    (D) Mississippi.

47. (A) A strong back.
    (B) A lot of money.
    (C) A promise of gold.
    (D) A permit.

48. (A) The prospectors.
    (B) The merchants.
    (C) The cattle ranchers.
    (D) The mule herder.

49. (A) A wife.
    (B) Strong sons.
    (C) A mule.
    (D) Good hands.

50. (A) They're uninhabited.
    (B) They now have zoos.
    (C) Gold has made them prosperous.
    (D) They are full of merchants.

THIS IS THE END OF THE LISTENING COMPREHENSION SECTION OF THE TEST

THE NEXT PART OF THE TEST IS SECTION 2. TURN TO THE DIRECTIONS FOR SECTION 2 IN YOUR TEST BOOK. READ THEM, AND BEGIN WORK. DO NOT READ OR WORK ON ANY OTHER SECTION OF THE TEST.

SECTION 2

STRUCTURE AND WRITTEN EXPRESSION

Time: 25 minutes

This section tests your ability to recognize language that is appropriate for standard written English. There are two types of questions in this section, with special directions for each type.

Directions: Questions 1–15 are incomplete sentences. Beneath each sentence you will see four words or phrases, marked (A), (B), (C), and (D). Choose the *one* word or phrase that best completes the sentence. Then, on your answer sheet, find the number of the question and fill in the space that corresponds to the letter of the answer you have chosen. Fill in the space so that the letter inside the oval cannot be seen.

Example I
   Vegetables are an excellent source _____ vitamins.
   (A) of
   (B) has
   (C) where
   (D) that

Sample Answer
● Ⓑ Ⓒ Ⓓ

The sentence should read, "Vegetables are an excellent source of vitamins." Therefore, you should choose answer (A).

Example II
   _____ in history when remarkable progress was made within a relatively short span of time.
   (A) Periods
   (B) Throughout periods
   (C) There have been periods
   (D) Periods have been

Sample Answer
Ⓐ Ⓑ ● Ⓓ

The sentence should read, "There have been periods in history when remarkable progress was made within a relatively short span of time." Therefore, you should choose answer (C).

Now begin work on the questions.

1. Powder when mixed with water _____.
   (A) dissolving
   (B) dissolves
   (C) dissolve
   (D) is dissolve

2. _____ is thought to be one of the best investments of the decade.
   (A) That the artist works
   (B) The artist's works
   (C) The work of that artist
   (D) That the artist's work

GO ON TO THE NEXT PAGE

3. Water boils _____ if there is a cover on the pan.
   (A) faster
   (B) more fast
   (C) as fast as
   (D) most fast

4. In one year rats eat 40 to 50 times _____ weight.
   (A) its
   (B) and
   (C) their
   (D) of

5. If there were life on Mars, such life forms _____ unable to survive on Earth.
   (A) would be
   (B) are
   (C) will be
   (D) would

6. Little is known about platinum _____ so little of it exists.
   (A) but
   (B) why
   (C) because
   (D) although

7. The damage was caused by either the earthquake _____ the subsequent explosions.
   (A) and
   (B) but
   (C) then
   (D) or

8. After _____, the supernova hurls its mass into the black void of space.
   (A) explode
   (B) exploding
   (C) explosive
   (D) explodes

9. Severe reactions to bee stings among adults _____ than once believed.
   (A) more are probably common
   (B) more common probably are
   (C) are more probably common
   (D) are probably more common

10. The vineyards are open all year except for August, which _____.
    (A) the best time to harvest is
    (B) is the best time to harvest
    (C) to harvest is the best time
    (D) the best time is to harvest

11. Because of intermittent charging by the _____, the lights flickered.
    (A) generating
    (B) generation
    (C) generator
    (D) generated

12. New research in geophysics disproved _____ had been a universally accepted truth.
    (A) that
    (B) which
    (C) whom
    (D) what

13. The static interference on the radio _____ an airplane.
    (A) was caused by
    (B) was causing
    (C) has caused
    (D) caused by

14. Water vapor _____ on a window pane produces condensation.
    (A) which accumulating
    (B) accumulating
    (C) accumulates
    (D) is accumulating

GO ON TO THE NEXT PAGE

15. The management requests that all personnel _____ their complaints to their immediate supervisor.
    (A) will direct
    (B) directs
    (C) directing
    (D) direct

Directions: In questions 16–40, each sentence has four underlined words or phrases. The four underlined parts of the sentence are marked (A), (B), (C), and (D). Identify the *one* underlined word or phrase that must be changed in order for the sentence to be correct. Then, on your answer sheet, find the number of the question and fill in the space that corresponds to the letter of the answer you have chosen.

Example I

A ray of light passing through the center of a thin lens keep its
                      A   **B**   **C**

original direction.
   D

Sample Answer
(A) (B) ● (D)

The sentence should read, "A ray of light passing through the center of a thin lens keeps its original direction." Therefore, you should choose answer (C).

Example II

The mandolin, a musical instrument that has strings, was proba-
                        A   **B**

bly copied from the lute, a many older instrument.
        C   **D**

Sample Answer
(A) (B) (C) ●

The sentence should read, "The mandolin, a musical instrument that has strings, was probably copied from the lute, a much older instrument." Therefore, you should choose answer (D).

Now begin work on the questions.

16. Because of the rising cost of living, more families today they are discovering that
             A   **B**

    both husband and wife must work.
           C   **D**

17. A team of specialists concluded that the patient's blindness was contemporary.
        A   **B**   **C**   **D**

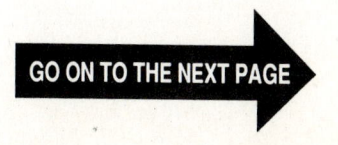

GO ON TO THE NEXT PAGE

18. After given the award, the recipient of the Peace Prize made a short acceptance speech,
    A   B

    which was followed by a standing ovation.
    C   D

19. When the Spanish constructed its missions in the New World, they incorporated
         A   B   C

    Moorish architectural features.
    D

20. Marcel Duchamp, who died in 1969, is known as the artist who has abandoned art for
                         A   B   C   D

    chess.

21. Although the country's military budget is insufficient, the army be expected
        A   B   C

    to perform well in war.
    D

22. After two weeks of intensive computer training, the new recruits were allowed to
    A   B

    write a program theirselves.
    C   D

23. The archaeologist believed which the tomb discovered in North Africa belonged to one of
        A   B   C   D

    Hannibal's generals.

24. Meteorologists have been using both computers or satellites to help make weather forecasts
                   A   B   C

    for two decades.
    D

25. There is a folk myth that an horsehair in a container of rainwater placed in the sunshine
        A   B C

    will develop into a snake.
    D

GO ON TO THE NEXT PAGE

26. The Arctic ice pack is 40 percent thin and 12 percent smaller in area than it was a half
    　　　A　　　　　　　　　B　　　　　　　　　　　　　　C　　　　　　　　D

    a century ago.

27. Crime prevention experts believe that if the possession of small firearms were limited,
    　　　　　　　　　A　　　　　　　　　　B　　　　　　C

    crime and violence decreased.
    　　　　　　　D

28. For nesting and shelter, the sparrow seeks out the seclusion and being secure offered by
    　　　A　　　　　　　　　　　　B　　　　　　　　　　　　C

    tangled vines and thick bushes.
    　　　　　　　　　D

29. The advent of calculators did fundamentally changed the teaching methods for
    　　A　　　　　　　　B　　　　　　　　　　　　C

    mathematics.
    　　D

30. Aluminum, which making up about 8 percent of the Earth's crust, is the most abundant
    　　　　　　　　A　　　　　　　　　　　　B　　　　　C　　　D

    metal available.

31. The screenwriter who provides the words for a film is acclaimed seldom, unlike the
    　　　　　　　　A　　　　　　　B　　　　　　　　C

    director and the actors and actresses.
    　　　　　　　　　D

32. The cowboy epitomizes the belief held by many Americans for rugged individualism and
    　　　　　　　　　　　A　　　　　　　　　B　　　C

    the frontier spirit.
    　　D

33. Most early immigrants are coming from an agricultural background found work on farms.
    　　　　　　A　　　B　　　　　　　C　　　　　　　　　　　　　　　D

34. Recently gasoline manufacturers have begun to develop additives will reduce the harmful
    　　A　　　　　　　　　　　　　　　　　　　　B　　　　　　　C

    emissions from automobile engines.
    　　　　　D

GO ON TO THE NEXT PAGE

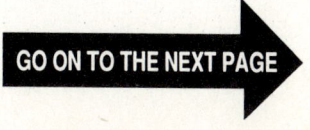

Practice Tests 89

35. People, when they sleep less than normal, awake more friendly and more aggression.
          A   B   C   D

36. As cooling slows the life process, blood cells in the laboratory is stored at
        A   B   C

    low temperatures.
        D

37. The lawyers for the administration met with the representative of the students had been
                A   B   C

    occupying the building for a week.
                          D

38. Restaurant patrons who stay after 11 o'clock will not be able to use public transportation to
                 A   B   C

    have returned home.
       D

39. The citizens, who been tolerant of the mayor's unsavory practices in the past,
             A   B

    finally impeached the amoral politician.
        C   D

40. During the Industrial Revolution, the birth rate in Europe declined, as the death rate.
         A   B   C   D

THIS IS THE END OF SECTION 2

IF YOU FINISH BEFORE TIME IS CALLED, CHECK YOUR WORK ON SECTION 2 ONLY.

DO NOT READ OR WORK ON ANY OTHER SECTION OF THE TEST. THE SUPERVISOR WILL TELL YOU WHEN TO BEGIN WORK ON SECTION 3.

SECTION 3

READING COMPREHENSION AND VOCABULARY

Time: 45 minutes

This section tests your comprehension of standard written English. There are two types of questions in this section, with special directions for each type.

Directions: In questions 1–30, each sentence has an underlined word or phrase. Below each sentence are four other words or phrases, marked (A), (B), (C), and (D). You are to choose the *one* word or phrase that *best keeps the meaning* of the original sentence if it is substituted for the underlined word or phrase. Then, on your answer sheet, find the number of the question and fill in the space that matches the letter you have chosen. Fill in the space so that the letter inside the oval cannot be seen.

Example   **Sample Answer**

Passenger ships and aircraft are often equipped with ship-to-shore   Ⓐ Ⓑ ● Ⓓ
or air-to-land radio telephones.
 (A) highways
 (B) railroads
 (C) planes
 (D) sailboats

The best answer is (C), because "Passenger ships and planes are often equipped with ship-to-shore or air-to-land radio telephones" is closest in meaning to the original sentence. Therefore, you should choose answer (C).

Now begin work on the questions.

1. The issue we are discussing concerns everyone who has children.
 (A) subject
 (B) book
 (C) article
 (D) equation

2. The evaluation stated that the secretary's work has been satisfactory.
 (A) whimsical
 (B) adequate
 (C) audacious
 (D) comprehensive

3. The hospital is looking for people willing to donate their organs.
 (A) sell
 (B) retrieve
 (C) give
 (D) show

4. Most teenagers think their actions are mature.
 (A) grown-up
 (B) intelligent
 (C) serious
 (D) childlike

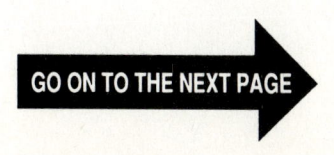

GO ON TO THE NEXT PAGE

5. The chorale wanted to rehearse the song before the performance.
   (A) delete
   (B) rewrite
   (C) introduce
   (D) practice

6. After an extended break, the class resumed.
   (A) continued
   (B) returned
   (C) repeated
   (D) receded

7. Prejudice toward minorities probably stems from fear of the unknown.
   (A) concerning
   (B) upon
   (C) through
   (D) around

8. The bank needed some assurance that the loan would be repaid.
   (A) contract
   (B) approval
   (C) guarantee
   (D) presence

9. The sign requested that we extinguish all fires before leaving the campground.
   (A) count
   (B) put out
   (C) remember
   (D) locate

10. Invitations were extended to everyone who had worked on the project.
    (A) offered to
    (B) mandated for
    (C) shown to
    (D) intended for

11. The roof of the house was practically falling in and the front steps were rotting away.
    (A) almost
    (B) obviously
    (C) always
    (D) conveniently

12. Their inept handling of our account made us reevaluate our relationship with them.
    (A) dishonest
    (B) clever
    (C) clumsy
    (D) competent

13. The article alluded to the devastation in the countryside, caused by the wind storms.
    (A) misrepresented
    (B) referred to
    (C) forgot about
    (D) recounted

14. The zealous demonstrators were ignored by the media.
    (A) ardent
    (B) colorful
    (C) rude
    (D) clever

15. No one ever knew the reason for the enmity between the two families.
    (A) relationship
    (B) hatred
    (C) friendship
    (D) remoteness

16. The teacher thought the aspiring writer's essays were verbose.
    (A) interesting
    (B) concise
    (C) clever
    (D) redundant

GO ON TO THE NEXT PAGE

17. The organizer's intransigent manner helped her get her way.
    (A) honest
    (B) stubborn
    (C) friendly
    (D) loud

18. The humidity made us more lethargic than usual.
    (A) thirsty
    (B) slow
    (C) warm
    (D) careless

19. People usually think cats are naturally ferocious, but it depends on the type of cat.
    (A) friendly
    (B) furry
    (C) savage
    (D) independent

20. Generosity is believed to be an innate quality of man.
    (A) a hidden
    (B) a benevolent
    (C) a natural
    (D) an unselfish

21. The greatest physical distinction between humans and apes is the hollow space humans have under their chins.
    (A) attraction
    (B) danger
    (C) comfort
    (D) difference

22. Physicists have made discoveries that challenge our most fundamental theories of the universe.
    (A) basic
    (B) permanent
    (C) interesting
    (D) ancient

23. The most recent research indicates that dinosaurs were warm-blooded animals.
    (A) disputes
    (B) insists
    (C) suggests
    (D) disproves

24. Contrary to popular belief, Cleopatra, the famous Egyptian queen, was Greek, spoke six languages, and was a brilliant military strategist.
    (A) an intelligent
    (B) a known
    (C) a professional
    (D) a popular

25. An archaeologist must know exactly where and when an artifact was found.
    (A) intuitively
    (B) immediately
    (C) briefly
    (D) precisely

26. The budget director wanted to be certain that his officers were aware of the deadline.
    (A) ask if
    (B) pretend that
    (C) make sure that
    (D) know if

27. The cab driver was discourteous.
    (A) handsome
    (B) rude
    (C) irritable
    (D) lost

28. The children in the neighborhood have a club that excludes everyone over eight.
    (A) laughs at
    (B) avoids
    (C) leaves out
    (D) invites

GO ON TO THE NEXT PAGE

29. What is the gist of the article?
    (A) ending
    (B) length
    (C) title
    (D) point

30. A good magician can make an elephant disappear.
    (A) behave
    (B) forget
    (C) learn
    (D) vanish

Directions: In the rest of this section you will read several passages. Each one is followed by several questions about it. For questions 31–60, you are to choose the *one* best answer, (A), (B), (C), or (D), to each question. Then, on your answer sheet, find the number of the question and fill in the space that matches the letter of the answer you have chosen.

Answer all questions following a passage on the basis of what is *stated* or *implied* in the reading passage.

Example passage and questions

The rattles with which a rattlesnake warns of its presence are formed by loosely interlocking hollow rings of hard skin, which make a buzzing sound when its tail is shaken. As a baby, the snake begins to form its rattles from the button at the very tip of its tail. Thereafter, each time it sheds its skin, a new ring is formed. Popular belief holds that a snake's age can be told by counting the rings, but this idea is fallacious. In fact, a snake may lose its old skin as often as four times a year. Also, rattles tend to wear or break off with time.

Example I

A rattlesnake's rattles are made of
(A) skin
(B) bone
(C) wood
(D) muscle

Sample Answer
● Ⓑ Ⓒ Ⓓ

According to the passage, a rattlesnake's rattles are made of rings of hard skin. Therefore, you should choose answer (A).

Example II

How often does a rattlesnake shed its skin?
(A) Once every four years
(B) Once every four months
(C) Up to four times every year
(D) Four times more often than other snakes

Sample Answer
Ⓐ Ⓑ ● Ⓓ

The passage states that "a snake may lose its old skin as often as four times a year." Therefore, you should choose answer (C).

Now begin work on the questions.

Questions 31–37

The names that admiring naturalists have given to hummingbirds suggest exquisite, fairylike grace and gemlike refulgence. Fiery-tailed awlbill, ruby-topaz hummingbird, glittering-bellied emerald—these are a few of the colorful names that I find applied to some of the 233 species of hummingbirds briefly described in Meyer de Schauenesee's scientific *Guide to the Birds of South America*.

One would expect one's first glimpse of a creature that bears one of these glamorous names to be a breathtaking vision of beauty. Often the birdwatcher is disappointed. To behold the hummingbird's most vivid colors, he or she may have to wait patiently before flowers that it habitually visits, until it turns squarely toward the viewer. Then the gorget or the crown—usually the male hummingbird's most glittering part—which at first appeared to be lusterless, suddenly gleams with the most intense metallic green, blue, violet, magenta, or ruby, like a sunbeam suddenly breaking through a dark cloud. The fiery glitter is often all too brief, for with the first turn of the hummer's body it expires as suddenly as it flared up. How different from the bright colors of such birds as tanagers, orioles, and wood warblers, which are visible at a glance and show to almost equal advantage from any angle.

31. Which of the following does the author mainly discuss?
    (A) Birds of South America
    (B) Hummingbirds
    (C) Tanagers, orioles, and wood warblers
    (D) Colors

32. According to the passage, which statement is true?
    (A) Hummingbirds are visible at a great distance.
    (B) Hummingbirds are found only in South America.
    (C) It's difficult to see the beautiful colors of hummingbirds.
    (D) Male hummingbirds are lusterless.

33. Which of the following does the author imply?
    (A) Orioles and hummingbirds have similar colors.
    (B) The male hummingbird is more colorful than the female.
    (C) There are only a few different types of hummingbirds.
    (D) Hummingbirds show their beautiful colors from every angle.

34. The words "he or she" (line 8) refers to
    (A) the hummingbird
    (B) Meyer de Schauenesee
    (C) a bird watcher
    (D) the author

35. The tone of the passage could best be described as
    (A) objective
    (B) reverential
    (C) critical
    (D) dismissive

36. The author compares the hummingbird with tanagers, orioles, and wood warblers because
    (A) they are colorful
    (B) they like flowers
    (C) they are frequently seen
    (D) they move quickly

37. What does the word "*it*" in line 14 refer to?
    (A) the fiery glitter
    (B) the first turn
    (C) a sunbeam
    (D) the hummer's body

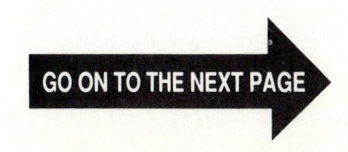

GO ON TO THE NEXT PAGE

Questions 38–43

At the worker level, technology can affect the social relationships among people by bringing about changes in such human elements as the size and composition of the work group or the frequency of contact with other workers. E. L. Trist and K. W. Bamforth discovered this when they conducted research among post-World War I coal miners. The miners initially worked in
small, independent, cohesive groups. However, advances in technology and equipment led to changes in the composition of these work groups, and the result was a decline in productivity. Only when management restored many of the social and small-group relationships did output again increase.

It is perhaps the greatest fear of workers faced with new technology that the machinery will
lead to the abolition of jobs or to the reduction of tasks to such simplistic levels that workers can hardly endure the stress of their new, extremely dull functions. Since the human being must be able to support one or more persons by means of work and since the mind resists its own belittling, such changes, brought about by advancing technology, have a profound effect on the psychosocial system. In order to prevent intolerable upheaval, management must be simultaneously and equally
aware of the social (human) and the technical (operational) aspects and needs of the organization.

38. What is the main idea of the passage?
    (A) Small groups work more efficiently than large ones.
    (B) Modern work methods are inhumane and degrading.
    (C) Efficiency in the workplace results from a balance of social and technological factors.
    (D) The technology of coal mining is constantly evolving.

39. The author's purpose in the passage is to
    (A) urge workers to form unions
    (B) suggest ways to prevent disruption in the workplace
    (C) argue for smaller work groups
    (D) discourage rapid technological change in the workplace

40. Which of the following best describes the author's attitude toward the workers?
    (A) Puzzled
    (B) Critical
    (C) Interested
    (D) Supportive

41. The author uses the word "output" (line 7) in the passage to mean
    (A) tasks
    (B) productivity
    (C) increase
    (D) advances

42. At which point does the author begin to discuss supporting evidence?
    (A) Line 1
    (B) Line 4
    (C) Line 9
    (D) Line 11

43. The paragraph immediately following the passage probably discusses
    (A) details about post-World War I miners
    (B) how workers support their families
    (C) details about social aspects and needs in the workplace
    (D) how to resist change in the workplace

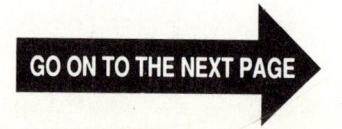

GO ON TO THE NEXT PAGE

Questions 44–50

Hospitals and surgery can be especially frightening for children, and to help lessen young patients' anxiety, one drug company has been experimenting with sedative "lollipops." Recently the U.S. Food and Drug Administration (FDA) gave the go-ahead to further testing of sweet-tasting fentanyl suckers on children, despite protests from a consumer health group that the lollipop form will give kids the idea that drugs are candy. Fentanyl, a widely used narcotic anesthetic agent, is 200 times more potent than morphine.

Fentanyl lollipops can ease kids' separation from their parents and make the administration of anesthesia go more smoothly, according to a member of the team that tested them. But the Public Citizen Health Research Group, alarmed by what it believes is a danger to children and a new opportunity for drug abuse, urged the FDA to call a halt to the experiments. Fentanyl is so addictive, according to the group's director, Dr. Sidney Wolfe, that its widespread availability could cause drug-abuse problems. He suggests that hospitals develop other ways to calm young patients, such as making greater use of play therapy and allowing parents to accompany children into the operating room.

Dr. Gary Henderson, a pharmacologist and an authority on fentanyl abuse, doubts that carefully controlled use of the drug in a hospital setting would pose a danger or suggest to kids that drugs are like candy. "Children will associate few things in the hospital with a pleasant experience," he says.

44. Which of the following is the best title for the passage?
  (A) Children's Fears
  (B) Play Therapy versus Fentanyl
  (C) Dangerous Medicines for Children
  (D) Narcotic Lollipops

45. According to the passage, why does the Public Citizen Health Research Group protest the use of fentanyl lollipops?
  (A) Testing for effectiveness has not been completed.
  (B) Fentanyl is addictive, and could therefore be abused.
  (C) The lollipops contain too much sugar, and could possibly affect the teeth of the children.
  (D) Morphine is preferable for sedating children.

46. According to the passage, what advantage do the lollipops have over regular anesthesia?
  (A) They are easier to administer.
  (B) They are less costly.
  (C) They are more potent.
  (D) They are safer.

47. Which of the following is NOT mentioned as a way of lessening young patients' anxieties regarding surgery?
  (A) Sedative lollipops
  (B) Play therapy
  (C) Parents' presence in the operating room
  (D) Children's books about anesthesia

GO ON TO THE NEXT PAGE

48. The passage supports which of the following conclusions?
    (A) Fentanyl lollipops have been declared safe for children.
    (B) Sedative lollipops have caused children to have no fears regarding surgery.
    (C) The use of sedative lollipops is controversial.
    (D) Medical doctors agree that fentanyl lollipops will be considered beneficial in the future.

49. Which of the following words best describes the tone of the passage?
    (A) Critical
    (B) Didactic
    (C) Informative
    (D) Insistent

50. The author uses the quote in the last sentence to indicate
    (A) that children are usually optimistic about hospital stays
    (B) there is always something memorable about hospitals
    (C) that young patients can be taught to enjoy hospitals
    (D) that children don't usually enjoy hospital stays

Questions 51–56

What issues are of concern to today's teenagers? How do they view themselves and the world in which they live? How do they rate their schools in terms of helping them prepare for adulthood? These were the basic questions answered by the 1988 American Home Economics Association's Survey of American Teenagers. Interviews with 510 high school juniors and seniors, selected to represent the U.S. high school population by sex and by race/ethnicity, indicated that the world of today's teenagers is a balance of positive and negative influences.

Teenagers identified issues relating to money, the future, and health as ones that worry them most. At least three in ten were "extremely" or "very" concerned about being able to pay for college, not earning enough money, making the wrong decisions about their futures, contracting AIDS, and the future of the United States. Issues relating to career choice, marriage, family financial well-being, combining work and family responsibilities, dealing with family crises, and nutrition and disease were of concern to at least one in five surveyed.

Further, teenagers reported that the schools are doing only an "adequate" job of teaching them the skills necessary for a responsible and productive life. Schools received the highest ratings in life-skill areas related to health concerns (substance abuse, human sexuality, and AIDS), choosing a career, and making important life decisions. But teenagers perceived that they were least prepared by schools in matters related to family life/parenting, choosing a marital partner, and dealing with family crises, such as death and divorce.

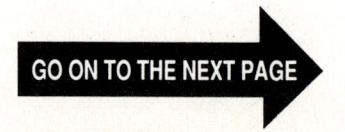

51. With which topic is the passage mainly concerned?
    (A) American teenagers' preparation for adulthood
    (B) Results of a survey of American teenagers
    (C) Positive and negative influences on American teenagers
    (D) Current home economics curricula

52. According to the passage, which of the following is considered one of the most worrisome issues facing teenagers today?
    (A) A decrease in academic skills
    (B) Racial problems
    (C) Future financial problems
    (D) The high rate of divorce

53. According to the passage, which of the following is NOT mentioned as an area in which schools are sufficiently preparing their teenagers?
    (A) Health
    (B) Careers
    (C) Drugs
    (D) Academics

54. It can be inferred from the passage that
    (A) the students surveyed were chosen for their academic abilities
    (B) those surveyed were from various parts of the United States
    (C) most of the students surveyed were in vocational studies
    (D) the teenagers surveyed were enrolled in home economics classes

55. With which of the following statements would the author of the passage be LEAST likely to agree?
    (A) Today's American teenagers are mostly pessimistic about their future.
    (B) American teenagers are satisfied with their educational programs.
    (C) The results of the survey reflect the consensus of most American teenagers.
    (D) American teenagers are somewhat dissatisfied with the current family life education programs available in their high schools.

56. The paragraph following the passage most probably discusses
    (A) the likelihood of increasing the number of academic course requirements
    (B) the need for additional funding for health-related courses
    (C) how the survey was administered and how the results were calculated
    (D) program improvement and curriculum in life-skills programs

GO ON TO THE NEXT PAGE

Questions 57–60

Stories are often told about telephone operators from all over the United States getting inquiries about foreign long-distance rates to New Mexico. The post office in Albuquerque receives U.S. mail affixed with international airmail stamps. The occasional first-time visitor will bring a passport. Although it has been a part of the U.S. since 1912, New Mexico's 122,000 square miles can seem like a foreign country to those unfamiliar with it. More than any other state, it has held on to—and nurtured—its historic roots. Spanish flows easily from the lips of residents. Native Americans still live in ancient cities built by their forbears and participate in age-old traditions.

Yet New Mexico, which has a history and culture traceable for thousands of years, is perhaps the most "American" of all the states; it could be said that it is the cradle of this country's civilization. Long before European feet trod on Plymouth Rock, they left footprints in New Mexico.

Although the presence of man in New Mexico can be traced back more than 25,000 years, it is generally thought that today's Pueblo Indians are descendants of the Anasazi, a culture that flourished from before the birth of Christ to the thirteenth century. The Anasazi and their descendants were mostly peaceful people, agrarian and social, who lived together in small villages.

57. What is the main topic of this passage?
 (A) The Anasazi way of life
 (B) The geography of the Southwest
 (C) A history of New Mexico
 (D) Various Native American tribes

58. According to the passage, when did man first appear in New Mexico?
 (A) About 25,000 years ago
 (B) At around the thirteenth century
 (C) At the time of the arrival of Europeans
 (D) Since 1912

59. The author implies, but does not state, that
 (A) the Anasazi preceded the Pueblo Indians
 (B) New Mexico is one of the largest states in the U.S.
 (C) many people consider New Mexico part of Mexico
 (D) the Anasazi were farmers

60. In the first paragraph, the phrase "Native Americans" could best be replaced by which of the following?
 (A) The Anasazi
 (B) Pueblo Indians
 (C) New Mexicans
 (D) Albuquerque residents

THIS IS THE END OF SECTION 3

DO NOT READ OR WORK ON ANY OTHER SECTION OF THE TEST.

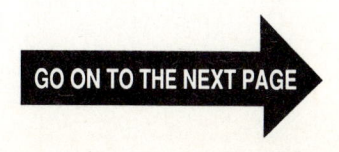

PRACTICE TEST 5

SECTION 1

LISTENING COMPREHENSION

The questions in Section 1 of the test are on a recording.

In this section of the test, you have an opportunity to demonstrate your ability to understand spoken English. There are three parts to this section, with special directions for each part.

Part A

Directions: For each question in Part A, you will hear a short sentence. Each sentence will be spoken just one time. The sentences you hear will not be written out for you. Therefore, you must listen carefully to understand what the speaker says.

After you hear a sentence, read the four choices in your test book, marked (A), (B), (C), and (D), and decide which *one* is closest in meaning to the sentence you heard. Then, on your answer sheet, find the number of the question and fill in the space that matches the letter of the answer you have chosen. Fill in the space so that the letter inside the oval cannot be seen.

Example I
    You will hear: *Mary swam out to the island with her friends.*
    You will read: (A) Mary outswam the others.
                     (B) Mary ought to swim with them.
                     (C) Mary and her friends swam to the island.
                     (D) Mary's friends owned the island.

Sample Answer
(A) (B) ● (D)

The speaker said, "Mary swam out to the island with her friends." Sentence (C), "Mary and her friends swam to the island," is closest in meaning to the sentence you heard. Therefore, you should choose answer (C).

Example II
    You will hear: *Would you mind helping me with this load of books?*
    You will read: (A) Please remind me to read this book.
                     (B) Could you help me carry these books?
                     (C) I don't mind if you help me.
                     (D) Do you have a heavy course load this term?

Sample Answer
(A) ● (C) (D)

The speaker said, "Would you mind helping me with this load of books?" Sentence (B), "Could you help me carry these books?" is closest in meaning to the sentence you heard. Therefore, you should choose answer (B).

GO ON TO THE NEXT PAGE

1. (A) The accountant is poor.
   (B) There isn't enough money in the account.
   (C) I have no faith in the accountant's judgment.
   (D) The man cannot count.

2. (A) We all walked 3 miles.
   (B) The coach walked 15 miles.
   (C) The coach only hiked 3 miles.
   (D) We only walked 13 miles.

3. (A) Larger jets make less noise than old, small ones.
   (B) The smaller the jet, the less noise it makes.
   (C) The noisiest aircraft are the newest.
   (D) The older jets are larger.

4. (A) The orphans were put in a home.
   (B) The windows were covered with dust.
   (C) Everyone remembers the feast we had.
   (D) Women honored their deceased husbands.

5. (A) The tenant agreed to rent the house from the landlord.
   (B) The landlord didn't want to rent to the tenant anymore.
   (C) The landlord still cannot understand the tenant's decision.
   (D) The landlord refused to rent the house.

6. (A) The engineer submitted the plans.
   (B) There was no disagreement.
   (C) Only one person disagreed.
   (D) The builder needed the city's plans.

7. (A) The nurse turned over as she slept.
   (B) The nurse woke late because of her clock.
   (C) She always does her duty.
   (D) The nurse shouldn't sleep on duty.

8. (A) She married a prince.
   (B) The prince married the princess.
   (C) She will marry a prince.
   (D) She could be a princess if she were married to a prince.

9. (A) Before the invention of clocks, people were unable to tell time.
   (B) People are constantly telling time by their clocks.
   (C) People used to tell time by the position of the stars.
   (D) You can tell time only during the day.

10. (A) The test starts at five o'clock.
    (B) Thirty people are taking the exam.
    (C) Twelve students are in the group.
    (D) Thirteen students will take the test.

11. (A) The highway department has enough men.
    (B) More laborers are required to finish the job.
    (C) The highways are wider than the roads.
    (D) More men are needed during the winter.

12. (A) Clothes must be put on in the dark.
    (B) Wear protective clothing at all times.
    (C) Do not turn on the electricity before the lid is off.
    (D) The electricity must be off before the cover is removed.

13. (A) She got an A without studying.
    (B) She didn't study and didn't get an A.
    (C) She changed her grade to an A.
    (D) She got an A because she studied.

14. (A) The wind blew the door open.
    (B) The door smashed the vase.
    (C) The wind blew the table over.
    (D) The wind knocked the vase over.

GO ON TO THE NEXT PAGE

15. (A) The Citizens Concert is a popular event.
    (B) The mayor is carefully supervised.
    (C) The consensus of the group may not count.
    (D) The citizens presented the mayor with a new watch.

16. (A) Hawking's study of endangered species is brilliant.
    (B) Hawking is studying hard to become a scientist.
    (C) Hawking continues to work, although he is physically disabled.
    (D) Although Hawking is a famous scientist, he wants to study crippling diseases.

17. (A) He is a wonderful conductor.
    (B) Swimming causes electrical charges.
    (C) Swimming is excellent conditioning
    (D) Electrical storms can be dangerous.

18. (A) Four of us heard the concert.
    (B) Only four of us went to the concert.
    (C) Thirteen of us couldn't get in.
    (D) Eight of us heard the concert.

19. (A) I was 10 minutes late.
    (B) I was 15 minutes late.
    (C) I slept until 8:13.
    (D) I slept past 8:30.

20. (A) The priest spoke well.
    (B) The minister was the first speaker.
    (C) We had not received his speech beforehand.
    (D) The audience didn't like the speech.

GO ON TO THE NEXT PAGE

Part B

Directions: In Part B you will hear short conversations between two speakers. At the end of each conversation, a third person will ask a question about what was said. You will hear each conversation and question about it just one time. The sentences you hear will not be written out for you. Therefore, you must listen carefully to understand what each speaker says. After you hear a conversation and the question about it, read the four possible answers in your test book and decide which *one* is the best answer to the question you heard. Then, on your answer sheet, find the number of the question and fill in the space that corresponds to the letter of the answer you have chosen.

Example

You will hear:

(first man) *Professor Smith is going to retire soon. What kind of gift shall we give her?*
(woman) *I think she'd like to have a photograph of our class.*
(second man) *What does the woman think the class should do?*

You will read: (A) Present Professor Smith with a picture.
(B) Photograph Professor Smith.
(C) Put glass over the photograph.
(D) Replace the broken headlight.

Sample Answer
● Ⓑ Ⓒ Ⓓ

From the conversation you learn that the woman thinks Professor Smith would like a photograph of the class. The best answer to the question "What does the woman think the class should do?" is (A), "Present Professor Smith with a picture." Therefore, you should choose answer (A).

21. (A) It's cool inside.
    (B) It's noisy outside.
    (C) The windows are bare.
    (D) The curtains need some care.

22. (A) At 6 a.m.
    (B) At 7 a.m.
    (C) At 8 a.m.
    (D) At 10 a.m.

23. (A) 46 cents each.
    (B) 92 cents.
    (C) From $4–$6.
    (D) $4.60.

24. (A) Eagerly.
    (B) Delicately.
    (C) Slowly.
    (D) Simply.

25. (A) The prices.
    (B) The company.
    (C) The restaurant.
    (D) The desserts.

26. (A) The man's.
    (B) The woman's.
    (C) The boss's.
    (D) His own.

27. (A) He practiced.
    (B) He ate a lot.
    (C) He rowed hard yesterday.
    (D) He didn't tire.

28. (A) Go to Paris.
    (B) Spend a weekend at home.
    (C) Go to London.
    (D) Visit her cousin.

GO ON TO THE NEXT PAGE ➡

29. (A) Napped.
    (B) Shopped.
    (C) Walked.
    (D) Dined.

30. (A) In a store.
    (B) At a party.
    (C) At a boxing match.
    (D) At a post office.

31. (A) It's not hard.
    (B) The language is too hard.
    (C) It's not difficult learning a language.
    (D) The woman should keep trying.

32. (A) In a car.
    (B) At a doctor's office.
    (C) In her office.
    (D) Over the phone.

33. (A) 8:05.
    (B) 9:06.
    (C) 9:13.
    (D) 9:30.

34. (A) Five.
    (B) Six.
    (C) Seven.
    (D) Fourteen.

35. (A) A store was robbed.
    (B) A car was taken.
    (C) A door was broken.
    (D) They heard a robber.

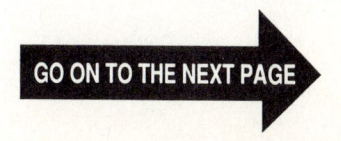

GO ON TO THE NEXT PAGE

1●1●1●1●1●1●1●1

Part C

Directions: In this part of the test, you will hear several short talks and conversations. After each of them, you will be asked some questions. You will hear the talks and conversations and the questions about them just one time. They will not be written out for you. Therefore, you must listen carefully in order to understand what each speaker says.

After you hear a question, read the four possible answers in your test book and decide which *one* is the best answer to the question you heard. Then, on your answer sheet, find the number of the question and fill in the space that corresponds to the letter of the answer you have chosen.

Answer all questions on the basis of what is *stated* or *implied* in the talk or conversation.

Listen to this sample talk.
    You will hear:
        (first man) *Balloons have been used for about a hundred years. There are two kinds of sport balloons, gas and hot air. Hot-air balloons are safer than gas balloons, which may catch fire. Hot-air balloons are preferred by most balloonists in the United States because of their safety. They are also cheaper and easier to manage than gas balloons. Despite the ease of operating a balloon, pilots must watch the weather carefully. Sport balloon flights are best early in the morning or late in the afternoon, when the wind is light.*

Sample Answer
Ⓐ ● Ⓒ Ⓓ

Now look at the following example.
    You will hear:
    (second man) *Why are gas balloons considered dangerous?*
    You will read: (A) They are impossible to guide.
                   (B) They may go up in flames.
                   (C) They tend to leak gas.
                   (D) They are cheaply made.

The best answer to the question "Why are gas balloons considered dangerous?" is (B), "They may go up in flames." Therefore, you should choose answer (B).

Now look at the next example.
    You will hear:
    (second man) *According to the speaker, what must balloon pilots be careful to do?*
    You will read: (A) Watch for changes in weather.
                   (B) Watch their altitude.
                   (C) Check for weak spots in their balloons.
                   (D) Test the strength of the ropes.

Sample Answer
● Ⓑ Ⓒ Ⓓ

The best answer to the question "According to the speaker, what must balloon pilots be careful to do?" is (A), "Watch for changes in weather." Therefore, you should choose answer (A).

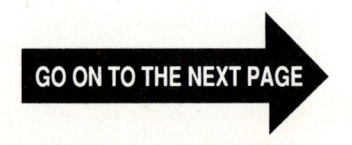

GO ON TO THE NEXT PAGE ➡

36. (A) Innovative.
    (B) Inaccessible.
    (C) Essential.
    (D) Risky.

37. (A) Multicolored graphics.
    (B) An understanding of reading skills.
    (C) A multitude of computer operations.
    (D) A tracking system.

38. (A) The ability to draw on many different skills.
    (B) The knowledge of a phonics system.
    (C) The ability to solve problems.
    (D) The awareness of linguistic skills.

39. (A) As a passive process.
    (B) As a psychological process.
    (C) As a linguistic process.
    (D) As an active process.

40. (A) Existing reading programs.
    (B) An electronic page-turner.
    (C) Problem-solving exercises.
    (D) Phonics drills.

41. (A) A chocolate factory.
    (B) An Italian town.
    (C) University courses.
    (D) Art history.

42. (A) Wife and husband.
    (B) Fellow university students.
    (C) Art history professor and student.
    (D) Personnel director and job applicant.

43. (A) In a classroom.
    (B) In front of an arch.
    (C) In an office.
    (D) Outside in the fresh air.

44. (A) Before a trip abroad.
    (B) In advance of a field trip.
    (C) During a class lecture.
    (D) During an interview.

45. (A) Talk about his work experience.
    (B) Make airline reservations.
    (C) End the conversation.
    (D) Offer to accompany the man.

46. (A) France.
    (B) Spain.
    (C) England.
    (D) Italy.

47. (A) Encouraging.
    (B) Cooperative.
    (C) Neutral.
    (D) Hostile.

48. (A) Mexico.
    (B) France.
    (C) Spain.
    (D) England.

49. (A) Required military service.
    (B) Rights for native Indians.
    (C) Limits on immigrations.
    (D) The right to name the capital.

50. (A) 1579.
    (B) 1821.
    (C) 1836
    (D) 1845.

THIS IS THE END OF THE LISTENING COMPREHENSION SECTION OF THE TEST

THE NEXT PART OF THE TEST IS SECTION 2. TURN TO THE DIRECTIONS FOR SECTION 2 IN YOUR TEST BOOK. READ THEM, AND BEGIN WORK. DO NOT READ OR WORK ON ANY OTHER SECTION OF THE TEST.

SECTION 2

STRUCTURE AND WRITTEN EXPRESSION

Time: 25 minutes

This section tests your ability to recognize language that is appropriate for standard written English. There are two types of questions in this section, with special directions for each type.

Directions: Questions 1–15 are incomplete sentences. Beneath each sentence you will see four words or phrases, marked (A), (B), (C), and (D). Choose the *one* word or phrase that best completes the sentence. Then, on your answer sheet, find the number of the question and fill in the space that corresponds to the letter of the answer you have chosen. Fill in the space so that the letter inside the oval cannot be seen.

Example I

Vegetables are an excellent source _____ vitamins.
(A) of
(B) has
(C) where
(D) that

Sample Answer
● Ⓑ Ⓒ Ⓓ

The sentence should read, "Vegetables are an excellent source of vitamins." Therefore, you should choose answer (A).

Example II

_____ in history when remarkable progress was made within a relatively short span of time.
(A) Periods
(B) Throughout periods
(C) There have been periods
(D) Periods have been

Sample Answer
Ⓐ Ⓑ ● Ⓓ

The sentence should read, "There have been periods in history when remarkable progress was made within a relatively short span of time." Therefore, you should choose answer (C).

Now begin work on the questions.

1. An employment survey revealed today that demand for high-level executives _____ increased this year.
   (A) have
   (B) be
   (C) has
   (D) were

2. Lawmakers are considering banning both beer _____ wine commercials from television.
   (A) also
   (B) than
   (C) or
   (D) and

GO ON TO THE NEXT PAGE

3. Every fall geese _____ over the house located directly on the bay.
   (A) fly
   (B) flies
   (C) flying
   (D) flown

4. Of the many opinions expressed to the council members by the various citizens' groups present, _____ was the only opinion that mattered.
   (A) their
   (B) their one
   (C) theirs
   (D) they

5. The Rosetta stone has provided scientists _____ a link to ancient civilizations.
   (A) of
   (B) to
   (C) by
   (D) with

6. If poisons like DDT _____ to control insects, there will be serious environmental repercussions.
   (A) use
   (B) uses
   (C) are used
   (D) used

7. Carnival sideshows often feature acrobats who juggle knives and balls _____ same time.
   (A) all at the
   (B) at all
   (C) all at a
   (D) all at some

8. Literature _____ provides only fragments of information about the Anglo Saxon period.
   (A) recorded in the century tenth
   (B) in the recorded tenth century
   (C) in the century tenth recorded
   (D) recorded in the tenth century

9. _____ the railroads were built, early settlers had organized an elaborate system of trails and canals.
   (A) After
   (B) During
   (C) While
   (D) Before

10. Technology has increased _____, or the amount of goods and services available.
    (A) produce
    (B) productivity
    (C) producers
    (D) products

11. National Park conservationists think _____ concession stands mar the natural beauty of the park.
    (A) of
    (B) about
    (C) that
    (D) a lot

12. The receptionist, _____ job it was to answer the phone, had laryngitis.
    (A) whose
    (B) who
    (C) who's
    (D) that

13. The climates of grasslands and deciduous forests are similar except that the former receives _____ rainfall.
    (A) least
    (B) few
    (C) less
    (D) fewer

14. The embezzler, _____ his actions, wanted to make restitution to the company.
    (A) were
    (B) regretful
    (C) was regretting
    (D) regretting

GO ON TO THE NEXT PAGE

15. _____ lunch, the finance committee resumed the meeting.
    (A) Having to eat
    (B) Have to eat
    (C) Having eaten
    (D) Having eat

Directions: In questions 16–40, each sentence has four underlined words or phrases. The four underlined parts of the sentence are marked (A), (B), (C), and (D). Identify the *one* underlined word or phrase that must be changed in order for the sentence to be correct. Then, on your answer sheet, find the number of the question and fill in the space that corresponds to the letter of the answer you have chosen.

Example I

A ray of light passing through the center of a thin lens keep its
                    A   B   C

original direction.
      D

Sample Answer
Ⓐ Ⓑ ● Ⓓ

The sentence should read, "A ray of light passing through the center of a thin lens keeps its original direction." Therefore, you should choose answer (C).

Example II

The mandolin, a musical instrument that has strings, was proba-
                         A   B

bly copied from the lute, a many older instrument.
         C   D

Sample Answer
Ⓐ Ⓑ Ⓒ ●

The sentence should read, "The mandolin, a musical instrument that has strings, was probably copied from the lute, a much older instrument." Therefore, you should choose answer (D).

Now begin work on the questions.

16. The system of time measured in 24-hour days is based upon used in ancient Babylon.
      A   B   C   D

17. Most automobile engine use a liquid, usually water, to maintain the engine at a constant
               A   B   C

operating temperature.
    D

18. Not able to type accurately would hurt a graduate's chances of finding a suitable job
    A   B   C

as a secretary.
  D

GO ON TO THE NEXT PAGE

19. Roman law had became the foundation for law codes that subsequently developed in
          A   B   C

    Europe and in other parts of the world.
           D

20. When the government eliminated funds for day care centers, many working parents
     A   B   C

    are obliged to take part-time jobs.
         D

21. The group of spectators was dispersed by the police who was at the scene of the accident
                    A   B   C

    within minutes.
         D

22. Dame Judith Anderson, an Australian actress, made his professional theater debut in
                          A   B   C

    Sydney in 1915.
           D

23. Cities which they have highly polluted air show the effects of weathering caused by acid
                  A   B   C   D

    rain on buildings, statues, and parks.

24. Trade relationships between the two countries have improved if their respective leaders can
                        A   B   C

    agree on the proposed quotas.
              D

25. The appropriate action to take could not be decided on by either the president nor the vice
                           A   B   C   D

    president.

26. Aristotle believed that any piece of matter could be infinitely cut into smaller and more
               A   B   C   D

    smaller pieces.

GO ON TO THE NEXT PAGE

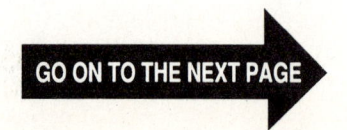

27. Jack London's tour of South Pacific was delayed by his illness and
          A   B   C

the San Francisco earthquake of 1906.
              D

28. Violent wind storms have caused more damaging than fires, floods, or other natural
       A   B   C

disasters combined.
         D

29. By the year 2010, the earth will inhabit twice as many people as it is today.
    A   B   C   D

30. High school students must be complete courses in math and science as well as history
                            A   B   C

before graduating.
       D

31. Working together, scientists and genetic researchers have made recently discoveries
    A   B

that are causing philosophical debates.
  C   D

32. At no time a student's cheating on a final examination can be condoned.
       A   B   C   D

33. A hush fell over the concert hall when the well-known classical guitarist in the world
       A   B   C

stepped onto the stage.
    D

34. In postindustrial society, factories became not so much places of hard physics labor as
                                               A   B

places of automated operation.
   C   D

GO ON TO THE NEXT PAGE

112 Practice Tests

35. The honeysuckle bush, which smells so sweetly when it blooms, was originally brought to
                                          A   B   C

    the U.S. from Japan.
             D

36. The Forest Service limits to cut trees to the amount that can be replaced in a single year.
                                 A   B   C   D

37. The guests were surprised by their host's furniture was made in Italy especially for the new
          A   B   C   D

    gallery.

38. Fish flour must be proved fitted for human consumption before it is allowed to be
                              A   B   C   D

    distributed to the public.

39. If banks were increase their loans to businesses, the additional funds would stimulate
                A   B   C

    investment.
    D

40. Parents, before they are moving to another state, should consider the effect the move may
                   A   B   C

    have on their children.
            D

THIS IS THE END OF SECTION 2

IF YOU FINISH BEFORE TIME IS CALLED, CHECK YOUR WORK ON SECTION 2 ONLY.

DO NOT READ OR WORK ON ANY OTHER SECTION OF THE TEST. THE SUPERVISOR WILL TELL YOU WHEN TO BEGIN WORK ON SECTION 3.

Practice Tests 113

SECTION 3

READING COMPREHENSION VOCABULARY

Time: 45 minutes

This section tests your comprehension of standard written English. There are two types of questions in this section, with special directions for each type.

Directions: In questions 1–30, each sentence has an underlined word or phrase. Below each sentence are four other words or phrases, marked (A), (B), (C), and (D). You are to choose the *one* word or phrase that *best keeps the meaning* of the original sentence if it is substituted for the underlined word or phrase. Then, on your answer sheet, find the number of the question and fill in the space that matches the letter you have chosen. Fill in the space so that the letter inside the oval cannot be seen.

Example

Passenger ships and aircraft are often equipped with ship-to-shore or air-to-land radio telephones.
(A) highways
(B) railroads
(C) planes
(D) sailboats

Sample Answer
Ⓐ Ⓑ ● Ⓓ

The best answer is (C), because "Passenger ships and planes are often equipped with ship-to-shore or air-to-land radio telephones" is closest in meaning to the original sentence. Therefore, you should choose answer (C).

Now begin work on the questions.

1. In spite of his many faults, Paul is very dedicated to his mother.
   (A) polite
   (B) devoted
   (C) agreeable
   (D) considerable

2. Mrs. Smith will demonstrate how this computer works.
   (A) guess
   (B) learn
   (C) estimate
   (D) show

3. The columnist's remarks were inappropriate and rude.
   (A) unsuitable
   (B) unnecessary
   (C) inconsistent
   (D) inarticulate

4. The argument, although understandable, was not very convincing.
   (A) persuasive
   (B) realistic
   (C) reliable
   (D) clear

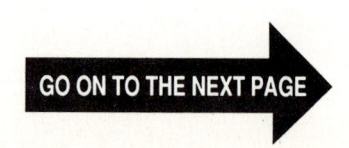

GO ON TO THE NEXT PAGE

114 Practice Tests

5. The judge would not hear the case because the evidence was not sufficient.
   (A) proper
   (B) legal
   (C) adequate
   (D) positive

6. Being meek, the stranger had difficulty making friends.
   (A) lonely
   (B) lazy
   (C) loud
   (D) humble

7. The gem is so rare it could be fake.
   (A) expensive
   (B) stolen
   (C) simulated
   (D) sold

8. An inexperienced driver is a potential danger.
   (A) possible
   (B) certain
   (C) actual
   (D) definite

9. When the wind died, the sailboat drifted toward the beach.
   (A) collapsed
   (B) floated
   (C) hurried
   (D) returned

10. This course focuses primarily on the history of early civilizations.
    (A) objectively
    (B) mainly
    (C) actively
    (D) subjectively

11. Success is most deserved by amiable people.
    (A) efficient
    (B) prestigious
    (C) good-humored
    (D) essential

12. An ulterior motive is behind the question.
    (A) A concealed
    (B) A good
    (C) An important
    (D) An exceptional

13. There is no resolution to this conflict.
    (A) decision
    (B) condition
    (C) action
    (D) disagreement

14. There was a long pause before the music began.
    (A) interval
    (B) introduction
    (C) prayer
    (D) play

15. A brisk walk in cool weather is invigorating.
    (A) short
    (B) long
    (C) lively
    (D) solemn

16. Some tall people often feel clumsy.
    (A) superior
    (B) ignored
    (C) noticed
    (D) awkward

17. All typing errors must be deleted from this memo.
    (A) erased
    (B) corrected
    (C) circled
    (D) determined

18. Animals in the wild seem more ferocious than they really are.
    (A) hairy
    (B) fierce
    (C) silly
    (D) callous

GO ON TO THE NEXT PAGE

19. The manager was found to be harassing his employees.
    (A) ridiculing
    (B) bribing
    (C) coaxing
    (D) bothering

20. The government will issue a statement about tax increases soon.
    (A) invent
    (B) deny
    (C) give out
    (D) propose

21. The garments of colonial times, if in good condition, are highly prized.
    (A) homes
    (B) pictures
    (C) clothes
    (D) tools

22. Children must learn to tolerate one another.
    (A) put up with
    (B) admire
    (C) trust
    (D) play with

23. More responsibility and higher salaries are incentives for on-the-job training.
    (A) implicit in
    (B) integral part of
    (C) privileges of
    (D) inducements for

24. The product to use to douse a grease fire is salt or baking soda.
    (A) extinguish
    (B) create
    (C) prolong
    (D) deter

25. The suspect is being held for arraignment without bail.
    (A) nonbeliever
    (B) judge
    (C) robber
    (D) accused

26. The quaint style of the homes is typical of this region.
    (A) curious
    (B) ancient
    (C) elaborate
    (D) ultramodern

27. Doctors discourage massive doses of drugs for infants.
    (A) light
    (B) huge
    (C) repetitive
    (D) infrequent

28. The provisions of the contract exclude any division of the property for 50 years.
    (A) writers
    (B) clauses
    (C) readers
    (D) lawyers

29. History has shown that rulers do not relinquish power easily.
    (A) abandon
    (B) hold
    (C) control
    (D) gain

30. Modern music is usually characterized by a remarkable dissonance.
    (A) melody
    (B) clarity
    (C) discord
    (D) volume

GO ON TO THE NEXT PAGE

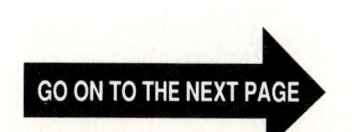

Directions: In the rest of this section you will read several passages. Each one is followed by several questions about it. For questions 31–60, you are to choose the *one* best answer, (A), (B), (C), or (D), to each question. Then, on your answer sheet, find the number of the question and fill in the space that matches the letter of the answer you have chosen.

Answer all questions following a passage on the basis of what is *stated* or *implied* in the reading passage.

Example passage and questions

The rattles with which a rattlesnake warns of its presence are formed by loosely interlocking hollow rings of hard skin, which make a buzzing sound when its tail is shaken. As a baby, the snake begins to form its rattles from the button at the very tip of its tail. Thereafter, each time it sheds its skin, a new ring is formed. Popular belief holds that a snake's age can be told by counting the rings, but this idea is fallacious. In fact, a snake may lose its old skin as often as four times a year. Also, rattles tend to wear or break off with time.

Example I

A rattlesnake's rattles are made of
(A) skin
(B) bone
(C) wood
(D) muscle

Sample Answer
● Ⓑ Ⓒ Ⓓ

According to the passage, a rattlesnake's rattles are made of rings of hard skin. Therefore, you should choose answer (A).

Example II

How often does a rattlesnake shed its skin?
(A) Once every four years
(B) Once every four months
(C) Up to four times every year
(D) Four times more often than other snakes

Sample Answer
Ⓐ Ⓑ ● Ⓓ

The passage states that "a snake may lose its old skin as often as four times a year." Therefore, you should choose answer (C).

Now begin work on the questions.

GO ON TO THE NEXT PAGE

Questions 31–35

The involved relation between the spelling of English words and their sounds has led to frequent suggestions for modifying the alphabet or for rationalizing the spelling system. To some extent both these intentions share the same misconceptions and difficulties. A number of contemporary linguists would deny that there is anything wrong with the way most words are spelled; they
5 argue that a good deal of information would be lost if spelling were touched.

Most of the apparent inconsistencies in English spelling have some historical basis; the spelling system may be complex, but it is not arbitrary—it has become what it is for quite systematic reasons. And because spelling is systematic and reflects something of the history of words, much more information is available to the reader than we normally realize.

10 Spelling reform might seem to make English words easier to pronounce, but only at the cost of other information about the way words are related to each other, so that rationalizing words at the phonological level might make reading more difficult at syntactic and semantic levels. As just one example, consider the silent *b* in words like *bomb, bombing, bombed,* which would be an almost certain candidate for extinction if spelling reformers had their way. But the *b* is something
15 more than a pointless appendage; it relates the previous words to others like *bombard, bombardier, bombardment,* in which the *b* is pronounced.

31. The writer of this passage probably supports
    (A) a modification of the alphabet for English
    (B) the phonetic systemization of English spelling
    (C) a rationalized English system of spelling
    (D) the retention of present English spelling

32. Which of the following features of language does the author NOT mention?
    (A) Rhetoric
    (B) Syntax
    (C) Phonology
    (D) Semantics

33. The author believes which of the following?
    (A) Inconsistent spelling systems should be reformed.
    (B) Historical vestiges in modern English spelling can mislead the reader.
    (C) The spelling of words can embody more than simply phonetic information.
    (D) The spelling of English is essentially arbitrary.

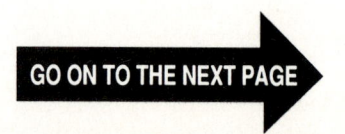

34. What does the passage mainly discuss?
    (A) the history of English spelling
    (B) the interrelationships of sound and meaning in English spelling
    (C) the uselessness of silent letters in English spelling
    (D) the importance of phonetics in English spelling

35. In line 13, the word "which" refers to
    (A) words
    (B) semantic levels
    (C) the silent *b*
    (D) bombed

Questions 36–41

Perhaps the most publicized environmental health issue to emerge in recent years is radioactive radon, or radon-222. Radon is a gas found virtually everywhere, because its predecessors—radium-226 and uranium-238—are ubiquitous in all rocks and soils. Outdoors, the concentration of radon in the air is typically less than 0.5 picoCuries per liter (pCi/L) and the gas represents a
5 negligible risk to health. But radon hazards to uranium miners, and to individuals living in areas where uranium wastes have been dumped, are well documented.

Mines and dumping grounds are easy problems to spot. But radon troubles are not always so obvious. Not only is radon invisible and odorless, but its presence cannot be predicted accurately from geological data. Houses that are safely below acceptable radon thresholds can sit right next to
10 houses with unacceptably high radon concentrations.

The discovery in 1985 that buildings in seemingly low-risk areas could have radon concentrations as high as 2,000 pCi/L caused widespread concern and even panic among homeowners who lacked the information they needed to cope with this problem. Suddenly the environment became suspect. Media coverage of the issue swung between extremes, from the sensationalism of
15 "The sky is falling!" to the ostrich-like "Ignore what you can't see." Neither attitude is compatible with good science.

36. Which of the following is the passage mainly about?
    (A) The explanation of pCi/L
    (B) Radioactive radon
    (C) Housing safety
    (D) Panicked homeowners

37. Which of the following is NOT mentioned as a reason for the difficulty of locating concentrations of radon gas?
    (A) Geographical areas are unpredictable.
    (B) We can't see radon.
    (C) There is no discernible smell.
    (D) Concentrations are often less than 0.5 pCi/L.

38. In the next paragraph, the author will most likely discuss
    (A) how to answer questions with "good science"
    (B) using books to help understand scientific concepts
    (C) where to locate radon diagnostic kits
    (D) the incorrect media coverage of radon hazards

39. The word "they" (line 13) in the last paragraph refers to
    (A) scientists
    (B) homeowners
    (C) miners
    (D) houses

GO ON TO THE NEXT PAGE

Practice Tests 119

40. How does the writer characterize the attitude of the news industry toward the radon problem?
    (A) Probing
    (B) Unfocused
    (C) Inconsistent
    (D) Cynical

41. Why is radon considered especially dangerous by homeowners?
    (A) Because of its odor
    (B) Because it appears most frequently in houses
    (C) Because it is so difficult to detect
    (D) Because of its corrosive effects

Questions 42–47

The foremost way for a manager to improve communication is to be sensitive to the needs and feelings of the subordinates. Although most superiors think they are sensitive, research shows they are neither as perceptive nor as sensitive as they believe.

If managers were made aware of and made to consider these findings seriously, it would be a start toward sensitizing them. So would the development of an awareness of nonverbal communication cues. These cues can take many forms. A listener who begins staring out the window may be telling the manager that he is either bored or unwilling to continue listening. A manager who frowns or shakes his head no is telling the speaker that he disagrees.

Yet it is not necessary to confine oneself to such obvious nonverbal cues. Consider the manager who pulls a chair around the desk and sits close to a subordinate while discussing a major memo that has just been sent down from top management. This physical closeness indicates that the manager trusts the subordinate, wants the person's input on how to deal with the situation, and is going to communicate openly and freely. This is in direct contrast to the superior who stands up and leans across the desk to reprimand a nervously cringing subordinate whose only wish is to sink through the chair.

All the above are examples of nonverbal communication, and there are many more. In fact, we learn something about people by the ways they walk, stand, move their eyes, or gesture. A manager who is to develop sensitivity must learn to recognize these nonverbal cues in his own behavior and in the behavior of others.

42. The passage focuses on the importance of
    (A) courtesy in the workplace
    (B) efficient office furniture arrangements
    (C) total communication in the workplace
    (D) listening to office workers' complaints

43. In line 4, the pronoun "them" refers to
    (A) subordinates
    (B) findings
    (C) managers
    (D) needs

44. With which one of the following statements would the author most likely agree?
    (A) Managers must do more than listen.
    (B) Workers may use nonverbal cues to mislead.
    (C) Most managers are sensitive to workers' needs.
    (D) Nonverbal communication is limited.

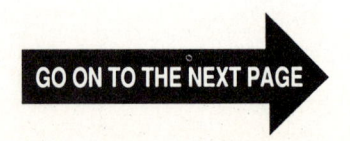

GO ON TO THE NEXT PAGE

45. According to the passage, nonverbal signals convey strong meaning only if
    (A) we use them openly and freely
    (B) they are accompanied by words
    (C) we learn to notice and interpret them
    (D) they are used sparingly

46. A manager's physical proximity to a worker during an office discussion implies
    (A) admiration
    (B) submissiveness
    (C) confidence
    (D) superiority

47. The passage is primarily intended to address potential communication deficiencies of
    (A) office workers
    (B) customers
    (C) supervisors
    (D) store clerks

Questions 48–53

Most children have achieved remarkably sophisticated language capabilities by the age of three. Their vocabularies have reached about 1,000 words, and they can use as many as five of those words in a single sentence. They make up new words, too. They can speak about the past and future as well as the present. They understand that some words have more than one meaning. They can *duck* when a ball is coming or see a *duck* on a lake. They've begun to use negatives ("That's not mine") and helping verbs ("I can do it myself").

Over the next two years, their vocabulary will more than double. They'll begin to play with words, to repeat silly sounds, to try out "toilet" words or even swear words, just to elicit an adult's reaction. Newly aware of the power of words, they'll begin to argue, and they'll start to tell jokes.

This language play carries on a process of experimentation that began when the child was an infant, first encountering language. At one time, experts thought children learned language simply by imitating adults. Nowadays, most linguists agree that children learn primarily by experimenting—by listening and thinking about what they hear, by making their own sounds, and then by observing the way others react.

Language comes first as a great garble of sound. Slowly, children learn to hear individual sound patterns, or words. They try out sounds. For example, babies babble "da da," and from adults' responses ("Yes, that's daddy"), learn which sounds enable them to communicate effectively.

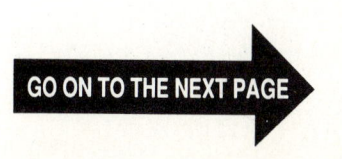

GO ON TO THE NEXT PAGE

48. Which of the following is the best title for the passage?
    (A) How to Increase Children's Vocabulary
    (B) The Development of Children's Language
    (C) Scientific Experiments for Children
    (D) The Importance of Imitation

49. Which of the following questions does the passage answer?
    (A) What should adults do to help children's language?
    (B) How should adults model their language?
    (C) How do children learn to communicate?
    (D) What reaction should parents have to swear words?

50. According to the passage, which sentence is true?
    (A) Children start to learn language at about the age of five.
    (B) Children start learning how to communicate when they are infants.
    (C) Children learn language by imitating adults.
    (D) Children are incapable of using language until around three years of age.

51. Which of the following is NOT mentioned as a linguistic capability of five-year-olds?
    (A) They have a vocabulary of about 2,000 words.
    (B) They tell jokes.
    (C) They develop prereading skills.
    (D) They get into arguments.

52. The passage tells us that, at about the age of five, children begin to experiment with
    (A) basic sound patterns
    (B) future-tense constructions
    (C) social dimensions of language
    (D) gestures in place of words

53. What does the passage tell us about a child's first recognition of words?
    (A) It is a gradual process.
    (B) It occurs only when the child can use them.
    (C) It happens suddenly at the age of three.
    (D) It means the child is ready to attend school.

Questions 54–60

The popular view of anthropology is that it is concerned with faraway places, strange peoples, and odd customs. This notion was neatly captured by a nineteenth-century wit who described the field as "the pursuit of the exotic by the eccentric." In recent decades many anthropologists have tried to shake this image. They see the exotic as dangerously close to the sensational and
5   therefore a threat to the respectability of a serious academic discipline. They argue that anthropology has solid theoretical bases, and that some anthropologists routinely work in cities right here in America. And they are right. Nevertheless, anthropologists are also as much involved with the exotic as ever, and I think that this concern actually works to the scholarship's advantage.

   This continuing involvement is a result of the most characteristic *modus operandi* of anthro-
10 pologists. First, we seek out the exotic, in the sense of something originating in another country or

GO ON TO THE NEXT PAGE

something "strikingly or excitingly different," as my dictionary puts it. Second, we try to fit this alien item—culture trait, custom, piece of behavior—into its social and cultural context, thereby reducing it to a logical, sensible, even necessary element. Having done that, we feel that we can understand why people do or say or think something instead of being divorced from them by what
15 they do, say, or think.

54. This passage is mainly concerned with
    (A) the *modus operandi* of anthropologists
    (B) the theoretical bases of anthropology
    (C) how anthropology is actually a serious academic discipline
    (D) why anthropologists should work in both urban and exotic sites

55. In the second sentence, the word "field" refers to
    (A) anthropological sites
    (B) anthropology
    (C) a faraway place
    (D) this notion

56. The author of the passage is
    (A) a researcher
    (B) a sociologist
    (C) an archaeologist
    (D) an anthropologist

57. The author implies that anthropologists
    (A) could be helpful in cross-cultural negotiations
    (B) should be doing more studies in exotic places
    (C) are content with their public image
    (D) should be seeking out more urban areas for study

58. According to the passage, anthropological theory
    (A) should de-emphasize the exotic
    (B) is valid for the study of modern urban life
    (C) does not adequately explain the illogical
    (D) uses different bases for urban and exotic societies

59. According to the passage, who objects to the perception of anthropology as an exotic field of study?
    (A) Many anthropologists
    (B) The general public
    (C) Foreigners
    (D) Eccentric scientists

60. In line 11, the word "it" refers to
    (A) something
    (B) *modus operandi*
    (C) the definition of exotic
    (D) another country

THIS IS THE END OF SECTION 3

IF YOU FINISH BEFORE TIME IS CALLED, CHECK YOUR WORK ON SECTION 3 ONLY.

DO NOT READ OR WORK ON ANY OTHER SECTION OF THE TEST.

1 ● 1 ● 1 ● 1 ● 1 ● 1 ● 1 ● 1

PRACTICE TEST 6

SECTION 1

LISTENING COMPREHENSION

The questions in Section 1 of the test are on a recording.

In this section of the test, you have an opportunity to demonstrate your ability to understand spoken English. There are three parts to this section, with special directions for each part.

Part A

Directions: For each question in Part A, you will hear a short sentence. Each sentence will be spoken just one time. The sentences you hear will not be written out for you. Therefore, you must listen carefully to understand what the speaker says.

After you hear a sentence, read the four choices in your test book, marked (A), (B), (C), and (D), and decide which *one* is closest in meaning to the sentence you heard. Then, on your answer sheet, find the number of the question and fill in the space that matches the letter of the answer you have chosen. Fill in the space so that the letter inside the oval cannot be seen.

Example I   **Sample Answer**
  You will hear: *Mary swam out to the island with her friends.*   Ⓐ Ⓑ ● Ⓓ
  You will read: (A) Mary outswam the others.
                 (B) Mary ought to swim with them.
                 (C) Mary and her friends swam to the island.
                 (D) Mary's friends owned the island.

The speaker said, "Mary swam out to the island with her friends." Sentence (C), "Mary and her friends swam to the island," is closest in meaning to the sentence you heard. Therefore, you should choose answer (C).

Example II   **Sample Answer**
  You will hear: *Would you mind helping me with this load of books?*   Ⓐ ● Ⓒ Ⓓ
  You will read: (A) Please remind me to read this book.
                 (B) Could you help me carry these books?
                 (C) I don't mind if you help me.
                 (D) Do you have a heavy course load this term?

The speaker said, "Would you mind helping me with this load of books?" Sentence (B), "Could you help me carry these books?" is closest in meaning to the sentence you heard. Therefore, you should choose answer (B).

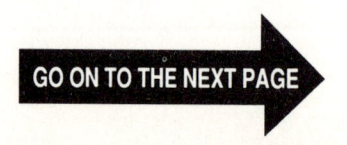

GO ON TO THE NEXT PAGE

1. (A) My daughter studies the sun.
   (B) My father has been studying my son.
   (C) My son has been helping his father.
   (D) My daughter is helping my son.

2. (A) The flight leaves at 7:40.
   (B) The flight leaves on the 20th at eight o'clock.
   (C) The flight leaves at 8:18 in the evening.
   (D) The flight 818 departs on the 18th.

3. (A) Rice is found on the lower shelf.
   (B) Fall is not my favorite season.
   (C) Prices are as low as they will go.
   (D) Nothing could surprise me any more.

4. (A) The flooded plain ruined the food crop.
   (B) Rice requires a lot of rain.
   (C) The drought raised the cost of food.
   (D) Eating on the train is expensive.

5. (A) We raised enough money.
   (B) The project needs more money to continue.
   (C) The project was cancelled.
   (D) The cancelled project was revived.

6. (A) There was a third off all merchandise.
   (B) Everything was sold.
   (C) The price tag said $11.00.
   (D) It cost $33.50.

7. (A) Trainees must be very careful about the details.
   (B) The critics did not listen carefully.
   (C) The trainees were paid a great deal.
   (D) There was a lot of criticism of the story.

8. (A) The janitor returned the briefcase to the teacher.
   (B) The teacher gave her briefcase to the principal to keep.
   (C) The principal found the janitor's suitcase.
   (D) The janitor found the teacher's briefcase.

9. (A) There were fewer books this year.
   (B) Major publishers always display their books.
   (C) The fair was attended by all publishers.
   (D) There were more books this year.

10. (A) The accident report is due right away.
    (B) Notify the police whenever you see an accident.
    (C) The police came upon the accident immediately.
    (D) The reporters caused the accident.

11. (A) Bill drank quickly.
    (B) Bill didn't enjoy his drink.
    (C) Bill enjoys drinking.
    (D) Bill drank slowly.

12. (A) We all went to the movies.
    (B) We all stayed home.
    (C) None of us went to the movies.
    (D) Half of us stayed home.

13. (A) Labels were passed around to the participants.
    (B) They were eating and feeling jovial.
    (C) The group met around the table.
    (D) The round table had a few empty seats.

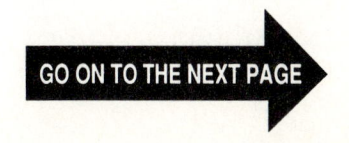

GO ON TO THE NEXT PAGE

14. (A) The payments are $49.40 each month.
    (B) Payments for four months are due.
    (C) The payment is due on the 14th of the month.
    (D) The first payment is due on the 4th.

15. (A) Our professor will never change his mind.
    (B) He did not believe the professor could change our minds.
    (C) We changed the professor's mind.
    (D) We thought he changed his mind.

16. (A) The ball missed the window.
    (B) The boy threw the ball.
    (C) The boy didn't catch the ball.
    (D) The boy sat in the window.

17. (A) My brother visits us by car.
    (B) My father and brother fixed the car.
    (C) My mother and father visited me last summer.
    (D) My uncle came last summer.

18. (A) We plan to eat at a restaurant.
    (B) It rained so we ate inside.
    (C) The picnic will go on regardless of the weather.
    (D) We won't have a picnic if it rains.

19. (A) The conductor waved from the train.
    (B) The conductor ran to the train and gave the signal.
    (C) The conductor signaled before he boarded.
    (D) The conductor didn't make the train.

20. (A) There is more money for defense than for education.
    (B) More money is spent on education than on health.
    (C) The education budget is equal to the defense budget.
    (D) Most money is spent on education.

GO ON TO THE NEXT PAGE

1●1●1●1●1●1●1●1

Part B

Directions: In Part B you will hear short conversations between two speakers. At the end of each conversation, a third person will ask a question about what was said. You will hear each conversation and question about it just one time. The sentences you hear will not be written out for you. Therefore, you must listen carefully to understand what each speaker says. After you hear a conversation and the question about it, read the four possible answers in your test book and decide which *one* is the best answer to the question you heard. Then, on your answer sheet, find the number of the question and fill in the space that corresponds to the letter of the answer you have chosen.

Example

Sample Answer

● B C D

You will hear:
(first man) *Professor Smith is going to retire soon. What kind of gift shall we give her?*
(woman) *I think she'd like to have a photograph of our class.*
(second man) *What does the woman think the class should do?*

You will read: (A) Present Professor Smith with a picture.
(B) Photograph Professor Smith.
(C) Put glass over the photograph.
(D) Replace the broken headlight.

From the conversation you learn that the woman thinks Professor Smith would like a photograph of the class. The best answer to the question "What does the woman think the class should do?" is (A), "Present Professor Smith with a picture." Therefore, you should choose answer (A).

21. (A) She bought a new light.
    (B) She got new shoes.
    (C) She ate a pear.
    (D) She painted her walls blue.

22. (A) 2
    (B) 10
    (C) 12
    (D) 22

23. (A) 6
    (B) 16
    (C) 60
    (D) 66

24. (A) Write the check.
    (B) Paint the shelves.
    (C) Fix a shelf.
    (D) Search for the pen.

25. (A) She'll stay.
    (B) She's going to leave.
    (C) She's going to eat there.
    (D) She's going to check it out.

26. (A) 25
    (B) 50
    (C) 100
    (D) 540

27. (A) Traffic on the bridge.
    (B) Dangerous drivers.
    (C) Ice on the bridge.
    (D) Slow traffic.

28. (A) He goes to college.
    (B) He works for his father.
    (C) He takes another test.
    (D) He chooses another school.

GO ON TO THE NEXT PAGE

Practice Tests 127

29. (A) Planning a party.
    (B) Going swimming.
    (C) Trying on clothes.
    (D) Having refreshments.

30. (A) A week.
    (B) Four days.
    (C) For 4 more days.
    (D) Ten days.

31. (A) The woman is afraid of dogs.
    (B) He doesn't know the house.
    (C) He is allergic to dogs.
    (D) There's no one home.

32. (A) One quarter-million dollars.
    (B) One half-million dollars.
    (C) One million dollars.
    (D) Two million dollars.

33. (A) In 5 minutes.
    (B) In about 15 minutes.
    (C) In about an hour.
    (D) At noon.

34. (A) She likes to collect old books.
    (B) She likes to reread her books.
    (C) She likes to write poetry.
    (D) She likes to drink wine.

35. (A) They can't agree.
    (B) The restaurant wasn't good.
    (C) Neither can cook.
    (D) They always go to the same restaurant.

GO ON TO THE NEXT PAGE

1•1•1•1•1•1•1

Part C

Directions: In this part of the test, you will hear several short talks and conversations. After each of them, you will be asked some questions. You will hear the talks and conversations and the questions about them just one time. They will not be written out for you. Therefore, you must listen carefully in order to understand what each speaker says.

After you hear a question, read the four possible answers in your test book and decide which *one* is the best answer to the question you heard. Then, on the your answer sheet, find the number of the question and fill in the space that corresponds to the letter of the answer you have chosen.

Answer all questions on the basis of what is *stated* or *implied* in the talk or conversation.

Listen to this sample talk.
  You will hear:
    (first man) *Balloons have been used for about a hundred years. There are two kinds of sport balloons, gas and hot air. Hot-air balloons are safer than gas balloons, which may catch fire. Hot-air balloons are preferred by most balloonists in the United States because of their safety. They are also cheaper and easier to manage than gas balloons. Despite the ease of operating a balloon, pilots must watch the weather carefully. Sport balloon flights are best early in the morning or late in the afternoon, when the wind is light.*

Sample Answer
Ⓐ ● Ⓒ Ⓓ

Now look at the following example.
  You will hear:
  (second man) *Why are gas balloons considered dangerous?*
  You will read: (A) They are impossible to guide.
    (B) They may go up in flames.
    (C) They tend to leak gas.
    (D) They are cheaply made.

The best answer to the question "Why are gas balloons considered dangerous?" is (B), "They may go up in flames." Therefore, you should choose answer (B).

Now look at the next example.
  You will hear:
  (second man) *According to the speaker, what must balloon pilots be careful to do?*
  You will read: (A) Watch for changes in weather.
    (B) Watch their altitude.
    (C) Check for weak spots in their balloons.
    (D) Test the strength of the ropes.

Sample Answer
● Ⓑ Ⓒ Ⓓ

The best answer to the question "According to the speaker, what must balloon pilots be careful to do?" is (A), "Watch for changes in weather." Therefore, you should choose answer (A).

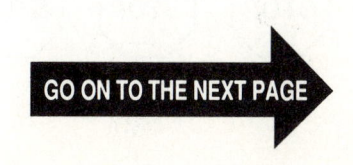

GO ON TO THE NEXT PAGE ➡

36. (A) Chief Engineer of America.
    (B) Chief Executive Officer.
    (C) President of Harvard College.
    (D) Father of Scientific Management.

37. (A) Germany.
    (B) France.
    (C) Transylvania.
    (D) The United States.

38. (A) He didn't pass the entrance exams.
    (B) His eyes were bad.
    (C) He wanted to join the family business.
    (D) He preferred Stevens Institute.

39. (A) Two years.
    (B) Four years.
    (C) Eight years.
    (D) Twelve years.

40. (A) He graduated from Harvard.
    (B) He took correspondence courses and home study.
    (C) He attended Phillips Exeter Academy.
    (D) He received a European degree.

41. (A) Egypt.
    (B) Africa.
    (C) The United States.
    (D) Southwest Asia.

42. (A) Companionship.
    (B) Hunting.
    (C) Sport.
    (D) Food.

43. (A) By air scent.
    (B) By ground scent.
    (C) By keen eyesight.
    (D) By accute hearing.

44. (A) Guarding.
    (B) Hunting.
    (C) Rescue.
    (D) Companionship.

45. (A) Their unquestioning loyalty.
    (B) Their independence.
    (C) Their sense of smell.
    (D) Their strength.

46. (A) Military battles.
    (B) Poetry.
    (C) Politics.
    (D) History.

47. (A) Timorous.
    (B) Punitive.
    (C) Unfinished.
    (D) Indicative.

48. (A) A drama.
    (B) Literature.
    (C) Natural law.
    (D) Etymology.

49. (A) Works of fiction.
    (B) Vague operations.
    (C) A maverick and its bloodlines.
    (D) A political boundary line.

50. (A) Carl Van Doren.
    (B) Dixon.
    (C) Mason.
    (D) Mavericks.

THIS IS THE END OF THE LISTENING COMPREHENSION SECTION OF THE TEST

THE NEXT PART OF THE TEST IS SECTION 2. TURN TO THE DIRECTIONS FOR SECTION 2 IN YOUR TEST BOOK. READ THEM, AND BEGIN WORK. DO NOT READ OR WORK ON ANY OTHER SECTION OF THE TEST.

SECTION 2

STRUCTURE AND WRITTEN EXPRESSION

Time: 25 minutes

This section tests your ability to recognize language that is appropriate for standard written English. There are two types of questions in this section, with special directions for each type.

Directions: Questions 1–15 are incomplete sentences. Beneath each sentence you will see four words or phrases, marked (A), (B), (C), and (D). Choose the *one* word or phrase that best completes the sentence. Then, on your answer sheet, find the number of the question and fill in the space that corresponds to the letter of the answer you have chosen. Fill in the space so that the letter inside the oval cannot be seen.

Example I

Vegetables are an excellent source _____ vitamins.
(A) of
(B) has
(C) where
(D) that

Sample Answer
● Ⓑ Ⓒ Ⓓ

The sentence should read, "Vegetables are an excellent source of vitamins." Therefore, you should choose answer (A).

Example II

_____ in history when remarkable progress was made within a relatively short span of time.
(A) Periods
(B) Throughout periods
(C) There have been periods
(D) Periods have been

Sample Answer
Ⓐ Ⓑ ● Ⓓ

The sentence should read, "There have been periods in history when remarkable progress was made within a relatively short span of time." Therefore, you should choose answer (C).

Now begin work on the questions.

1. The organizers of the convention have arranged accommodations for those participants _____ from out of town.
   (A) who comes
   (B) which will come
   (C) are coming
   (D) coming

2. The farmers recruited to work in the paper mill complained that they were not accustomed _____ a timecard.
   (A) to punching
   (B) to punch
   (C) by punching
   (D) having punched

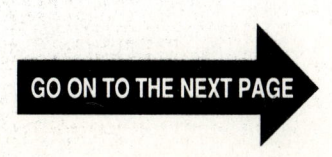

GO ON TO THE NEXT PAGE

3. The playground supervisor reprimanded _____ for our shouting.
   (A) ourselves
   (B) us
   (C) ours
   (D) we

4. _____ the lawyer's opinion, the case should not go to trial.
   (A) By
   (B) On
   (C) In
   (D) With

5. The job applicant was worried about the interview _____ he was well prepared.
   (A) because
   (B) if
   (C) unless
   (D) even though

6. _____ the predicament and solving it are two different problems.
   (A) Identification
   (B) Identifying
   (C) It is identifying
   (D) To identify

7. The human rights activist considered it _____ honor to be nominated for the award.
   (A) an
   (B) a
   (C) the
   (D) this

8. The spectators breathed a sign of relief when _____.
   (A) the whistle has blown
   (B) the referee blows the whistle
   (C) they heard the final whistle
   (D) the whistle blows

9. Although the members of the faculty seem inflexible, _____ to suggestions.
   (A) they are always open
   (B) always they are open
   (C) open they are always
   (D) they are open always

10. _____ rain now, the farmers will have to postpone the harvest.
    (A) It should
    (B) Will it
    (C) Should it
    (D) When it will

11. Some consider Las Vegas _____ city in the world to live in.
    (A) the bad
    (B) worse
    (C) worst
    (D) the worst

12. The phonograph next door was so loud that we could _____ hear the television in our own room.
    (A) hard
    (B) harder
    (C) hardly
    (D) hardy

13. The parent scolded the child and made her promise _____ again.
    (A) never to do that
    (B) what to do never
    (C) that never to do that
    (D) so never to do that

14. The motivation of the workers _____ not a monetary reward, but the satisfaction of a job well done.
    (A) was
    (B) were
    (C) should be
    (D) could be

15. Energetic, ambitious people often _____ more hours in a day.
    (A) needing
    (B) need
    (C) needed
    (D) are needing

GO ON TO THE NEXT PAGE

Directions: In questions 16–40, each sentence has four underlined words or phrases. The four underlined parts of the sentence are marked (A), (B), (C), and (D). Identify the *one* underlined word or phrase that must be changed in order for the sentence to be correct. Then, on your answer sheet, find the number of the question and fill in the space that corresponds to the letter of the answer you have chosen.

Example I

A ray of light passing <u>through</u> <u>the center</u> of a thin lens <u>keep</u> its
                                A   **B**   **C**

<u>original</u> direction.
   D

Sample Answer
Ⓐ Ⓑ ● Ⓓ

The sentence should read, "A ray of light passing through the center of a thin lens keeps its original direction." Therefore, you should choose answer (C).

Example II

The mandolin, a musical <u>instrument</u> <u>that has</u> strings, was proba-
                                A   **B**

bly copied <u>from</u> the lute, a <u>many</u> older instrument.
           C   **D**

Sample Answer
Ⓐ Ⓑ Ⓒ ●

The sentence should read, "The mandolin, a musical instrument that has strings, was probably copied from the lute, a much older instrument." Therefore, you should choose answer (D).

Now begin work on the questions.

16. The <u>use of computers</u>, potentially <u>powerful</u> educational tools, <u>it will not</u> be widespread
        A   **B**   **C**

until <u>prices come down</u>.
     D

17. Recent <u>studies done</u> by the Department of Labor <u>have shown</u> that <u>nonsmoking are</u> more
             A   **B**   **C**

productive than those who <u>smoke</u>.
                         D

18. The <u>new, more stringent</u> requirements <u>for obtaining</u> a driving license <u>has resulted</u> in
         A   **B**   **C**

<u>a decrease</u> in traffic accidents.
    D

19. We all thought the office <u>manager</u> had gone <u>too far</u>, but his staff <u>did supported him</u>.
     A   **B**   **C**   **D**

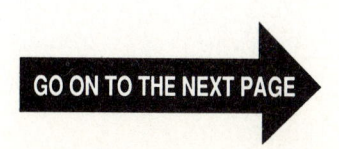

GO ON TO THE NEXT PAGE

20. Hearing the fire alarm sound, the librarian requested those reading to leave their books and
    ___A___   ___B___   ___C___

    headed for the nearest exit.
    ___D___

21. The scientific experiments conducted by the class was placed on the center table for the
                                 ___A___   ___B___   ___C___   ___D___

    judges to evaluate.

22. Ms. Amelia Earhart, like many of the world's greatest heroes, sacrificed their life for the
                        ___A___   ___B___   ___C___

    sake of adventure, glory, and country.
    ___D___

23. The anthropologists reviewed its findings and discovered that a fossil previously
                                 ___A___   ___B___

    thought to date from the Mesozoic period was a current forgery.
    ___C___   ___D___

24. Satellite technology has helped journalists gather and spread information on the world.
                        ___A___   ___B___   ___C___   ___D___

25. The general's political judgment or his ability to analyze a situation accurately were both
    ___A___   ___B___   ___C___

    as remarkable as his military skill.
    ___D___

26. Welcoming the astronaut to the community and prepare a big banquet were important
                             ___A___   ___B___   ___C___

    responsibilities for the newly formed citizens group.
                             ___D___

27. The freezing point and boiling point of water are standard reference points used in
        ___A___   ___B___   ___C___

    calibrating thermometer.
    ___D___

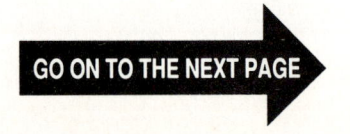

GO ON TO THE NEXT PAGE

134 Practice Tests

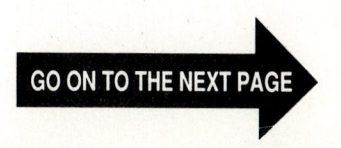

28. Sacajawea, the woman Indian who accompanied Lewis and Clark on their journey, has
       　　　　A　　　　　　　B　　　　　　　　　　　　　　　C
    been the inspiration for countless romantic legends.
    　　　　　　　　　　　　　　D

29. Ceramic materials, taken directly from the Earth's crust have used as building materials
    　　　　　　　　　　A　　　　　　　　　　　　　　　　B　　　　　C
    since time immemorial.
    　D

30. People which follow the pseudoscience astrology believe that stars govern man's fate.
    　　　A　　B　　　　　　　　　　　　　　　　C　　　　　　　　　　D

31. The force of gravity becomes least as one goes farther from the center of the Earth.
    　　　　　　　A　　　　　　B　　　　C　　　　　　　　　　　　　　　　　D

32. Using herbal medicines, treat doctors more illness for less cost.
    　A　　　　　　　　　　　B　　　　　　C　　　　D

33. The letters of Elizabeth Charlotte presents an unparalleled contemporary view of the court
    　　　　　A　　　　　　　　　B　　　　　　C　　　　　　D
    of Louis XIV.

34. Child labor laws were instituted to protect the neglected long rights of children.
    　　　A　　　　　　　　B　　　　　　　　　　　C　　　　　　　D

35. If excess air was pumped into an elastic cylinder, the cylinder will explode.
    　　A　　　　B　　　　　C　　　　　　　　D

36. English, is spoken by slightly more than 8 percent of the world's population, is
    　　　　　A　　　　　　B　　　　　　　　　　　　C
    the most common language after Chinese.
    　　　　D

37. Many people, physicians included, fail to appreciate that can bee stings have fatal results in
    　　　　　　A　　　　　　　B　　　　　　　　　C　　　　　　　D
    minutes.

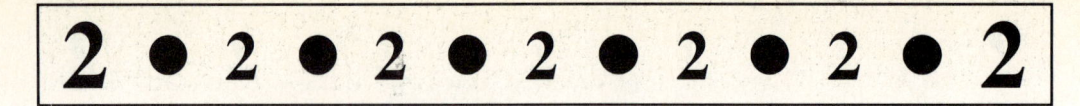

38. Today's playing cards, what are modeled after eighteenth-century English design, trace
           A   B

    their roots to Turkey.
         C   D

39. The brain's left hemisphere controls logic and language, while the right controlling
                    A   B   C

    intuitive talents and musical ability.
                                   D

40. Upon immigrants arriving in America at the turn of the century, most immigrants
          A   B   C

    passed through Ellis Island.
         D

THIS IS THE END OF SECTION 2

IF YOU FINISH BEFORE TIME IS CALLED, CHECK YOUR WORK ON SECTION 2 ONLY.

DO NOT READ OR WORK ON ANY OTHER SECTION OF THE TEST. THE SUPERVISOR WILL TELL YOU WHEN TO BEGIN WORK ON SECTION 3.

136 Practice Tests

SECTION 3

READING COMPREHENSION AND VOCABULARY

Time: 45 minutes

This section tests your comprehension of standard written English. There are two types of questions in this section, with special directions for each type.

Directions: In questions 1–30, each sentence has an underlined word or phrase. Below each sentence are four other words or phrases, marked (A), (B), (C), and (D). You are to choose the *one* word or phrase that *best keeps the meaning* of the original sentence if it is substituted for the underlined word or phrase. Then, on your answer sheet, find the number of the question and fill in the space that matches the letter you have chosen. Fill in the space so that the letter inside the oval cannot be seen.

Example

Passenger ships and aircraft are often equipped with ship-to-shore or air-to-land radio telephones.
(A) highways
(B) railroads
(C) planes
(D) sailboats

Sample Answer

(A) (B) ● (D)

The best answer is (C), because "Passenger ships and planes are often equipped with ship-to-shore or air-to-land radio telephones" is closest in meaning to the original sentence. Therefore, you should choose answer (C).

Now begin work on the questions.

1. If one has an open mind, it is not difficult to appreciate another's point of view.
   (A) understand
   (B) agree with
   (C) contradict
   (D) apprise

2. There are some people who advocate relaxation over work.
   (A) insist on
   (B) recommend
   (C) appreciate
   (D) deplore

3. An employer must verify that the applicants have the proper qualifications.
   (A) credentials
   (B) measurements
   (C) forms
   (D) attire

4. Allowing books to be sold at the exhibition would set a precedent for future conventions.
   (A) start a fad
   (B) establish a pattern
   (C) upset the applecart
   (D) inhibit change

GO ON TO THE NEXT PAGE

Practice Tests 137

5. The lawyers obliged the newspaper to retract its allegations.
   (A) withdraw
   (B) deny
   (C) reprint
   (D) change

6. It is often difficult to reveal one's true feelings.
   (A) divulge
   (B) assess
   (C) discover
   (D) recognize

7. Since the beginning of time, there have been people who predict that the end of the world is near.
   (A) are sure that
   (B) agree
   (C) forecast
   (D) are afraid

8. The size of our staff was reduced to reflect the change in the budget.
   (A) implemented
   (B) augmented
   (C) decreased
   (D) reevaluated

9. Some people can eat large quantities of food, yet never gain any weight.
   (A) varieties
   (B) plates
   (C) items
   (D) amounts

10. The building is so well constructed that it will survive even the strongest earthquake.
    (A) guaranteed
    (B) built
    (C) located
    (D) insured

11. Jane looked at an assortment of necklaces before choosing one with green beads.
    (A) inexpensive
    (B) high-quality
    (C) multicolored
    (D) a variety of

12. The caterers must know approximately how many people are expected.
    (A) about
    (B) exactly
    (C) confidentially
    (D) truthfully

13. The chart showed the amount of money spent on food compared with the amount spent on recreation.
    (A) necessities
    (B) education
    (C) incidentals
    (D) amusement

14. The woman, who sponsored the civic art show, has not been seen recently.
    (A) anywhere
    (B) inside
    (C) lately
    (D) outside

15. The man's brother accompanied him to the corner and then went in a different direction.
    (A) went with
    (B) sent
    (C) followed
    (D) helped

16. When I heard the alarm, I was prepared to run!
    (A) anxious
    (B) going
    (C) afraid
    (D) ready

GO ON TO THE NEXT PAGE

138 Practice Tests

17. History is best learned from contemporary sources.
    (A) ancient
    (B) concurrent
    (C) modern
    (D) several

18. This flag symbolizes what is important to our country.
    (A) summarizes
    (B) reveals
    (C) contains
    (D) represents

19. It is advisable to have an alternative plan.
    (A) a substitute
    (B) a better
    (C) an easier
    (D) an equal

20. One is not always able to choose one's associates.
    (A) colleagues
    (B) neighbors
    (C) superiors
    (D) students

21. Reports of the discovery were telegraphed to the waiting nation.
    (A) election
    (B) find
    (C) district
    (D) dance

22. The film rights were negotiated by the author's lawyers.
    (A) rejected
    (B) suggested
    (C) demanded
    (D) arranged

23. The results of experiments on the intelligence of monkeys have not been conclusive.
    (A) understood
    (B) final
    (C) valid
    (D) predicted

24. A recent census of home-buying patterns shows that many people under 30 are still renting.
    (A) survey
    (B) group
    (C) number
    (D) newspaper

25. The use of the microcomputer is as pedestrian as the use of the telephone.
    (A) unusual
    (B) newsworthy
    (C) common
    (D) public

26. The price of gold fluctuated and then plummeted on the world market last quarter.
    (A) varied
    (B) rose
    (C) stabilized
    (D) decreased

27. Congressional debate over the passage of this controversial bill was inevitable.
    (A) popular
    (B) personal
    (C) disputatious
    (D) biased

28. The picture illustrates the compassion the artist has for his native land.
    (A) feeling
    (B) distrust
    (C) revulsion
    (D) knowledge

GO ON TO THE NEXT PAGE

29. The drought caused escalation of prices and <u>depletion</u> of supplies.
    (A) craving
    (B) exhaustion
    (C) hoarding
    (D) maintenance

30. The worker's <u>aggressive</u> personality kept him from having many friends.
    (A) assertive
    (B) depressed
    (C) unstable
    (D) insecure

Directions: In the rest of this section you will read several passages. Each one is followed by several questions about it. For questions 31–60, you are to choose the *one* best answer, (A), (B), (C), or (D), to each question. Then, on your answer sheet, find the number of the question and fill in the space that matches the letter of the answer you have chosen.

Answer all questions following a passage on the basis of what is *stated* or *implied* in the reading passage.

Example passage and questions

The rattles with which a rattlesnake warns of its presence are formed by loosely interlocking hollow rings of hard skin, which make a buzzing sound when its tail is shaken. As a baby, the snake begins to form its rattles from the button at the very tip of its tail. Thereafter, each time it sheds its skin, a new ring is formed. Popular belief holds that a snake's age can be told by counting the rings, but this idea is fallacious. In fact, a snake may lose its old skin as often as four times a year. Also, rattles tend to wear or break off with time.

Example I

A rattlesnake's rattles are made of
(A) skin
(B) bone
(C) wood
(D) muscle

Sample Answer
● Ⓑ Ⓒ Ⓓ

According to the passage, a rattlesnake's rattles are made of rings of hard skin. Therefore, you should choose answer (A).

Example II

How often does a rattlesnake shed its skin?
(A) Once every four years
(B) Once every four months
(C) Up to four times every year
(D) Four times more often than other snakes

Sample Answer
Ⓐ Ⓑ ● Ⓓ

The passage states that "a snake may lose its old skin as often as four times a year." Therefore, you should choose answer (C).

Now begin work on the questions.

GO ON TO THE NEXT PAGE

140   Practice Tests

Questions 31–36

Since the laser is an intense, highly directional source of light, some of its energy will be absorbed by the material it strikes. This absorption can result in a temperature increase of the surface and/or the interior of the object. If the object placed in the path of the laser is the human body, then extra precautions should be taken.

The eye is much more vulnerable to injury from laser radiation than the skin. When a laser beam directly hits the eye, visible light is transmitted through the cornea and lens and is focused to a small spot on the retina. This is true for direct viewing (looking into the laser) as well as specular reflections of the beam (reflection off mirrorlike surfaces).

Both Class I and II Helium-Neon lasers can be used for classroom demonstrations because of the low potential for injury to the user or viewer. However, the Laser Institute of America lists the following safety precautions when operating Class II lasers:

- Do not permit a person to stare into the laser.

- Do not point the laser at a person's eye.

- Keep beam paths above or well below either sitting or standing eye level.

- Permit only experienced personnel to operate the laser, and do not leave an operable laser unattended.

- Eliminate unnecessary specular surfaces from the vicinity of the beam path.

31. What is the main topic of the passage?
    (A) Eye operations using lasers
    (B) Using lasers in the classroom
    (C) The hazards of lasers
    (D) Problems using lasers

32. Which of the following is NOT listed as a precaution for using lasers?
    (A) Keep mirrorlike surfaces away from the path of the laser.
    (B) Make sure the laser path is not directed at anyone's eye.
    (C) Allow only specular reflection when experimenting with eyes.
    (D) Make sure that only experienced laser operators use the lasers.

33. According to the passage, what happens to the surface or the interior of an object after laser treatment?
    (A) It becomes hot.
    (B) It is absorbed by the light.
    (C) It gets injured.
    (D) It freezes.

34. According to the passage, which of the following statements is true?
    (A) Lasers can increase surface temperatures.
    (B) Lasers should never be used on the human body.
    (C) The Laser Institute of America forbids classroom demonstrations of laser use.
    (D) Lasers are harmless.

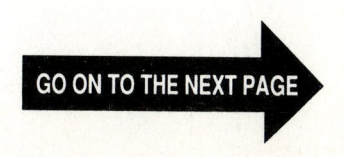

GO ON TO THE NEXT PAGE

35. In what way does a Helium I laser differ from a Helium II laser?
    (A) It cannot be directed.
    (B) It does not reflect off surfaces.
    (C) It is not recommended for classroom use.
    (D) It is less dangerous.

36. Which of the following will probably produce a specular reflection of a laser?
    (A) A windowpane
    (B) A blackboard
    (C) A wooden door
    (D) A carpet

Questions 37–42

Businesses engaged in frequent external communication must look for the most practical means of communicating. In addition to mail and telephone, telex and TWX (teletypewriter exchange) sending/receiving systems are widely used.

Telex and TWX communications offer several advantages. They are rapid: the message is sent immediately, like a telephone call. Also, they provide both the sender and the receiver with a printed record of each message. These two advantages combine the most desirable elements of both telephone call and letter. There are also cost advantages. Generally speaking, telex and TWX messages are inexpensive. Charges are by the minute, but the resulting cost is about one cent per word. The TWX is even cheaper. Both machines print at the end of the message exactly how much time was used in sending the message. Thus, the user is immediately provided with a statement of costs for each message. This, of course, is useful in accounting for expenses and budgeting. As a result, telex and TWX communication systems are highly desirable as a means of communication across long distances, since they provide written records of all correspondence and costs and communicate quickly and economically.

In order to write good telex or TWX messages, some basic principles should be followed. Since long messages are more expensive, you will want to conserve words and be as concise as possible. However, if your message is so short as to be unclear, it is wasted expense. Similarly with abbreviations—a careful use of abbreviations is helpful in reducing costs, but overuse of them will prevent your reader from understanding, and will in the end result in costs of additional communications and lost time.

37. Which of the following does the author mainly discuss?
    (A) Basic principles for writing telex or TWX messages
    (B) The most cost-efficient communication systems
    (C) Ways of preventing wasted expense
    (D) The advantages of telex and TWX communication systems

38. Which of the following questions does the passage answer?
    (A) What is the most economical way of communicating long distance?
    (B) What problems might one encounter with telex and TWX systems?
    (C) Which long-distance communication systems are used by most businesses?
    (D) How much money is saved by switching to telex and TWX communication systems?

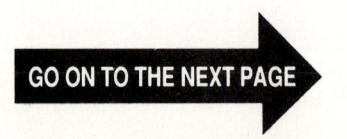

GO ON TO THE NEXT PAGE

39. Which of the following words best describes the tone of the passage?
    (A) Ambivalent
    (B) Critical
    (C) Persuasive
    (D) Disapproving

40. According to the passage, which statement is true?
    (A) Using the mail and telephone is the most practical means of long-distance communication.
    (B) Writing concise telex or TWX messages is important.
    (C) The telex system is the most inexpensive way to send long-distance communications.
    (D) It's best not to use abbreviations in telex messages.

41. What is the author's attitude toward the use of abbreviations in telex/TWX messages?
    (A) Cautious
    (B) Negative
    (C) Enthusiastic
    (D) Skeptical

42. Which of the following would the author probably advise someone using telex or TWX?
    (A) Avoid abbreviations whenever possible.
    (B) Use a telephone for long-distance communication.
    (C) Take time to formulate your message.
    (D) Send a duplicate copy of your message by mail.

Questions 43–49

Biology has begun to provide clear answers to problems that once seemed beyond the reach of science, and each of the new answers has brought along new and more puzzling questions, especially about the nature of man and his place in the living world. The universe has become a far stranger place for the physicists, and now the life within that universe is turning into an even stranger phenomenon for the biologists. At the center of all puzzles is the connectedness of the Earth's life. Ever since Darwin, we have known that the wide varieties of species on the planet are in some sense related to each other, but now we must face the fact that they comprise, all together, one form of life, a coherent system of life, a living mass in which we humans have the look of working parts.

From our point of view, the human being is the highest achievement of the natural world, the best thing on the face of the Earth. Or at least this is the way we have always tended to view ourselves and our place, masters of all we survey. There are risks for us in this point of view, however. We need reminding that we are a very young species, only recently down from the trees, still preoccupied by the new gift of language, and still trying to figure out what we mean and what the world means. We are juvenile, as species go. We seem to be a stunning success in biological terms, already covering more of the Earth than any other single form of life since the famous trilobites, whose fossils abound everywhere, but we should be going warily into our future. We may be error-prone at this stage of our development, apt to fumble and drop things, too young to have our affairs in order. If we get things wrong, we could be leaving a very thin layer of fossils ourselves, and radioactive at that.

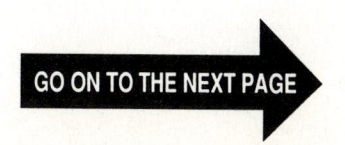

GO ON TO THE NEXT PAGE

43. Which of the following does the author mainly discuss?
    (A) The nature of man and his place in the living world
    (B) The wide varieties of species on the planet
    (C) Our preoccupation with the new gift of language
    (D) Human beings as the highest achievement of the natural world

44. Which of the following is NOT mentioned as descriptive of human beings?
    (A) We are a relatively young species.
    (B) We have populated a large portion of the Earth.
    (C) We could possibly make serious errors.
    (D) We have put our affairs in order.

45. Which of the following statements would the author most likely agree with?
    (A) We have been absolutely successful.
    (B) We must be cautious.
    (C) We will learn from our mistakes.
    (D) We should give biologists more recognition.

46. According to the passage, humanity's traditional view of its place on Earth has been that it is
    (A) youthful
    (B) error-prone
    (C) superior
    (D) immortal

47. The author implies that humanity could be destroyed by
    (A) famine
    (B) overpopulation
    (C) young people
    (D) nuclear conflict

48. The author implicitly compares the human race to
    (A) a fossil
    (B) a child
    (C) an old person
    (D) a tree

49. According to the passage, Darwin helped us to see that
    (A) human beings are error-prone
    (B) physicists can best explain the universe
    (C) all life is interconnected
    (D) language is found in all species

Questions 50–55

This should have been a good year for the gypsy moths of New England. But instead of feeding happily on tree leaves throughout the Northeast, huge populations of the caterpillars were felled by a mysterious illness.

Last week, after four months of detective work that included examining 300 caterpillar
5 cadavers in ten states, U.S. Department of Agriculture scientists in Ithaca, New York, announced that they had identified the culprit: an all-but-forgotten fungus brought to the United States from the Far East in 1909.

The fungus, known as *Entromophaga maimaiga*, is highly effective against gypsy moths in its native Japan, but when tested in six Boston suburbs against the caterpillars common to North
10 America, it was thought by scientists to be a failure. They were wrong. Over the next 80 years, the fungus—which secretes enzymes that invade and devour the insides of caterpillars—slowly

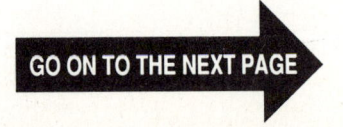

GO ON TO THE NEXT PAGE

spread over the surrounding region and adapted to New England's climate. This year, after an ideal, cool and wet spring, it struck, killing so many moths that USDA entomologists began an investigation.

50. Which of the following does the author mainly discuss?
    (A) Caterpillar cadavers
    (B) A USDA investigation
    (C) Entomologists
    (D) A Japanese fungus

51. It can be inferred from the passage that
    (A) the fungus originated in Boston
    (B) organisms adapt to change
    (C) the *Entromophaga maimaiga* is a failure
    (D) it is sometimes impossible to identify causes of illnesses

52. Where in the passage does the author explain how the fungus destroys its victim?
    (A) Line 8
    (B) Line 11
    (C) Line 13
    (D) Line 14

53. The paragraph following the passage probably discusses
    (A) entomology
    (B) New England climate
    (C) the investigation
    (D) the enzymes

54. The fungus *Entromophaga maimaiga* had almost been forgotten because
    (A) it was effective only against gypsy moths
    (B) it was considered ineffective
    (C) it was imported so long ago
    (D) it adapted to the New England climate

55. The best title for this passage would be
    (A) From Caterpillar to Gypsy Moth
    (B) An Imported Gypsy Moth Deterrent
    (C) The Fight to Save the Gypsy Moths
    (D) Japanese Gypsy Moths Invade New England

Questions 56–60

Washington, D.C., began as a planned city. It did not spring up around a fort or trading post like Pittsburgh, nor on a natural harbor like New York City. In the manner of Brasilia, the fabricated capital of Brazil, it was hewn out of wilderness on a designated spot. However, there was no large government subsidy for its completion as there was for Brasilia, nor was it an "instant city"
5 like the new town of Columbia, Maryland. Washington City grew slowly, and at times painfully, on swamp and farmland on the Potomac River near the flourishing ports of Georgetown and Alexandria, Virginia.

In 1789, when George Washington became President, one of the many pressing problems of the new government was to find a site for a capital that would be acceptable to various factions.
10 Back in 1783, there had been an unfortunate confrontation when a group of unpaid Revolutionary War veterans menaced the Continental Congress at Philadelphia. Local authorities refused to protect Congress, which was forced to move to Princeton, New Jersey. As a result, Congress decided that a city must be created far from the influence of local or national politics, thereby insuring safety to the government, which presumably would be subject to the physical violence of excited
15 pressure groups. At the time it was a sound idea. Now, however, thanks to rapid air and surface transportation, the capital city can qualify as the Pressure Group Center of the western world.

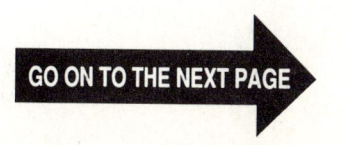

56. What is the main topic of this passage?
    (A) Why the nation's capital is located where it is
    (B) How Washington deals with pressure groups
    (C) How the natural terrain influenced the design of Washington
    (D) Why the national capital should be located elsewhere today

57. In what way did Brasilia develop that is different from the way Washington developed?
    (A) It was developed out of wilderness.
    (B) It was built on a specifically chosen site.
    (C) It was built very slowly.
    (D) It was completed using government funds.

58. Why was Washington's present location chosen?
    (A) Because of its climate
    (B) To avoid political extremists
    (C) To ensure gradual growth
    (D) Because of hostility in Princeton

59. The writer characterizes some of the early growth of Washington as
    (A) rapid
    (B) efficient
    (C) difficult
    (D) violent

60. In line 15, the word "it" refers to
    (A) the time
    (B) to isolate the new capital city
    (C) a city
    (D) the influence of local or national politics

THIS IS THE END OF SECTION 3

IF YOU FINISH BEFORE TIME IS CALLED, CHECK YOUR WORK ON SECTION 3 ONLY.

DO NOT READ OR WORK ON ANY OTHER SECTION OF THE TEST.

3

LISTENING TARGETS

◼ STATEMENTS

Purpose
You will have to recognize a written paraphrase of an oral statement.

Words/Phrases to Look for

	Examples
Numbers:	1962, 2nd, etc.
Quantities:	two pounds, a lot, few
Street names:	2614 1st. Avenue
Ages:	15 years old
Contractions:	it's, let's
Common American names:	Bill Jones, Miss Betsy Smith
Idioms:	to carry on, to take a break

Sample Statements

Affirmative:	We've been waiting for the bus for over 15 minutes.
Negative:	The school won't open until 8:30.
Imperative:	Turn left at the second light.

STRATEGIES FOR THE TOEFL

1. Do NOT listen to the general directions. Use that time (approximately 3 minutes) to read the answer choices.

2. Read the four answer choices quickly before you listen to the statement. There is 12 seconds between each statement on the tape.

3. Anticipate the oral statement. Look at the answer choices and try to guess what the statement will be.

4. When the statement starts, do NOT read—only listen.

5. Listen to the statement carefully. Try to repeat it to yourself. Do NOT read the answer choices while you are listening. You have 12 seconds to answer the question.

6. Answer every question. If you aren't sure, GUESS!

7. When you hear the speaker on the tape say the number of the next question (for example, question 2), STOP and LISTEN. Do NOT read or mark in your book.

STRATEGY-BUILDING ACTIVITY

1. Practice these strategies in the Skill-Building Exercises section below.
2. Listen to the tape without looking at the book.
3. Repeat the questions you hear.

SKILLS TO DEVELOP

1. Learn to distinguish between words with similar sounds.
2. Learn to distinguish between numbers with similar pronunciation. (Note: All numbers on the TOEFL go in ascending order. This will make it easier for you to locate the right answer.)
3. Learn to recognize synonyms.
4. Learn to hear negative markers: *no, not, don't,* etc.
5. Learn to use context to help you understand.
6. Learn to understand cause and effect.
7. Learn to understand conditional statements.
8. Learn to recognize correct chronological order.
9. Learn to recognize comparisons.

SKILL-BUILDING EXERCISES

The following exercises will help you develop these skills. Do the following exercises on statements. Listen to the tape carefully.

SIMILAR SOUNDS

Similar sounds are words that sound almost alike, such as *bit* and *beat; beet* and *bet; candidate* and *cannot eat; car* and *cart; tin* and *ten.*

In the following listening exercises, you will hear a statement. You must choose the sentence that most closely restates the original.

1. (A) He goes to sleep early.
   (B) He is surly at bedtime.
   (C) It is better that he have a hobby.
   (D) His rabbit is in the flower garden.

2. (A) He became wealthy writing rhymes.
   (B) His health prevents long hours at work.
   (C) He helps his fellow workers.
   (D) He ruined his health working with lime.

3. (A) He kept her clothes for her.
   (B) They were close to the pier.
   (C) She couldn't hear the convocation.
   (D) Near her, he overheard them talking.

4. (A) The icing on the cake is almost melted.
   (B) The heat will melt the ice.
   (C) We met the nicest people on our walk.
   (D) These are the nicest seats in the house.

5. (A) We needed our boots on the farm.
   (B) The boat fared well during the storm.
   (C) She bought the boots from the store.
   (D) The storm sank the boat fast.

Listening Targets 149

NUMBER DISCRIMINATION

Many numbers sound alike. Be careful to listen for the differences between numbers, such as 13 and 30 or 15 and 50.

In the following questions, you will hear a statement. You must choose the sentence that most closely restates the original. These are difficult. They will test your understanding as well as your short-term memory. Read the answer choices before you listen to the statement.

1. (A) Books should be opened to page 16.
   (B) There were six pages in the book.
   (C) Sixteen books were opened.
   (D) The books were on page 60.

2. (A) The flight leaves at 8:13.
   (B) There are 13 flights at 8:30.
   (C) Flight 30 departs at half-past eight.
   (D) The Madrid flight leaves at 8:30.

3. (A) There are 80 graduates in our class.
   (B) The eighth is graduation day for 18 of us.
   (C) Eight of us will graduate.
   (D) The graduation is on the 18th.

4. (A) John was born on the 15th.
   (B) John was born on the 30th.
   (C) John was born in 1980.
   (D) John was born in 1930.

5. (A) The teams appear at 9:20.
   (B) Nineteen teams appear on the field.
   (C) Twenty teams of nine each appear.
   (D) The teams arrive before 9.

150 Listening Targets

SYNONYMS

You may be asked to identify words that have a similar meaning, such as *careless* and *inattentive*; *rational* and *reasonable*; *quick* and *swift*.

In the following questions, you will hear a statement. You must choose the sentence that most closely restates the original.

1. (A) She put the empty box in the elevator.
   (B) The package was empty.
   (C) She was too young to dress herself.
   (D) She had difficulty moving the package.

2. (A) Cages make practical homes for all bears.
   (B) Bears are kept in outdoor cages.
   (C) The forest is the only habitat for bears.
   (D) Most bears taken from the wild live in cages.

3. (A) We dropped the envelope in the fog.
   (B) We missed the mailbox off to the side.
   (C) The fog made it impossible to see our companions.
   (D) She missed the envelope, although it was in sight.

4. (A) We'd also planned a raft trip.
   (B) Conditions forced us to cancel the expedition.
   (C) We tripped over the height of the raft.
   (D) We'd carefully planed the surface of the raft.

5. (A) She had little time to recover before having to travel again.
   (B) She had to fly on her business trip.
   (C) She had no choice between taking a boat and a plane.
   (D) She was about over her illness.

Listening Targets   151

NEGATION

Words like *not, no,* and *any* are sometimes difficult to distinguish. Be aware of these potential problems.

In the following questions, you will hear a statement. You must choose the sentence that most closely restates the original.

1. (A) We doubt they invited the boys.
   (B) All the boys got an invitation.
   (C) We think the boys went away.
   (D) They asked the boys but not us.

2. (A) There are more people than chairs.
   (B) There are too many empty seats.
   (C) There are never enough people.
   (D) There are more than enough seats.

3. (A) I would not want to fall asleep here.
   (B) Nobody would sleep during this performance.
   (C) Not many people fall asleep during the show.
   (D) I would expect people to fall asleep watching this.

4. (A) He can call me any time he wants.
   (B) I am never here when he calls.
   (C) I pretend I'm not home each time he calls.
   (D) I am never out when he calls.

5. (A) Marjorie had no books about reasoning.
   (B) Marjorie bought the book without thinking.
   (C) The book was not for sale.
   (D) There was no need for her to buy it.

CONTEXTUAL REFERENCE

To answer some of the questions, you will have to identify appropriate antecedents or referents. A pronoun refers to some noun in the sentence. Don't confuse the pronoun related to the subject with one related to the object.
Pay attention to:

1. Gender (*John . . . his, Sally . . . hers*)
2. Number (*children . . . they, the boy . . . his*)

In the following questions, you will hear a statement. You must choose the sentence that most closely restates the original.

1. (A) They thought my route was quicker.
   (B) I found their route faster.
   (C) They thought their route was faster.
   (D) Anne found Claire's route more direct.

2. (A) Bill's brother was Jim's best friend.
   (B) Bill was closer to his brother.
   (C) Paul and Jim were brothers.
   (D) Jim is no relation to Paul.

3. (A) I lent my car to George's mother.
   (B) George lent my mother his car.
   (C) My mother is picking up George's laundry.
   (D) I lent my mother his car for the weekend.

4. (A) My father and my brother visited my sister.
   (B) My father visited my brother at camp.
   (C) My father and his brother saw their sister.
   (D) My father and my uncle saw my sister.

5. (A) Karen gives me her answers.
   (B) John gives Karen the answers.
   (C) I give John her answers.
   (D) John wants both our answers.

Listening Targets 153

CAUSE AND EFFECT

Cause-and-effect statements show the result of a particular action. One part of the sentence will state a situation, which is followed by its effect.

Pay attention to:

1. Verb tense
2. Subject of each sentence
3. Words like *any* and *not*
4. Words that sound alike

In the following questions, you will hear a statement. You must choose the sentence that most closely restates the original.

1. (A) The heavy traffic made me arrive late at the airport.
   (B) The plane was late, so I didn't catch a taxi.
   (C) I caught a taxi on a side lane.
   (D) The taxes on the plane ticket were high.

2. (A) It rained on the birds.
   (B) The birds sang until it rained.
   (C) The rain made the birds sing with joy.
   (D) Birds like what the rain brings.

3. (A) She missed Sam so much it made her sick.
   (B) It was a bad day to take an exam.
   (C) She could not take the test because she was sick.
   (D) She felt bad about missing the exam.

4. (A) My smiling won his confidence.
   (B) He smiled warmly at me.
   (C) He can talk openly about me.
   (D) He walked a mile in the open.

5. (A) At present, he has no plans for the program.
   (B) He was new in the program, unlike her.
   (C) The change in the program astonished him.
   (D) His being on the program made her rearrange her schedule.

CONDITIONALS

A conditional statement is one of the most difficult English structures. It consists of two clauses and can express the following conditions:

(A) *Factual condition:* If you turn the key, the motor starts.
(B) *Future condition:* If he comes after six, we'll be gone.
(C) *Imaginative condition:* If my mother could see me now, she'd be very proud.

In the following questions, you will hear a statement. You must choose the sentence that most closely restates the original.

1. (A) We left before it rained.
   (B) The rain prevented us from leaving.
   (C) They bet the rain would stop soon.
   (D) She hated the rain as much as we did.

2. (A) Noise is on the increase these days.
   (B) The door closed and it was quiet.
   (C) Closing the door will muffle the sound.
   (D) The noisy door needs grease.

3. (A) I would repeat the same mistakes.
   (B) It's a mistake to want to be younger.
   (C) I make mistakes because I am young.
   (D) I would do things differently if I were young again.

4. (A) The defective product will be reclaimed.
   (B) Voters must register by calling the polling office.
   (C) The telephone office received the most complaints.
   (D) No one asked about the quality of the produce.

5. (A) Her arrival means she longs for a walk.
   (B) Where we're walking, it will be dusty.
   (C) The dust makes the walk seem longer.
   (D) If she comes before twilight, we'll go walking.

Listening Targets 155

CHRONOLOGICAL ORDER

The questions below require you to determine the order of events—that is, what happened *first, second, third,* and so on.

Pay attention to:

1. Words that modify actions, such as *second . . . two, third . . . three,* etc.
2. Words that indicate order, such as *before, after,* etc.

In the following questions, you will hear a statement. You must choose the sentence that most closely restates the original.

1. (A) The waitress told the diners to finish their trays first.
   (B) They finished their trays after the waitress tried to take them away.
   (C) The waitress finished their trays for them.
   (D) The waitress removed the trays when the diners were done.

2. (A) We built the fire before we went skiing.
   (B) After we skied, we relaxed by the fire they started for us.
   (C) They went skiing as we built the fire.
   (D) We relaxed by the fire before going skiing.

3. (A) While dinner was cooking, we went to the store.
   (B) We cooked dinner, visited the store, and slept.
   (C) After shopping, we had dinner and slept.
   (D) We ate and then were too tired to shop.

4. (A) The guest room was painted for his visit.
   (B) He came because the guest room was painted.
   (C) He painted the guest room when he came.
   (D) We painted the room, then went to see him.

5. (A) She went to the concert, then the party.
   (B) The party ended before the concert.
   (C) The party stopped her from going to the concert.
   (D) She went to the party, then the concert.

156 Listening Targets

COMPARISONS

A comparison shows how two things are similar or different.

Noun

Different: Bill has fewer *cavities* than Jack.

Similar: Jack has as many *cavities* as Rosalind.

Verb

Different: John *studies* more than Bill.

Similar: Bob *talks* as much as George.

Adverb

Different: We speak more *quickly* than they.

Similar: She drives as *slowly* as my mother.

Adjective

Different: Betty is *shorter* than Raymond.

Similar: This car is as *expensive* as a house.

In the following questions, you will hear a statement. You must choose the sentence that most closely restates the original.

1. (A) The bridge was too narrow.
   (B) The engineer thought the bridge was too wide.
   (C) At the engineer's insistence, they leveled the bridge.
   (D) All agreed the bridge was too high.

2. (A) I think Joe used to be better than Cliff.
   (B) I do better than Joe and Cliff.
   (C) Cliff seems to test better than Joe.
   (D) Joe does better than Cliff on the exams.

3. (A) Urban malls are growing larger.
   (B) Shops in the city are not doing well.
   (C) Suburban trains contribute to the growth.
   (D) Stores make more money downtown.

4. (A) There are longer runways in the Western Hemisphere.
   (B) The new runway is not the longest.
   (C) The long runway runs toward the land.
   (D) The runway is long but in need of repair.

5. (A) Winter has longer days.
   (B) Days are longer in the summer.
   (C) Winter days are longer than summer days.
   (D) Summer days are shorter than winter days.

Listening Targets 157

■ SHORT DIALOGS

Purpose

You will have to understand social, or everyday, informal English conversation.

Words/Phrases to Look for

	Examples
Contractions:	*they're, didn't, etc.*
Common American names:	*Jane, Bob, etc.*
Everyday vocabulary:	*go to work, get ready, etc.*
Specific vocabulary:	*nonsmoking section, round-trip ticket*
Question words:	*who, what, when, where, why, how*
Idioms	

Sample Questions

Most common question:	What does the man/woman mean?
Other question types:	Where does this conversation take place?
	What will the man/woman do next?
	What are the men/women talking about?

STRATEGY-BUILDING ACTIVITY

Can you guess what kind of question you will hear by reading the answer choices? Read the answer choices in the Skill-Building Exercises that follow and guess what the questions are. You can find the correct question in the Tapescripts in the Appendix.

SKILLS TO DEVELOP

1. Learn to distinguish between words with similar sounds.
2. Learn to distinguish between numbers with similar pronunciation. (Note: All numbers on the TOEFL go in ascending order. This will make it easier for you to locate the right answer.)
3. Learn to recognize synonyms.
4. Learn to hear negative markers: *no, not, don't,* etc.
5. Learn to use context to help you understand.
6. Learn to understand cause and effect.
7. Learn to understand conditional statements.
8. Learn to recognize correct chronological order.
9. Learn to recognize comparisons.

SKILL-BUILDING EXERCISES

The following exercises will help you develop these skills. Do the following exercises on short dialogs. Listen to the tape carefully.

SIMILAR SOUNDS

In the following questions, you will hear a short dialog followed by a question about the dialog. You must choose the appropriate answer.

1. (A) Spread a rumor.
   (B) Miss someone.
   (C) Herd some cattle.
   (D) Tell a joke.

2. (A) He's become hoarse.
   (B) Someone beat the horse.
   (C) He doesn't eat beets.
   (D) He wouldn't gamble on the horse.

3. (A) The clapping.
   (B) The curtain.
   (C) The toys.
   (D) The boys.

4. (A) To be rich.
   (B) A light.
   (C) His sight.
   (D) To be liked.

5. (A) Potted plants.
   (B) A song.
   (C) Ants.
   (D) Planets.

NUMBER DISCRIMINATION

In the following questions, you will hear a short dialog followed by a question about the dialog. You must choose the appropriate answer.

1. (A) 8:30
   (B) 8:13
   (C) 8:33
   (D) 3:30

2. (A) 13
   (B) 14
   (C) 30
   (D) 40

3. (A) 8th
   (B) 9th
   (C) 15th
   (D) 18th

4. (A) 9
   (B) 15
   (C) 50
   (D) 90

5. (A) 16
   (B) 18
   (C) 60
   (D) 88

SYNONYMS

In the following questions, you will hear a short dialog followed by a question about the dialog. You must choose the appropriate answer.

1. (A) Ice storm.
   (B) Hard bed.
   (C) Tornado.
   (D) Thunderstorm.

2. (A) Coarse sand.
   (B) Calm water.
   (C) A stormy ocean.
   (D) Being sad.

3. (A) Dinner on shore.
   (B) Lunch in port.
   (C) Port wine with dinner.
   (D) Dinner on board.

4. (A) Alternate jobs.
   (B) Go to bed.
   (C) Run a factory.
   (D) Quit work.

5. (A) Objective.
   (B) Timid.
   (C) Hostile.
   (D) Sympathetic.

NEGATION

In the following questions, you will hear a short dialog followed by a question about the dialog. You must choose the appropriate answer.

1. (A) The man did not study.
   (B) The man is not nervous.
   (C) The woman did not study.
   (D) The woman is as nervous as the man.

2. (A) Contrary.
   (B) Malicious.
   (C) Angry.
   (D) Apologetic.

3. (A) Don't use ice cubes.
   (B) Be nice.
   (C) Boil the water first.
   (D) Lose some weight.

4. (A) Watching television.
   (B) In a furniture store.
   (C) At a gymnasium.
   (D) At a theatre.

5. (A) The woman agrees with the man.
   (B) They have never met before.
   (C) They've met before.
   (D) The woman remembers him.

CONTEXTUAL REFERENCE

In the following questions, you will hear a short dialog followed by a question about the dialog. You must choose the appropriate answer.

1. (A) Kate.
   (B) The man's brother.
   (C) Kate's brother.
   (D) The woman's brother.

2. (A) On the weekend.
   (B) Within 2 days.
   (C) Tomorrow.
   (D) Yesterday.

3. (A) Laura.
   (B) The woman.
   (C) Joan.
   (D) Himself.

4. (A) Only George.
   (B) George's family.
   (C) The man's family.
   (D) The man's grandfather.

5. (A) Susan's.
   (B) Sidney's.
   (C) The man's.
   (D) The woman's.

CAUSE AND EFFECT

In the following questions, you will hear a short dialog followed by a question about the dialog. You must choose the appropriate answer.

1. (A) He couldn't get a job.
   (B) He had to come back later.
   (C) He couldn't take the test.
   (D) He had to take the test now.

2. (A) She prefers apples.
   (B) There was nothing else to eat.
   (C) She's on a diet.
   (D) It's only a snack.

3. (A) Feet.
   (B) Shoes.
   (C) Solvent.
   (D) Work.

4. (A) Everything.
   (B) Grapefruit.
   (C) Running.
   (D) Quick eating.

5. (A) Fall.
   (B) Spring.
   (C) Winter.
   (D) Summer.

CONDITIONALS

In the following questions, you will hear a short dialog followed by a question about the dialog. You must choose the appropriate answer.

1. (A) A driving permit.
   (B) A new watch.
   (C) A new car.
   (D) An empty road.

2. (A) Overseas.
   (B) Czechoslovakia.
   (C) To the bank.
   (D) Anywhere.

3. (A) Vengeful.
   (B) Dishonest.
   (C) Fair.
   (D) Unreasonable.

4. (A) Bald.
   (B) Overweight.
   (C) Thin.
   (D) Sallow.

5. (A) Borrow some money.
   (B) Ask if he's forgotten borrowing money.
   (C) Ask if he needs a loan.
   (D) Repay him.

CHRONOLOGICAL ORDER

In the following questions, you will hear a short dialog followed by a question about the dialog. You must choose the appropriate answer.

1. (A) Before the man came home.
   (B) After the man came home.
   (C) After the woman left.
   (D) When both were home.

2. (A) In an hour.
   (B) After Sally arrives.
   (C) When they return.
   (D) Before Sally arrives.

3. (A) Go to bed.
   (B) Has breakfast.
   (C) Tour museums.
   (D) Rest.

4. (A) They left with the man.
   (B) They didn't wait for the man.
   (C) The man arrived too early.
   (D) The man waited for them.

5. (A) Next year.
   (B) Soon.
   (C) When he finishes writing.
   (D) After he visits her.

COMPARISONS

In the following questions, you will hear a short dialog followed by a question about the dialog. You must choose the appropriate answer.

1. (A) The light bulb.
   (B) The shade.
   (C) The wattage.
   (D) The power.

2. (A) The mountain's height.
   (B) The woman's height.
   (C) The view.
   (D) Their ages.

3. (A) A big country.
   (B) Increasing deafness.
   (C) A growing debt.
   (D) Escalating rents.

4. (A) Shopping for clothes.
   (B) Taking a trip.
   (C) Exercising.
   (D) Studying.

5. (A) This play is shorter.
   (B) Last year's play is shorter.
   (C) The plays are of equal length.
   (D) Last year's play was longer.

■ MINI-TALKS AND DIALOGS

Purpose

You will have to understand two or three listening passages of 130 to 230 words that last for 40 to 70 seconds and answer four to eight questions on the passages. The English tested here is more formal and academic than in the previous two sections.

Words/Phrases to Look for

Vocabulary related to university life, American history, geography, or science.

Definitions
Descriptions
Explanations
Question words: *who, what, when, where, why, how*
Sums of money
Dates, amounts, statistics
Cause and effect

Listening Targets 163

Sample Questions

With slight variations, these questions are found in both the mini-talks and dialogs.

What is the main topic of the conversation?
Who is the speaker?
What is the speaker's profession?
Where does the conversation take place?
Whom is the speaker talking to?
What will the man/woman probably do next?
What is the relationship of the speakers?
When did the conversation take place?

STRATEGIES FOR THE TOEFL

1. Do NOT listen to the general directions. Use that time (approximately 3 minutes) to read the answer choices.

2. Read the answer choices to get a basic idea of the passage before the passage starts.

3. Anticipate the question. Look at the answer choices and try to guess what the question is.

4. When the passage starts, do NOT read—only listen.

5. Listen for the details in the passage.

6. Again, anticipate the questions.

7. Listen to the question carefully. Try to repeat it to yourself. Do NOT read the answer choices while you are listening. You have 12 seconds to answer the question.

8. Answer every question. If you aren't sure, GUESS!

9. When you hear the speaker on the tape say the number of the question (for example, question 37), STOP and LISTEN. DO NOT read or mark in your book.

STRATEGY-BUILDING ACTIVITY

Can you guess what kind of question you will hear by reading the answer choices? Read the answer choices in the Skill-Building Exercises that follow and guess what the questions are. You can find the correct question in the Tapescripts in the Appendix.

SKILLS TO DEVELOP

1. Learn to identity the main topic.
2. Learn to determine the identity of the speakers.
3. Learn to recognize contextual clues regarding location.
4. Learn to make assumptions.

SKILL-BUILDING EXERCISES

The following exercises will help you develop these skills. Do the following exercises on mini-talks and dialogs. Listen to the tape carefully.

MINI-TALKS

1. (A) Just before they are born.
   (B) The first few hours after birth.
   (C) Adolescence.
   (D) Middle age.

2. (A) Neonatologists.
   (B) Small children.
   (C) Survivors.
   (D) High-risk babies.

3. (A) Women over the age of 40.
   (B) Women between the ages of 18 and 40.
   (C) Women who are doctors.
   (D) Unmarried women.

4. (A) The first three months of life.
   (B) Hospital administration.
   (C) Care of small children.
   (D) Life-saving equipment.

5. (A) 10%.
   (B) 25%.
   (C) 75%.
   (D) 90%.

6. (A) Real.
   (B) Fabulous.
   (C) Adventurous.
   (D) Depressing.

7. (A) History.
   (B) Morality.
   (C) Spirituality.
   (D) Comedy.

8. (A) Private authors.
   (B) Small publishers.
   (C) Literary critics.
   (D) Major publishing houses.

9. (A) Early twentieth century.
   (B) Late twentieth century.
   (C) Eleventh century.
   (D) Late eighteenth century.

10. (A) The Romantics.
    (B) The Classicists.
    (C) The Enlightenment.
    (D) The famous.

Listening Targets 165

11. (A) Cost.
    (B) Length.
    (C) Hyperbole.
    (D) Naturalness.

12. (A) Regulated them.
    (B) Gave them an example.
    (C) Hindered them.
    (D) Imprisoned them.

13. (A) Sculpture.
    (B) Painting.
    (C) Ceramics.
    (D) Textiles.

14. (A) Cubists.
    (B) Impressionists.
    (C) Expressionists.
    (D) Transcendentalists.

15. (A) Euphoria.
    (B) Patriotism.
    (C) Disillusion.
    (D) Disinterest.

16. (A) Realist.
    (B) Abstract.
    (C) Symbolist.
    (D) Pointillist.

17. (A) No.
    (B) Yes.
    (C) Doesn't know.
    (D) Doesn't say.

18. (A) Casual preparation.
    (B) High fats.
    (C) Large portions.
    (D) Lower calories.

19. (A) West Coast.
    (B) East Coast.
    (C) South.
    (D) Midwest.

DIALOGS

1. (A) Johnny.
   (B) Preschools.
   (C) Creative play.
   (D) Philosophy.

2. (A) Casual friends.
   (B) Teacher and assistant.
   (C) Mother and daughter.
   (D) Two philosophers.

3. (A) A school of philosophy.
   (B) An academic institution.
   (C) A school of etiquette.
   (D) A playschool.

4. (A) Easy.
   (B) Complicated.
   (C) Impossible.
   (D) Fun.

5. (A) Food.
   (B) Music.
   (C) A party.
   (D) New people.

6. (A) The music.
   (B) The dancing.
   (C) The discussions.
   (D) The company.

7. (A) Fun-loving.
   (B) Introverted.
   (C) Serious.
   (D) Difficult.

8. (A) There was no percussion.
   (B) He wouldn't play music.
   (C) The music was too loud.
   (D) No one would dance with her.

9. (A) A dancer.
   (B) A musician.
   (C) A disc jockey.
   (D) A restaurant owner.

10. (A) Large.
    (B) Black.
    (C) Male.
    (D) Small.

11. (A) In the zoo.
    (B) At the office.
    (C) In the park.
    (D) On a bus.

12. (A) The man threw soot at her.
    (B) She was chasing something.
    (C) She heard a loud noise.
    (D) The woman called to her.

13. (A) That he hold the leash firmly.
    (B) That they look for the dog.
    (C) That he change the dog's name.
    (D) That he stay out of the park.

14. (A) Small.
    (B) Color.
    (C) A name.
    (D) Size.

15. (A) Zoo.
    (B) Museum.
    (C) School.
    (D) Restaurant.

16. (A) Pencils.
    (B) Tape recorders.
    (C) Lunches.
    (D) Papers.

17. (A) He wasn't in class Friday.
    (B) He wasn't hungry.
    (C) He would eat at the zoo.
    (D) He only eats dinner.

Listening Targets

4

STRUCTURE AND WRITTEN EXPRESSION TARGETS

■ INCOMPLETE SENTENCE

Purpose

You will be tested on your knowledge of English structure as it is used in academic settings.

There are 15 questions in this part. Each sentence will have a blank space. You are to choose a word or phrase from the four possible answer options to complete the sentence. The choices represent the most common errors made by students.

Words/Phrases to Look For

Academic English

Academic Content

Famous American names: *George Washington, Amelia Earhart*

Famous American landmarks: *Grand Canyon, Broadway*

Sample Incomplete Sentence

The new instructor came _____ if the books had been delivered.

(A) seeing

(B) having seen

(C) to see

(D) and saw

The answer is (C). *To see* best completes the sentence.

STRATEGY-BUILDING ACTIVITY FOR INCOMPLETE SENTENCE

Practice these strategies in the Skill Building Exercise section. Try to fill in the blank without looking at the answer choices.

SKILLS TO DEVELOP FOR INCOMPLETE SENTENCE

1. Learn to recognize parts of speech.
2. Learn to recognize grammatical agreement.
3. Learn to recognize grammatical form.
4. Learn to recognize appropriate usage.
5. Learn to recognize correct word order.
6. Learn to appreciate parallel structures.
7. Learn to recognize potential wrong answers.

■ INCORRECT SENTENCE PART

Purpose

You will be tested on your knowledge of English structure as it is used in academic settings.

There are 25 questions in this part. A sentence will have four words or groups of words underlined. You are to choose the underlined part that should be changed to make the sentence grammatically correct.

Words/Phrases to Look For

Academic English

Academic content

Famous American names: *George Washington, Amelia Earhart*

Famous American landmarks: *Grand Canyon, Broadway*

Sample Incorrect Sentence Part

This <u>is</u> an example <u>of</u> a sentence with <u>an error</u> <u>underlining</u>.
     A   B   C   D

The answer is *D*. The correct word would be *underlined*.

STRATEGY-BUILDING ACTIVITY FOR INCORRECT SENTENCE PART

Practice these strategies in the Skill Building Exercise section. Try to fill in the blank without looking at the answer choices.

SKILLS TO DEVELOP FOR INCORRECT SENTENCE PART

1. Learn to recognize parts of speech.
2. Learn to recognize grammatical agreement.
3. Learn to recognize grammatical form.
4. Learn to recognize appropriate usage.
5. Learn to recognize correct word order.
6. Learn to appreciate parallel structures.
7. Learn to recognize potential wrong answers.

STRATEGIES FOR THE TOEFL

1. Do NOT read the general directions. Use that time to start the test.
2. For incomplete sentences, try to fill in the blank before you read the answer choices. See which answer choice is closest to what you thought was correct.
   For incorrect sentence part, look at each of the underlined words to see which are correct.
3. Be aware of common mistakes and avoid them.
4. Answer every question. If you aren't sure, GUESS!

SKILL-BUILDING EXERCISES

The following exercises will help you develop these skills. Each of the exercises in this book focuses on the most common errors made by students learning English.

Before you do these exercises, you should have done one of the Practice Tests and completed your Personalized Study Plan. This plan will help you determine which of the grammar structures you should study first.

☐ Subject

The subject of a sentence or clause is a noun, which can be in the form of a **word, a phrase,** or **a clause.** The subject usually precedes the verb and answers the question **Who?** or **What?** It agrees in number with the verb.

Every sentence in English must have a subject. The subject of a sentence can be a noun, a noun phrase, a gerund, a noun clause, or words like *it* and *there*.

SUBJECT	SENTENCE
Noun	<u>Mountains</u> are high.
Noun Phrase	<u>The Rocky Mountains of Colorado</u> are high.
Gerund	<u>Climbing mountains</u> is exciting.
Noun Clause	<u>Why he climbed the mountain</u> is a mystery to me.
It	<u>It</u> is a mystery to me.
There	<u>There</u> are many mountains.

POTENTIAL PROBLEMS

1. The subject may be omitted.

   Incorrect: I'll meet him <u>when comes.</u>
   Correct: I'll meet him when <u>he</u> comes.

2. The subject may be repeated.

   Incorrect: Telling their professor the truth, <u>this</u> made them feel better.
   Correct: Telling their professor <u>the truth made</u> them feel better.

SUBJECT OMITTED

In the sentences below, identify the one underlined phrase that is incorrect.

1. <u>Carrying</u> the equipment easily, <u>rounded</u> the corner and <u>entered</u> the <u>restricted-access</u>
    A   B   C   D

   laboratory.

2. Since <u>the 1830s have trekked</u> to Hot Springs and its 4,000-acre <u>park to bathe in</u> 143-degree
           A   B

   mineral water, <u>enjoy the view</u> from the 216-foot observation <u>towers, and sail</u> the nearby
                    C   D

   Diamond Lake.

3. <u>Has issued</u> <u>a proposal</u> that <u>could</u> have a devastating <u>effect</u> on some landmark districts.
      A   B   C   D

Structure and Written Expression Targets 171

4. Usually read more novels in the summer than they do during the school year when
   A   B

   schoolwork takes up their time.
   C   D

5. Captain John Smith found the Potomac River sparkling clean and full of fish when sailed
                         A   B   C

   upriver to what is now Washington, D.C., at the beginning of the seventeenth century.
           D

6. Moved lightly up the steps that curved around the sides of the garden wall topped by
   A   B   C

   clusters of climbing roses.
               D

7. This is the last time the Harrisons plan to go to the country since grows cold in the fall,
                                        A   B

   and heating the house becomes difficult.
       C   D

8. Given the circumstances, does not seem strange that the caller would have left us this
                            A   B

   message without giving us her phone number or telling us where she could be reached.
                                                D

SUBJECT REPEATED

In the sentences below, identify the one underlined phrase that is incorrect.

1. The book of formulas it was kept a secret for many years, and no one, not even the chemist
                        A   B   C

   in charge of the project, knew where it was hidden.
                                        D

2. The computer, it is a twentieth-century invention, has created startling technological
                 A   B

   changes in the way we organize and produce information.
   C   D

172 Structure and Written Expression Targets

3. The escalating inflation rate, which it has been fodder for political speeches, has shown
        A   B   C

   no sign of stabilizing.
    D

4. Agreeing to the treaties, which they were signed early this morning, the two superpowers
                            A   B

   pledged not to reveal their contents to the press, who had been waiting at the door.
                     C   D

5. New computerized technologies have given doctors diagnostic and surgical tools offering a
       A   B   C

   precision that until recently it was only a tantalizing dream.
                               D

6. A square dance it is merely the act of going round and round in a circle of dancers
                  A   B   C

   composed of four couples.
    D

7. Originally designed to carry only cargo, the *Alexandria*, a 125-foot three-masted trading
        A   B

   schooner built in Sweden in 1929, it has been refitted for passengers.
        C   D

8. Economics, a subject which it has caused many college students problems in the
      A   B

   past, continues to be one of the least attended courses.
     C   D

9. The visiting delegation which inspected the new facilities was surprised to find the
           A   B   C

   building it was so large.
    D

10. The typewriter, which it is one of the world's great inventions, has not yet been
        A   B   C

    replaced by the word processor.
     D

Structure and Written Expression Targets

Verbs

The verb in a sentence or a clause shows action, being, or state of being of the subject. Every sentence in English must have a subject and a verb. The verb of a sentence can be a single verb or a verb phrase. It usually follows the subject. It also agrees in number with the subject. Subject-verb agreement is discussed in detail in the next Target section.

Single word as verb:
   The climber <u>rested</u> at the mountain top.
Verb phrase:
   The climbers <u>will be</u> tired when they return.

A verb phrase consists of a verb (the main verb) and its auxiliaries.

Subject	Auxiliaries	Main Verb
Students	must	study.
The sun	was	shining.
She	will	sing.

A verb tense shows the "time" of the verb—that is, when the action takes place. Verb tenses in English are the simple present, the simple past, the present continuous, the past continuous, the future, the present perfect, or the past perfect. You will not need to know these labels for the TOEFL, but you will need to know the correct verb tense.

Simple Present Tense

Form:
The simple present tense is the simple form of the verb. Note the addition of "-s" in 3rd person singular.

   I <u>swim</u> everyday.
   He <u>swims</u> everyday.

Use:

1. The simple present tense shows a routine or habitual action.
      We <u>study every evening</u>.
      They <u>usually drive</u> to work.
2. The simple present tense is used with "stative" verbs to show present time; that is, something that is happening now.
      I <u>love</u> you.
      The cake <u>smells</u> good.

174   Structure and Written Expression Targets

Some stative verbs					
to be					
be	have	like	own	smell	understand
believe	hear	love	see	sound	want
hate	know	need	seem	taste	weigh

Present Continuous Tense

Form

The present continuous tense is formed by adding an auxiliary (the verb *to be*) to the main verb plus *-ing*.

Subject + *am* + [verb + *ing*]
is
are

Use

1. The present continuous tense shows an action that is happening now.
    The children are sleeping now.
    Dinner is being prepared now.

2. The present continuous tense *also* shows an action that will take place in the future.
    We are going to California tomorrow.
    The teacher is walking out the door at four o'clock.

Simple Past Tense

Form

The simple past tense is formed by adding *-ed* to regular verbs. Irregular verbs form the past tense by either changing their spelling or by using the simple verb form.

Look at the following verb charts.

Common Regular Verb Patterns

Pattern 1 When the simple form of a verb ends in *e*, only *-d* is added.	<u>Simple</u> change live	<u>Past</u> changed lived
Pattern 2 When a one-syllable verb ends in a single consonant (except *c, w, x,* or *y*) preceded by a single vowel, the final consonant is doubled and *-ed* is added. Verbs that end with *c* add *k* before *-ed*.	<u>Simple</u> drop ship picnic	<u>Past</u> dropped shipped picnicked
Pattern 3 When a verb with more than one syllable ends in a single consonant preceded by a single vowel, the final consonant is doubled when the final syllable is stressed. The final consonant is not doubled when the final syllable is unstressed.	<u>Simple</u> omit occur listen visit	<u>Past</u> omitted occurred listened visited
Pattern 4 When the simple form of a verb ends in *y* preceded by a consonant, the *y* is changed to *i* before adding *-ed*.	<u>Simple</u> dry apply study	<u>Past</u> dried applied studied
Pattern 5 All other regular verbs form the past tense by adding *-ed* to the simple form.	<u>Simple</u> accept talk need	<u>Past</u> accepted talked needed

Common Irregular Verb Patterns

PATTERN 1: The past tense form is the same as the simple form.

Simple	Past	Simple	Past
bet	bet	quit	quit
bid	bid	rid	rid
burst	burst	set	set
cost	cost	shed	shed
cut	cut	slit	slit
hit	hit	split	split
hurt	hurt	spread	spread
let	let	wed	wed
put	put	wet	wet

PATTERN 2: The final consonant changes to *t*.

Simple	Past
bend	bent
build	built
lend	lent
send	sent
spend	spent

PATTERN 3: The past tense ends in *-ought* or *-aught*.

Simple	Past
bring	brought
buy	bought
catch	caught
fight	fought
teach	taught
think	thought

Common Irregular Verb Patterns

PATTERN 4: The sound of the vowel changes from [i] to [ɛ].

Simple	Past	Simple	Past
bleed	bled	kneel	knelt
breed	bred	lead	led
creep	crept	leave	left
deal	dealt	mean	meant
dream	dreamt	meet	met
feed	fed	read	read
feel	felt	sleep	slept
flee	fled	sweep	swept
keep	kept	weep	wept

PATTERN 5: The vowel changes from [I] to [ʌ].

Simple	Past
dig	dug
spin	spun
stick	stuck
sting	stung
string	strung
swing	swung
win	won
wring	wrung

PATTERN 6: The vowel changes from [ai] to [au].

Simple	Past
bind	bound
find	found
grind	ground
wind	wound

Common Irregular Verb Patterns

PATTERN 7: Unpredictable change from simple to past form.

Simple	Past	Simple	Past
come	came	run	ran
have	had	say	said
hear	heard	sell	sold
hold	held	shine	shone
lay	laid	shoe	shod
light	lit	shoot	shot
lie	lay	sit	sat
lose	lost	slide	slid
make	made	stand	stood
pay	paid	strike	struck
		tell	told

Use

The simple past tense is used for an action that was completed in the past. The action is finished.

The students studied last night.
We went to New York last week.
They bought their books yesterday.

Yesterday	Today
Simple past	Present continuous
	Simple present

Past Continuous Tense

Form

The past continuous tense is formed by adding the past tense of an auxiliary (the verb *to be*) plus *-ing* to the main verb.

subject + *was* + [main verb + *-ing*]
         were

Structure and Written Expression Targets 179

Use

1. The past continuous tense shows an action that occurred at a specific time in the past that lasted for some time.

   I <u>was reading</u> a book <u>at six o'clock</u>.
   Why <u>were</u> you <u>practicing</u> the piano <u>at four o'clock in the morning</u>?

2. The past continuous tense shows two actions that occurred at the same time.
   While I <u>was typing</u>, the dog <u>was sleeping</u>.
   The radio <u>was playing</u> while we <u>were dancing</u>.

3. The past continuous tense can also show one action that was interrupted by another.
   I <u>was talking</u> on the phone when the doorbell rang.
   When the music started, we <u>were</u> still <u>eating</u>.

Present Perfect Tense

Form

The present perfect tense is formed by adding the present tense of an auxiliary (the verb *to have*) plus the past participle of the main verb.

> Subject + *has* + [past participle of the verb]
>   *have*

Study the past participles of common regular and irregular verbs in the section above.

Use

1. The present perfect tense is used to show when an action happened more than once in the past.

   She <u>has won</u> the lottery ten times in the last three years.
   We <u>have passed</u> every test this semester.

2. The present perfect tense is used to show an action that began in the past and continues in the present.

   The scientists <u>have worked</u> in this lab for six years.
   Our neighbors <u>have lived</u> in their house for two months.

3. The present perfect tense is used to show an action that took place at an unknown time in the past.

>He <u>has read</u> all the books in his library.
>They <u>have thought</u> about retiring to Hawaii.

Present Perfect Continuous Tense

Form

The present perfect continuous tense is formed by adding the present tense of an auxiliary (the verb *to have*) plus the past participle of the verb *to be* plus (the main verb + *-ing*).

>Subject + *has* + been + [main verb + *-ing*]
>   *have*

Use

The present perfect continuous tense, like the present perfect tense, can be used to show an action that began in the past and continues in the present.

>The scientists <u>have been working</u> in this lab for six years.
>Our neighbors <u>have been living</u> in their house for two months.

Past Perfect Tense

Form

The past perfect tense is formed by adding the past tense of an auxiliary (the verb *to have*) plus the past participle of the main verb.

>Subject + *had* + [past participle of main verb]

Use

1. The past perfect tense is used to show an action that began before another action in the past.

>The students <u>had studied</u> all night before they took the exam.
>The students did well on the exam because they <u>had studied</u>.

Structure and Written Expression Targets **181**

2. The past perfect tense is used to show an action that continued for a time in the past, but stopped at some point also in the past.

> We had kept our old records until we changed apartments.
> The student had studied all night just before he took the exam.

Past Perfect Continuous Tense

Form

The past perfect continuous tense is formed by adding the past tense of an auxiliary (the verb *to have*) to the past participle of the verb *to be* and the main verb plus *-ing*.

$$\text{Subject} = had + been + [\text{main verb} + \textit{-ing}]$$

Use

The past perfect continuous tense (like the past perfect tense) is used to show an action that continued for a time in the past, but stopped at some point also in the past.

> We had been keeping our old records until we changed apartments.
> The student had been studying all night just before he took the exam.

POTENTIAL PROBLEMS

1. Verbs may be omitted in part.
   Incorrect: The students will completed the essay by the end of the class.
   Correct: The students will have completed the essay by the end of the class.

2. There may be an additional, unnecessary auxiliary (form) with the verb.
   Incorrect: The messenger did delivered the package.
   Correct: The messenger delivered the package.

3. Verbs may be in the wrong tense.
   Incorrect: I'm going to eat as soon as the cafeteria will open.
   Correct: I'm going to eat as soon as the cafeteria opens.

VERB OMITTED

In the sentences below, identify the one underlined phrase that is incorrect.

1. As California's population has increased, <u>concern grown</u> over the <u>possible</u> <u>effects</u> of a
                                                   A   B   C

   large-scale earthquake <u>in the area</u>.
                              D

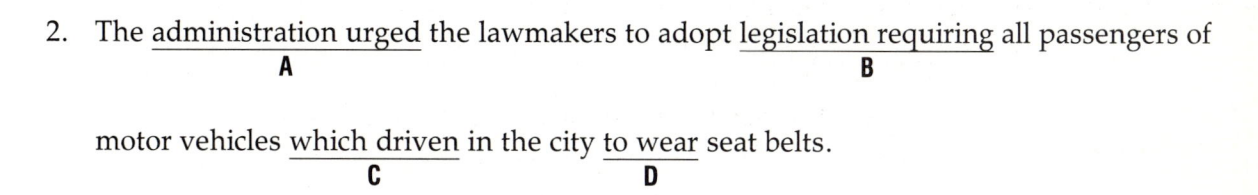

2. The <u>administration urged</u> the lawmakers to adopt <u>legislation requiring</u> all passengers of
               A   B

   motor vehicles <u>which driven</u> in the city <u>to wear</u> seat belts.
                        C   D

3. Whenever John <u>thinks</u> <u>about quitting work</u> and going back to school, he becomes
                        A   B

   <u>worried that</u> he <u>won't able</u> to pay the rent.
        C   D

4. Cairo University, the Arab <u>world's first secular</u> university, <u>founded in 1925</u> <u>with seven main</u>
                                     A   B   C

   faculties <u>and colleges</u>.
                D

5. We <u>should to</u> a routine <u>by establishing</u> patterns <u>useful</u> <u>in meeting</u> deadlines.
          A   B   C   D

6. The assistant manager <u>asked</u> the clerk <u>to help him</u> <u>move the supplies</u>, but the clerk
                            A   B   C

   <u>claimed he too</u> busy.
         D

7. The new head of the <u>Park Service promised</u> <u>to protect and expand</u> the park system even
                                A   B

   <u>if it raising fees</u> and <u>sometimes closing</u> the gates because of overcrowding.
            C   D

Structure and Written Expression Targets

8. To catch our colleague at home, you must early in the morning because he leaves at 7 a.m.
      A   B   C

   to go to work.
   D

9. In spite of fewer hours in class, tenth graders continuing to score
      A   B

   higher than the national average on reading tests.
        C   D

10. Even though the guest did not like sleeping on a hard bed, she managed to fall asleep
                                         A   B   C

    because she so tired.
            D

VERB WITH UNNECESSARY FORM

In the sentences below, identify the one underlined phrase that is incorrect.

1. During the fire, most of the injured were been trampled or crushed when the
                                            A   B

   spectators raced for the exits.
         C   D

2. Thinking through their plan thoroughly did convinced the committee they were wrong to
     A   B   C

   believe that no one else would find fault with their logic.
                              D

3. The journalist, who had not slept for 36 hours, was obliged to must drive through the
                         A   B   C

   fog to interview the union leader.
   D

4. Some mammals that live in the wild have thick skins or hides which are protect them from
         A   B   C   D

   the weather and their enemies.

5. Music is an international language and a way for newly arrived immigrants to be assimilate
   A   B   C

   themselves into the cultural activities of the community.
                       D

6. In spite of recent advances in modern medicine, the long-sought cure for cancer
                      A   B

   has not been found, and the incidence of the disease is being increasing.
   C   D

7. Many service personnel like being plumbers and repairmen charge high prices and do an
                         A   B   C

   inadequate job unworthy of their qualifications.
              D

8. Working hard may have been good for the new recruit, but it tired him out so much that
                 A   B   C

   he was collapsed.
   D

9. Tokyo, founded in the sixteenth century, is older than New York, but because of fires,
   A   B

   earthquakes, and war destruction, much less is remains of old Tokyo than of old New York.
                                                C   D

10. Each of the owners of the building had took a look at the terrain before they agreed
                                        A   B

    to landscape it and put in a road.
    C   D

Structure and Written Expression Targets 185

INAPPROPRIATE VERB TENSE

In the sentences below, identify the one underlined phrase that is incorrect.

1. My book <u>is having</u> three torn pages, which <u>I tried</u> <u>to tape</u> before I <u>left</u> home.
              A   B   C   D

2. This area <u>seldom</u> <u>is experiencing</u> rain in summer, when the <u>heat breaks all</u> <u>maintained</u> records.
               A   B   C   D

3. Insects in the garden can best <u>have been</u> controlled by <u>using</u> nontoxic pesticides and by <u>destroying</u> their <u>breeding</u> grounds.
                                A   B
      C   D

4. The student <u>protests</u> that <u>has erupted</u> first in 1968 <u>continued</u> throughout <u>the decade</u>.
            A   B   C   D

5. A labor <u>survey revealed</u> that <u>less than</u> 4 or 5 percent of the labor force <u>is doing</u> its <u>work at</u> home last year.
              A   B   C   D

6. The voters' <u>attitude</u> <u>toward</u> the political system after the war <u>tended</u> to be less complacent than it <u>has been</u> in the past.
            A   B   C
      D

7. Businesses <u>are looking</u> for software that they <u>can adapt</u> and <u>applied immediately</u> to their own <u>accounting procedures</u>.
              A   B   C
      D

8. <u>Improved</u> health standards and preventive medicine have <u>been forced</u> a <u>decline</u> in the world's <u>death rate</u>.
       A   B   C
      D

186 Structure and Written Expression Targets

9. When the printing press was <u>invented</u>, the price of books decreased and more people
               A

   <u>have access</u> to knowledge once <u>restricted</u> to the <u>learned few</u>.
       B   C   D

10. Workmen <u>clear</u> brush away from the cave entrance <u>when</u> they suddenly saw what turned
            A   B

    out to be the first <u>unspoiled</u> Indian burial chamber <u>to be unearthed</u> in Utah.
                            C   D

EXTRA EXERCISES

Choose the one answer that best completes the sentence.

1. Most universities _____ only people entering the freshman class.
   (A) will be accepted
   (B) accept
   (C) although it accepts
   (D) accepting

2. _____, the examinees knew it was time to stop.
   (A) Hearing the bell
   (B) Heard the bell
   (C) To have been heard the bell
   (D) To hear the bell

3. The debate _____ by the partisan review drew a large crowd.
   (A) sponsored
   (B) was sponsored
   (C) has sponsored
   (D) sponsoring

4. If the superintendent does not _____ his mind, there is nothing more to be done.
   (A) changes
   (B) have changed
   (C) change
   (D) to change

5. The permission that was needed to build the roads _____.
   (A) it will be granted
   (B) was granted
   (C) was being granted
   (D) have been granted

6. The pilots _____ the most direct route to save fuel.
   (A) although choosing
   (B) when they chose
   (C) was to choose
   (D) chose

7. The song had a melody that _____ like this.
   (A) was gone
   (B) went
   (C) is to go
   (D) had went

8. One's success cannot always _____ in terms of money.
   (A) be measured
   (B) being measured
   (C) to measure
   (D) measure

Structure and Written Expression Targets 187

Subject-Verb Agreement

The subject of a sentence and its verb must agree in person and number. Except for the irregular verbs *be* and *have,* the rule is very easy: You add an *s* to the main verb. Only the third-person singular, present tense, is written differently.

You must be careful with *be* and *have* in all tenses, especially when they are used as auxiliary verbs. They will always be irregular in form.

**Irregular verb: *to be*
Present Tense**

Singular			
1st person	I	am	studying for the TOEFL.
2nd person	You	are	studying for the TOEFL.
3rd person	He/She	is	studying for the TOEFL.
	The student	is	studying for the TOEFL.

Plural			
1st person	We	are	studying for the TOEFL.
2nd person	You	are	studying for the TOEFL.
3rd person	They	are	studying for the TOEFL
	The students	are	studying for the TOEFL

**Regular verb: *to study*
Present Tense**

Singular			
1st person	I	study	every evening.
2nd person	You	study	every evening.
3rd person	He/She	studies	every evening.
	The student	studies	every evening.

Plural			
1st person	We	study	every evening.
2nd person	You	study	every evening.
3rd person	They	study	every evening.
	The students	study	every evening.

Structure and Written Expression Targets

POTENTIAL PROBLEMS

1. The subject and verb are separated by one or more prepositional phrases.

> Subject + prepositional phrase(s) + verb

Singular subject
   The series of articles was very interesting.

Plural subject
   The aftershocks of the recent earthquake are frightening.

2. The subject and verb are separated by one or more clauses.

> subject + clause(s) + verb

Singular subject
   The committee, which is composed of four senators, meets every Friday.

Plural subject
   The buildings that were constructed before World War II are no longer standing.

3. If the subject of the sentence is a gerund, the verb is singular.

> gerund as subject + singular verb

Walking six miles a day is good exercise.
Exploring the oceans requires a knowledge of currents.

Structure and Written Expression Targets

4. Certain expressions do not change the number of the subject.

> along with   as well as
> accompanied by   together with

The student, accompanied by his parents, is receiving a prize.

The chair, along with the desk, is being given away.

5. Certain nouns always take a plural verb.

> glasses   pants   scissors
> jeans   pliers   shorts

His glasses are on the desk.

The jeans are on sale.

6. Certain pronouns always take a singular verb.

> any + [singular noun]   every   some + [singular noun]
> anybody   everybody   somebody
> anyone   everyone   someone
> anything   everything   something
>
> nobody   each
> no one
> nothing

Anyone who is late is counted absent.

Everyone who brought his lunch is welcome.
(Note that these pronouns require singular pronouns, too.)

Somebody is missing his umbrella.

Each of the new students is studying for the TOEFL.

7. The articles *a* and *the* in the expression *a(the) number of* can change the "number" of the verb.

> *a number of* + plural noun + plural verb

A number of decisions were made at the meeting.

> *the number of* + plural noun + singular verb

The number of cells is less than the biologist expected to find.

8. The expletives *there* and *here* take either singular or plural verbs. The subject follows the verb.

> *There* + plural verb (*are*) + plural subject
> *Here* + plural verb (*are*) + plural subject

There are opportunities to become successful.

Here are the documents you asked for.

> *There* + singular verb (*is*) + singular subject
> *Here* + singular verb (*is*) + singular subject

There is enough evidence to convict the thief.

Here is the opportunity we have been waiting for.

9. The pronouns *either* and *neither* are singular unless they are followed by *or* or *nor*. The number of the verb depends on the "number" of the closest noun.

> *either* + singular verb
> *either* + singular noun + singular verb
> *either* + noun + *or* + singular noun + singular verb
> *either* + noun + *or* + plural noun + plural verb

<u>Either</u> <u>is</u> acceptable.

<u>Either</u> <u>plan</u> <u>is</u> acceptable.

<u>Either</u> plan A <u>or</u> <u>plan B</u> <u>is</u> acceptable.

<u>Either</u> my plan <u>or</u> their <u>plans</u> <u>are</u> acceptable.

> *neither* + singular verb
> *neither* + singular noun + singular verb
> *neither* + noun + *nor* + singular noun + singular verb
> *neither* + noun + *nor* + plural noun + plural verb

<u>Neither</u> <u>is</u> acceptable.

<u>Neither</u> <u>plan</u> <u>is</u> acceptable.

<u>Neither</u> plan A <u>nor</u> plan B <u>is</u> acceptable.

<u>Neither</u> my plan <u>nor</u> their <u>plans</u> <u>are</u> acceptable.

10. The pronouns *some, none* and *no* are dependent on the "number" of the closest noun.

> *None* + *of the* + noncount noun + singular verb
> *None* + singular verb (when antecedent is a noncount noun)

<u>None</u> of the milk <u>was</u> spilled.

<u>None</u> <u>was</u> spilled. (The antecedent *milk* is understood.)

> *None* + *of the* + plural noun + plural verb
> *None* + plural verb (when antecedent is plural noun)

<u>None</u> of the students <u>were</u> late.

<u>None</u> <u>were</u> late.

> *No* + singular noun + singular verb

No <u>problem</u> <u>was</u> unanticipated.

No <u>solution</u> <u>was</u> found.

> *No* + plural noun + plural verb

No <u>problems</u> <u>were</u> left unsolved.

No <u>solutions</u> <u>were</u> found.

11. Words that represent groups of people, animals, time, money, and measurements are usually singular.

army	crowd	organization
class	family	public
club	government	team
committee	jury	
Congress	minority	

The <u>army</u> <u>is</u> always prepared.

The <u>class</u> <u>is</u> made up of six men and ten women.

Structure and Written Expression Targets 193

> flock of sheep   pack of dogs   school of fish
> herd of cattle   pride of lions

A <u>pack of dogs</u> <u>roams</u> the streets at night.

The <u>school of fish</u> <u>is</u> being studied for behavioral changes.

> cents   seconds   inches
> dollars   minutes   feet
>   hours   miles

<u>Forty cents</u> <u>is</u> too much for a candy bar.

<u>There</u> <u>is</u> <u>45 minutes</u> remaining to finish the test.

<u>Six feet</u> <u>is</u> as long as the sofa can be.

12. The word *majority* will take either a singular or plural verb. If the word is followed by a plural noun, it will take a plural verb.

> *majority* + singular verb
>
> *majority* + plural noun + plural verb

The <u>majority</u> <u>controls</u> the election.

The <u>majority</u> of the voters <u>control</u> the election.

194   Structure and Written Expression Targets

AGREEMENT I

In the sentences below, identify the one underlined phrase that is incorrect.

1. The boys is thought to be one of the most gifted children in the class.
      A   B   C   D

2. The advent of low-cost, high-speed data processing facilities have provided school
                   A   B   C

   administrators with resources not available a few years ago.
                          D

3. Splashing water from waterfalls produce a negative charge in the atmosphere which causes
      A   B   C

   a feeling of well-being.
             D

4. The law, which is in effect in 20 of the 50 states, safeguard against tax abuse by small
          A   B   C   D

   corporations.

5. Professor Janes has told the class repeatedly that we has no business in that room
                          A   B   C

   and should never use it to study.
        D

6. Banks in economically depressed areas has demonstrated their reluctance to
                        A   B

   extend the loans of borrowers who have not met their monthly payments.
       C   D

7. The appearance of fresh molten rock on a volcano's lava dome indicates that eruptions of
         A   B   C

   new lava flow is imminent.
         D

8. Medical researchers <u>have discovered</u> a <u>way</u> in which the nervous systems of
                                       A   B

   <u>primates appears</u> to <u>communicate</u> with their immune systems.
          C   D

9. <u>Arms control</u> is a major <u>issue</u> of this decade since all of mankind <u>live</u> under the shadow of
       A   B   C

   nuclear <u>war</u>.
           D

10. This is <u>an idea</u> <u>researchers</u> hope will <u>bring</u> to them the financial and moral support they
             A   B   C

    <u>deserves</u>.
      D

AGREEMENT II

In the sentences below, identify the one underlined phrase that is incorrect.

1. My English grade, which for many <u>reasons was</u> not deserved, <u>were sent</u> to my
                                             A   B

   <u>parents, who chose</u> not to <u>comment on it</u>.
           C   D

2. The monuments in <u>Washington was built</u> through the years and consequently <u>do not share</u>
                               A   B

   a common theme like those <u>built</u> and <u>designed</u> during one period.
                                 C   D

3. There <u>were</u> no clear-cut sides in the Civil War unless the local <u>stories which tend to</u>
           A   B

   <u>propagate partition</u> <u>is considered</u>.
          C   D

4. The counselors from <u>the college feels</u> it is <u>unwise</u> for students to select a major before
                               A   B

   <u>they have</u> <u>the opportunity to experience</u> different academic subjects.
      C   D

5. Telling ghost stories is one of my grandfather's favorite hobbies, and when he begins to
   A   B   C

   whisper, it send chills up and down my spine.
           D

6. Several authors whose publishers rejected their finished manuscripts and demanded
                    A   B

   they return their advances has prevailed in court in recent years.
      C   D

7. The camel, which shuffles its feet and nod its head, has been, as the desert tribes know, a
               A   B   C   D

   true beast of burden.

8. The pedestrian passing the construction site fell in the hole where the crew has been
        A   B   C

   working to replace the cover that protect the spot.
                                 D

9. Violence at recent soccer matches is causing city officials to reevaluate security
                                 A   B

   measures which has proved ineffectual.
       C   D

10. The political power at stake in the upcoming elections are small, considering that none of
                    A   B   C

    the three opposition parties is supporting a candidate.
                       D

Articles

There are **definite** and **indefinite** articles. The definite article (*the*) can be used before a singular or plural count noun. Sometimes the article is omitted before a plural count noun. The indefinite article (*a* or *an*) is used only before singular count nouns or adjectives. *An* precedes nouns beginning with a vowel sound.

Count Nouns

A count noun is one that can be counted:

> chair: one chair, two chairs, three chairs . . .
> page: one page, two pages, three pages . . .
> question: one question, two questions, three questions . . .

With count nouns, you can use the articles *a*, *an*, and *the*.

Noncount Nouns

A noncount noun is one that cannot be counted:

> News: no plural
> air: no plural
> money: no plural

With noncount nouns, you can use expressions of quantity, such as *some, a lot of, much, a little,* etc.

Some common noncount nouns:

air	dirt	grammar	literature	music	sand
advertising	economics	grass	machinery	news	scenery
advice	equipment	hair	mail	noise	soap
atmosphere	food	history	mathematics	poetry	stuff
cash	fruit	homework	measles	politics	traffic
change	furniture	information	meat	postage	water
clothing	garbage	jewelry	money	physics	work

198 Structure and Written Expression Targets

1. *A* and *an* come only before singular count nouns.

   A building must be made of good material to last.
   An eagle builds its nest high in the mountains.
   A comes before words beginning with a consonant sound:

a ball	a moment
a house	a uniform
a home	a university
a heavy brick	a universal symbol
a half of a grapefruit	a union

   An comes before words beginning with a vowel sound:

an apple	an igloo
an elephant	an opening
an hour	an uncle
an heir	an umbrella

2. *The* comes before nouns with an established reference.

   There is an apple on the desk. (a general apple/a specific desk)
   The apple belongs to me. (a specific apple with a specific reference)

3. If the noun is a noncount noun and the reference is general, do not use *the*.

   Music soothes the savage beast. (general music)
   The music in the elevator drives me crazy. (specific music)

4. *The* normally does not come before plural count nouns when the noun refers to the entire group.

   Stamps and coins are fun to collect. (all stamps and coins)
   Computers are becoming more widespread. (all computers)

Structure and Written Expression Targets 199

5. In American English, *the* does not come before the following words unless the meaning is restricted.

breakfast	church
lunch	home
dinner	hospital
	school

6. Study the following general guidelines for using *the*.

the	oceans, rivers, seas, gulfs, plural lakes	the Atlantic Ocean, the Hudson river, the Gulf of Mexico, the Great Lakes
No *the*	singular lakes	Lake Mead, Lake Tahoe

the	mountains	the Appalachian Mountains
No *the*	mounts	Mount Hood

the	Earth, moon, sun	the Earth, the moon
No *the*	other planets, and constellations	Jupiter, Mercury

the	ordinal numbers before nouns	the Second World War, the second page
No *the*	cardinal numbers after nouns	World War II, page two

the	countries with more than one word (exception: Great Britain)	the United States, the USSR
No *the*	countries of one word	Norway, Thailand
	continents	North America, Asia
	states	Iowa, New York

200 Structure and Written Expression Targets

the	historical documents	the Constitution, the Bill of Rights
	ethnic groups	the Chinese, the Japanese

No *the*	sports	football, tennis
	abstract nouns	liberty, love
	general subject matter	biology, chemistry
	holidays	New Year's Day, Thanksgiving

POTENTIAL PROBLEMS

1. Addition of an article

    Incorrect: <u>The</u> New York City is the largest city in New York.

    Correct: <u>New York City</u> is the largest city in New York.

2. Omission of an article

    Incorrect: The newspaper is <u>on table</u>.

    Correct: The newspaper is on <u>the</u> table.

3. Inappropriate use of an article

    Incorrect: <u>A</u> sugar spilled on the floor.

    Correct: <u>The</u> sugar spilled on the floor.

ARTICLES I

Choose the one answer that best completes the sentence. If no article is appropriate (or required), select (D) 0.

1. _____ eagle is the national bird of the United States.
    - (A) A
    - (B) An
    - (C) The
    - (D) 0

2. _____ Nantucket Island is a superb spot for watching the eclipse.
    - (A) A
    - (B) An
    - (C) The
    - (D) 0

3. The cat is _____ independent animal.
   (A) a
   (B) an
   (C) the
   (D) 0

4. _____ university must be accredited to grant degrees.
   (A) A
   (B) An
   (C) The
   (D) 0

5. Families like _____ Rockefellers have become synonymous with wealth.
   (A) a
   (B) an
   (C) the
   (D) 0

6. Mrs. James wanted to buy _____ umbrella.
   (A) a
   (B) an
   (C) the
   (D) 0

7. _____ University of Chicago has an excellent law school.
   (A) A
   (B) An
   (C) The
   (D) 0

8. Western art of the nineteenth century shows the influence of _____ Far East.
   (A) a
   (B) an
   (C) the
   (D) 0

9. _____ Finland is known for its beautiful forests and seacoasts.
   (A) A
   (B) An
   (C) The
   (D) 0

10. _____ Air and Space Museum has the highest attendance record of all the museums in the world.
    (A) A
    (B) An
    (C) The
    (D) 0

ARTICLES II

In the sentences below, identify the one underlined phrase that is incorrect.

1. The sugar the cook left on shelf was eaten by a mouse as large as a rat.
      A   B   C   D

2. To design a house the architect needs only a ruler, a pencil, piece of paper, and an eraser.
          A   B   C   D

3. Some people prefer <u>hotels</u> to <u>apartment buildings</u>, but most like <u>the houses</u> the best of
                               A   B   C

   <u>the three</u>.
     D

4. There are <u>103 universities</u> in <u>the Tokyo</u> with more than <u>one-half million students</u> from all
                     A   B   C

   parts <u>of Japan</u>.
          D

5. People who dislike concerts prefer listening to <u>records</u>, but musicians insist that
                                                      A

   <u>an orchestra</u> must be heard in person to appreciate <u>the strength</u> and subtleties of <u>a music</u>.
         B   C   D

6. <u>Television</u> replaced radio as <u>the most</u> widely enjoyed <u>form</u> of <u>the broadcasting</u> in the
       A   B   C   D

   United States.

7. <u>The biology teacher</u> suggested <u>class</u> collect <u>sea shells</u>, rocks, wildflowers, or <u>fossils</u>.
             A   B   C   D

8. <u>The new doorman</u> has <u>the problem</u> remembering <u>the names</u> of the people with offices
          A   B   C

   <u>in the building</u>.
       D

9. <u>All travelers</u> should carry <u>change of clothes</u>, extra money, and their passport in
         A   B

   <u>a small bag</u> that can be carried <u>on the plane</u>.
       C   D

10. <u>A computer</u> with <u>a terminal</u>, <u>monitor</u>, and printer is often referred to as <u>work station</u>.
         A   B   C   D

Word Order

There are three forms of word order that are often difficult: **subject-verb**, **adjective-noun**, and **adverb-adjective**. Generally, in affirmative statements the subject precedes the verb, the adjective precedes the noun, and the adverb precedes the adjective it modifies.

Many of the problems associated with word order are discussed in other sections. Because English sentences derive most of their meaning from word order, it is important to have extra practice in this area.

POTENTIAL PROBLEMS

1. The subject precedes the verb when *wh* or *yes/no* questions are added to an independent clause

    Incorrect: They wondered where *was* he.

    Correct: They wondered where *he was*.

2. The verb precedes the subject with expletive *there* or *it*

    Incorrect: There the door is.

    Correct: There is the door.

3. The verb precedes the subject with an initial prepositional phrase of place and an intransitive verb

    Incorrect: Around the table the directors sat.

    Correct: Around the table sat the directors.

4. The Auxiliary precedes the subject with *only* and an adverbial phrase or clause

    Incorrect: Only if he comes, I will come, too.

    Correct: Only if he comes, will I come, too.

5. The auxiliary precedes the subject in certain conditional sentences

    Incorrect: He had come, we would have finished.

    Correct: Had he come, we would have finished.

6. The auxiliary precedes the subject following a negative adverb

    Incorrect: Never he has done that.

    Correct: Never has he done that.

7. Adjectives follow nouns and pronouns when the pronoun ends in *-one, -body, -thing*

    Incorrect: Intelligent anyone could do it.

    Correct: Anyone intelligent could do it.

8. Adjectives follow nouns and pronouns when the modifier is a prepositional phrase

   Incorrect: <u>In the short dress</u>, the boy talked to the girl.

   Correct: The boy talked to the girl <u>in the short dress</u>.

   Note: Sentences can, of course, begin with a prepositional phrase, but the prepositional phrase, usually a reduced adjective clause, must be close to the noun it is modifying.

   Example:

   <u>On time</u>, the students took their place.

   (Being) <u>on time</u>, the students took their place. (reduced adjective clause)

9. Adverbs precede adjectives they modify

   Incorrect: The event was <u>well-planned extremely</u>.

   Correct: The event was <u>extremely well-planned</u>.

   Note: This applies only to adverbs that modify adjectives. Adverbs that modify verbs may, of course, be placed at the beginning or the end of the sentence or by the modified verb.

   Example:

   The student's work has been poor recently.

   Recently the student's work has been poor.

   The student's work recently has been poor.

10. Adjectives may be in the wrong order

    Incorrect: He used a <u>Japanese, new, lightweight, black, compact</u> camera.

    Correct: He used a <u>compact, lightweight, new, black, Japanese</u> camera.

Subject and Verb Placement

Choose the one answer that best completes the sentence.

1. Never _____ such a night.
   - (A) I did see
   - (B) have I seen
   - (C) have seen I
   - (D) I saw

2. There _____ the proofreader overlooked on this page.
   - (A) a mistake is
   - (B) is a mistake
   - (C) a mistake be
   - (D) be mistake

3. _____ that the days seem to be getting shorter.
   - (A) My imagination it is not
   - (B) It is not my imagination
   - (C) Isn't it my imagination
   - (D) My imagination isn't

4. So little _____ that the neighbors could not settle their differences.
   - (A) they agreed
   - (B) agreed did they
   - (C) did they agree
   - (D) they did agree

5. Only once before _____.
   (A) has happened this
   (B) happened this
   (C) this has happened
   (D) has this happened

6. Close by the door _____.
   (A) the spy listen
   (B) listening the spy
   (C) listened the spy
   (D) the listening spy

7. He was told under no circumstances _____ the computer.
   (A) he may use
   (B) he use may
   (C) may he use
   (D) may use

8. Only when it rains _____.
   (A) does the river overflow
   (B) the river does overflow
   (C) overflows does the river
   (D) overflow the river

ADJECTIVE AND ADVERB PLACEMENT I

Choose the one answer that best completes the sentence.

1. _____ are often used for laboratory experiments.
   (A) Gray small mice
   (B) That gray small mice
   (C) They are small gray mice
   (D) Small gray mice

2. The cost of _____ of both scientific and commercial interest can be prohibitive.
   (A) large-scale projects research
   (B) research large-scale projects
   (C) projects research large-scale
   (D) large-scale research projects

3. The young artist creates _____.
   (A) translucent marble sculptures
   (B) marble translucent sculptures
   (C) marble sculptures translucent
   (D) translucent sculptures marble

4. The biological factor in food design requires _____.
   (A) safe food and nutritious
   (B) safe and nutritious food
   (C) food safe and nutritious
   (D) safe and food nutritious

5. My father, the _____ person, managed to fix the toaster.
   (A) world's least mechanical
   (B) least mechanical in the world
   (C) least world's mechanical
   (D) least mechanical world's

6. _____ would have known the answer.
   (A) Anyone is clever
   (B) Clever anyone
   (C) Anyone clever
   (D) Clever is anyone

206 Structure and Written Expression Targets

7. The woman who lost the key hoped the finder would turn it over to _____.
   (A) anyone official
   (B) official anyone
   (C) official
   (D) anyone officially

8. Nuclear power _____ is a risk to civilization.
   (A) as a system total
   (B) as a total system
   (C) total system
   (D) system total

9. The trash can behind the juice stand was full of _____.
   (A) ripe banana skins
   (B) banana ripe skins
   (C) ripe skins banana
   (D) skins banana ripe

10. The shore is the home of the new rich and is dotted with _____.
    (A) big great houses
    (B) great big houses
    (C) houses big great
    (D) houses great big

ADJECTIVE AND ADVERB PLACEMENT II

In the sentences below, identify the one underlined phrase that is incorrect.

1. The <u>new company</u> <u>develops and markets</u> a series of high-quality, inexpensive
         A   B

   <u>products peripheral</u> for both <u>micro- and minicomputers</u>.
           C   D

2. <u>Strong winds</u> <u>flow naturally</u> from areas of <u>greater energy</u> concentration to areas of
        A   B   C

   <u>concentration less</u>.
           D

3. A <u>particular natural event</u> <u>called a phenomenon</u> is used by scientists in
            A   B

   <u>making guesses intelligent</u> <u>called hypotheses</u>.
              C   D

4. <u>Long after sewing machines were ubiquitous</u> <u>in American life</u>, <u>quilts continued</u> to be
                    A   B   C

   <u>by hand made</u>.
         D

5. The <u>brilliant star</u> that shone <u>that first night</u> was <u>barely visible</u> on the <u>clear evening next</u>.
              A   B   C   D

Structure and Written Expression Targets 207

6. Greatly the hotel strike inconvenienced the extremely elderly patrons who
      A   B   C

   unwillingly and ungraciously made their own beds.
                   D

7. Upon further examination it was discovered that your shipment, which late arrived, was
           A   B

   incomplete and incorrectly labeled.
       C   D

8. The simple charity organized by the patron wealthy is now the biggest in the state with
          A   B   C

   hundreds of loyal volunteers.
                   D

9. Illegally cars parked will be towed at the owner's expense and may not be retrieved until
       A   B   C

   the following week.
         D

10. The doctor, unprepared for the difficult operation, brought in two special assistants to help
                    A   B   C

    in areas dangerous where he was not an expert.
        D

▢ Pronouns

There are five types of pronouns: **subject, object, possessive, possessive adjective,** and **reflexive.**

1. Subject pronouns

   Subject pronouns act as subjects of sentences or clauses.
      I will be late if I stay here any longer.
      They have given their report.

Subject Pronouns	
I	we
you	you
he, she, it	they

208 Structure and Written Expression Targets

2. Object pronouns

   Object pronouns are used as direct or indirect objects or as objects of prepositions.
   　The college accepted <u>him</u> without an entrance exam.
   　The newspaper wrote about <u>us</u>.

Object Pronouns	
me	us
you	you
him, her, it	them

3. Possessive pronouns

   Possessive pronouns are used to replace a noun understood from context.
   　You can give your books away, but I will keep <u>mine</u>.
   　Your class always gets out early, but <u>ours</u> always stays late.

Possessive Pronouns	
mine	ours
yours	yours
his, hers, its	theirs

   Note: Possessive adjectives are commonly confused with pronouns.
   　<u>Your</u> speech will never be forgotten.
   The senator hoped <u>her</u> colleagues would agree with her.

Possessive Adjectives	
my	our
your	your
his, hers, its	their

4. Reflexive pronouns
   Reflexive pronouns are used when the subject and object are the same, or are used to show emphasis.
   　They drove <u>themselves</u> home.
   　We had no one to thank but <u>ourselves</u>.

Reflexive Pronouns	
myself	ourselves
yourself	yourselves
himself, herself, itself	themselves

Structure and Written Expression Targets

POTENTIAL PROBLEMS

1. The pronoun may not refer to the appropriate noun.

   Incorrect: Since it was their vacation, it should be their decision how to spend *them*.
   Correct: Since it was their vacation, it should be their decision how to spend *it*.

2. One type of pronoun may be substituted for another.

   Incorrect: Compared to you and *I*, Maureen is extremely studious.
   Correct: Compared to you and *me*, Maureen is extremely studious.

3. The pronoun may be omitted.

   Incorrect: The problem was a complex one, so we needed ample time *to discuss*.
   Correct: The problem was a complex one, so we needed ample time to discuss *it*.

4. The pronoun may be repeated.

   Incorrect: John and his roommate, they have to get up early to get to class on time.
   Correct: John and his roommate have to get up early to get to class on time.

AGREEMENT

Choose the one answer that best completes the sentence.

1. The more students understand the concepts of geometry, the easier it is for _____ to appreciate the scientific achievements built on these formulas.
   (A) one
   (B) them
   (C) him
   (D) her

2. Using computers is the best way to become acquainted with _____ features.
   (A) our
   (B) its
   (C) their
   (D) his

Structure and Written Expression Targets

3. When the contest was over and the results were posted, the team members were so exhausted they couldn't even read _____.
   (A) it
   (B) them
   (C) themselves
   (D) us

4. The way he talked, you would have thought the prize was his, although it was obviously _____, since I won it in front of them.
   (A) yours
   (B) theirs
   (C) ours
   (D) mine

5. The child to _____ she was kind grew up to be one of our most distinguished teachers in this area.
   (A) whom
   (B) which
   (C) us
   (D) them

6. If you ask me for _____ next week, I will have time to find one.
   (A) it
   (B) our
   (C) whom
   (D) you

7. Have you ever caught us giving _____ undeserved praise for doing well on a project?
   (A) yourself
   (B) themselves
   (C) ourselves
   (D) itself

8. The politician's friends did not want him to retire from Congress since _____ feared a replacement would be hard to find.
   (A) they
   (B) it
   (C) we
   (D) you

9. The clients have only _____ to blame if the paper does not include the advertisement, because they submitted it too late for the advertising agency to use.
   (A) themselves
   (B) ourselves
   (C) itself
   (D) yourself

10. The jaws of the shark were so huge that we estimated a small craft could be damaged if _____ had the misfortune to encounter the beast in the ocean.
    (A) he
    (B) it
    (C) you
    (D) they

Structure and Written Expression Targets 211

FORM

Choose the one answer that best completes the sentence.

1. We hoped _____ being there would give our cause credibility.
   (A) he
   (B) his
   (C) him
   (D) himself

2. The senator collects facts for his memoirs by writing notes to _____.
   (A) his own
   (B) his
   (C) himself
   (D) he

3. _____ arrival made it easier for us.
   (A) Him
   (B) He
   (C) Himself
   (D) His

4. One of _____ has to take responsibility for the act.
   (A) our
   (B) us
   (C) we
   (D) ourselves

5. In her notebook, _____ has written herself a short note.
   (A) her
   (B) her one
   (C) hers
   (D) she

6. They taught _____ to read Latin from the old grammar book.
   (A) themselves
   (B) they
   (C) their
   (D) there

7. We don't like to think of _____ in that way.
   (A) us
   (B) we
   (C) ourselves
   (D) our

8. Knowing one's score on the first test, _____ is apt to do better the second time.
   (A) one
   (B) it
   (C) she
   (D) he

9. _____ ears could not believe what I was hearing.
   (A) Mine
   (B) My
   (C) Myself
   (D) Me

10. Giving credit where _____ was deserved, the principal handed over the award.
    (A) it
    (B) itself
    (C) it's
    (D) its

212 Structure and Written Expression Targets

EXTRA EXERCISES

In the sentences below, identify the one underlined phrase that is incorrect.

1. Management and Data Systems, a course for business executives and <u>their</u> employees,
                                                                        A

   offers <u>their</u> own approach to financial planning so that class members can learn what <u>they</u>
          B   **C**

   need to know for <u>their</u> jobs.
                     D

2. The district council and <u>its lawyers</u>, who met with the mayor, <u>they discussed</u> the issue of
                              A   **B**

   pay increases <u>for themselves</u> but did not resolve <u>it</u>.
                  C   **D**

3. Outdoing <u>himself</u> came in first in the marathon, beating the <u>favorite</u> <u>whom</u> we all hoped
             A   **B**   **C**

   <u>would win</u>.
   D

4. The geologists used <u>their new instrument</u> to determine how deep the well was, but
                        A

   <u>its scale</u> proved unreliable <u>and they</u> <u>could</u> not be used to measure.
   B   **C**   **D**

5. Each time <u>I</u> caught <u>sight of he</u> was standing <u>with his back</u> <u>to me</u>.
              A   **B**   **C**   **D**

6. The professor's reputation <u>is</u> based on <u>your</u> ability to meet <u>the</u> expectations of
                               A   **B**   **C**

   <u>his colleagues</u> and his family.
   D

7. He told <u>me</u> that <u>I would</u> have to speak <u>to herself</u>.
   A   **B**   **C**   **D**

8. If <u>you</u> thought about, <u>you would</u> see that <u>I am right</u> and <u>he is wrong</u>.
       A   **B**   **C**   **D**

Prepositions and Two-/Three-Word Verbs

A preposition connects the object of a preposition to other structures in the sentence or clause. There are prepositions of place, time, direction, cause, and location.

Some of these prepositions are listed below.

Place	Time	Direction	Cause	Location
on	on	at	of	next to
in	for	from	in	opposite
among	until	into	to	on
between	during	up	due to	across
on top of	within	down	because of	behind
opposite	since	out (of)	for	near

As prepositions have different meanings in different contexts, it is important to pay attention to how they are used when you see and hear them.

When prepositions are added to certain verbs, they are called two-word or three-word verbs. They can change the meaning of the verb. There are two groups of these verbs: separable and nonseparable.

1. Separable

Separable two-/three-word verbs can be separated by a noun.

Example:
 called off = cancelled
 The administration called off the test.
 The administration called the test off.

If a two-/three-word verb is separable, a pronoun, if used, always comes between the verb and the preposition. It NEVER follows a separable two-/three-word verb.

Example:
The administration called it off.

Look at this partial list of two-/three-word verbs that can be separated. Words with an asterisk (*) change their meaning if they are separated. Some two- or three-word verbs may have other meanings.

214 Structure and Written Expression Targets

ask out	to invite
break off	to terminate
bring up	to initiate a discussion
call back	to return a call; to cause a product to be returned
call off	to cancel
call up	to telephone
care for*	to like
check off	to cross off a list
check out	to examine
cross out	to draw a line across something
do over	to repeat
draw up	to write
figure out	to solve
fill in	to complete
fill out	to complete a form
fill up	to fill completely
find out	to discover
give back	to return something
give up	to resign
hand in	to turn in
hand out	to give out
hang up	to end a telephone call; to put something on a hook
leave out	to omit
look up	to research
make up	to invent
pass out*	to distribute
pay back	to return money or a favor
pick out	to choose
pick up	to lift
point out	to indicate
put away	to return something to its place
put back	to return something to its place
put down	to stop carrying or holding
put off	to postpone
put on	to put clothes on

Structure and Written Expression Targets 215

put out	to place outside
shut off	to turn off a valve
start over	to begin again
take off*	to remove
take over	to take charge
take over for	to substitute
talk over	to discuss
talk over with	to discuss with someone
try out*	to test
tear down	to destroy
tear off	to detach
tear out of	to detach a page from a book
tear up	to tear into pieces
throw away	to discard
throw out	to discard
try on	to test some article of clothing
turn down	to lower or not to accept
turn in*	to submit
turn off	to stop power
turn on	to start power
turn up	to make louder
wake up	to stop sleeping
write down	to write

2. Nonseparable

   Nonseparable two-/three-word verbs cannot be separated by a noun.
   Example:
   get off = disembark
   The passengers *got off* the boat.

Look at this partial list of two-/three-word verbs that cannot be separated. Words with an asterisk (*) change their meaning if separated.

call on	to visit
care for	to look after
check out*	to leave
check out of*	to leave a hotel
check up on	to investigate
close in on	to become nearer
come along with	to accompany
come down with	to become (sick with something)
count on	to depend on
do away with	to discard
drop in	to visit
drop in on	to visit someone
drop out	to stop going (to school)
fool around	to have fun
fool around with	to play with someone
get along with	to be good friends with
get back from	to return from
get by	to manage to survive
get in	to be accepted
get into	to go inside
get off	to disembark
get off of	to disembark from something
get out	to leave
get out of	to leave from somewhere
get over	to recover
get through	to finish
get through with	to finish with something
go along with	to accompany; to agree
hold onto	to grasp
hold up	to cause someone to wait
grow up	to become older
grow up in	to be raised in a place
keep on	to continue
look after	to take care of
look out	to be careful
look out for	to care for
pass out*	to faint

run across	to meet by chance
run into	to meet by chance
run out of	to have no more of something (gas/paper)
see about	to consider
take off*	a plane, to leave the ground
turn in*	to go to bed
watch out	to be cautious
watch out for	to be on the lookout for

POTENTIAL PROBLEMS

1. An inappropriate preposition may be used.

   Incorrect: The books were left <u>in</u> the table.
   Correct: The books were left <u>on</u> the table.

2. They may be omitted wholly or in part.

   Incorrect: I run into him <u>time to time</u>.
   Correct: I run into him <u>from time to time</u>.

3. They may be used unnecessarily.

   Incorrect: The audience <u>came from out</u> of the auditorium.
   Correct: The audience <u>came out of</u> the auditorium.

PREPOSITIONS I

Choose the one answer that best completes the sentence.

1. The chemist placed the bowl _____ the two test tubes.
   (A) among
   (B) between
   (C) in
   (D) through

2. The doctor sat _____ to the exit in case he had to leave early.
   (A) next
   (B) through
   (C) out
   (D) to

218   Structure and Written Expression Targets

3. Each day 500 million tons of garbage is _____.
   (A) put back
   (B) thrown on
   (C) thrown away
   (D) put back

4. The bird flew _____ the treetops.
   (A) opposite
   (B) with
   (C) up
   (D) over

5. The rain fell so heavily that it leaked _____ the ceiling.
   (A) at
   (B) over
   (C) since
   (D) through

6. The moment the curtain fell, the audience rushed _____ the steps.
   (A) on
   (B) through
   (C) up
   (D) out

7. Some of the land originally taken from Native Americans has been _____.
   (A) given to
   (B) given back
   (C) handed out
   (D) handed in

8. The politician's constituency was very upset _____ his announcement.
   (A) out of
   (B) from
   (C) by
   (D) behind

9. The irate citizen kept a record of all the unauthorized buses that came _____ the residential street.
   (A) at
   (B) for
   (C) above
   (D) down

10. The parking lot _____ the restaurant was full.
    (A) across from
    (B) out of
    (C) between
    (D) from

PREPOSITIONS II

In the sentences below, identify the one underlined phrase that is incorrect.

1. The instructions <u>in</u> the manual state that the equipment must be placed <u>in</u> a flat surface
                     A   **B**

   and <u>in</u> a climate-controlled room free <u>of</u> dust.
       C   **D**

Structure and Written Expression Targets   219

2. An important advance <u>in</u> the treatment <u>of</u> arthritis is the disclosure that certain enzymes
                                       A   **B**

   <u>bring with</u> the pain and damage <u>in</u> body joints.
      C   **D**

3. The young politician brings to her work <u>on</u> the city council the expertise that makes her
                                                A

   stand out <u>in</u> a crowd, puts her <u>above</u> the competition, and places her <u>under</u> her rivals.
              B   **C**   **D**

4. My efforts to change the <u>procedures of the council</u> were not <u>met enthusiasm</u> <u>by</u> my
                                    A   **B**   **C**

   colleagues <u>on</u> the board.
            D

5. The students looking <u>through</u> their binoculars <u>saw to</u> the birds sitting <u>on</u> the branch <u>of</u> the
                          A   **B**   **C**   **D**

   cherry tree.

6. <u>Local governments</u> were urged <u>to</u> cut <u>forward</u> on their own construction plans in order <u>to</u>
        A   **B**   **C**   **D**

   reduce high housing costs.

7. All <u>since</u> the night, the bandleader hoped for a clear sky <u>at</u> dawn, as his plans <u>for</u> the
      A   **B**   **C**

   parade depended <u>on</u> it.
                      D

8. My best student <u>of</u> my grammar class speaks <u>with</u> an accent, but she will have no
                   A   **B**

   <u>trouble</u> getting a job <u>with</u> her strong references.
        C   **D**

9. Recent studies show that <u>during</u> a volcanic eruption, ash spreads <u>by</u> the sky, lava flows
                              A   **B**

   <u>down</u>, and hot winds travel <u>for</u> miles, disturbing weather patterns.
    C   **D**

220   Structure and Written Expression Targets

10. The implementation <u>of</u> several treaties <u>for increased</u> trade <u>between</u> the U.S. and the
    　　　　　　　　　　A　　　　　　　　　　　　B　　　　　　　　　　C

　　U.S.S.R. were <u>put over</u> until the leaders could meet face to face.
　　　　　　　　　　D

◻ Subordinate Clauses

Subordinate (or dependent) clauses cannot stand alone. There are **noun, adjective,** and **adverb clauses.** Noun clauses are used as subjects, objects, and objects of prepositions. Adjective clauses modify nouns, and adverb clauses modify verbs.

NOUN CLAUSES

A noun clause is used in the same way as a noun: as a subject, object, or object of preposition. A noun clause is made up of a subject and verb. It must have both.

　　Noun clauses may be introduced by these markers:

that	why	whether	how
who	when	if	
whom	where	that	

Note these examples:

　　Noun clause as subject

$$\underbrace{\text{marker} + \text{subject}_2 + \text{verb}_2}_{\text{subject}_1} + \text{verb}_1 + \text{complement}$$

Note: When used as a subject, the noun clause takes a singular verb.
　<u>Whether the team wins or loses</u> is not important.

　　Noun clause as object

$$\text{subject}_1 + \text{verb}_1 + \underline{\text{marker} + \text{subject}_2 + \text{verb}_2}$$

The story told <u>why the revolution started</u>.

Noun clause as object of preposition

subject₁ + marker + subject₂ + verb₂ + verb₁

The article on how photosynthesis occurs was well written.

POTENTIAL PROBLEMS

1. The verb may come before the subject.

    Incorrect: He asked what time was it.
    Correct: He asked what time it was.

2. A subject noun clause may lack an introductory word.

    Incorrect: The research had been easy astounded him.
    Correct: That the research had been easy astounded him.

3. A plural verb may be used after a single noun clause.

    Incorrect: Whose essays were missing were on everyone's mind.
    Correct: Whose essays were missing was on everyone's mind.

NOUN CLAUSES

Choose the one answer that best completes the sentence.

1. _____ was not the way the event happened.
    (A) What the press reported
    (B) What reported the press
    (C) What reported
    (D) The press reported

2. No announcement has been made concerning _____ on the next shuttle flight.
    (A) who the person is going
    (B) the person is going
    (C) is the person going
    (D) who is going

3. _____ is a fact.
    (A) That we all have to eat
    (B) We all have to eat
    (C) What do we all have to eat
    (D) Whether we all have to eat

4. Regarding our current Director of Finance, _____ is of no consequence to me.
    (A) he goes or stays
    (B) whether he goes or stays
    (C) whether he go or stays
    (D) he goes whether he stays

222   Structure and Written Expression Targets

5. _____ is his own decision.
   (A) When leaving
   (B) When does he leave
   (C) When he leaves
   (D) He leaves

6. The prosecutor questioned the witness about _____.
   (A) what knew he
   (B) what did he know
   (C) he knew
   (D) what he knew

7. The reporter was unable to make an appointment with the celebrity _____.
   (A) she had hoped to interview
   (B) to interview she had hoped
   (C) she to interview had hoped
   (D) had hoped she to interview

8. _____ the election is the question both political parties are asking.
   (A) Who's candidate will win
   (B) Whose candidate will win
   (C) Whose will win the candidate
   (D) Candidate will win

9. How the _____ fascinated the reader of the mystery.
   (A) crime solved the detective
   (B) detective solved the crime
   (C) crime
   (D) crime solved

10. The reasons given for postponing the meeting until next week suggested _____ unprepared.
    (A) the managers
    (B) to the managers
    (C) how the managers were
    (D) that the managers were

Adjective Clauses

An adjective clause is a dependent clause that modifies a noun or noun phrase. It is made up of a subject and a verb. It must have both.

Adjective clauses may be introduced by these markers:

that	who	where	after
which	whome	why	before
	whose		when

These markers substitute for the duplicate noun or noun phrase.

> **Sentence 1:** The bell is over a hundred years old.
> **Sentence 2:** The bell hangs in the library.
>
> The bell, <u>which hangs in the library</u>, is over a hundred years old.
>
> subject₁ + [adjective clause marker + verb₂] + verb₁
>   bell = which

Structure and Written Expression Targets 223

Examples:
  The picnic was cancelled.
  We had planned the picnic for weeks.

  The picnic *that* we had planned for weeks was cancelled.

$$\text{subject}_1 + who + \text{verb}_2 + \text{verb}_1$$

The students will attend college in the fall.
The students did well on the exam.

The students *who* did well on the exam will attend college in the fall.

$$\text{subject}_1 + whom + \text{subject}_2 + \text{verb}_2 + \text{verb}_1$$

I gave the book to Margaret.
Margaret is my best friend.

Margaret, to *whom* I gave the book, is my best friend.

$$\text{subject}_1 + whose + \text{subject}_2 + \text{verb}_2 + \text{verb}_1$$

The Mississippi is a long river.
The mouth of the Mississippi is in Louisiana.

The Mississippi, *whose* mouth is in Louisiana, is a long river.

POTENTIAL PROBLEMS

1. The subject or verb may be omitted.

   Incorrect (subject): His name, which had known before, escaped me.

   Correct: His name, which I had known before, escaped me.

   Incorrect (verb): They took the steps because of the elevator, which broken.

   Correct: They took the steps because of the elevator, which was broken.

2. The subject may be repeated.

   Incorrect: We beckoned to the waitress who she was so busy.

   Correct: We beckoned to the waitress who was so busy.

3. The clause marker may be omitted.

   Incorrect: The book was required reading was being held at the reference desk.

   Correct: The book that was required reading was being held at the reference desk.

4. There may be no independent clause.

   Incorrect: The campus, which had become desolate and deserted during the holidays.

   Correct: The campus, which had become desolate and deserted during the holidays, suddenly came to life again.

5. The marker may be inappropriate.

   Incorrect: The girls which won were honored by their friends.

   Correct: The girls who won were honored by their friends.

ADJECTIVE CLAUSES I

Choose the one answer that best completes the sentence.

1. Buildings _____ of brick last longer than those made of mud.
   - (A) which
   - (B) which they are made
   - (C) which are made
   - (D) are made

2. The team _____ waiting for finally arrived.
   - (A) who been
   - (B) whom we had
   - (C) who we
   - (D) we had been

3. Statistics _____ substantiated by research are considered valid.
   - (A) are
   - (B) which
   - (C) which are
   - (D) that be

4. The corporation whose _____ first will host the delegation for lunch.
   - (A) plant we visit
   - (B) visit plant we
   - (C) visit we plant
   - (D) we plant visit

5. The economic recession was the focus of the debate, _____.
   - (A) surprises to no one
   - (B) no one was surprised
   - (C) which surprised no one
   - (D) to no one was surprised

6. The president refused to accept the decision _____.
   - (A) which the committee proposed
   - (B) proposed the committee
   - (C) which proposed the committee
   - (D) who the committee proposed

Structure and Written Expression Targets 225

7. Trade relations among the states, _____ improving, are currently at an ebb.
   (A) constantly are
   (B) which are constant
   (C) which constantly
   (D) which are constantly

8. The author eagerly anticipates the time _____ finished, and she can start a new one.
   (A) when her book
   (B) when her book is
   (C) her book be
   (D) her will be

ADJECTIVE CLAUSES II

In the sentences below, identify the one underlined phrase that is incorrect.

1. Mr. Jacobs, who immigrated to a country which was known for its business opportunities,
       A   B

   always wanted his partners, of whom my father was one, to continue the firm
                               C

   which started.
       D

2. Miami, which is known for its temperate winters, has become the home of many retired
     A   B

   citizens which left their homes in the North, where winters were too severe.
           C   D

3. The exhibition, toured in major cities, has returned to the Boston Museum, where it
         A   B

   originated and where it will be on view for another month.
                    C   D

4. The metric system, which introduced in England where it met strong resistance, is a
                        A   B

   system of measurement which uses the unit 10 as a standard.
                          C   D

5. A new running shoe monitors the runner's motion and calculates time, average speed,
         A   B

   distance, and caloric expenditures is currently on the market.
            C   D

6. The officers who were from the corporation that it sponsored the golf tournament felt
           A   B

   that announcing the name of a rival as the next sponsor of the tournament was
                 C   D

   inappropriate.

7. Restaurants where people smoke, parks where people play loud radios, pools that are too
              A   B   C

   crowded, and grass isn't mowed annoy many people.
                    D

8. The gardeners who the grounds have maintained which surround the hospital have gone
                   A   B   C

   on a strike that threatens to last through the summer.
         D

9. The accountant is known for his honesty was troubled by the discrepancy which he
        A   B   C

   discovered in the ledgers that he examined.
                   D

10. Rome is a city where the streets are crowded with sights attract tourists, where churches
           A   B   C

    are magnificently decorated, and where the language has its own music.
                                               D

☐ Adverb Clauses

An adverb clause is a dependent clause that modifies a verb. It can express **time, place, cause and effect, opposition,** or **condition**. An adverb clause is made up of a subject and a verb. It must have both. A reduced adverb clause may have neither a subject nor a verb. This is discussed in the next section.

Adverb clauses may be introduced by these markers (subordinating conjunctions):

after	whereas	where	so	ever since	while
before	although	if	as	as if	
because	when	since	whenever	though	

Look at these examples. The adverb clause can come before, inside, or after the main clause.

> marker + subject₂ + verb₂, subject₁ + verb₁
> subject₁ + verb₁ + marker + subject₂ + verb₂

Time

Note: The future tense is not generally used in adverb clauses. The simple present tense is used to refer to future time.

Whenever you are ready, we will go.
The lecture will start when the speaker arrives.

Place

The earthquake occurred where the ground fault was the widest.
Wherever the guide went, the tour group went.

Cause and Effect

Since there was no rain, the crops died.
   Cause   Effect
The students did well on the exam because they studied.
   Effect   Cause

Opposition

Although the movie had started, the audience kept talking.
We ordered more to eat even though we were not hungry.

Condition

As you are the oldest member of the group, you may speak for us all.
We cannot do this experiment since we don't have the right materials.

POTENTIAL PROBLEMS WITH ADVERB CLAUSES

1. The subject or verb may be omitted

   Incorrect (subject): Although witnessed the theft, no one would testify.

   Correct: Although some witnessed the theft, no one would testify.

   Incorrect (verb): They took a small gift in case she depressed.

   Correct: They took a small gift in case she was depressed.

2. The clause marker may be omitted.

   Incorrect: Classes were cancelled there was so much snow.

   Correct: Classes were cancelled because there was so much snow.

3. A wrong verb form may be used.

   Incorrect: Because the community was prepare for potential disaster, the fire caused less destruction than it could have.

   Correct: Because the community was prepared for potential disaster, the fire caused less destruction than it could have.

4. An inappropriate marker may be used.

   Incorrect: We will be ready to start while he comes.

   Correct: We will be ready to start when he comes.

ADVERB CLAUSES I

Choose the one answer that best completes the sentence.

1. While tomatoes are in season, _____.
   - (A) and inexpensive
   - (B) they are inexpensive
   - (C) inexpensive
   - (D) besides inexpensive

2. The applicant was turned down by the college _____ were too low.
   - (A) his test scores
   - (B) because
   - (C) because his test scores
   - (D) if test scores

3. The governess agreed to teach the temperamental child _____ she was given complete authority.
   - (A) whether
   - (B) for
   - (C) that
   - (D) provided

4. _____ the rain has stopped, the field will dry out.
   - (A) Though
   - (B) While
   - (C) Even if
   - (D) Now that

5. _____, the graduate student who was late every day will still take the test.
   - (A) You think it wise
   - (B) You think it wise who
   - (C) Whether or not you think it wise
   - (D) Whether it wise

6. The service attendant filled the tires _____ could ride our bikes.
   - (A) as we
   - (B) so that we
   - (C) even if we
   - (D) so that

7. _____ my brother, I don't have to believe everything he says.
   - (A) Even though he is
   - (B) So he is
   - (C) As
   - (D) Where he is

8. The meeting was postponed _____.
   - (A) although no reason was given
   - (B) no reason given
   - (C) why no reason was given
   - (D) although given no reason

Structure and Written Expression Targets   229

ADVERB CLAUSES II

1. The burning of trash left a residue, there would always be some material that had
   　　　　　　　　　　　A　　　　B　　　　　　　　　　C

   to be buried.
   　　D

2. Before the motion was approved and while it was being debated, the opposition tried to
   　　A　　　　　　　　　　　　　　　　B

   influence the chairman although he had refused to hear arguments the motion was
   　　　　　　　　　　　　　　　C　　　　　　　　　　　　　　　　　D

   made.

3. The first English settlers in the New World quickly established living patterns
   　　　　　　　　　　　　　　　　　　　　　　　　　　A

   based on their various backgrounds, the conditions they had left, and those in which
   　　　B　　　　　　　　　　　　　　　　　　　　　　　C

   they found themselves when arrived.
   　　　　　　　　　　　　D

4. The merchandise arrived before was expected, and since no one was home, the postman
   　　　　　　　　　　　　A　　　　　　　　　　　B　　　　　　　　　　　　C

   left it in front of the door.
   　　　D

5. Even though laws protecting many species of rare animals, common animals, like rats
   　　　A　　　　　B

   and mice, continue to be used for medical experiments.
   　　　　　　　C　　　　　　　　　　　D

6. Even though maintained a united front, the migrant workers quarreled among
   　　　　A　　　　　　　　　　　　　　　　　　　　　　　　　　　B

   themselves until the strike ended and they returned to work.
   　　　　　　C　　　　　　　　　　　D

230　Structure and Written Expression Targets

7. The <u>rain</u> had not stopped, the roads would have been inundated and <u>no</u> travelers,
      A   B

   unless <u>they</u> rode in amphibious vehicles, would have <u>been</u> able to pass.
          C   D

8. After the immigration quotas were <u>being changed</u>, there was <u>increased</u> <u>immigration</u>
                                             A   B   C

   from non-European countries, <u>especially</u> from China.
                                    D

☐ Reduced Adjective Clauses

An adjective clause can be made shorter several ways. Look at the following examples.

1. Subject pronoun + verb *to be* omitted

   Adjective clause
      The man who <u>is walking in the rain</u> will get sick.

   Reduced adjective clause
      The man <u>walking in the rain</u> will get sick.

2. Subject pronoun + verb *to be* omitted

   Adjective clause
      The chair <u>which is next to mine</u> is occupied.

   Reduced adjective clause as prepositional phrase
      The chair <u>next to mine</u> is occupied.

3. Subject pronoun and one or more auxiliaries omitted

   Adjective clause in passive voice
      The law <u>which had been passed by Congress</u> was vetoed by the President.

   Reduced adjective clause
      The law <u>passed by Congress</u> was vetoed by the President.

4. Subject pronoun omitted and progressive passive tense reduced to *being* plus the past participle

   Adjective clause in passive voice
      The building <u>which was being built when the earthquake struck</u> will be finished soon.

   Reduced adjective clause
      The building <u>being built when the earthquake struck</u> will be finished soon.

POTENTIAL PROBLEMS

1. The subject may be added.

   Incorrect: The student he having quit school found a job.
   Correct: The student, having quit school, found a job.

2. A *to be* form may be added.

   Incorrect: The winner was ecstatic about the results, jumped up and down.
   Correct: The winner, ecstatic about the results, jumped up and down.

3. The clause marker may be added.

   Incorrect: He was proud to see his grades which posted on the bulletin board.
   Correct: He was proud to see his grades posted on the bulletin board.

4. The incorrect participle may be used.

   Incorrect: The teacher, reviewed for the test, asked if there were any questions.
   Correct: The teacher, reviewing for the test, asked if there were any questions.

REDUCED ADJECTIVE CLAUSES I

Choose the one answer that best completes the sentence.

1. The phone _____ started ringing.
   - (A) which next door
   - (B) was next door
   - (C) next door
   - (D) it was next door

2. The chessmen, _____, are displayed in a glass case.
   - (A) which from ivory
   - (B) which carved from ivory
   - (C) carved from ivory
   - (D) carving from ivory

3. The man _____ the wheelbarrow ignored our calls.
   - (A) who pushing
   - (B) pushing
   - (C) was pushing
   - (D) pushed

4. The noise of the trains _____ into the station was deafening.
   - (A) that come
   - (B) which was coming
   - (C) coming
   - (D) that coming

5. The letter _____ our guests' intention to visit came after their arrival.
   - (A) it announcing
   - (B) announcing
   - (C) had announced
   - (D) that announcing

6. A political campaign _____ will be costly.
   - (A) which for months last
   - (B) lasts for months
   - (C) lasting for months
   - (D) will last for months

7. My best friend, _____ quickly, told the teacher I was home sick.
   (A) who thinking
   (B) be thinking
   (C) think
   (D) thinking

8. The barn, _____ with hay, went up in flames.
   (A) loaded
   (B) loading
   (C) it was loaded
   (D) which loaded

REDUCED ADJECTIVE CLAUSES II

In the sentences below, identify the one underlined phrase that is incorrect.

1. Cape Cod <u>Canal, is said</u> <u>to be</u> the widest sea-level <u>canal anywhere</u>, is cluttered during the
                 A   B   C

   summer season with as many as 300 or more pleasure craft's a day, <u>most coming</u> from
                                                                                  D

   Boston.

2. The boys <u>who were</u> first in line <u>were given</u> the T-shirts <u>donating</u> by the philanthropist
                  A   B   C

   <u>who has</u> always supported our charity.
      D

3. The physical matter in a "black hole" in the galaxy is so <u>dense that it creates</u> a gravitational
                                                                      A

   <u>pull which strong</u> enough <u>to prevent anything</u>, even <u>light, from escaping</u>.
         B   C   D

4. The <u>crowd, anxiously await</u> the arrival of the soccer <u>team, pressed</u> against the fence
                  A   B

   <u>separating them</u> from the <u>playing field</u>.
         C   D

5. The <u>flights were not being</u> allowed to take off until the control tower <u>which monitoring</u>
                  A   B

   <u>the changing weather</u> felt <u>it was safe</u>.
         C   D

Structure and Written Expression Targets

6. The talks promote the expansion of trade between the two neighboring countries were
          A   B

   discontinued after certain protocol agreements were violated.
        C   D

7. The delays are caused by the striking longshoremen cost the steamship companies millions
        A   B   C

   every day their ships were not allowed to dock.
                         D

8. Muttering to herself, the woman, being hot and was weary, sat down on a stump
       A   B   C

   next to the road.
     D

9. The freezing rain made driving dangerous was obliging many motorists to use public
         A   B   C   D

   transportation.

10. The statement made by the press was implying that the senator was a fool was
                                        A   B

    retracted the following morning with an apology.
         C   D

▢ Reduced Adverb Clauses

An adverb clause can be reduced if the subject of the adverb clause and the subject of the independent clause are the same. These reduced adverb clauses are also called participial phrases.

Adverb Clause

   While I was visiting New York, I met many people.

Reduced Adverb Clause

   While visiting New York, I met many people.

234 Structure and Written Expression Targets

POTENTIAL PROBLEMS

1. The subject may be added.

   Incorrect: While <u>she</u> singing the anthem, she had tears in her eyes.
   Correct: <u>While singing</u> the anthem, she had tears in her eyes.

2. A *to be* form may be added.

   Incorrect: Daniel waited, <u>was</u> getting more and more nervous until the moment arrived.
   Correct: Daniel <u>waited, getting</u> more and more nervous until the moment arrived.

3. The subjects may not be the same.

   Incorrect: <u>The alarm</u> going off, <u>Victor</u> got out of bed.
   Correct: <u>Hearing</u> the alarm go off, <u>Victor</u> got out of bed.

4. An incorrect participle may be used.

   Incorrect: <u>Listened</u> to the speech, the audience was restless.
   Correct: <u>Listening</u> to the speech, the audience was restless.

REDUCED ADVERB CLAUSES I

Choose the one answer that best completes the sentence.

1. _____, flowers need a lot of sun and water.
   (A) When growth
   (B) When they growing
   (C) They are growing
   (D) When growing

2. Pedestrians should look to the left and right _____ the street.
   (A) when crossing
   (B) when they be crossing
   (C) they cross
   (D) when to cross

3. The sailor, home at last, is happy _____.
   (A) he be sitting in the garden
   (B) sitting in the garden
   (C) in the garden sitting
   (D) sit in the garden

4. _____, the nurse checked the patient's temperature.
   (A) Called the doctor
   (B) Before calling the doctor
   (C) The doctor calling
   (D) Before the doctor calling

5. _____, the commissioners like to take a walk.
   (A) After they eating
   (B) They after eating
   (C) After eating
   (D) After to be eaten

6. _____ asleep, the young child was really awake and listening.
   (A) Although pretending to be
   (B) Being
   (C) To be
   (D) Although pretended to be

7. _____, the mind lets suppressed thoughts surface.
   (A) While dream
   (B) While dreaming
   (C) While our dream
   (D) While the mind it dreams

8. The deadline, _____, had been extended to accommodate our schedule.
   (A) passing
   (B) although past
   (C) while being past
   (D) past

REDUCED ADVERB CLAUSES II

In the sentences below, identify the one underlined phrase that is incorrect.

1. Although <u>they frequently misinterpreted</u>, <u>these laws</u> apply in part to groups <u>seeking</u>
              A   B   C
   redress for wrongs <u>without their having</u> to hire a lawyer.
                              D

2. The extension services of the university, while <u>it is</u> providing an opportunity for the
                                                    A
   community <u>to take</u> courses, <u>offer</u> full-time students greater flexibility <u>in arranging</u> their
                  B   C   D
   schedules.

3. <u>After signing it</u>, the insurance policy covers illness <u>on or off</u> the company grounds,
        A   B
   <u>where</u> most accidents are likely <u>to occur</u>.
      C   D

4. Although <u>is nutlike</u> in shape, the cashew, <u>grown</u> in many tropical <u>regions</u>, <u>is</u> actually a
                A   B   C   D
   legume.

5. Athletes, when <u>they competing</u> in international events, <u>are</u> challenged <u>to do</u> their best if
                        A   B   C
   they <u>want</u> to bring honor to their country.
           D

236 Structure and Written Expression Targets

6. When <u>coming</u> to school, the children need <u>to think</u> before <u>they crossing</u> the streets
      A   B   C

   <u>where</u> there is no crossing guard.
     D

7. <u>Before design</u> the building, the architect <u>studied</u> the <u>plans of</u> other buildings <u>built near</u>
      A   B   C   D

   the site.

8. <u>Conserving</u> heat in the winter and <u>reduce heat</u> in the summer, deciduous trees
      A   B

   <u>planted at the west</u> and south parts of a house <u>are natural</u> energy savers.
          C   D

9. When <u>they traveling</u> long distances, <u>tourists should</u> <u>reduce</u> caloric intake and
            A   B   C

   <u>limit consumption</u> of alcohol.
          D

10. Since <u>they moving</u> to the East Coast, the Parsons have not <u>been able</u> <u>to find</u> a home
              A   B   C

    <u>large enough</u> for their family.
         D

☐ Parallel Structures and Conjunctions

Although the TOEFL does not have many parallel structure questions on the exam, it is good to study this section because it provides a review of other grammatical targets.

In a parallel sentence, all items in a series are equal. They are either all adjectives, all adverbs, all nouns, etc. You should not mix grammatical structures in a series.

A conjunction connects identical grammatical structures in a series. There are **coordinating conjunctions** (*and, but, or, nor*), **paired conjunctions** (*both . . . and; not only . . . but also; either . . . or; neither . . . nor*), and **comparative conjunctions** (*than; and so; and . . . too; and . . . either; and . . . neither*).

Look at these charts. These are examples of a series.

> **Adjectives**
> subject + verb + adjective, adjective, and adjective.

Not parallel

The book was long, boring, and <u>without a plot</u>.

Parallel

The book was long, boring, and <u>plotless</u>.

> **Adverbs**
> subject + verb + adverb, adverb, + adverb.

Not parallel

The dancer moved with <u>grace</u>, rhythmically, and beautifully.

Parallel

The dancer moved <u>gracefully</u>, rhythmically, and beautifully.

> **Nouns**
> subject + verb + noun, noun, and noun.

Not parallel

My father was an officer, a gentleman, and <u>he did magic tricks</u>.

Parallel

My father was an officer, a gentleman, and <u>a magician</u>.

> **Gerunds**
> subject + verb + gerund, and gerund.

Not parallel

Most children enjoy swimming, boating, and to eat.

238 Structure and Written Expression Targets

Parallel

Most children enjoy swimming, boating, and eating.

> **Verbs**
> subject + verb, verb, and verb.

Not parallel

We watched TV, ate dinner, and <u>are going to bed</u>.

Parallel

We watched TV, ate dinner, and <u>went to bed</u>.

POTENTIAL PROBLEMS

1. The forms may connect nonparallel structures.

   Incorrect: The suggestion was <u>to skim</u> and then <u>scanning</u> for information.
   Correct: The suggestion was <u>to skim</u> and then <u>to scan</u> for information.

2. The meaning of the forms may be confused.

   Incorrect: It didn't matter <u>whether</u> the report was typed <u>and</u> handwritten.
   Correct: It didn't matter <u>whether</u> the report was typed <u>or</u> handwritten.

PARALLEL STRUCTURES

In the sentences below, identify the one underlined phrase that is incorrect.

1. An <u>element</u> cannot be formed from simpler <u>substances</u>, nor can it be <u>decomposed</u> with
      A   B   C

   <u>more simple</u> varieties of matter.
      D

2. Electric eels <u>use</u> charges to detect prey and also <u>stunning</u> it <u>before</u> <u>they</u> eat it.
                    A   B   C   D

3. <u>Without</u> entering the body and <u>cause</u> damage, the CT is <u>far</u> superior to the X-ray or
      A   B   C

   <u>exploratory</u> surgery.
      D

Structure and Written Expression Targets 239

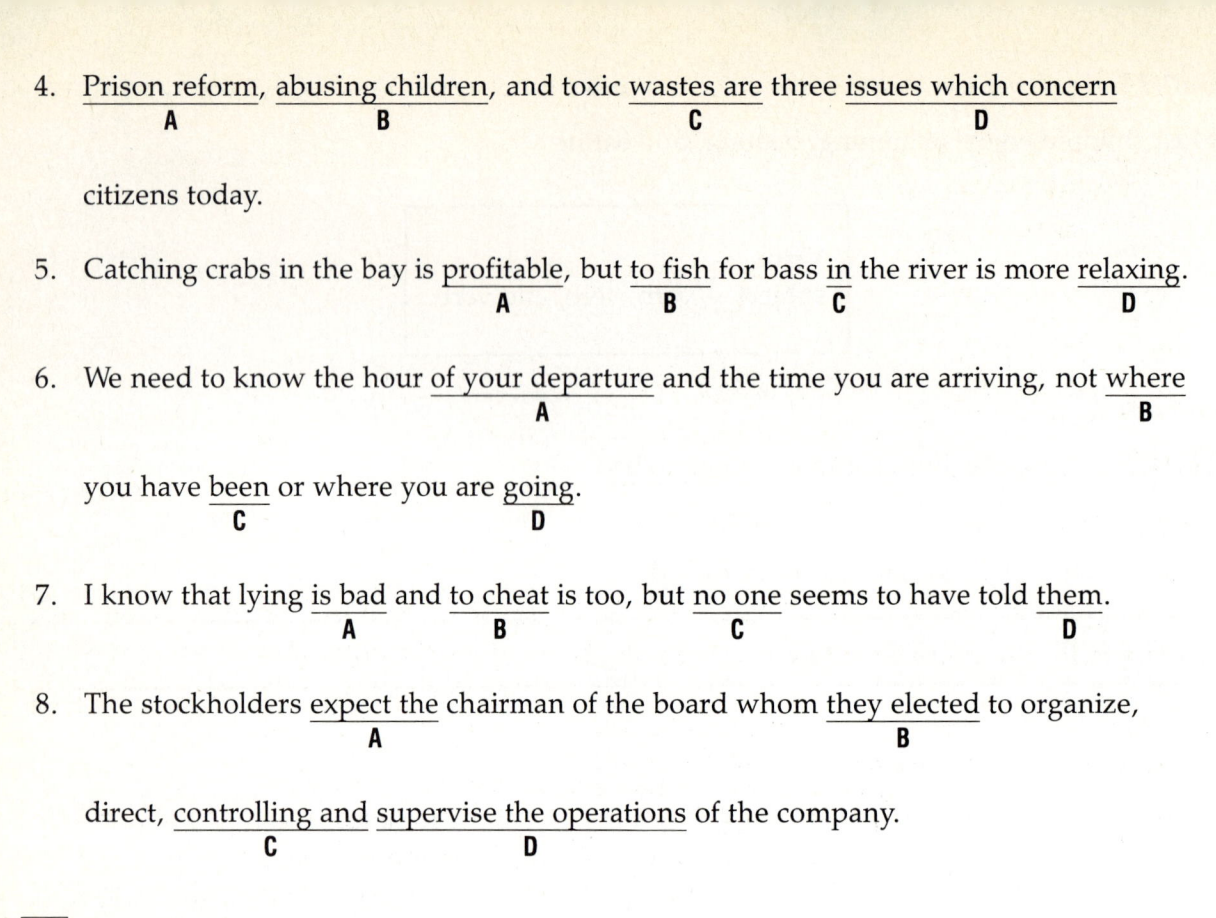

4. Prison reform, abusing children, and toxic wastes are three issues which concern
   　　　A　　　　　　　　　B　　　　　　　　　　　C　　　　　　　　　　　D

   citizens today.

5. Catching crabs in the bay is profitable, but to fish for bass in the river is more relaxing.
   　　　　　　　　　　　　　　A　　　　　　　　B　　　　　　　C　　　　　　　　D

6. We need to know the hour of your departure and the time you are arriving, not where
   　　　　　　　　　　　　　A　　　　　　　　　　　　　　　　　　　　　　　　　　B

   you have been or where you are going.
   　　　　C　　　　　　　　　　D

7. I know that lying is bad and to cheat is too, but no one seems to have told them.
   　　　　　　　　A　　　　　B　　　　　　　　C　　　　　　　　　　　　　D

8. The stockholders expect the chairman of the board whom they elected to organize,
   　　　　　　　　　A　　　　　　　　　　　　　　　　　　　B

   direct, controlling and supervise the operations of the company.
   　　　　　　C　　　　　　　D

▢ Gerunds and Infinitives

Gerunds are *-ing* words used as nouns. Consequently, the gerund can act as a subject, object, or object of preposition.

The base form of a verb is called an infinitive. An infinitive is introduced by *to*. Used as a noun, the infinitive can also act as a subject or object.

Study the following charts to learn more about gerunds and infinitives.

1. Some verbs can be followed by either a gerund or an infinitive in place of a noun.

> subject + verb + object (noun)
> He likes the swimming pool.
>
> subject + verb + object (infinitive)
> He likes to swim.
>
> subject + verb + object (gerund)
> He likes swimming.

240　Structure and Written Expression Targets

These verbs can be followed by either a gerund or an infinitive.

begin	like
continue	love
dread	prefer
hate	start

The newscaster continued <u>to read</u> the news after the break.
The newscaster continued <u>reading</u> the news after the break.

It started <u>to rain</u> just before we left.
It started <u>raining</u> just before we left.

2. Some verbs can only be followed by a gerund.

admit	finish	regret
appreciate	mind	report
avoid	miss	resent
consider	postpone	resist
delay	practice	resume
deny	quit	risk
enjoy	recall	suggest

The team <u>practiced kicking</u> the ball.
The villagers <u>reported seeing</u> an unidentified flying object.

3. Some verbs can only be followed by an infinitive.

agree	intend	tend
attempt	learn	try
claim	need	want
decide	offer	wish
demand	plan	
desire	prepare	
fail	pretend	
forget	refuse	
hesitate	seem	
hope	strive	

The government <u>planned to raise</u> taxes.
The teacher <u>forgot to mention</u> there would be an exam tomorrow.

4. A verb plus a preposition is always followed by a gerund.

> verb + preposition + gerund

Here are some examples of verbs plus prepositions.

approve of	keep on	think of
confess to	look forward to	worry about
count on	object to	
depend on	put off	
give up	rely on	
insist on	succeed in	
	think about	

We <u>thought about not studying</u> for the exam.
We <u>worried about passing</u> the exam.

5. A noun plus a preposition is followed by a gerund.

> noun + preposition + gerund

Here are some examples of nouns plus prepositions.

choice of	possibility of
excuse for	reason for
intention of	
method for	

There was no <u>excuse for losing</u> the race.
The <u>possibility of not doing</u> well did not even occur to us.

6. An adjective plus a preposition is followed by a gerund.

> adjective + preposition + gerund

Here are some examples of adjectives plus prepositions.

accustomed to	intent on
afraid of	interested in
capable of	successful at
fond of	tired of

242 Structure and Written Expression Targets

The singer was capable of singing high notes.
The teacher was tired of hearing excuses.

7. Some adjectives are followed by the infinitive. Do not confuse the *to* of the infinitive with the preposition *to*.

> adjective + infinitive

Study the following list.

able	good
anxious	pleased
boring	prepared
common	ready
dangerous	strange
difficult	usual
hard	
eager	
easy	

It was too dangerous to proceed on the ice.
They were prepared to leave at dawn.

8. The pronoun before an infinitive will be an object pronoun.

> subject + verb + object pronoun + infinitive

The following verbs plus infinitives usually require an object pronoun.

allow	invite	remind
ask	order	urge
beg	permit	want
convince	persuade	
expect	prepare	
instruct	promise	

The teacher advised the students to study before the exam.
The college permitted them to take extra classes.

Structure and Written Expression Targets   243

9. The pronoun before a gerund will be a possessive pronoun.

> subject + verb + possessive pronoun + gerund

We <u>counted on their being</u> on time.
She <u>recalled his saying</u> he would be late.

POTENTIAL PROBLEMS WITH GERUNDS

1. An inconsistent form may be used.

   Incorrect: Michelangelo is known for his painting, sculpting, and <u>for his ability to write</u>.
   Correct: Michelangelo is known for his <u>painting</u>, <u>sculpting</u>, and <u>writing</u>.

2. An incorrect form may follow one of the verbs listed above.

   Incorrect: Most physicians <u>suggest to take</u> vitamins on a full stomach.
   Correct: Most physicians <u>suggest taking</u> vitamins on a full stomach.

3. In negative sentences with infinitives, the *not* may be misplaced.

   Incorrect: Consumer groups advise holiday shoppers <u>to not overcharge</u> on their credit cards.
   Correct: Consumer groups advise holiday shoppers <u>not to overcharge</u> on their credit cards.

GERUNDS AND INFINITIVES 1

1. Mother Teresa's followers intend _____ care of "the poorest of the poor."
   (A) taking
   (B) to take
   (C) have taken
   (D) to have taken

2. Renaissance masters were able to complete commissions by _____ assistants.
   (A) employment of
   (B) having employed
   (C) employing
   (D) to employ

3. _____ and revising are critical steps in creative writing.
   (A) To edit
   (B) Having edited
   (C) Editing
   (D) To have edited

4. Jane Goodall prefers _____ alone among the chimpanzees of Gombe National Park.
   (A) living
   (B) to have lived
   (C) to have been living
   (D) lived

244 Structure and Written Expression Targets

5. Amnesty International wants us _____ the victims of international terrorism.
   (A) to not forget
   (B) not to forget
   (C) not forgetting
   (D) forget not

6. _____ the consequences of the final decision, the committee approved the proposal.
   (A) To not realize
   (B) Realizing not
   (C) Not to realize
   (D) Not realizing

7. _____ to be alone, Monet married his sister-in-law after the death of his wife.
   (A) Not to want
   (B) Not wanting
   (C) To not want
   (D) To want not

8. Language students need practice in speaking, listening, and _____.
   (A) written
   (B) to write
   (C) writing
   (D) write

GERUNDS AND INFINITIVES II

1. Organizations are being established nationwide to help people quit to smoke.
                                   A   B   C   D

2. To commute to the city and fighting rush-hour traffic is a boring but necessary routine for
         A   B   C

   many working suburbanites.
         D

3. Most teachers attempt to motivate students by using materials that are interesting to them
                               A   B   C

   and will inspire them succeeding.
                            D

4. The hostess appreciated to your contributing your time and effort into making the party a
                                        A   B   C

   smashing success.
   D

5. Educators indicate that preschoolers are able to practice social skills by taking turns,
                                                          A   B

   solving conflicts, and to verbalize their problems.
    C   D

Structure and Written Expression Targets

6. The Budget Committee regretted not to put enough energy into reducing the costs for the
       A   B   C

   upcoming year.
     D

7. The secretary hesitated asking the invited guests if they would mind to smoke in the
           A   B   C

   designated areas of the building.
     D

8. Engaged couples in prematrimony classes are encouraged to look ahead and anticipating
    A   B   C

   handling common marital problems before they occur.
     D

☐ Participles

The present or past participle of a verb can serve as an adjective.

> verb + *-ing* = present participle
> verb + *-ed/-en* = past participle

1. The present participle is used when the noun it modifies is the "doer" of the action.
   The singing waiter dropped the tray.
   (The waiter is the man who sings.)

   The barking dog scared the robber.
   (The dog is the animal that barks.)

2. The past participle is used when the noun it modifies received the action.
   We couldn't go through the locked door.
   (Someone else locked the door. The door did not lock itself.)

   The wounded man called for help.
   (Someone else wounded the man.)

A participial phrase acts as an adjective. It contains either a present participle (*-ing*) or a past participle (*-ed/-en*).

POTENTIAL PROBLEMS

A present participle may be used instead of a past participle, and vice versa.

Incorrect: <u>Given</u> out all his presents, Santa Claus made sure every child had something to open.

Correct: <u>Giving</u> out all his presents, Santa Claus made sure every child had something to open.

PARTICIPLE FORM

1. Because of the drama at the finish line, it was _____ race we'd ever seen.
   (A) a very interested
   (B) the most interesting
   (C) a most interested
   (D) an interestingly

2. It was Halloween, so there were many _____ noises in the neighborhood.
   (A) fright
   (B) having fright
   (C) frightened
   (D) frightening

3. As a child, Albert Einstein was not considered a particularly _____ student.
   (A) advanced
   (B) advancing
   (C) advancement
   (D) advancer

4. _____ by her tutor, Helen Keller went on to graduate from Radcliffe College.
   (A) Encourage
   (B) Encouraging
   (C) Encourages
   (D) Encouraged

5. The _____ spectators watched the space shuttle take off and disappear into space.
   (A) amaze
   (B) amazing
   (C) amazingly
   (D) amazed

6. _____ his promise, the dictator stopped the ceasefire.
   (A) Breaking
   (B) Broke
   (C) Broken
   (D) Breaks

7. _____ around the actress, the fans were hardly able to let her pass.
   (A) Crowds
   (B) Crowding
   (C) To crowd
   (D) Crowd

8. The storyteller was surrounded by _____ children who listened to every word he said.
   (A) fascinated
   (B) fascinatingly
   (C) fascinating
   (D) fascinate

Structure and Written Expression Targets

Conditionals

Conditional sentences are put into two categories: **the real** and **the unreal.**

1. The **real conditional** expresses an idea that could happen.

   If Mary loans Bob $5.00, he can take a taxi home.
   (It is possible that Mary will loan Bob $5.00. That is something that is real. He can then take a taxi home.)

2. The **unreal conditional** expresses an idea that did not, is not, or will not happen.

   If Mary had $5.00 to loan to Bob, he could have taken a taxi home.
   (This is difficult because the unreal conditional seems to contradict itself. *If Mary had $5.00* uses the positive verb form, yet its meaning is negative: Mary does not have $5.00 to loan Bob.)

   If the war had ended sooner, there would have been fewer casualties.
   (The war did not end sooner. There were many casualties.)

   If I were rich, I would buy a house.
   (I am not rich. I can't buy a house now.)

Conditional Tense Forms: Real Conditions

1. Future

   > *if* + subject + simple present . . . + *will* + [simple verb form]
   >   can
   >   may
   >   must

   If you are going to the grocery store, will you buy some milk?
   If the singer wins this contest, he will get a scholarship.
   We might finish on time if the computers cooperate.

2. Habitual

   > *if* + subject + simple present . . . + simple present tense

We always <u>watch</u> the news if we are home by six.
<u>If you see the bus pass the window</u>, it means I am late again.

3. Command

> *if* + subject + simple present . . . + command

Please <u>ask if you need more money</u>.
<u>If you want something special for dinner, say</u> so now.

Conditional Tense Forms: Unreal Conditions

1. Present or future

> *if* + subject + simple past . . . + *would* + [simple verb form]
> *could*
> *might*

<u>If they studied more</u>, they <u>would do</u> better in school.
(They don't study enough.) (They don't do well in school.)

<u>If the copier wasn't broken, I could leave</u> early.
(The copier is broken.) (I can't leave early.)

<u>If the days were longer</u>, we <u>might finish</u> this project.
(The days aren't longer.) (We won't finish this project.)

2. Past

> *if* + subject + past perfect . . . + *would* + *have* + [past participle]
> *could*
> *might*

<u>If they had anticipated the reaction</u>, they <u>would have made</u> the announcement sooner.
(They didn't anticipate the reaction.) (They made the announcement later.)

Structure and Written Expression Targets 249

If the teacher hadn't asked such hard questions, we could have passed the test.
(The teacher asked hard questions.) (We didn't pass the test.)

We would have been on time if we hadn't missed the bus.
(We were late.) (We missed the bus.)

POTENTIAL PROBLEMS

1. Inappropriate sequence of tenses.

   Incorrect: If I know his number, I'd call him now.
   Correct: If I knew his number, I'd call him now.

   Incorrect: If she helped, we would have finished.
   Correct: If she had helped, we would have finished.

2. Inappropriate introductory marker.

   Incorrect: We had known, we would have brought a gift.
   Correct: Had we known, we would have brought a gift.
                 (and) If we had known, we would have brought a gift.

3. The incorrect form of *to be* in the first and third person singular may be used.

   Incorrect: I would answer truthfully if I was you.
   Correct: I would answer truthfully if I were you.

   Incorrect: If he was younger, he would join.
   Correct: If he were younger, he would join.

CONDITIONALS I

Choose the one answer that best completes the sentence.

1. If they _____ overworked in the beginning, the volunteers would have helped finish the project.
   (A) were not
   (B) was not
   (C) had not been
   (D) have not been

2. If Marie _____, tell her I will call her back as soon as I return.
   (A) calls
   (B) called
   (C) will call
   (D) is going to call

250 Structure and Written Expression Targets

3. The supervisors could have prevented this problem _____ it beforehand.
   (A) if they knew
   (B) had they known
   (C) if had they known
   (D) whether

4. The boy's parents knew he _____ if he had passed the final exam.
   (A) graduated
   (B) would graduate
   (C) could have graduated
   (D) will graduate

5. Because Mr. Gleason worked only a month, the personnel director would not write a recommendation for him even if he _____.
   (A) could ask
   (B) ask
   (C) asked
   (D) will ask

6. If _____ enough interest, the proposed flexible work schedule will be implemented.
   (A) there be
   (B) there will be
   (C) there are
   (D) there is

7. The teaching assistant's explanations to the class will be more understandable if he _____ more clearly next time.
   (A) speaks
   (B) spoke
   (C) will speak
   (D) has spoken

8. If it _____ to rain, the band members will have to cover their instruments.
   (A) will start
   (B) starts
   (C) started
   (D) had started

9. Had the damage been worse, the insurance company _____.
   (A) would pay
   (B) paid
   (C) would have paid
   (D) had paid

10. If the art dealer _____ the money, he would have bought the painting.
    (A) had had
    (B) has
    (C) had
    (D) would have

CONDITIONALS II

In the sentences below, identify the one underlined phrase that is incorrect.

1. If the terms <u>had been</u> better, the borrower <u>would accept</u> the bank's proposal, <u>even though</u>
                  A   B   C

   he <u>disagreed</u> with some of the conditions.
         D

2. It <u>is</u> not impossible to overcome the difficulties <u>of learning</u> a new language <u>if</u> one <u>will have</u>
      A   B   C   D

   the right attitude.

3. <u>Had they known</u> the snowstorm <u>would</u> be so treacherous, the hikers <u>did not venture</u> into
          A   B   C

   <u>it</u> without proper equipment.
    D

4. If more low-cost housing <u>is available</u>, the poor would <u>have</u> shelter and <u>would not</u> have
                                 A   B   C

   <u>to live</u> on the street.
      D

5. If <u>going</u> to that restaurant is Jeff's choice, <u>then</u> we automatically <u>vetoed</u> it because
       A   B   C

   <u>he is consistently</u> too extravagant for our tastes.
        D

6. If the <u>resources</u> of forest and water power were more <u>fully developed</u>, the economy would
           A   B

   <u>not have been</u> so <u>dependent on</u> imports.
        C   D

7. If the new student <u>followed</u> the rules as they <u>were explained</u> <u>to</u> him, he <u>would not</u> have
                    A   B   C   D

   been in such a predicament.

8. I think I would enjoy the movie we went to last night even more if I had read the book
   — A —— — B ——   — C ——
   before seeing it.
          — D —

9. If the library is closed over the holidays, it would be very difficult to finish the research
   A   — B —   — C —   — D —
   project.

10. If all the members of the committee who are present would agree, the proposal will go into
    A   — B —   — C —
    effect immediately.
           — D —

☐ Comparisons

A comparison shows how different two nouns or two verbs are from one another. The comparison could be equal or unequal.

Comparing Adjectives and Adverbs

1. An equal comparison shows how two nouns or two verbs are the same. Equal comparisons can be either positive or negative.

   Positive

   subject + verb + *as* + adjective + *as* + noun
                                       adverb   pronoun
                                                                   clause

   Negative

   subject + verb + not + *as* + adjective + *as* + noun
                                             adverb   pronoun
                                                                    clause

The boys are as old as the girls.
Our new ballet teacher teaches as well as the previous one.
We did as well as we had expected.

Dinner was not as good as lunch.
These shoes are not as comfortable as my old ones.
The river did not flood as much as we had feared.

2. A comparison can also be made using the expressions *the same as* and *different from*.

>   subject + verb + *the same* + (noun) + *as* + noun
>   pronoun
>   clause

This river is as long as the Nile.
   This river is the same length as the Nile.
This new blanket is as light as my old one.
   This new blanket is the same weight as my old one.

>   subject + verb + *different from* + noun
>   pronoun
>   clause

The tests are different from each other.
Their voices sound different from one another.

3. A comparison can also show how two nouns or two verbs are similar or dissimilar.

>   subject + verb + adjective + -er + *than* + noun
>   adverb + -er   pronoun
>   *more* + adjective/adverb   clause
>   *less* + adjective/adverb

Florida is hotter than Minnesota.
She arrived later than I.
The food is more expensive than I am used to.
There is less time to finish than we need.

254 Structure and Written Expression Targets

4. A comparison can be emphasized by adding the words *far* or *much* before the comparative adjective or by adding *far more* or *much more* before the comparative adjective or adverb.

> subject + verb + *far* +   adjective +   *-er* + *than* + noun
>   *far more* + adjective/adverb + *-er*   pronoun
>   *far less* + adjective/adverb   clause

Florida is hotter than Minnesota.
She arrived much later than I.

Comparing Nouns

1. Nouns can be compared using the *as . . . as* pattern with these comparative markers: *many, much, little, few*.

> subject + verb + *as* + *many* + noun + *as* + noun
>   *few*
>   *much**   pronoun
>   *little**   clause

*use with noncount nouns.

We sleep as many hours now as we did when we were children.
The flowers cost as much money as perfume.
He has as few vacations days as I.

2. Nouns can also be compared using the *-er* pattern with these comparative markers: *more, fewer, less*

> subject + verb + *more** + noun + *than* + noun
>   *fewer*   pronoun
>   *less***   clause

*use with either count or noncount nouns.
**use with noncount nouns.

There is less sugar in this coffee than I like.
I have more free time than you do.
There are fewer chairs in this room than there are people.

3. Nouns can also be compared with numbers.

> subject + verb + number + *as* + adjective/adverb + *as* + noun
> pronoun
> clause

or

> subject + verb + number + *as* + *much* + noun + *as* + noun
> *many* pronoun
> clause

The phone bill was twice as high as I expected.
My ticket cost half as much as yours.
We wrote eight times as many letters as you did.

Comparing Clauses

1. Clauses can also be compared.

> *the* + comparative + subject + verb + *the* + comparative + subject + verb

The stronger the coffee is, the better I like it.
The longer the play, the less I enjoy it.

> *the more* + subject + verb + *the* + comparative + subject + verb

The more you study, the better you will do on the TOEFL.
The less you worry, the happier your life will be.

Superlative Comparisons

When you are comparing more than two nouns or two verbs, you use the superlative form. Look at the following chart.

Base Word	Comparative	Superlative
satisfactory	more satisfactory	most satisfactory
quickly	more quickly	most quickly
quietly	more quietly	most quietly
softly	less softly	least softly
deep	deeper	deepest
wide	wider	widest
cheap	cheaper	cheapest
easy	easier	easiest

```
subject + verb + the  adjective + -est  + in + single count noun
                      most + adjective    of + plural count noun
                      least + adjective
```

The armies fought the longest battle of the war.
We are the most prepared of all the students.
This essay is the least carefully written of all the papers I read.

POTENTIAL PROBLEMS

1. *More* or *most* may be added incorrectly.

   Incorrect: The deck is more longer than the couch.
   Correct: The deck is longer than the couch.

2. The comparative and superlative forms may be incorrect.

   Incorrect: Today's lectures was most stimulating than ever before.
   Correct: Today's lecture was more stimulating than ever before.

3. There may be a double comparative.

   Incorrect: Today's computers are more faster than adding machines.
   Correct: Today's computers are faster than adding machines.

4. *Then* or *that* may be used for *than*.

   Incorrect: The student studies harder that she used to.
   Correct: The student studies harder than she used to.

5. *Less* and *fewer* may be used incorrectly. *Less* is used with noncount nouns; *fewer* with count nouns. (See the section on count and noncount nouns under Articles.)

   Incorrect: There are less people here now than before.
   Correct: There are fewer people here now than before.

COMPARISONS I

Choose the one answer that best completes the sentence.

1. It took five men to carry the tree, which was _____ than a three-story building.
   (A) taller
   (B) as tall
   (C) more taller
   (D) the tallest

2. One of the _____ inventions of the century was the holograph.
   (A) cleverest than
   (B) cleverer
   (C) more clever
   (D) most clever

3. The plan to use existing resources was considered the _____ solution.
   (A) good
   (B) most better
   (C) best
   (D) more better

4. During the experiment, volunteers slept _____ usual.
   (A) as longer that
   (B) longer than
   (C) longer that
   (D) longer

5. Since their organization had not followed the budgetary reforms we did, their gross revenues were less this year _____ ours.
   (A) that
   (B) as
   (C) than
   (D) but

6. The plan calls for a _____ defense than the one we currently have.
   (A) stronger
   (B) most strongest
   (C) stronger than
   (D) as stronger

7. The appreciation of platinum is _____ subject than that of gold to the vagaries of international circumstances.
   (A) less
   (B) few
   (C) fewer
   (D) least

8. The risk the financial commission is taking is _____.
   (A) greater than the bank
   (B) as greater than the bank's
   (C) greater than the bank's
   (D) as greater as the bank's

9. Although we have reason to believe otherwise, the editors believe they can write _____.
   (A) as well as we do
   (B) as well we do
   (C) well as we do
   (D) as well than we do

10. This particular comet, which comes every ten years, does not move _____ light.
    (A) as quicker than
    (B) as quickly as
    (C) but quickly than
    (D) as quickly

COMPARISONS II

In the sentences below, identify the one underlined phrase that is incorrect.

1. The days become <u>more long</u> as the sun moves into a <u>wider</u> orbit <u>farther</u> from the earth.
                             A   B   C   D

2. The competition was <u>the easy</u> the swimmer could remember, although <u>the other</u>
                           A   B

   <u>contestants</u>, who were <u>younger</u>, thought it was hard.
      C   D

3. The <u>strange</u> sound that came through <u>the thick</u> walls separating <u>the two</u> buildings seemed
        A   B   C

   to be <u>as closest as</u> the next room.
           D

4. The <u>lengthy</u> report was given <u>more directly</u> to the <u>responsible</u> supervisor, who read it
        A   B   C

   <u>without haste</u>.
    D

5. A study <u>released last week indicates</u> that college <u>students, particularly</u> men, regard female
                       A   B

   teachers <u>as less</u> worthy <u>of male</u> teachers.
         C   D

6. The <u>more rapid changes</u> in <u>modern</u> technology have left <u>many computer owners</u> with
          A   B   C

   <u>obsolete</u> equipment.
      D

7. A <u>greater</u> number of doctors in <u>fewest</u> hospitals indicates another <u>significant</u> change in the
       A   B   C

   status of health care for the <u>low-income</u> family.
                                  D

8. The industrial community should be <u>closer enough</u> to the <u>crowded</u> centers, but <u>distant</u>
                                             A   B   C

   enough to reduce <u>potential</u> hazards.
                 D

9. Before dental care became <u>more widespread</u>, people looked <u>older</u> before their time since so
                                A   B

   <u>many</u> lost their teeth at <u>an early</u> age.
     C   D

10. The plane's instrument console, <u>one</u> of its <u>more</u> intricate design features, is <u>lowest</u> in the
                                         A   B   C

    compartment than usual, especially for those crew members <u>as tall as</u> those doing the
                                                                           D

    testing of the plane.

☐ Subjunctive

The subjunctive verb form is used in noun clauses that express **suggestion, possibility,** or **requirement.** The clause is always introduced by *that* and the verb is in the simple form, regardless of the tense of the verb in the main clause.

> subject + verb (any tense) + *that* + subject + verb (subjunctive)

The word *that* is always used in a subjunctive clause.

> They suggested that I leave immediately.
> The contract stipulated that we sell the house with the furniture.

1. The following verbs are generally followed by the subjunctive.

advise	demand	prefer	require
ask	insist	propose	stipulate
command	move	recommend	suggest
decree	order	request	urge

2. The subjunctive form of the verb is often used with some adjectives, similar in meaning to the verbs above.

advised	obligatory	suggested
important	proposed	urgent
mandatory	recommended	imperative
necessary	required	

> *it* + *be* (any tense) + adjective from the above list + *that* + subject + [verb in simple form]

> It was advised that we reconsider our first offer.
> It is imperative that all personnel leave the building immediately.

POTENTIAL PROBLEMS

1. The subjunctive may not be used after verbs and nouns that require it.

   Incorrect: It was necessary that he knew the formula.
   Correct: It was necessary that he know the formula.

2. The incorrect tense may be used.

   Incorrect: It will be recommended that she will get the job.
   Correct: It will be recommended that she get the job.

SUBJUNCTIVE I

Choose the one answer that best completes the sentence.

1. The woman being charged with tax evasion has insisted that her lawyer and accountant _____ present.
   (A) have been
   (B) be
   (C) were
   (D) are

2. Before a member can make a motion, it is necessary that he _____ the presiding officer.
   (A) rise and address
   (B) will rise and address
   (C) rises and addresses
   (D) rise and addresses

3. The final recommendation was that the employee on probation _____ a special night class for one semester.
   (A) has attended
   (B) attended
   (C) attends
   (D) attend

4. The committee voted that all its members _____ a raise next year.
   (A) will be given
   (B) are going to be given
   (C) be given
   (D) have been given

5. The building contractors have asked that the unfinished project _____.
   (A) is extended
   (B) will be extended
   (C) has been extended
   (D) be extended

6. It is important that someone searching for a job _____ all the prospects.
   (A) consider
   (B) be considering
   (C) considers
   (D) will be considering

7. The politician urged that all citizens _____ to the polls on election day.
   (A) goes
   (B) went
   (C) must go
   (D) go

8. The U.S. Immigration Service requires that all passengers _____ a passport.
   (A) will have
   (B) have
   (C) must have
   (D) should have

9. The fire department ordered that the elevator _____.
   (A) be turned off
   (B) turn off
   (C) was turned off
   (D) turned off

10. The ad hoc committee proposed that the chairman _____.
    (A) promote
    (B) was promoted
    (C) be promoted
    (D) be promoting

SUBJUNCTIVE II

In the sentences below, identify the one underlined phrase that is incorrect.

1. School counselors <u>are convinced</u> that <u>it</u> will be obligatory that all applicants <u>must have</u>
                           A   B   C

   computer training to <u>enter</u> the job market in the future.
                        D

2. The suggestion that taxes <u>were cut</u> <u>was vetoed</u> by the mayor, who <u>foresaw</u> a deficit that
                                         A   B   C

   <u>was</u> not yet public knowledge.
    D

3. Educators are now <u>recommending</u> that reasoning skills <u>are emphasized</u> in the classroom
                               A   B

   since recent tests <u>indicate</u> that many teachers in the past <u>have ignored</u> these skills.
                         C   D

4. After the man looking for work <u>completed</u> the application, he <u>was told</u> that it <u>was</u>
                                           A   B   C

   necessary that he <u>included</u> a resume.
                     D

5. The requirement that all students <u>paying</u> an activities fee <u>was met</u> with protests from the
                                      A   B

   students who <u>would not</u> benefit because they only <u>attended</u> classes at night.
                  C   D

6. The stubborn young man <u>did not follow</u> the advice that he <u>reflected</u> on his behavior since
                                A   B

   he <u>refused</u> to believe he <u>had done</u> anything wrong.
       C   D

7. The lawyers for the <u>defense made</u> the recommendation to the judge that the trial <u>will be</u>
                        A   B

   delayed until the <u>missing</u> <u>witness was found</u>.
                    C   D

8. Before renovation could <u>continue</u>, <u>it was</u> imperative that the owner <u>approve</u> the work and
                              A   B   C

   <u>will suggest</u> additional improvements.
       D

9. It is the requirement of the personnel director that the <u>applicant is</u> a college graduate, even
                                                                  A

   though <u>the director</u> <u>has never felt</u> the need <u>to go</u> to college herself.
              B   C   D

10. The federal <u>government recommends</u> that local civic <u>groups will accept</u> the responsibility
                          A   B

    of <u>welfare disbursement</u> <u>to the needy</u>.
              C   D

☐ Word Families

Many **nouns, verbs, adjectives,** and **adverbs** are related. They come from the same *root* word; that is, they are from the same word family.

Verb	*Noun*	*Adjective*	*Adverb*
repeat	repetition	repeated	repeatedly
persuade	persuasion	persuasive	persuasively
destruct	destruction	destructive	destructively
beautify	beauty	beautiful	beautifully

POTENTIAL PROBLEMS

The appropriate word may be replaced by another word in the same family.

Incorrect (*noun substitution*): The ocean was two miles <u>depth</u> at that point.
Correct: The ocean was two miles <u>deep</u> at that point.

Incorrect (*adverb substitution*): The fruit tasted <u>bitterly</u>.
Correct: The fruit tasted <u>bitter</u>.

264   Structure and Written Expression Targets

WORD FAMILIES I

Choose the one answer that best completes the sentence.

1. The naïve man _____ believed what he read in the papers.
   - (A) foolish
   - (B) foolishly
   - (C) fool
   - (D) fooled

2. After _____ attempts, the police were able to enter the building.
   - (A) repeating
   - (B) repetition
   - (C) repeatedly
   - (D) repeated

3. The gardens that were planted this spring should _____ the roadway.
   - (A) beautifully
   - (B) beautiful
   - (C) beauty
   - (D) beautify

4. The values of a society are reflected in its _____.
   - (A) traditional
   - (B) traditions
   - (C) traditionally
   - (D) traditionalize

5. The major _____ were reported by the press without bias.
   - (A) eventual
   - (B) eventfully
   - (C) eventful
   - (D) events

6. Although the couch looks _____, it is extremely hard.
   - (A) comfortable
   - (B) comfortably
   - (C) comfortableness
   - (D) comfort

7. The bodybuilder _____ tossed the child into the air.
   - (A) easily
   - (B) easy
   - (C) ease
   - (D) eased

8. The _____ of landing men on the moon is unsurpassed in modern technology.
   - (A) achieve
   - (B) achiever
   - (C) achievement
   - (D) achievable

9. The first in _____ was the general who served his country only during peacetime.
   - (A) commander
   - (B) commandment
   - (C) commanding
   - (D) command

10. A family with ten children in a small restaurant is easily _____.
    - (A) noticed
    - (B) notice
    - (C) notify
    - (D) notification

Structure and Written Expression Targets 265

WORD FAMILIES II

In the sentences below, identify the one underlined phrase that is incorrect.

1. Our partner, being business <u>oriented</u>, <u>provided</u> us with the <u>information</u> we needed to start
                                        A   B   C

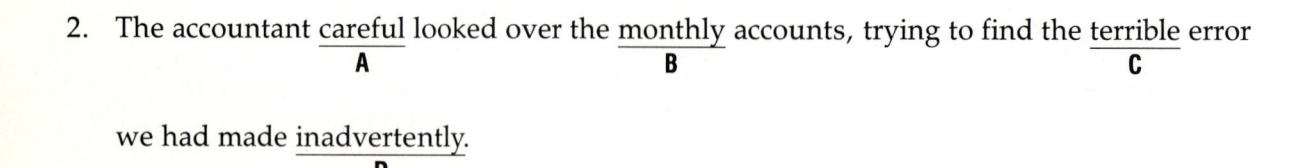

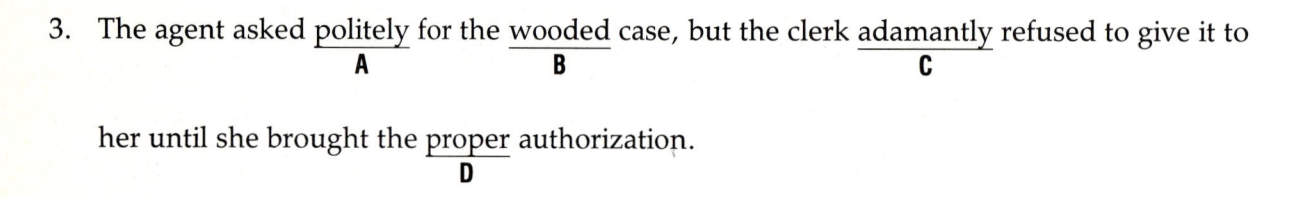

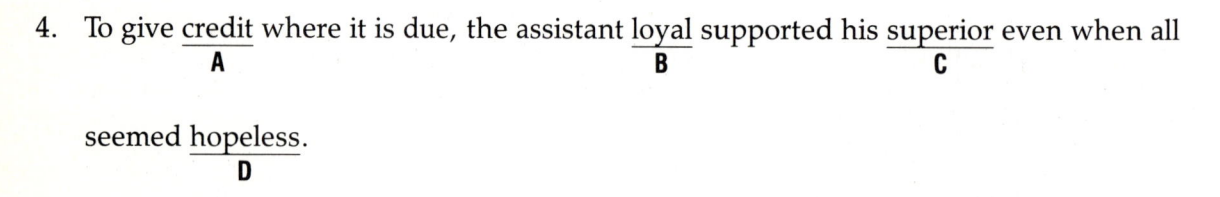

   our own <u>commerce</u> venture.
             D

2. The accountant <u>careful</u> looked over the <u>monthly</u> accounts, trying to find the <u>terrible</u> error
                   A   B   C

   we had made <u>inadvertently</u>.
                   D

3. The agent asked <u>politely</u> for the <u>wooded</u> case, but the clerk <u>adamantly</u> refused to give it to
                    A   B   C

   her until she brought the <u>proper</u> authorization.
                                   D

4. To give <u>credit</u> where it is due, the assistant <u>loyal</u> supported his <u>superior</u> even when all
           A   B   C

   seemed <u>hopeless</u>.
           D

5. The lecturer <u>smilingly</u> addressed the <u>massively</u> audience in the <u>city</u> auditorium without
                     A   B   C

   using her <u>numerous</u> notes.
               D

6. Energy <u>resources</u> like the sun and water have to date not been exploited because of the
     A   B

   <u>abundant</u> of cheap <u>oil</u>.
       C   D

7. The major <u>investors</u> decided <u>without warn</u> to withdraw their large contribution and
              A   B

   <u>refused</u> to <u>elaborate</u> on the decision.
     C   D

8. The journalist asked the <u>elected</u> official <u>present</u> to make a statement, but he <u>refused</u> to <u>commentary</u>.
   A   B   C
   D

9. The government's <u>obligation</u> to its <u>constituency</u> prompted it to <u>resume</u> local food distribution <u>immediate</u>.
                      A   B   C
                            D

10. For the <u>first time</u> the <u>unpopular</u> regulations were <u>temporarily</u> <u>suspension</u> during the week-long celebration.
            A   B   C   D

☐ Active/Passive Verbs

Sentences are either in the active voice (or mode) or passive voice. The subject is the **doer** of the action in an active voice sentence. The subject is the **receiver** in a passive construction. The passive construction consists of *be* + *-ed/-en*.

Congress <u>passed</u> a law.
   (doer)   (action)
A law was passed <u>by</u> congress.
     (action)   (doer)

> **Active**
> subject + verb + object
>
> **Passive**
> object + *to be* + verb (past participle form) + *by* + subject

The tense of the verb *to be* matches the tense of the original action verb. Note the examples below.

1. Simple present

> *am* + [verb (past participle form)]
> *is*
> *are*

Active

Birds collect twigs to make nests.

Passive

Twigs are collected by birds to make nests.

2. Simple past

> was + [verb (past participle form)]
> were

Active

The gardener cut the grass yesterday.

Passive

The grass was cut by the gardener yesterday.

3. Present continuous

> am + being + [verb (past participle form)]
> is
> are

Active

The community is building several parks.

Passive

Several parks are being built by the community.

4. Past continuous

> was + being + [verb (past participle form)]
> were

Active

The director was reading the play when the lights went out.

Passive

The play was being read by the director when the lights went out.

5. Present perfect

> has + been + [verb (past participle form)]
> have

Active

The volunteers have donated their time and money.

Passive

Time and money have been donated by the volunteers.

6. Past perfect

> had + been + [verb (past participle form)]

Active

The president had not signed the proclamation by midnight.

Passive

The proclamation had not been signed by midnight.

7. Modals

> modal + *be* + [verb (past participle form)]

Active

The housekeeper must clean the house before she leaves.

Passive

The house must be cleaned by the housekeeper before she leaves.

Structure and Written Expression Targets 269

8. Modals + perfect tense

> modal + *have* + *been* + [verb (past participle form)]

Active

We should have started this project long ago.

Passive

This project should have been started long ago.

POTENTIAL PROBLEMS

1. One voice form may be substituted for the other.

   Incorrect: She couldn't consult the map because it was packing away.
   Correct: She couldn't consult the map because it was packed away.

2. The auxiliary may not agree in tense or number.

   Incorrect: The people was given small party favors.
   Correct: The people were given small party favors.

ACTIVE/PASSIVE I

Choose the one answer that best completes the sentence.

1. Although the mission was to be kept a secret, it _____ to the press.
   (A) reveals
   (B) revealed
   (C) was revealed
   (D) reveal

2. The secretary opened the mail which _____ that morning.
   (A) had delivered
   (B) delivered
   (C) had been delivered
   (D) is delivered

3. The congressional committee _____ all foreign aid funds.
   (A) were cut
   (B) was cut
   (C) cut
   (D) cut it

4. In spite of popular support, the radio program _____ off the air very soon.
   (A) had taken
   (B) will be taken
   (C) takes
   (D) were taken

5. The stockholder _____ questions to the board in a belligerent tone.
   (A) poses
   (B) was posed
   (C) were posed
   (D) posed

6. Seemingly reasonable people _____ strange things under stress.
   (A) have done
   (B) does
   (C) is done
   (D) are done

7. The commissioners told the journalists that the problem _____ care of already.
   (A) has been taken
   (B) had been taken
   (C) will take
   (D) will be taken

8. Some people believe that giving gifts is one way _____ by others.
   (A) to love
   (B) love
   (C) to be loved
   (D) is loved

9. The early settlers _____ the land for pasture.
   (A) were cleared
   (B) cleared
   (C) were being cleared
   (D) clearing

10. Government control of the press _____ by every concerned citizen.
    (A) has been opposed
    (B) has opposed
    (C) has been opposing
    (D) opposed

ACTIVE/PASSIVE II

In the sentences below, identify the one underlined phrase that is incorrect.

1. Although some <u>difficulty was expected</u>, the extent of the problem <u>was not known</u> until the
          A   B

   <u>project completed</u> and the final report was <u>distributed</u>.
          C   D

2. Metal <u>must be hammered</u>, worked, and <u>cooled rapidly</u> <u>to relieve</u> internal <u>stresses causing</u>
              A   B   C   D

   by heating.

3. To add distilled water to the test tube, the technician was inserted a large-gauge hollow
        A   B
   needle through a cork in the base made of opaque material.
            C   D

4. Inventors were applied theories to everyday phenomena to create products for man's use.
                A   B   C   D

5. A stain that has first been soaked in solvent can then easily removed by adding water
                 A   B   C
   which has been distilled.
                 D

6. Spacecraft destined for orbit will be propelling from Earth by rockets developed by a
               A   B   C
   West Coast engineering firm.
                   D

7. The well-known, well-advertised products developed by major corporations have become
            A   B   C
   an industry standard to emulated rather than improved upon.
                         D

8. Meteorologists have been detected a gradual warming of the Earth's atmosphere that
                       A   B
   will cause rising water levels.
              C   D

9. Risks that are taking by today's entrepreneurs are considerable and, while
                A   B   C
   stimulating, pose threats to their financial security.
                D

10. Oil and gold, both of which had an unparalleled price increase in the 90s, have not been
                                A   B
    popular recently and not placed on the most favored stock lists.
                           C   D

272   Structure and Written Expression Targets

GRAMMAR REVIEW I

Choose the one answer below that best completes the sentence.

1. Both abstract and realistic paintings were _____ at the art show.
   - (A) exhibit
   - (B) exhibits
   - (C) exhibited
   - (D) exhibiting

2. The city of New Orleans would be under water if the river banks _____ unprotected.
   - (A) left
   - (B) were left
   - (C) leave
   - (D) were leaving

3. _____ who attend good schools usually earn more money as adults.
   - (A) The child
   - (B) Children
   - (C) Children those
   - (D) Any child

4. The art of storytelling is as _____ as the art of drawing.
   - (A) creative
   - (B) create
   - (C) creating
   - (D) creates

5. The workers are paid _____.
   - (A) by the hour
   - (B) to each hour
   - (C) with the hour
   - (D) by each hour

6. Cancer causes more deaths than all other _____.
   - (A) is illnesses added together
   - (B) illnesses add together
   - (C) illnesses added together
   - (D) adding illnesses together

7. _____ colonial pottery was intended for everyday use, few pieces have survived intact.
   - (A) Usually
   - (B) Since
   - (C) Although
   - (D) Regarding

8. The beaver, _____ many to work all day, is actually a nocturnal animal.
   - (A) believed
   - (B) are known
   - (C) believed by
   - (D) which

9. It has never been understood _____ the dinosaur became extinct.
   - (A) by
   - (B) why
   - (C) if
   - (D) there

10. Parking spaces in large cities are difficult to find; _____ taking public transportation is the alternative to owning a car.
    - (A) nevertheless
    - (B) therefore
    - (C) however
    - (D) moreover

Structure and Written Expression Targets

11. _____ the Philadelphia statesman Benjamin Franklin active in politics, but he was an inventor and publisher as well.
    (A) Not was only
    (B) Not only was
    (C) Only not was
    (D) Only was not

12. The U.S. Meteorological Service provides information on climatic changes for _____, regional, and international weather bureaus.
    (A) locally
    (B) local
    (C) locality
    (D) location

13. The maple tree has a five-pointed leaf, and _____ roots do not extend as much as other trees.
    (A) they
    (B) their
    (C) it
    (D) its

14. Many adults feel _____ easy to learn a language.
    (A) isn't it
    (B) because it's
    (C) although it's
    (D) it isn't

15. _____ no real difference between a statesman and a diplomat.
    (A) Theirs
    (B) There's
    (C) They're
    (D) There

16. Lead is much _____ than aluminum.
    (A) heavy
    (B) heavier
    (C) heaviest
    (D) most heavy

17. Furniture is made from wood and _____ is manufactured from wood pulp.
    (A) a paper
    (B) papers
    (C) paper
    (D) the paper

18. Metallurgy had its _____ in decorative objects like necklaces rather than useful objects like knifes.
    (A) original
    (B) originality
    (C) originally
    (D) origin

19. Fluorescent lighting, even though _____ inexpensive, may be dangerous to your health.
    (A) is
    (B) it is
    (C) they are
    (D) are

20. The average life span of a cat is _____ years.
    (A) from 10 and 12
    (B) through 10 and 12
    (C) from 10 until 12
    (D) between 10 and 12

GRAMMAR REVIEW II

In the sentences below, identify the one underlined phrase that is incorrect.

1. The introduction <u>of the tomato</u> from the New World <u>changed</u> the <u>cuisines</u> of Europe
                   A   B   C

   <u>in an instant</u>, thoroughly, and irrevocably.
        D

2. <u>High</u> fences <u>surrounded by</u> military bases <u>and other</u> <u>government</u> areas.
     A   B   C   D

3. Frank Lloyd Wright <u>is well-known</u> architect whose <u>private</u> homes and public buildings are
                           A   B

   <u>primarily made</u> of <u>natural materials</u>.
       C   D

4. The history <u>of</u> civilization <u>has been greatly</u> affected <u>the invention of</u> the steam engine and
               A   B   C

   <u>the Industrial Revolution</u>.
            D

5. <u>The more visited</u> museum <u>in</u> the world <u>is</u> the Air and Space Museum <u>in</u> Washington, D.C.
         A   B   C   D

6. <u>To chew</u> gum is <u>sold</u> <u>in packets</u> of five, ten, or twenty-five <u>sticks</u>.
       A   B   C   D

7. Benjamin Franklin, <u>who an inventor</u> <u>as well as</u> a statesman, had a <u>central</u> role
                          A   B   C

   <u>in the drafting</u> of the Constitution.
        D

8. Each man or woman <u>must</u> do <u>their</u> part and <u>vote</u> in the <u>national</u> elections.
                      A   B   C   D

9. <u>Geology</u> professors <u>do not agree</u> <u>on</u> <u>caused</u> the Ice Age.
     A   B   C D

Structure and Written Expression Targets

10. Even though weather conditions are not always predictable, farmers must have alternate
            A   B   C

    plans in case of drought or flood.
          D

11. Mules are stubborn, working hard animals that have greatly increased in numbers
                 A   B   C

    in recent years.
        D

12. The Lewis and Clark Expedition was the first group of explorers to travel, map, and
                                  A   B

    giving descriptions of the northwestern part of the United States.
        C   D

13. Its amazes people when they observe how porpoises can be trained to interact with
     A   B   C   D

    humans.

14. Most book lovers agree that it is no other university like Harvard for the variety and
     A   B   C   D

    volume of its library collections.

15. How it is possible to determine the age of an antique without comparing it to
        A   B   C   D

    contemporary examples?

16. Every year rainforests as larger as Tennessee are cut down.
        A   B   C D

17. The practice of bringing gifts are not as common today as in the past.
              A   B   C   D

18. Today, Washington, D.C. has the most trees than any other city in the world.
                       A   B   C   D

19. Although the summers in Florida are very hot, the state was still a popular vacation spot
    A   B   C

    for tourists all year round.
        D

20. The Alaskan landscape is character by tundra and glaciers.
        A   B   C   D

5

VOCABULARY TARGETS

■ VOCABULARY QUESTIONS

Purpose

You will be tested on your knowledge of vocabulary. You will have to match an underlined word with its synonym. There are 30 questions in this part.

Words/Phrases to Look for

Academic English

Sample Vocabulary Item

The ingredients when blended were toxic.
- (A) purchased
- (B) dissolved
- (C) heated
- (D) mixed

The correct answer is (D). *Mixed* is a synonym of *blended*.

STRATEGIES FOR THE TOEFL

1. Do NOT read the general directions. Use that time to begin the exercises.

2. Look only at the underlined word. Think of a synonym and try to find that synonym among the four answer choices.

3. It is usually not necessary to read the sentence. The sentence will not provide any extra clues.

4. Look for clues in the underlined word. What is the root of the word? What is the meaning of the prefix or suffix?

5. Read through each question quickly. You will want to save time for the Reading Comprehension section that follows.

6. Answer every question. If you aren't sure, GUESS!

STRATEGY-BUILDING ACTIVITIES

Before you take the TOEFL, there are some techniques and exercises you can use to increase your vocabulary. Remember that using a word will help you remember it.

1. **Read! Read! Read!**
   There is no substitute for a systematic approach to reading. The more you read, the more words you will discover. The more often you read, the more frequently you will see these words. You should read in a variety of subject matter areas. You should read books, magazines, newspapers, time schedules, letters, and so on. You will find new words each time you pick up something to read.

2. **Keep a Notebook**
   Once you find a new word, write it down in a notebook. Later, look up the word in the dictionary and write synonyms for the word in your notebook next to the word. You must train yourself to recognize synonyms, not translations. Whenever you have a spare moment, pull out your Word Notebook and study a few words and their synonyms.

3. **Make Flash Cards**
   Find a block of heavy paper (index or file) cards that are a convenient size. Write a new word on one side and the synonym or synonyms on the reverse. Carry these flash cards with you and give yourself mini-tests whenever you have spare time. Show yourself the word and guess the synonyms. Show yourself the synonyms and guess the word.

4. **Study Word Lists**
   Some word lists are included in this section. Each day transfer some words and their synonyms from these lists into your Word Notebook or onto your flash cards.

   It is difficult to memorize words on a word list. These lists, however, draw your attention to a word. You will soon notice words that you saw on the list as you read. As you increase the amount you read, you will see the new words more frequently. The more you practice, the larger your vocabulary will become.

5. **Study This Section**
   In the Vocabulary Target section are lists of words and prefixes that will help you prepare for the TOEFL. Study the following lists; then do the Vocabulary Target exercises that follow the lists.

SKILLS TO DEVELOP

1. Learn to identify synonyms.
2. Learn to recognize common prefixes.
3. Learn to recognize negative prefixes.

SKILL-BUILDING EXERCISES

The following exercises will help you develop these skills. By recognizing common prefixes and synonyms and by identifying synonyms and root words, you will be better prepared for the TOEFL. In addition, keeping a Word Notebook with all the words you learn and preparing flash cards of these words will help you improve your vocabulary.

The TOEFL vocabulary questions test your ability to recognize words and their synonyms. Study the following sections and do the exercises carefully.

Beware!

The words in this book are not the only words in the English language and not the only words that you will see on the TOEFL. You must improve your vocabulary by reading a variety of English books, magazines, and newspapers.

☐ Synonyms

Word	Synonym	Synonym
accord	agree	grant
affluent	plentiful	rich
amenable	agreeable	favorable
apathetic	dispirited	lifeless
astonish	confound	overwhelm
augment	add	enlarge
awkward	graceless	inept
barren	desolate	sterile
betray	deceive	fool
bitter	acrid	sour
bliss	happiness	joy
bold	daring	fearless
bother	annoy	irritate
brilliant	clever	intelligent
budget	allot	plan
caricature	cartoon	imitation
category	classification	division
chaotic	disordered	messy
circumvent	avoid	go around
compensate	balance	recompense
conceive	design	plan
contradict	deny	oppose
courteous	polite	well-mannered
credulous	confident	trustful

280 Vocabulary Targets

Word	Synonym	Synonym
dare	challenge	defy
decent	honorable	pure
designate	name	select
disclose	announce	reveal
durable	constant	lasting
eager	earnest	keen
elaborate	embellish	enhance
eminent	distinguished	prominent
endure	last	persist
essential	basic	necessary
evaluate	appraise	judge
exhilarated	cheerful	zestful
fastidious	exacting	particular
feeble	weak	infirm
feud	argument	dispute
flatter	compliment	praise
frivolous	inconsequential	trivial
furious	angry	outraged
genuine	actual	real
gloomy	cheerless	dim
grasp	grab	hold
guarantee	assure	pledge
habitual	customary	regular
harass	annoy	disturb
harsh	hard	coarse
haughty	arrogant	pretentious
hygiene	cleanliness	sanitation
idle	lazy	unoccupied
illogical	incongruent	rambling
imitate	copy	mimic
impartial	candid	impersonal
implicate	accuse	insinuate
inadvertent	accidental	unintentional
jargon	argot	slang
judge	evaluate	referee
juvenile	adolescent	immature
label	brand	classify
lead	direct	guide
leave	abandon	desert

Vocabulary Targets

Word	Synonym	Synonym
liberal	lenient	open-minded
lucid	clear	understandable
mad	furious	irate
manipulate	control	shape
match	agree	correspond
meditate	ponder	think
mention	allude	refer to
narrow	confined	restricted
necessary	mandatory	requisite
negligent	careless	remiss
nice	affable	benign
novice	beginner	nonprofessional
obedient	faithful	loyal
obligatory	compulsory	required
obvious	conspicuous	definite
offer	bid	proposal
omit	exclude	remove
pacify	appease	placate
paramount	chief	leading
passive	inactive	lethargic
perpetuate	endure	preserve
persecute	inflict	harass
radical	basic	fundamental
rank	arrange	classify
recalcitrant	obstinate	stubborn
reconcile	atone	conciliate
reliable	dependable	trustworthy
scope	aim	extent
settle	adjust	compromise
shrewd	careful	calculating
slight	delicate	slender
spread	expand	diffuse
tame	domesticate	subdue
temper	mood	nature
term	cycle	duration
tough	aggressive	unyielding
tumult	agitation	commotion
vain	boastful	inflated
variety	assortment	diversity

SYNONYM EXERCISES

Replace the underlined word with the appropriate synonym.

1. The contractor abandoned the project before it was complete.
   (A) changed
   (B) criticized
   (C) evaluated
   (D) discarded

2. Affluent neighborhoods usually have good schools.
   (A) Rich
   (B) Close
   (C) Riverside
   (D) Urban

3. The bank teller wanted the customer's signature verified.
   (A) authenticated
   (B) repeated
   (C) forged
   (D) legible

4. A brisk walk is good for your heart.
   (A) slow
   (B) fast
   (C) long
   (D) short

5. If you want my candid opinion, your work needs improvement.
   (A) naive
   (B) own
   (C) honest
   (D) critical

6. The warning was explicit: Do not smoke here.
   (A) illegible
   (B) loud
   (C) written
   (D) definite

7. The pictures stored in the damp cellar were ruined.
   (A) dark
   (B) small
   (C) nearest
   (D) wet

8. The illegal aliens were detained at the border.
   (A) kept
   (B) introduced
   (C) turned back
   (D) finished

9. Very intelligent people, especially geniuses, are quite often eccentric.
   (A) untrustworthy
   (B) idiosyncratic
   (C) personable
   (D) annoying

10. The well-read philosopher was quite erudite on the subject.
    (A) adamant
    (B) learned
    (C) ignorant
    (D) vocal

11. No one knows what started the longstanding feud between the two females.
    (A) fence
    (B) dispute
    (C) friendship
    (D) discussion

12. The miser led a very frugal life.
    (A) prudent
    (B) unhappy
    (C) quiet
    (D) prosperous

Vocabulary Targets   283

13. The gloomy atmosphere was depressing.
    (A) homey
    (B) cramped
    (C) roomy
    (D) cheerless

14. The gullible lad bought the Brooklyn Bridge.
    (A) rich
    (B) credulous
    (C) guilty
    (D) nice

15. The returning employees were harassed by the strikers.
    (A) annoyed
    (B) encouraged
    (C) wounded
    (D) questioned

16. The students' lack of respect humiliated the teacher.
    (A) embarrassed
    (B) honored
    (C) encouraged
    (D) worried

17. The monkeys imitated the actions of the humans.
    (A) impeded
    (B) observed
    (C) ignored
    (D) copied

18. The lawyers called the man's defense illogical.
    (A) baseless
    (B) weak
    (C) incongruent
    (D) credible

19. Most disciplines have their own jargon.
    (A) employees
    (B) slang
    (C) rules
    (D) cars

20. The student's juvenile behavior disappointed the chaperons.
    (A) immature
    (B) modest
    (C) adult
    (D) careless

21. A bird watcher needs a keen eye and a lot of patience.
    (A) fast
    (B) blind
    (C) questioning
    (D) observant

22. The accident victim, although severely injured, was still lucid.
    (A) understandable
    (B) cheerful
    (C) nervous
    (D) bleeding

23. His imagination has no limitations.
    (A) credibility
    (B) value
    (C) boundaries
    (D) purpose

24. The robot was able to manipulate the machine's setting.
    (A) control
    (B) determine
    (C) calculate
    (D) cancel

25. The newspaper article didn't mention the date of the crash.
    (A) predict
    (B) refer to
    (C) correct
    (D) forget

26. The managers negotiated a new contract with the workers.
    (A) cancelled
    (B) wanted
    (C) discussed
    (D) bargained for

27. The barking dog was a real nuisance.
    (A) beauty
    (B) annoyance
    (C) champion
    (D) thoroughbred

28. The soldiers followed their commander obediently.
    (A) quietly
    (B) diligently
    (C) loyally
    (D) quickly

29. The owner rejected their last offer.
    (A) dollar
    (B) bid
    (C) design
    (D) plan

30. The mediator tried to pacify the warring factions.
    (A) placate
    (B) divide
    (C) isolate
    (D) organize

31. The foundation will perpetuate the widow's legacy.
    (A) glorify
    (B) dissolve
    (C) spend
    (D) preserve

32. The children were ranked in order of age.
    (A) taught
    (B) thanked
    (C) shown
    (D) arranged

33. The babysitter was considered reliable.
    (A) dependable
    (B) expensive
    (C) insolent
    (D) honest

34. A valid passport is required for international travel.
    (A) A new
    (B) An autographed
    (C) A current
    (D) An authorized

35. The pilot asked us to fasten our seat belts during turbulent weather.
    (A) calm
    (B) predictable
    (C) violent
    (D) snowy

Common Prefixes

Pre in Latin means **before**. *Fix* is a Latin root meaning **to fix**, or **position**. Prefix means **placed before**. The prefixes below came into the English language from either the Latin or Greek languages. Knowing one Latin or Greek prefix can help you recognize up to 50 English words. Knowing 40 Latin or Greek prefixes can help you recognize up to 2,000 English words.

Prefix	Meaning	Examples
a-, an-,	without or not	asexual, amoral, anarchy, antonym
a-	to, toward	aloud, ameliorate, akin, aground
ab-, abs-	off, away from	abstain, absence, abnormal
ad- (ac-, ag-, al-, an-, as-, at-)	to	adhere, account, aggregate, allocate, anchor, assure, attach
ambi-, amphi-	on both sides	ambivalent, amphibious, ambidextrous
ante-	before	antecedent, anteroom, antebellum
anti-	against, opposite	antidote, antibody
bi-	twice, two	bicycle, bilateral, bilingual
bio-	life	biology, biosphere
circum-	around, about	circumspect, circumvent
com- (con-, co-, cog-, col-, cor-)	together or with	compare, constant, cohabitate, cognate, collect, correlate
contra- (contro-, counter-)	against, opposing	contradiction, controversial, counterproductive
de-	from, off, down	deter, descend, decimate
di-	twice, two	divide, dilemma
dis-, dif-, di-	apart, away, not	disappear, different, digest
en-, em-	cause to be, put into	encircle, empower, entrust
ex-, e-	from, out of	except, egress, exit
extra-, extro-	outside, beyond	extraterritorial, extravagant
fore-	before	foreseen, forecast
in-, im-, it-, ir-	not	insufferable, impotent, illogical, irrefutable
in-, im-	in	ingest, imbibe
inter-, intro-	between, together	intermingle, introduction
intra-	within	intrastate

Prefix	Meaning	Examples
macro-	big	macrosystem
mal-	bad, wrong	malcontent, malevolent
mega-	big	megahertz, megaphone
meta-	changed	metastasis
micro-	small	microscope, microbiology
mid-	middle	midlife, midstream
mini-	small	minicar, miniscule
mis-	ill, wrong	misdeed, miserable
mono-	one	monolingual, monocle
multi-	many	multiply, multilingual
non-	non, lacking	nonsense, nondescript
ob-(oc-, of-, op-)	toward, against, to	obtuse, occur, offer, oppress
over-	more than required	overcome, overdo
para-	near, beyond, beside	paragraph, paradox, paralegal
per-	throughout, completely	persuade, perversion
poly-	many	polygamy, polyglot
post-	after, behind	postpone, posterior, posthumous
pre-	before	preclude, predate, prevent
pseudo-	false	pseudoscience
re-	again, back	reverse, return
retro-	backward	retrospective, retrograde
semi-	half, part	semiannual, semicircle
sub-	under	substandard
super-, sur-	over	superman, supervisor
syn- (sym-)	together	synchronize, symbolic
trans-	across	transoceanic, transport, transcontinental
ultra-	excessive	ultrafine, ultrasensitive
un-	not	undone, unhappy

Vocabulary Targets **287**

Negative Prefixes

A negative prefix added to a word implies the opposite of the word.

unsolicited	not solicited
disabled	not able/handicapped
incompatible	not compatible
impatient	not patient
irrelevant	not relevant
nonviolent	not violent
misspelled	not spelled correctly

Examples of words with these prefixes are listed below:

unaware	imbecile	irreconcilable	nonalcoholic
unbearable	immaterial	irredeemable	nonconformist
uncomplicated	immature	irrefutable	noneffective
undecided	immortal	irreligious	nonpolitical
unfit	impatient	irremovable	nonpoisonous
ungrammatical	impolite	irreparable	nonproductive
uninteresting	impossible	irresistible	nonrestrictive
unpleasant	improbable	irrational	nonsense
unreliable	improper	irregular	nonstop
unsolicited	impure	irresponsible	nonviolent

disadvantage	inapplicable	misbehave
disburse	incapable	miscalculate
discharge	indecent	misconduct
disembark	inexact	misfire
disfavor	infallible	misfortune
dishonest	inhuman	misgiving
disinfect	inimitable	misinterpret
disjointed	inoffensive	mislay
dislocate	insatiable	misplace
displeasure	invalid	mispronounce

Vocabulary Targets

PREFIX EXERCISE

Select the one word or phrase that most closely matches the meaning of the underlined word.

1. People said that the personalities of the young married couple were incompatible.
   (A) discordant
   (B) harmonious
   (C) lovable
   (D) blissful

2. The newspaper described the amoral activities of the terrorist group in detail.
   (A) erotic
   (B) unproductive
   (C) philanthropic
   (D) unethical

3. The debate team found their opponents' arguments illogical and consequently irrefutable.
   (A) interesting
   (B) challenging
   (C) irritating
   (D) incontrovertible

4. The enraged manner of the speaker caused the committee to reconsider the issue.
   (A) stubborn
   (B) angry
   (C) forthright
   (D) charming

5. The fundraisers claim their motives are apolitical.
   (A) pure
   (B) laudable
   (C) unbiased
   (D) nonpartisan

6. The antidote was not where the doctor had left it.
   (A) prescription
   (B) bandage
   (C) anecdote
   (D) remedy

7. The house, although not unusually small, made us feel uncomfortable.
   (A) dirty
   (B) immobile
   (C) uneasy
   (D) impractical

8. The disadvantage of winning is the notoriety one receives.
   (A) pleasure of
   (B) goal to
   (C) drawback to
   (D) purpose of

9. The students' actions toward the substitute teacher were distasteful.
   (A) inappropriate
   (B) unpleasant
   (C) inconsiderate
   (D) inhuman

10. The insufficient supply of food did not worry the villagers.
    (A) increased
    (B) abundant
    (C) inadequate
    (D) diminishing

11. The manager does not tolerate imperfections in himself or in others.
    (A) shyness
    (B) stupidity
    (C) misbehavior
    (D) defects

12. The recluse's mistreatment of animals did not go unnoticed.
    (A) cruelty to
    (B) protection of
    (C) hatred of
    (D) loyalty to

13. The reporter wondered how impartial the decision really was.
    (A) unprejudiced
    (B) bigoted
    (C) one-sided
    (D) insensitive

14. The directions to the museum were not what most people would call uncomplicated.
    (A) difficult
    (B) simple
    (C) illegible
    (D) impractical

15. The soldiers' disobedience made them subject to disciplinary action.
    (A) habit
    (B) tardiness
    (C) dishonor
    (D) insubordination

16. The speech, contrary to what we all expected, was inoffensive.
    (A) incomprehensible
    (B) interminable
    (C) ridiculous
    (D) harmless

17. We all, at times, wish we were invisible.
    (A) wealthy
    (B) more powerful
    (C) nonviolent
    (D) inconspicuous

18. Inorganic items are catalogued by their Latin names.
    (A) Nonmusical
    (B) Inanimate
    (C) Animated
    (D) Chemical

19. We saw he was displeased, but there was not enough time to do anything about it.
    (A) undressed
    (B) far away
    (C) hungry
    (D) annoyed

20. My aunt's reasoning was clever but invalid.
    (A) unjust
    (B) unsubstantiated
    (C) twisted
    (D) evasive

GENERAL VOCABULARY EXERCISE

Select the one word or phrase that most closely matches the meaning of the underlined word.

1. Parents should establish certain rules for their children.
   - (A) increase
   - (B) offer
   - (C) determine
   - (D) justify

2. There are numerous customs that dictate one's diet.
   - (A) popular
   - (B) many
   - (C) religious
   - (D) special

3. The teacher wanted to provide the class with enough work to keep them busy.
   - (A) supply
   - (B) irritate
   - (C) overwhelm
   - (D) exhaust

4. A botanist can identify a flower by its shape and its scent.
   - (A) name
   - (B) size
   - (C) color
   - (D) smell

5. Since an amoeba's old cell will divide into two new cells, it may be called immortal.
   - (A) duplicitous
   - (B) immoral
   - (C) biological
   - (D) undying

6. As instructed, the pilot precisely followed the control tower's directions.
   - (A) exactly
   - (B) purposely
   - (C) only
   - (D) always

7. Eating and drinking too much increase the size of the abdomen.
   - (A) headache
   - (B) gathering
   - (C) belly
   - (D) hangover

8. In times of war, the army will draft all able-bodied men.
   - (A) handsome
   - (B) single
   - (C) young
   - (D) strong

9. Notification of taxes due will be sent in the near future.
   - (A) Announcement
   - (B) Annotation
   - (C) Clarification
   - (D) Amplification

10. The comedian has a tendency to be more absurd than funny.
    - (A) late
    - (B) greedy
    - (C) ridiculous
    - (D) proud

11. Few <u>bachelors</u> live in this family neighborhood.
    (A) intelligent people
    (B) unmarried men
    (C) strangers
    (D) peers

12. Regular <u>maintenance</u> of an auto will improve its efficiency.
    (A) washing
    (B) upkeep
    (C) protection
    (D) driving

13. Children may <u>ridicule</u> other children new to a neighborhood.
    (A) become tired of
    (B) play with
    (C) make fun of
    (D) be shy around

14. <u>Instead of</u> raising taxes, the administration looked for different sources of revenue.
    (A) Rather than
    (B) Before
    (C) After
    (D) In addition to

15. My grandmother always had <u>kind</u> words to say about everyone she knew.
    (A) good
    (B) simple
    (C) similar
    (D) clever

16. The terrier was <u>kind of</u> short with long, black hair.
    (A) considered
    (B) described as
    (C) somewhat
    (D) captured

17. Twins usually wear the same <u>kind</u> of clothing.
    (A) size
    (B) color
    (C) type
    (D) outfit

18. The <u>probability</u> of the strike's ending before the tourist season is not high.
    (A) likelihood
    (B) idea
    (C) result
    (D) controversy

19. Violators who <u>are ignorant of</u> the parking laws must still pay their fines.
    (A) are tired of
    (B) are respectful of
    (C) know nothing of
    (D) want to change

20. The court <u>nullified</u> the agreement after months of debate.
    (A) heard
    (B) annulled
    (C) ratified
    (D) recognized

6

READING TARGETS

READING QUESTIONS

TYPES OF READING COMPREHENSION QUESTIONS

There are ten kinds of questions generally found on the TOEFL. The first five types are asked most frequently (75 to 80 percent of all questions); the last five types are asked much less frequently (20 to 25 percent of all questions). Examples of each are given below.

> **Most Frequently Asked Questions**
> 1. Main idea questions
> 2. Factual questions—positive
> 3. Factual questions—negative
> 4. Inference questions—specific applications
> 5. Inference questions—general applications
>
> **Less Frequently Asked Questions**
> 6. Analogy questions
> 7. Written expression questions
> 8. Organization questions
> 9. Follow-on questions
> 10. Viewpoint questions

There is usually one main idea question for each passage. The most important type of question is the factual question. Most of the questions for each passage are factual questions.

Main Idea Questions

Purpose

You will be asked to identify the main idea or topic of the whole passage. There is usually only one main idea.

Note: This is a very important question type. Each passage usually has one main idea question.

Words/Phrases to Look for

main point
mainly discuss
main idea
best title
main purpose
mainly concerned
main topic

Sample Questions

What is the main idea of this passage?
With which of the following is the passage mainly concerned?
What is the main part of the passage?
Which of the following does the author mainly discuss?
Which of the following would be the best title?

Factual Questions—Positive

Purpose

You will be asked for specific information discussed in the passage.

Note: This is a very important question type. Each passage usually has several factual questions.

Words/Phrases to Look for

According to the author, . . .
According to the passage, . . .
Who, what, when, where, why, how, which

Sample Questions

Which of the following questions does the passage answer?
According to the passage, which statement is true?
When did "something" happen?
Who did "something"?

☐ Factual Questions—Negative

Purpose
You will be asked to identify information NOT discussed in the passage.

   Note: This is a very important question type. Each passage usually has several factual questions.

Words/Phrases to Look for
   NOT
   EXCEPT
   LEAST
   MOST

Note: These words are always capitalized on the TOEFL.

Sample Questions
   The author discusses all of the following in the passage EXCEPT . . .

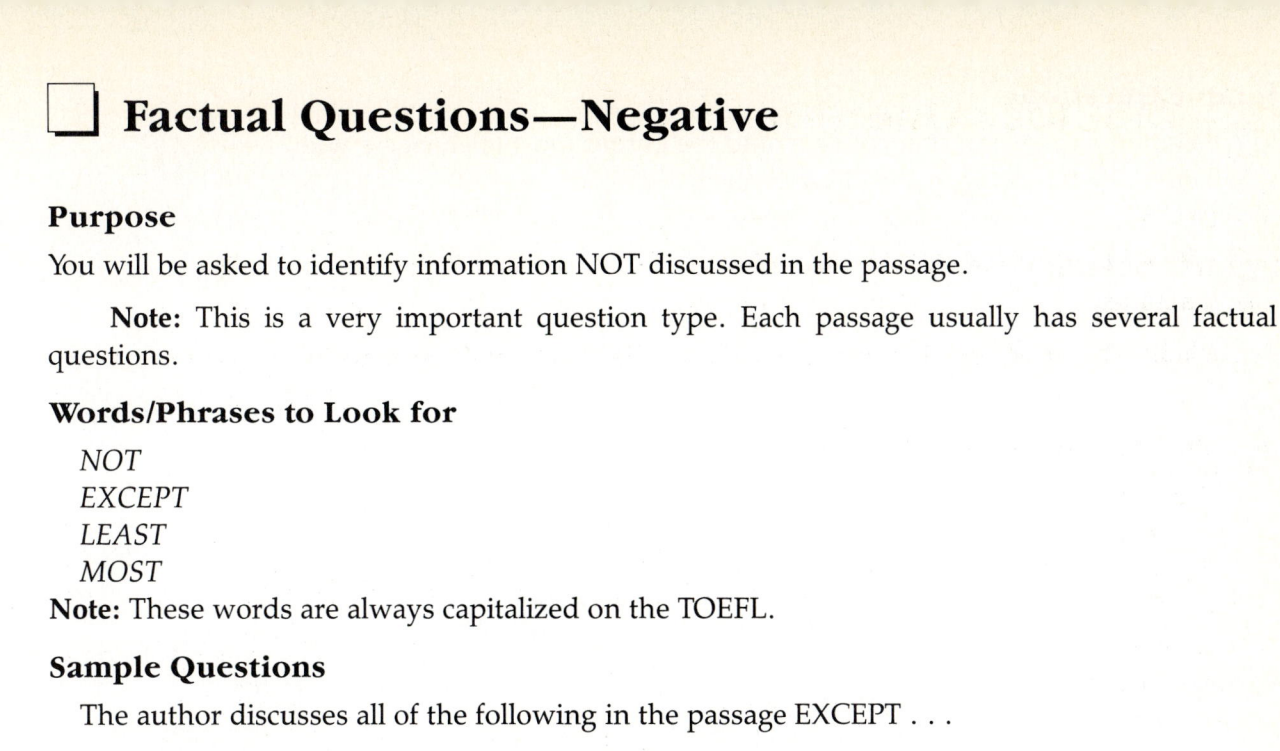

   According to the passage, which is the MOST likely reason?

   Which of the following is NOT mentioned in the passage?

☐ Inference Questions—Specific Applications

Purpose
You will be asked to form a conclusion based on information discussed in the passage.

Words/Phrases to Look for
   It can be inferred that . . .
   The author implied that . . .

Sample Questions
   Which of the following does the author imply?
   Which of the following can be inferred from the passage?

☐ Inference Questions—General Applications

Purpose
You will be asked to apply information from the passage to general situations outside the passage.

Words/Phrases to Look for
   likely agree with . . .
   most likely to . . .

Reading Targets 295

Sample Questions

Which of the following statements would the author most likely agree with?
Which of the following is most likely to be true?

☐ Analogy

Purpose

You will be asked to compare the questions's answer choices to ideas discussed in the passage.

Words/Phrases to Look for

similar to
comparable to
analogous to
like

Sample Questions

Which of the following is like the "main idea?"
Doing "something" is analogous to which of the following?

☐ Written Expression Questions

Purpose

You will be asked the meaning of words in the context of a passage or the referents (antecedents) for pronouns.

Words/Phrases to Look for

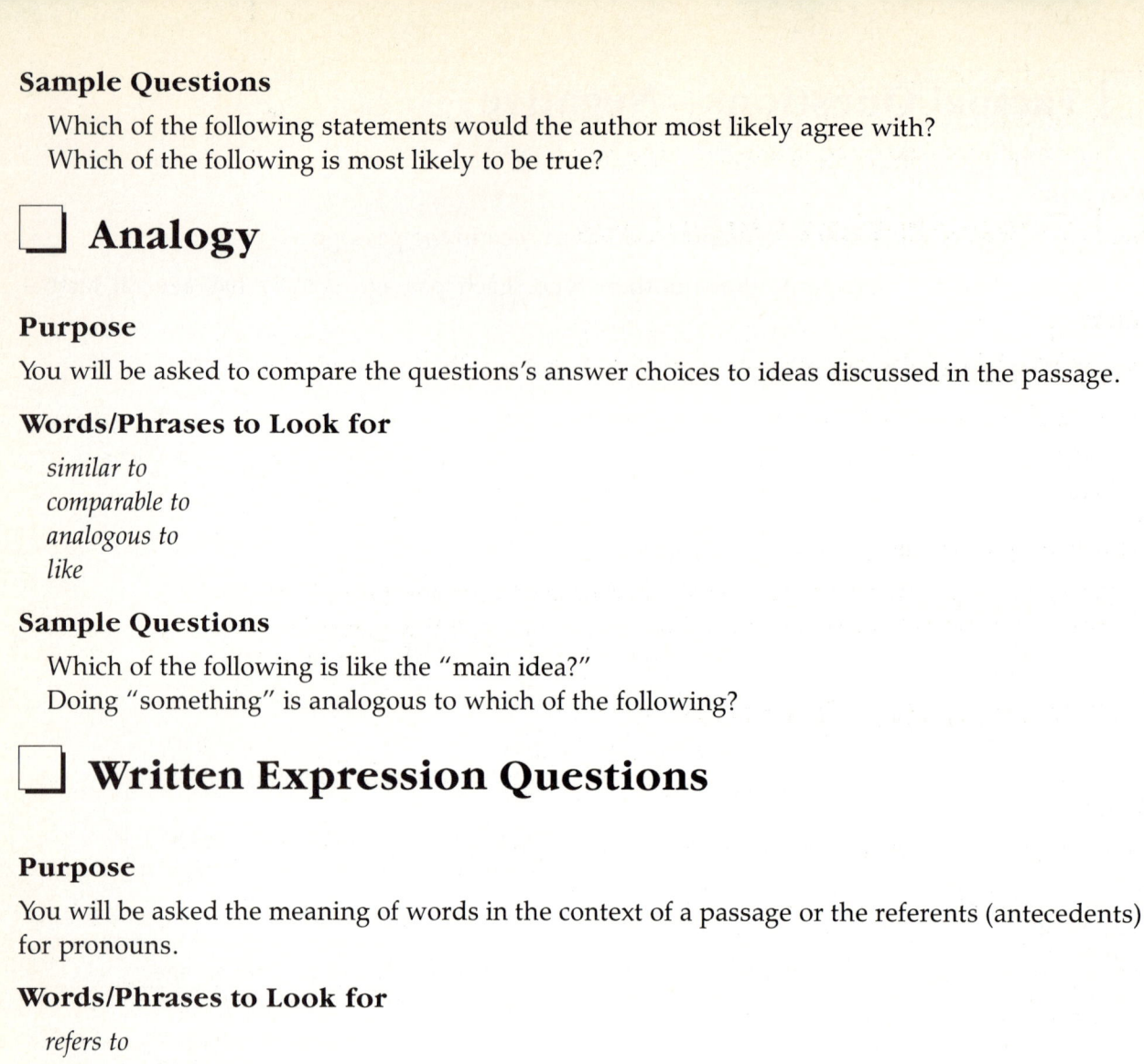

refers to
means in this context

Sample Questions

The word "this" in the last sentence refers to . . .
What does "word" mean in the context of this passage?

☐ Follow-On Questions

Purpose

You will be asked to guess what information might follow the passage.

Words/Phrases to Look for

In the next paragraph, . . .
Next sentence

Sample Questions

In the next paragraph, the author will most likely mention . . .
How might the author conclude the discussion?

☐ Organization Questions

Purpose
You will be asked to determine how the author presented the information.

Words/Phrases to Look for
which details
present this discussion

Sample Questions
Which of the following details does the author use to support his opinion?
How would you characterize the author's presentation of the material?

☐ Viewpoint Questions

Purpose
You will be asked to determine the author's tone, attitude, or purpose.

Words/Phrases to Look for
point of view
author's purpose
author's attitude
general tone
feel

Sample Questions
How does the author feel about the characters mentioned in the passage?
Which of the following best describes the author's purpose?
What is the general tone of the passage?

STRATEGIES FOR THE TOEFL

1. Learn to recognize the question type. If you know what the question is asking you to do, it will be easy to answer it.
2. Pay attention to what you are reading. Use the Skill-Building Exercises to help you focus on the passage.
3. Pay attention to the first sentence. It usually gives the main idea of the passage.
4. Read the questions first; when you read, look for the answer.
5. Answer every question. If you aren't sure, GUESS.

STRATEGY-BUILDING ACTIVITIES

Read this sample passage and note the questions that follow.

Questions 1–10 refer to the following passage.

In 1980, a new theory about the extinction of the dinosaurs was announced to the world. The theory generated a series of new and exciting ideas. It also sparked an intense debate within the scientific community.

The theory was the work of Luis and Walter Alvarez, a father-and-son team. In 1977, geologist Walter Alvarez discovered the element iridium in a 65-million-year-old layer of clay. The discovery was significant because iridium is rare on Earth but common in extraterrestrial objects, such as comets and asteroids. Using this and other evidence, Walter and his Nobel-Prize-winning father Luis formulated their theory. According to the Alvarezes, an asteroid struck the earth 65 million years ago. The impact created huge dust clouds, which blocked out light from the sun. The lack of sunlight and the resulting cold temperatures caused the death of many species of plants and animals as would a global nuclear war. Included among these were the dinosaurs. This theory became known as the asteroid-impact theory.

Main Idea

1. What is the best title for the passage?
   - (A) The Discovery of Asteroids
   - (B) Father and Son Geologists
   - (C) What Killed the Dinosaurs
   - (D) The Importance of Sunlight

Factual Question—Positive

2. According to the passage, asteroids
   - (A) are 65 million years old
   - (B) contain iridium
   - (C) create huge dust clouds
   - (D) were discovered by Alvarez

Factual Question—Negative

3. Which of the following was NOT mentioned as a result of the asteroid impact?
   - (A) Huge dust clouds
   - (B) Lack of sunlight
   - (C) Cold temperature
   - (D) Creation of new species

Inference Question—Specific Application

4. Which of the following is most necessary to sustain life forms?
   - (A) Sunlight
   - (B) Iridium
   - (C) Asteroids
   - (D) Geologists

Inference Question—General Application

5. Which of the following would most likely help geologists date changes in the Earth?
   (A) Minerals in the Earth's layers
   (B) Nobel Prize theories
   (C) Periods of cold temperatures
   (D) Extraterrestrial objects

Analogy Question

6. The events leading to the mass extinction of the dinosaurs are most comparable to which of the following?
   (A) World War I
   (B) Demise of plant forms
   (C) Scientific debates
   (D) Global nuclear war

Written Expression Question

7. The word "it" in the third sentence refers to
   (A) the new theory
   (B) the extinction
   (C) the series
   (D) the debate

Organization Question

8. In which of the following ways does the author present the discussion of the asteroid-impact theory?
   (A) As a description of the evidence
   (B) As a criticism of Alvarez
   (C) As a summary of scientific theories
   (D) As a comparison of comets and asteroids

Follow-On Question

9. In the next paragraph, the author will probably discuss
   (A) the debate in the scientific community
   (B) why Dr. Alvarez won the Nobel Prize
   (C) the extinction of other life forms
   (D) how sunlight affects mankind

Viewpoint Question

10. Which of the following best describes how the author would characterize the asteroid-impact theory?
    (A) Irrelevant
    (B) Significant
    (C) Uninspired
    (D) Predictable

Reading Targets 299

SKILLS TO DEVELOP

1. Learn to make reading a habit.

    The only way you can become a good reader is through practice. You cannot read a few paragraphs in your English book once a week and become a fluent reader. You need to read constantly. You should carry something to read with you wherever you go. Tear out pages of English magazines, for example, and carry them in your pocket. Whenever you have the chance, pull out a page and read a paragraph or two.

    You should read in as many different subject areas as you can. Try to find English books on different subjects and read a few paragraphs in each chapter in each book. Your eyes and mind need to practice. Your eyes need to practice moving quickly across the page from left to right, and your mind needs to practice making quick associations between the printed word and the meaning.

2. Learn to read with a purpose.

    When you begin to read you should ask yourself a basic question: *Why am I reading this?*

    If you are reading to practice your English, you will read in a certain way. You will read slowly and concentrate on the relationship between the words and the grammatical structures. If you are reading for information about a particular subject, you will read in another way. You will focus on main parts and supporting facts. You use the grammar of the passage as a means, not an end.

3. Learn to study English while practicing reading.

    Reading to practice English is the way most foreign students read English. In school you do not read English to learn about a particular subject; for example, you do not read English to learn history. You read English to learn how a sentence is put together, how the verbs agree with the subject, what the clause is, etc. This is the way you have to read for the Structure and Written Expression section of the TOEFL, but it is not the way you should read for the Reading Comprehension section.

4. Learn to read for specific information.

    Reading for information is the kind of reading you do in your own language. You do not stop to analyze tenses and clauses when you pick up a book written in your native language. You understand structure without thinking about it. It is second nature to you.

    Now you must develop this skill in English. You must be able to read beyond the clause markers and prepositions and other structure clues. You must learn to read for meaning.

    A reading comprehension test measures how well you understand the meaning of a passage. It measures your ability to understand the author's main idea and the facts used to support the main idea. It measures your ability to read "between the lines" and use contextual clues to infer what the author implied. It measures your ability to do this as quickly as a native speaker of English.

    To improve your reading comprehension, you have to develop certain skills. These skills include skimming or scanning a reading passage; identifying the main idea and supporting statements; making inferences; and using context clues to help you guess.

5. Learn to skim and scan.

   Scanning means looking over a passage very quickly to find specific information, such as a date, a name, or a particular word. Skimming means getting a quick, general overview of the passage. Both are techniques you will begin to use today and continue to use each time you read something in English or your own language. Every time you read you should use a technique called SQ3R: Survey, Question, Read, Review, and Recall.

SQ3R and the TOEFL

Survey

A good survey of a reading passage is very important. When you walk into a strange house at night, you may have no idea how large it is until you go through all the rooms, opening doors that lead into other rooms. Starting to read line by line is like exploring a house in the dark. You won't know what it's all about until you get to the end. Most people would feel more comfortable if they had some idea of how large the house was without walking through every room. Similarly, most people would feel more comfortable knowing what a book is about before they begin to read.

To survey a reading passage, read the first and last lines and let your eye pick up as many words as it can in a few seconds. A survey should take no more than five or ten seconds.

This survey will give you a *general idea* of the passage you are reading. You are preparing your brain for *specific information*. You can generally tell from your survey the main subject and the time frame of the passage.

Question

When you finish your survey, you know something, but not very much. You do not know **who, when, what, where,** and **why.** So you begin to formulate some questions that are of interest to you. For example, if in your survey you noticed the words **invention, 19th century,** and **Atlantic Ocean,** your questions might be:

Who invented something?
Did they invent it in the 19th century?
What did they invent?
Where did they live?
Did the invention cross over/above/under the ocean?
Why was this important?

The reading passage may or may not answer these questions. That is not important. What is important is that you have a specific goal for reading and that you read toward that goal. Knowing that the answers are *not* in the passage is as important as finding the answers in the passage.

Read

Once you have made your survey and asked yourself questions to give yourself a goal for reading, you read. You read to find specific information that will answer your questions or that will create new questions. You have become an active reader with a purpose. You now read quickly and efficiently.

> **Review and Recall**
>
> If a text is important enough to read once, it is important enough to read again. So skim the passage again to pick up missing details and remind yourself of what was important. Tomorrow or later try to recall what you read. You should learn to test your reading comprehension. What did the author want to say?
>
> *What generalizations did he make?*
> *With what facts did he support them?*
> *What did he imply?*

In the TOEFL, there will be reading passages on a variety of topics. Some will interest you more than others. But you have to treat them as if they were equally important.

First, survey the comprehension questions and answer choices. Look for key words that will help you when you survey the passage. What do the questions ask you to do?

What do they expect of me?
Do they ask for the main idea?
Do they ask for details?
Do they ask for a definition?
Do they ask for the author's opinion?
Do they ask for my opinion?

After you have surveyed the passage and formulated some questions, begin to read. **BUT READ QUICKLY! DO NOT READ WORD BY WORD.** Read phrase by phrase, idea by idea. Finish quickly and try to answer the questions.

If you cannot remember the answers, **SCAN** for the particular information. **DON'T READ EVERY WORD! SCAN THE PASSAGE!** Keep your eyes moving quickly, looking for specific information.

SKILL-BUILDING EXERCISES

The following exercises will help you develop these skills.

1. Before you read the passages, try to identify the question types. Look at the questions in the reading passages in this section and write beside them the type of questions they are. **DO NOT READ THE PASSAGE. DO NOT READ THE ANSWER CHOICES. DO NOT ANSWER THE QUESTIONS.** Read only the questions, not the passages or answer choices. The answers for this exercise are at the back of the book.

2. Practice skimming and scanning. You should always work as fast as possible on the TOEFL. The sooner you finish, the more time you have to check your work.

    In the Reading Comprehension section, you will have 55 minutes to answer 60 questions. That's less than a minute for each question! Use this timetable as a guide.

Section	Questions	Minutes
Vocabulary	30	10
Reading Comprehension	30	45

This means you will have to do at least three vocabulary questions in one minute. In the Reading Comprehension section, you will have to spend less than one minute on each question, because you will need three to five minutes for each reading passage. Because of this very short time, you **MUST** practice your skimming and scanning skills.

4. Now, you can read the passages as if you were taking the TOEFL. Practice the strategies you learned earlier.

HUMANITIES

Questions 1–6

The word *icon* means image, picture, or likeness. Originally, the term referred to all depictions of religious subjects; now, its significance has become restricted, and it denotes a portable religious picture, either painted on a wooden panel, or in enamel on metal, or executed in mosaic. Unless made for use in processions, most wooden panels were painted on one side only.

The selection of wood was of the greatest importance, as resinous wood was apt to harbor woodworm. Most favored were the nonresinous woods, such as lime, alder, birch and cypress; pine was used in Russia, where it tended to be less resinous than in the Mediterranean. The panel was cut to size, and in most cases a flat surface was hollowed out from the center in order to provide a raised border. This practice also made warping less likely. However, some icons have a completely flat surface.

The next step was to cover the panel with a sheet of loosely woven canvas that was treated with a mixture of gesso and powdered alabaster, or the finest grade of chalk. This was laid on in layers, each of which was allowed to dry before the application of the next, until there were about eight layers. On the resulting smooth surface the artist painted.

Finally, the finished painting was given a coat of varnish. Since the varnish absorbs dust and soot from its surroundings, the brilliant colors soon began to darken and recede, and the custom of covering an icon with an ornate sheet of precious metal developed, so that only the most significant parts were left visible. It is possible to remove the ancient varnish, so as to restore the colors to their original brilliance.

1. What does the passage mainly discuss?
   (A) The etymology of the word *icon*
   (B) Customs surrounding icons
   (C) The making of icons
   (D) The history of icons

2. According to the passage why were nonresinous woods preferable?
   (A) Nonresinous woods were more available.
   (B) Pines were less resinous in the Mediterranean areas.
   (C) Nonresinous woods did not warp.
   (D) Resinous woods could be damaged by woodworm.

3. According to the passage, on what type of surface did the artist actually paint?
   - (A) A flat surface hollowed out from the wood
   - (B) A canvas treated with gesso and powdered alabaster
   - (C) On top of a coat of varnish
   - (D) On a sheet of precious metal

4. In the last paragraph, what is said about the varnish?
   - (A) It restored the colors of the original painting.
   - (B) It protected the painting from fading.
   - (C) It caused changes in the colors of the icon.
   - (D) It made the colors of the painting shiny.

5. Which of the following best describes the organization of the passage?
   - (A) A definition and several examples
   - (B) A step-by-step description
   - (C) The history of iconography
   - (D) Directions for restoring icons

6. Which of the following phrases could be substituted for the phrase "so as" in the last paragraph without changing the meaning of the passage?
   - (A) So there
   - (B) And in so doing
   - (C) Because of
   - (D) Meanwhile

Questions 7–12

Social life is essential to human existence. We remain in the company of other people from the day we are born to the time of our death. People teach us to speak. They show us how to relate to our surroundings. They give us the help and the support we need to achieve personal security and mental well-being. Alone, we are relatively frail, defenseless primates; in groups we are astonishingly adaptive and powerful. Yet despite these advantages, well-organized human societies are difficult to achieve. Some species manage to produce social organization genetically. But people are not like bees or ants. We lack the genetically coded directions for behavior that make these insects successful social animals. Although we seem to inherit a general need for social approval, we also harbor individual interests and ambitions that can block or destroy close social ties. To overcome these divisive tendencies, human groups organize around several principles designed to foster cooperation and group loyalty. Kinship is among the strongest of these.

Whether large or small, kinship systems always include families. Usually these consist of at least an adult couple and their children. This nuclear family, as it is called, is characteristic of American society, and it lasts only as long as its members continue to remain at home. In a great many societies, the ideal family size is much larger than this. The Chinese family often consists of a couple, their sons and their sons' wives, and their grandchildren and any other unattached children. Extended families of this sort provide a very different style of life than do our small families.

7. What would be the best title for this passage?
   (A) American and Chinese Family Structures
   (B) Learning to Speak
   (C) Kinship Systems
   (D) Human and Insect Societies

8. How does the author illustrate some of his or her points?
   (A) By analogy
   (B) With recent theories
   (C) Through contrast
   (D) With historical examples

9. What does the author mainly intend to do in this passage?
   (A) To define human social order
   (B) To argue for larger families
   (C) To encourage social organization
   (D) To propose a new kinship system

10. The author believes that successful social grouping among humans can sometimes be impeded by
    (A) kinship
    (B) nuclear families
    (C) individualism
    (D) loyalty

11. Who does the word "our" refer to in the last sentence?
    (A) Humans
    (B) Chinese
    (C) Americans
    (D) Students

12. What does the paragraph immediately following the passage probably discuss?
    (A) Specific differences between nuclear and extended families
    (B) Why small families are better than extended families
    (C) How Chinese families spend their time
    (D) How single people maintain family ties

Questions 13–18

Culture is learned. At the moment of birth, the human being lacks a culture—a system of beliefs, knowledge, patterns of customary behavior. But from that moment until we die, each of us participates in a kind of universal schooling that teaches us our native culture. Laughing and smiling are genetic responses, but the infant soon learns when to smile, when to laugh, and even how to laugh. Crying is an inborn behavior, but every infant soon learns the rules for crying in a particular culture.

During the first few years of life, cultural learning proceeds at an intense and rapid rate. Informally, without thinking about it, children in every society learn their native language, kinship terms, family structure, how and when to eat, etiquette for everyday life, what goals are worth achieving, and hundreds of other things. Culture is a kind of social heredity; passed on from one generation to the next, it is acquired through learning.

The customs we acquire as members of a society have a curious effect on us. Though we find them hard to learn, with practice we conform and eventually we come to feel that these customs are right and natural. In time, the explicit rules for customary behavior fade from awareness. Most people are not conscious of the culture that guides their behavior. Conformity is effortless; it feels comfortable and secure. For example, each of us speaks a native language fluently, yet we are usually unable to state the rules of its grammar. Similarly, people abide by the rest of their culture with confidence, yet they lack a knowledge of its structure. We say then that culture has a tacit, taken-for-granted quality.

13. What does the passage mainly discuss?
    (A) Rules for a particular culture
    (B) Culture and its structure
    (C) Why we learn culture so slowly
    (D) How we acquire culture

14. Which of the following is NOT mentioned as a part of culture?
    (A) Geography
    (B) Manners
    (C) Personal goals
    (D) Language

15. According to the passage, why do we accept our own culture so effortlessly?
    (A) Because it is a genetic response
    (B) Because we learn it informally from society
    (C) Because it is unique
    (D) Because we are curious

16. According to the passage, when do we begin to learn culture?
    (A) After the first few years of life
    (B) From the moment of birth
    (C) As soon as we become aware of culture itself
    (D) When we start school

17. The author implies that when people feel comfortable in their culture, they
    (A) feel no need for etiquette
    (B) rarely conform to cultural expectations
    (C) usually cannot explain the culture structure
    (D) advance socially at a fast pace

18. How long does a person participate in the learning of his native culture, according to the passage?
    (A) Throughout infancy
    (B) Until middle age
    (C) All his/her life
    (D) During childhood

HISTORY

Questions 1-6

Perhaps fifteen to twenty thousand years ago man first trod American soil, crossing from Siberia to Alaska via the Bering Strait. We can guess at the habits of the first invaders of this continent by comparing them with their fellow men who lived at the same period in western Europe. This is a very hazardous experiment, as the mere fact that two peoples are contemporaneous does not imply that they are on the same cultural level. However, in all probability, there was a general resemblance between Upper Paleolithic man of western Europe and the invader of America, and so he may serve as our type. He lived either out in the open or in the entrances of caves, and dressed in the skins of the animals he slew with his stone- or bone-pointed spear, propelled by a spear-thrower. He employed flint for his weapons, but had not yet learned to polish hard stone. He had no pottery, agriculture, or domestic animals, and depended entirely on hunting for his food.

Probably the first immigrants drifted across in small bands, and their descendants traveled southward, populating in the course of thousands of years all of the American continents. Their remains found in caves in Brazil and Chile demonstrate that they had exceedingly long heads and low, retreating foreheads. Broad-headed people followed by the same route in sufficient numbers to swamp their predecessors. Later arrivals undoubtedly brought with them new arts and crafts, new religious conceptions, and new forms of social organization.

1. What does the passage mainly discuss?
   (A) The influence of ancient Europe in America
   (B) Aggression in prehistoric America
   (C) Contrasts between prehistoric Europeans and Americans
   (D) The population of ancient America

2. How many migrations to the Americas does the writer refer to?
   (A) Only one
   (B) Three
   (C) Fifteen
   (D) Thousands

3. The author considers his comparison of ancient Europeans to American migrants to be
   (A) inexact
   (B) sensitive
   (C) comprehensive
   (D) intuitive

4. In line 7, the pronoun "he" refers to
   (A) the invader of America
   (B) a male animal
   (C) a Brazilian
   (D) a Chinese

5. In line 12, the word "bands" means
   (A) orchestras
   (B) vehicles
   (C) groups
   (D) areas

6. According to the passage, what evidence is there of the physical attributes of the first immigrants?
   (A) Careful inspection of their arts and crafts gives clues.
   (B) There is no tangible evidence.
   (C) Educated guesses are based on the customs of the people.
   (D) Their skeletons have been found.

Questions 7–9

The popular mind was excited by Einstein's Theory of Relativity. So far as Einstein could be understood, he was saying that it was no longer possible for ordinary people to comprehend the universe, and that what scientists actually did understand was strange and unsettling. Time, space, matter, energy—all these dissolved, shifted, blurred. Everything depended on where the observer was located; relativity replaced fixity; ultimate things were hidden.

7. Another way to say what Einstein was saying is that
   (A) nobody would ever be able to study the nature of the universe
   (B) nonscientists would no longer be able to comprehend the universe, but scientists would
   (C) even scientists would have trouble comprehending the universe
   (D) people should give up trying to understand the universe

8. Which of the following would be strange to a scientist?
   (A) The dissolution of energy
   (B) Matter
   (C) Time-space shifts
   (D) All of the above

9. The author implies, but does not directly state, that
   (A) Einstein was a very strange man
   (B) people were drawn to Einstein's work because it was unfathomable
   (C) relativity is the final word in physics
   (D) man will never prove that God exists

Questions 10–13

In the early 1930s a new religious voice burst on the American scene, that of Reinhold Niebuhr. Soon he became the most influential thinker in American Protestantism. Niebuhr had watched national and international developments from his pastorate in Detroit in a mood of growing disenchantment. The war had horrified him. The facts of industrial life in Detroit convinced him that it was fruitless to preach sermons about love and kindness, for the actual conditions of survival made it impossible for people to be always loving and kind.

10. Reinhold Niebuhr must have been
    (A) a war activist
    (B) a theologian
    (C) a disenchanted politician
    (D) a stoic

11. Niebuhr came to prominence from
    (A) a European background
    (B) his military background
    (C) an American religious post
    (D) a university post

12. The event which horrified Niebuhr must have been
    (A) World War I
    (B) the actual conditions of survival
    (C) the Great Depression
    (D) the downfall of American Protestantism

13. According to the passage, which of the following best describes Niebuhr?
    (A) Niebuhr converted to a different religion.
    (B) Niebuhr urged men to be loving and kind.
    (C) Niebuhr stopped being loving and kind.
    (D) Niebuhr gave up the idea that man could always be loving and kind.

EDUCATION

Questions 1–6

Many teachers today believe that they teach thinking skills. In most instances, however, what they actually do involves putting students into situations where they are simply made to think and expected to do it as best they can. Most methods teachers customarily use to "teach" thinking are indirect, rather than direct. These methods are based on the questionable assumption that by doing thinking, students automatically learn how to engage in such thinking.

Educational researchers have pointed out time and again that learning how to think is not an automatic by-product of studying certain subjects, assimilating the products of someone else's thinking, or simply being asked to think about a subject or topic. Nor do youngsters learn how to engage in critical thinking effectively by themselves. There is little reason to believe that competence in critical thinking can be an incidental outcome of instruction directed, or that appears to be directed, at other ends. By concentrating on the detail of the subject matter being studied, most common approaches to teaching critical thinking so obscure the skills of how to engage in thinking that students fail to master them.

If we want to improve student proficiency in thinking, we must use more direct methods of instruction than we now use. First, we must establish as explicit goals of instruction, the attitude, skill, and knowledge components of critical thinking. Second, we must employ direct, systematic instruction in these skills prior to, during, and following student introduction to and use of these skills in our classrooms.

1. The author believes that the teaching of thinking is inadequate today because
   (A) the students ask few questions
   (B) it is taught indirectly
   (C) students are not put into "thinking" situations
   (D) the concept is too complicated to communicate

2. According to the passage, who points out that thinking must be taught?
   (A) Critics
   (B) The youngsters themselves
   (C) Educational researchers
   (D) Most parents

3. How many steps does the author suggest to teach thinking?
   (A) 2
   (B) 3
   (C) 4
   (D) 5

4. Which of the following best describes the attitude of the author toward his topic?
   (A) Cynical
   (B) Persuasive
   (C) Neutral
   (D) Desperate

5. With which of the following statements would the writer disagree?
   (A) Critical thinking is a natural by-product of academic achievement.
   (B) Uses of critical thinking should be taught before their application.
   (C) The ability to think critically must be consciously cultivated.
   (D) Critical thinking skills must be constantly reinforced.

6. The paragraph immediately following this passage probably discusses
   (A) ways to impart the attitude, skills and knowledge components of critical thinking
   (B) after-class activities to reinforce critical thinking
   (C) ways to concentrate attention on details of a subject area
   (D) teaching critical thinking by using indirect methods

Questions 7–12

When we try to teach children anything from how to count to how to take a bath, we can experience the frustrations of having youngsters, occasionally or often, reject these efforts. Children, in turn, are often frustrated by parents who think teaching is a matter of imposing some learning on them. Children may be "born learners," though they certainly won't display this all the time.
5 Many parents are not "born teachers" at any time.

To be a good teacher, patience is essential, but it's not enough. A good teacher needs to be able to work up and down a scale of greater and lesser difficulty. For example, let's say you're reading a book about trucks to your child. With a very young child, first you might ask your child to point to the bigger truck. Then you prompt your child to move to "yes" and "no" responses.
10 The next move is to whole-sentence answers and finally to your asking, "Tell me about this truck."

Creativity and intelligence thrive on discussion. Sometimes adults, who need the practice least, do most of the talking, while children sit by passively. This is unfortunate, because it is the

interplay of discussion and experience that encourages children to use their minds actively to
formulate ideas. Probably the best teaching tip is, "Don't talk too much!"

A good teacher keeps explanations short and backs them up with tangible demonstrations. If you are teaching measurement, actually measure a room. If you are teaching science, let children relive the drama and excitement of discovery.

7. According to the passage, a successful teacher should always
   (A) make use of "yes" and "no" questions
   (B) provide a comfortable learning environment
   (C) engage the student in conversation
   (D) make use of guided role-playing

8. The best title for the passage would be
   (A) The Uses of Natural Intelligence
   (B) Methods to Ensure Learning
   (C) The Importance of Children's Play
   (D) Discussion Topics for Today's Teacher

9. How does the author recommend that teachers present material to the child?
   (A) Infrequently
   (B) Uncritically
   (C) Progressively
   (D) Subliminally

10. The tone that the author uses in this passage might best be described as
    (A) academic
    (B) conversational
    (C) scientific
    (D) humorous

11. In line 13, the word "this" refers to
    (A) discussion
    (B) talkative adults and passive children
    (C) interplay
    (D) discussion and experience combined

12. Which of the following does the author believe to be an essential quality needed by an effective teacher?
    (A) A sense of authority
    (B) Patience
    (C) A sense of humor
    (D) Expressiveness

Reading Targets 311

Questions 13–18

I was drawn to the computer because it has a number of obvious advantages as a teaching tool—speed of operation, memory capacity, and flexibility—and some not-so-obvious advantages, like the opportunity it offers to limit the errors that can be made in the presentation of material. It can help teachers serve the greatest number of children by making maximum use of their time. I wasn't looking for something "teacher-proof," because the role of the adult, of the teacher in the classroom, is critically important to the success of any educational system. I didn't envision a sterile room where children are taught in isolation, surrounded by whirring technology.

What I did see was the shift away from methods of teaching centered on and solely dependent upon the quality of a teacher. Teaching remains an excessively labor-intensive activity. There is nothing inherently wrong in a school where the only technology is the teacher, a book, a piece of chalk, and a blackboard; but large classes, transient student populations, insufficient operating budgets, and erratic use of technology limit teachers' effectiveness.

On the other hand, I was also keenly aware that the computer industry and some educators were making outrageous predictions about the future of computers and education. There was talk of the awesome power of the computer and the ability of the high-tech revolution to create massive changes in education. In the face of these blustery arguments, I tried to keep in mind what John Dewey said many years ago: "Beware of the argument that proves too much."

13. Which of the following would be the best title for the selection?
    (A) Why Students Enjoy Computers
    (B) Modern Educational Methods
    (C) Why Teach with Computers
    (D) Classroom Techniques versus Technology

14. According to the passage, which of the following statements is true?
    (A) The advantages of computers are more extensive than we realize.
    (B) A teacher's performance determines the degree of success in a classroom.
    (C) Children seem to do best when they are left on their own with computers.
    (D) No teacher needs to be present when computers are used in class.

15. In which type of book would the passage be most likely to appear?
    (A) A science workbook
    (B) An encyclopedia
    (C) An education text
    (D) A computer manual

16. The author of this passage probably works in the field of
    (A) payroll services
    (B) computer marketing
    (C) psychological counseling
    (D) teacher training

17. The word "their" (line 4) refers to
    (A) children
    (B) errors
    (C) computers
    (D) teachers

18. The author of the passage believes that
    (A) early expectations for computers in schools were overblown
    (B) computers should give a teacher more free time
    (C) a school with minimal supplies is by definition deficient
    (D) today's teachers are more effective than those in the past

SCIENCE

Questions 1–6

Crack open an acorn and find a world of creatures that call this nut home. At least 30 kinds of animals and plants may take up residence in a single acorn while it grows on the tree and decays on the ground. Wireworms, springtails, fly maggots, cheese mites, and minute fungus beetles eat the decaying nutmeat and fungi. Millipedes, slugs, and snails scavenge; centipedes and other scavengers attack these inhabitants. And slave-making ants sometimes make their abode in hollowed-out shells.

Often the first animal to invade an acorn is the acorn weevil, which strikes while the nut is still on the tree. Using tiny teeth at the tip of a long slender snout, the 1-centimeter-long weevil cuts through the nut's tough shell. The weevil eats the nutmeat that enters its hollow snout during the drilling. A female may lay one egg deep inside each tiny channel she excavates. When a larva hatches, it eats a larger chamber into the acorn, which continues developing until it falls from the tree. The jolt of the acorn as it hits the ground often signals a fully grown weevil larva to emerge.

How long an acorn survives invasion depends on its size and the sequence of insects involved. As acorns die, more animals move in.

Acorns are not sought solely by creatures tiny enough to live in them. More than 80 North American birds and mammals make fresh acorns part of their diet.

1. With which of the following is the passage mainly concerned?
    (A) Acorn weevils
    (B) Worms and parasites
    (C) Acorns
    (D) Insects

2. According to the passage, when does the acorn weevil enter the acorn?
    (A) After it hits the ground
    (B) While still on the tree
    (C) When parasites attack
    (D) After the acorn dies

3. According to the passage, which of the following statements is NOT true?
   (A) Acorns are attacked both on the tree and on the ground.
   (B) Birds eat acorns.
   (C) It is common for many animals to live in an acorn.
   (D) Animals cannot survive in dead acorns.

4. Which of the following could be inferred from the passage?
   (A) Ants have tiny teeth similar to the acorn weevil.
   (B) Acorn weevils depend on acorns exclusively.
   (C) Most birds and mammals rely on acorns for their diet.
   (D) Acorns contain protein.

5. According to the passage, an acorn is
   (A) an egg
   (B) a tree
   (C) a fruit
   (D) a nut

6. How many birds and mammals eat fresh acorns?
   (A) None
   (B) All of them
   (C) More than 80
   (D) Less than 80

Questions 7–11

The human tongue is like a squid tentacle. It's not as long, usually, but it is almost as maneuverable and, more significantly, both violate one of the widely repeated teachings of elementary biology.

Beginning texts often claim that skeletons are necessary for muscles to produce useful motion. The biceps, for example, move the lower arm by contracting and pulling a tendon that runs from the muscle, which is in the upper arm, around the elbow to the lower arm. Without the upper arm bone as braced framework, the contracting biceps would simply shrivel the arm lengthwise.

If that's so, how can the utterly boneless squids and octopuses move their arms so precisely, grabbing swimming shrimps in less than a tenth of a second?

William Kier, a professor at the University of North Carolina, pursued this curiosity and discovered a previously unrecognized mechanical principle that operates not only in soft-bodied invertebrates but also in vertebrate tongues and in elephants' trunks.

When a muscle flexes, it shortens in length but grows in thickness, maintaining a constant volume. Kier found that while bulging, a muscle generates a powerful force that pushes in a direction perpendicular to the pulling force of the muscle contracting.

Vertebrates generally waste this bulging force but Kier found that invertebrates such as the octopus use it to provide the braced framework over which other muscles work. The inside of a tentacle, like the inside of a tongue, has muscles running in three directions—lengthwise, sideways (at right angles to the lengthwise muscles), and helically around the outside of the organ.

No matter which way the animal wants to extend or bend the tentacle or tongue, sets of muscles contract to create a bulging, rigid framework and then pull over that framework.

7. Which of the following is the best title for the passage?
   (A) The Human Tongue versus the Squid Tentacle
   (B) Vertebrates and Invertebrates
   (C) Muscles: Using the Bulging Force
   (D) The Principles of Mechanics

8. According to the passage, what violation of biology does the human tongue have in common with the squid tentacle?
   (A) They are capable of maneuverability but are boneless.
   (B) They exploit muscles in three different directions.
   (C) They produce movement by alternately pulling and contracting a muscle.
   (D) They utilize a mechanical principle that operates in vertebrates and invertebrates.

9. In the second paragraph, the word "skeletons" could best be replaced by which of the following?
   (A) Specimens
   (B) Basic systems
   (C) Bones
   (D) Proteins

10. At what point in the passage does the author first discuss supportive research?
    (A) Second paragraph
    (B) Third paragraph
    (C) Fourth paragraph
    (D) Sixth paragraph

11. Where in the passage does the author offer a comparison of the insides of the tentacle and tongue?
    (A) First paragraph
    (B) Second paragraph
    (C) Third paragraph
    (D) Sixth paragraph

Questions 12–15

The basic idea of spontaneous generation can be easily understood. If food is allowed to stand for some time, it putrefies, and when the putrefied material is examined microscopically, it is found to be teeming with bacteria. Where do these bacteria come from, since they are not seen in fresh food? Some people said they developed from seeds or germs that entered the food from the air, whereas others said that they arose spontaneously.

Spontaneous generation would mean that life could arise from something nonliving, and many people could not imagine something so complex as a living cell arising spontaneously from dead materials. The most powerful opponent of spontaneous generation was the French chemist Louis Pasteur, whose work on this problem was the most exacting and convincing. His precise, faultless experiments earned the support of many people.

12. Spontaneous generation is defined as
    (A) the process by which food gets rotten
    (B) the microscopic examination of bacteria
    (C) the view that bacteria grow from seeds or germs in the air
    (D) life arising from something nonliving

13. Louis Pasteur was an opponent of which of the following?
    (A) Germs are microscopic in size.
    (B) Germs entered food from the atmosphere.
    (C) Life could arise from dead materials.
    (D) Food should be examined microscopically for bacteria.

14. The author's view of Pasteur's work is that
    (A) Pasteur convinced everyone that he was correct
    (B) Pasteur was quite careful and precise
    (C) Pasteur made some basic mistakes
    (D) Pasteur could not disprove the theory of spontaneous generation

15. The reason why many people tended to agree with Pasteur is that
    (A) the alternative view seemed probable
    (B) Pasteur rarely made mistakes
    (C) his explanation was consistent with their religious views
    (D) Pasteur was the greatest scientist of his day

APPLIED SCIENCE

Questions 1–6

Parents probably have the most effect on children's abilities and inclinations for mental development. Concerned parents model thinking; their language engages differential cognitive structures. Often what we do in schools to teach thinking is remedial for those students whose parents do not provide this mediation.

Principals are the primary link between schools and the community. They have the opportunity to involve parents in decision making, interpret school programs to the community, and educate parents in their dominant role as mediators of their children's cognitive development.

Some parents believe that schools should teach only the basics. They may judge modern education in terms of their experience as students—during a time when the value of thinking was not necessarily recognized. Principals can help parents enhance their aspirations for their children by stressing that reasoning is basic for survival in the future, critical thinking is required for college entrance and success, cognitive processes are prerequisite to mastery in all school subjects, and career security and advancement are dependent on innovation, insightfulness, and cooperation.

Many parents appear to be realizing that reasoning is the fourth "R," and there is a definite trend toward increased parental concern for children's cognitive development. Principals should engage parents to search for ways to encourage children to use thinking by stimulating their interest in school and learning, environmental issues, time and money planning, and so on.

1. According to the third paragraph, many parents
   (A) are concerned about the costs of education
   (B) prefer a dominant role in their children's education
   (C) did not study reasoning as students
   (D) provide adequate examples for their children's development

2. The best title for this passage would be
   (A) Instruction in Reasoning in Today's Schools
   (B) Parental Involvement in Schools Brings Success
   (C) Innovation in the Schools via Community Outreach
   (D) The Importance of Principals in a Child's Development

3. The author would probably agree with which one of the following statements?
   (A) Schools are interested in criticism from the community.
   (B) Education in the past was inferior to today's.
   (C) A principal can do nothing unless he or she knows a child's parents.
   (D) Cognitive development does not occur spontaneously.

4. Which of the following is NOT mentioned as an area in which the ability to reason is important?
   (A) Success in college
   (B) Career advancement
   (C) Artistic development
   (D) Financial planning

5. Critical thinking can be defined as
   (A) Cognitive development
   (B) Manual skills
   (C) Reasoning
   (D) High scores

6. In the phrase "their dominant role" (line 7), the word "their" refers to
   (A) parents
   (B) principals
   (C) students
   (D) schools

Questions 7–12

In a study reported recently in the Harvard Medical School Mental Health Letter, adults who had been raised with harsh physical discipline were found to be almost three times as likely to develop depression or alcoholism as were those whose parents had brought them up with gentler rules.

Researchers interviewed a group of 200 St. Louis residents about their psychiatric history and the parental discipline they'd experienced as elementary school children. One hundred of the subjects either had suffered a major episode of depression or had a history of alcohol abuse; the other half of the study group had no psychiatric diagnosis at all.

Of those with a history of depression or alcoholism, 40 percent said they had been beaten by their parents. Only 14 percent of the others told of receiving harsh, unfair, or inconsistent punishment.

In general, the study also revealed mothers are milder disciplinarians than fathers. But in households where one parent does all the disciplining—whether the mother or the father—punishment is likely to be more severe.

Parents should try to be more lenient in their day-to-day handling of misbehavior, suggests Julia Cohen, a family therapist. "If discipline overwhelms the quality of the parent's relationship with a child, it puts the emphasis on control rather than on fostering the growth of the child."

7. What is the author's main point?
   (A) Alcoholic adults consistently have a history of physical abuse.
   (B) More research needs to be done on the effect of parental alcoholism on children.
   (C) Physical abuse toward children can affect their mental health as adults.
   (D) Children raised with little discipline tend to experience depression and alcoholism as adults.

8. It can be inferred from the passage that
   (A) fathers are more physical disciplinarians than mothers
   (B) most parents discipline in a physical manner
   (C) control is more important than nurturing after a certain age
   (D) children of alcoholics experience physical abuse more than children of nonalcoholic parents

9. Which of the following does the author mention as a possible cause of mental depression or alcoholism?
   (A) Psychiatric diagnosis
   (B) Harsh physical abuse
   (C) Alcoholic parents
   (D) Misbehavior in elementary schools

10. With which of the following would the author of the passage be most likely to agree?
    (A) Resolve the problem through words, not actions.
    (B) Human beings are too tentative.
    (C) Children should be seen but not heard.
    (D) Alcoholism is a disease.

11. Why does the author mention the family therapist?
    (A) To contradict to the research
    (B) To state a rationale for harsh physical abuse
    (C) To illustrate how to discipline properly
    (D) To support the author's thesis

12. In the first sentence, the phrase "physical discipline" could best be replaced by which of the following?
    (A) Exercise
    (B) Teachers
    (C) Therapeutic exercises
    (D) Beatings

Questions 13–16

We now define psychology as the study of human behavior by scientific methods. "Behavior," as used here, refers to more than conduct, deportment, or manner. It includes all normal and abnormal activities of the whole organism, even those of the mentally retarded and mentally ill. The purposes of studying behavior are to explore the roles of behavior in self-discovery and the varied
5 beneficent behavioral patterns the individual can develop. The aims of applied psychology are the description, prediction, and control of human activities in order that we may understand and intelligently direct our lives and influence the lives of others.

13. The main purpose of this passage is to
    (A) explain behavior
    (B) introduce the scientific method
    (C) define some key terms
    (D) define applied psychology

14. The primary difference between the ordinary use of the term "behavior" and its special sense here is that the
    (A) ordinary use is broader
    (B) ordinary use is narrower
    (C) special sense is more useful
    (D) special sense is more correct

15. The writer's use of the term "self discovery" in line 4 suggests that he or she
    (A) wants people to examine their own behavior
    (B) wants humans to develop better behavioral patterns
    (C) plans to delineate a new theory
    (D) believes that psychology has its limits

16. One of the subjects which an applied psychologist would NOT be directly interested in would be
    (A) behavior modification
    (B) control of human behavior
    (C) animal behavior
    (D) the description of normal human activity

GENERAL READINGS

Questions 1–4

Even the most accomplished gardener must sometimes face the challenges of weeds, insects, animals, and plant diseases. Plant pests of one sort or another are present everywhere, and they may seem overwhelming to the new gardener. Although even the best-tended garden can suddenly be plagued by aphids or mildew, good gardening techniques will help reduce the damage caused by plant pests. This is because plants that are well cared for are healthy and vigorous and are better able to resist pests and diseases. Also, techniques such as weeding and garden cleanup eliminate the places where many plant pests breed, greatly reducing the likelihood of attack in the first place.

However, certain measures and techniques must be used to effectively combat some pests. For instance, a hungry rabbit will most likely be enticed, not deterred, by a healthy, carefully grown lettuce plant. And if you've planted roses susceptible to mildew in an area where mildew is severe, even the best of growing conditions will not prevent infection.

Once you've learned about plant pests and the special techniques for controlling them, you'll be able to easily add them to your regular garden care routine.

1. What is the best title for the passage?
   (A) How to Maintain a Healthy Garden
   (B) Ridding the Garden of Pests
   (C) The Value of Pesticides in Gardening
   (D) Techniques for Eliminating Garden Insects

2. Which of the following questions does the passage answer?
   (A) What will deter hungry rabbits?
   (B) How do you control plant pests?
   (C) What birds come to well-tended gardens?
   (D) How do you cut roses?

3. According to the passage, what will reduce the damage caused by plant pests?
   (A) Planting roses
   (B) Good gardening techniques
   (C) Good growing conditions
   (D) Aphids and rabbits

4. In the last sentence, what does the word "them" refer to?
   (A) Growing conditions
   (B) Plant pests
   (C) Roses
   (D) Special techniques

Questions 5–9

Although the Constitution organized the American states into what was then the largest free-trade zone in the world, geographical constraints sorely inhibited trade and commerce. Enormous physical obstacles and great distances divided the republic. Henry Adams wrote, "No civilized country had yet been required to deal with physical difficulties so serious, nor did experience warrant the conviction that such difficulties could be overcome." From colonial times to the beginning of the nineteenth century, the movement of goods from the places of production to the points of sale continued to be a major problem for merchants and consumers alike. Throughout much of the nation, goods were transported by water from coastal port to coastal port and along navigable rivers and streams. Some freight moved over primitive, rutted roads, but in many areas the absence of roads meant that commodities could be transported only by pack horse. The cost of shipping items in such fashion often exceeded their value. Conditions for travelers were equally bad. A five-day trip north from Philadelphia would take a traveler only as far as Connecticut. The political and economic leaders of the country recognized the obstacles to commerce that distance and geographical barriers presented. Entrepreneurs and politicians proposed many internal development schemes to improve transportation. In most instances these involved local and state improvements, and the projects called invariably for the expenditure of substantial amounts of capital.

5. Which statement most accurately restates the main idea of this paragraph?
   (A) The U.S. Constitution was responsible for restrictions on business during colonial times.
   (B) The size and physical nature of the U.S. slowed the expansion of trade and commerce from colonial times to the early 1800s.
   (C) Businessmen and politicians were successful in their attempts to improve transportation.
   (D) Transportation projects were extremely expensive before 1800.

6. The quote from Henry Adams states that
   (A) the U.S. was the only civilized country with physical difficulties
   (B) Americans believed that they could overcome their physical difficulties
   (C) in the past no country had overcome such geographical constraints
   (D) he was opposed to the expansion of trade and commerce

7. Which of the following statements is true?
   (A) It was more expensive to ship items by water than by land.
   (B) Shipping items by water was less efficient than shipping by land.
   (C) The cost of shipping items by pack horse was frequently more expensive than the goods which were being supplied.
   (D) Little capital was required for transportation improvements.

8. Traveling was
   (A) much easier than shipping
   (B) more difficult than shipping
   (C) just as difficult as shipping
   (D) necessary if you wanted to buy goods

9. The passage implies, but does not directly state, that
   (A) transportation problems prior to 1800 caused many businessmen to give up
   (B) improvement of trade and commerce in early U.S. history required hard work and imagination by entrepreneurs and businessmen
   (C) small countries have fewer economic problems than big countries
   (D) big countries with no geographic constraints have few commercial problems

Questions 10–15

A revolution is under way in the store-dominated world of retailing. The instigators are nonstore retailers who are appearing in new forms, proliferating in numbers, and gaining market share from store-based retailers. Although accurate sales figures for this nonstore growth are hard to come by, one source estimates that nonstore annual sales are expanding from three to five times faster than those of traditional store outlets. Here are some examples of the rise of nonstore retailing:

- The increasing volume of telephone- and mail-generated orders received by traditional store retailers;
- The increased popularity of in-flight shopping catalogs of major airline companies;
- The expanding selection of merchandise offerings made to credit customers by major credit card companies.

It is expected that this trend toward nonstore retailing will accelerate rapidly with the development of telecommunication retail systems. Consumers with accounts at the telecommunication merchandiser will shop at home for a variety of products and services. Using an in-home video display catalog, they will order products from a participating retailer. When the order is received on its computer, this retailer will assemble the goods from a fully automated warehouse. Simultaneously, funds will be transferred from the customer's to the retailer's bank account. Customers will choose between picking up the order at a nearby distribution point or having it delivered to their door. There will be no fee for picking up the order. However, there may be a delivery charge of approximately $5. The charge will depend on the amount of the order and delivery time requirements.

Most people will move steadily toward the convenience of telecommunication shopping, though the other types of shopping will never completely disappear.

10. With which of the following is the passage mainly concerned?
    (A) Shopping using an in-home video display catalog
    (B) The trend toward nontraditional shopping
    (C) The importance of telecommunication in the future
    (D) Reasons for using telecommunication retail systems

11. The author discusses all of the following in the passage EXCEPT
    (A) making a purchase through your credit card company
    (B) placing an order over the telephone
    (C) ordering through your personal computer
    (D) buying from a street merchant

12. According to the passage, which sentence is true?
    (A) Telecommunication shopping is less expensive.
    (B) In the future, shopping will become more convenient for consumers.
    (C) The success of nonstore retailing will depend on the delivery charge.
    (D) Traditional store outlets will always be considered the most reliable way of shopping.

13. Which of the following best describes the author's purpose?
    (A) Persuasive
    (B) Critical
    (C) Informative
    (D) Laudatory

14. According to the passage, a consumer will need which of the following to shop from a telecommunication retailer?
    (A) A major credit card
    (B) An account with the merchandiser
    (C) A VCR
    (D) An in-flight shopping catalog

15. Which of the following will probably be true of nontraditional shopping?
    (A) It will grow very slowly in the immediate future.
    (B) Cash will rarely be used in transactions.
    (C) Store-based retailers will have it halted.
    (D) Goods and services will be quite limited.

7

ESSAY TARGETS

■ TEST OF WRITTEN ENGLISH

Purpose

The Test of Written English (TWE) tests your ability to write a cohesive essay. It is offered with the TOEFL four times a year. It is not given at every administration. If you are required to take the TWE, be sure you choose the correct test date.

On the TWE, you will be required to write a 250- to 300-word essay in 30 minutes. You will not have a choice of topics. You will be given a topic that you must develop into a cohesive, grammatical essay in the allotted time.

Scoring

Your essay will be read by two experienced, trained evaluators who will each give your essay a score of 1 to 6. The average of these two scores will be your score. If the readers' interpretations of your essay differ by more than 2 points, a third evaluator will read your essay.

The institutions that receive your score reports will not receive a copy of your essay. They will receive only the TWE score report with the essay score 1 to 6.

- 6 Excellent
- 5 Very Good
- 4 Good
- 3 Needs improvement
- 2 Needs improvement
- 1 Needs improvement

The descriptive interpretation above is NOT an official TOEFL Program interpretation, and those descriptions will not accompany the scores. The descriptions (excellent, good, needs improvement) are to help you understand the ranking.

The essay graders will evaluate your ability to:

1. Understand all parts of the question
2. Address all parts of the question
3. Develop the topic appropriately
4. Use appropriate details

The essay should contain:

1. A coherent structure
2. A clear, succinct presentation
3. A fluent style
4. Varied vocabulary
5. Varied grammatical structures
6. Standard punctuation

SCORING GUIDE

The TWE essay graders use the following Test of Written English Scoring Guide to assign a grade to your essay.

Scoring Guide*

The Test of Written English is the thirty-minute writing test administered at the September, October, March, and May TOEFL administrations. This is the scoring guide readers use to score the TWE.

Scores

6 **Clearly demonstrates competence in writing on both the rhetorical and syntactic levels, though it may have occasional errors.**

A paper in this category
—is well organized and well developed
—effectively addresses the writing task
—uses appropriate details to support a thesis or illustrate ideas
—shows unity, coherence, and progression
—displays consistent facility in the use of language
—demonstrates syntactic variety and appropriate word choice

5 **Demonstrates competence in writing on both the rhetorical and syntactic levels, though it will have occasional errors.**

A paper in this category
—is generally well organized and well developed, though it may have fewer details than does a 6 paper
—may address some parts of the task more effectively than others
—shows unity, coherence, and progression

—demonstrates some syntactic variety and range of vocabulary
—displays facility in language, though it may have more errors than does a 6 paper

4 **Demonstrates minimal competence in writing on both the rhetorical and syntactic levels.**

A paper in this category
—is adequately organized
—addresses the writing topic adequately but may slight parts of the task
—uses some details to support a thesis or illustrate ideas
—demonstrates adequate but undistinguished or inconsistent facility with syntax and usage
—may contain some serious errors that occasionally obscure meaning

3 **Demonstrates some developing competence in writing, but it remains flawed on either the rhetorical or syntactic level, or both.**

A paper in this category may reveal one or more of the following weaknesses:
—inadequate organization or development
—failure to support or illustrate generalizations with appropriate or sufficient detail
—an accumulation of errors in sentence structure and/or usage
—a noticeably inappropriate choice of words or word forms

*Copyright © 1988 by Educational Testing Service. All rights reserved.

2 Suggests incompetence in writing.

A paper in this category is seriously flawed by one or more of the following weaknesses:

—failure to organize or develop
—little or no detail or irrelevant specifics
—serious and frequent errors in usage or sentence structure
—serious problems with focus

1 Demonstrates incompetence in writing.

A paper in this category will contain serious and persistent writing errors, may be illogical or incoherent, or may reveal the writer's inability to comprehend the question. A paper that is severely underdeveloped, or one that exhibits no response at all, also falls into this category.

DIRECTIONS FOR THE TWE

The following directions are the actual directions used on the TWE. Read them carefully. Note the rules in direction #4.

TEST OF WRITTEN ENGLISH (TWE)

ESSAY QUESTION

30 Minutes

DO NOT OPEN UNTIL THE SUPERVISOR TELLS YOU TO DO SO.

The TWE Essay Question is inside. You will have 30 minutes to plan, write, and correct your essay. Your essay will be graded on its overall quality.

1. When the supervisor tells you to begin, open this sheet and read the Essay Question carefully.

2. Think before you write. Making notes may help you to organize your essay. Below the essay question is a space marked NOTES. Use only this area to outline your essay or make notes.

3. Write only on this topic. If you write an essay on a different topic, it will not be scored. Write clearly and precisely. Use examples to support your ideas. How well you write is much more important than how much you write, but to cover the topic adequately, you may want to write more than one paragraph.

4. Start writing your essay on the first line of Essay Page Side 3. Use Side 4 if you need more space. Extra paper will not be provided. Write neatly and legibly. Do <u>not</u> skip lines. Do <u>not</u> write in very large letters or leave large margins.

5. Check your work. Allow a few minutes <u>before</u> time is called to read over your essay and make small changes.

6. After thirty minutes, the Supervisor will tell you to stop. You must stop writing and put your pencil down. If you continue to write, it will be considered cheating.

STOP! WAIT FOR THE SUPERVISOR'S INSTRUCTIONS.

© 1988 Educational Testing Service.

Sample Student Essays

The following essays were written by foreign students applying to study at a U.S. university. The essays have been scored as if the students had taken the Test of Written English. The quality of the essays and the corresponding score will give you an idea of the level of writing expected. These scores are not official ETS scores.

> **Essay Question:** Is higher education a right or a privilege?

Essay Score 1

Demonstrates incompetence in writing.

A paper in this category will contain serious and persistent writing errors, may be illogical or incoherent, or may reveal the writer's inability to comprehend the question. A paper that is severely underdeveloped, or one that exhibits no response at all, also falls into this category.

Example:

My opinion: I Thingk college is better for every people want to estudin everey They want, have money o not have, but the problem is tritucion for pay teacher utilities and other espenses but I Thingk the inteligence is first for the estudin have volutad for Learned.

The estud is of best for every body and have a god future and gue god Life to of family.

Essay Score 2

Suggests incompetence in writing.

A paper in this category is seriously flawed by one or more of the following weaknesses:

   —failure to organize or develop
   —little or no detail, or irrelevant specifics
   —serious and frequent errors in usage or sentence structure
   —serious problems with focus

Example:

> I think College-level education should be available to all students. Because. For example. In Japan. Every one want to go the college or University. When They graduate the high school. But almost student can't go to the College. But They have a enough money and intelligence Eeuery student know better than to get lower education. and lower privilege. I want to get higher And Higher Education is a right education. because
>
> I got a high education Today, Japan's high school has the highest education level So I want to get higher education in the University. and it will be privilege for me. If I don't have a liance which graduated the University. I will not get the job. All the time I think that higher the better. when I was a senior, I hated to study because high student
> So I couldn't go to the better high school. So I think all the time. Higher the better And. Higher education is a privilege for every thing.

328   Essay Targets

Essay Score 3

Demonstrates some developing competence in writing, but it remains flawed on either the rhetorical or syntactic level, or both.

A paper in this category may reveal one or more of the following weaknesses:

- inadequate organization or development
- failure to support or illustrate generalizations with appropriate or sufficient detail
- an accumulation of errors in sentence structure and/or usage
- a noticeably inappropriate choice of words or word forms

Example:

Higher education is a privilege. It is a matter of ones own choice to acheive that. It depens on persons ambisiosness and desire. Some peoples goal is to get a higher education to serve other peoples, to solve the existing problems in the world. Problems like Cancer or Aids gives idea and challenge to get a high education in medicin to overcome these problem. Natural catastroff like Volkano and earth-quick is another challenge for people to get higher education. To reach to a better world, to end most of the worlds problem is again someothers reasons for that. These are matters which make a higher education a privilege.

College-level education should be available to all student and not only to those who have sufficient money or intelligence, because some students need to get this level al education and if it is available more and more will get the encourage and the ability for higher education otherwise many, many will give up totaly for college-level and the society will suffer for that reason. So lets har the college-level available for everybody.

Essay Score 4

Demonstrates minimal competence in writing on both the rhetorical and syntactic levels.

A paper in this category

- is adequately organized
- addresses the writing topic adequately but may slight parts of the task
- uses some details to support a thesis or illustrate ideas
- demonstrates adequate but undistinguished or inconsistent facility with syntax and usage
- may contain some serious errors that occasionally obscure meaning

Example:

In general, higher education helps people in many ways, such as make life easier, make ready for real world. And But, those example do not mean that higher education is right to everybody. In my opinion it is a myth. Education is privilege for the people who have money or intelligence.

First, a higher education such as College or graduate school, costs a numorous amounts of money. In real, a salary for undergraduate is about 20.000 ~ 25.000, but a net income would be much less. The net income from salary does not compensate his or her spending to tuition, room and board, books. He or she needs 5~6 yrs in college years. Saving in order to make balance between earning from higher education, and spending to higher education, without spending a penny.

Secondly, higher education need time in order to achieve.
It is a kind of privilege, who have time also. Thirdly, we need money in order to get it.
- to have at least average GPA, SAT score or ACT high school score in order to get a college. From the stand point of evaluation of admission, education is a privilege for the students who have at least average grade or average score from the test. Finally, higher education can give a short cut to the people, but it can not deliver basic personalities such as diligent and Innocent and so on. We often judge people from their personality not by their education.

In conclusion, higher education is nice to have, but it is not a right. It is more likely privilege for those who have excess of time, money and intelligence

Essay Score 5

Demonstrates competence in writing on both the rhetorical and syntactic levels, though it will have occasional errors.

A paper in this category

- is generally well organized and well developed, though it may have fewer details than does a 6 paper
- may address some parts of the task more effectively than others
- shows unity, coherence, and progression
- demonstrates some syntactic variety and range of vocabulary
- displays facility in language, though it may have more errors than does a 6 paper

Example:

Is Higher Education a Right or a Privilege?

A college education cannot be a privilege for the rich, but an opportunity for the qualified, and something available for every citizen. College education is not only a luxury because of its high prices, but also because of its competitive environment, where the intelligent and smart reign. This fact leads us to a problem that is getting more and more difficult to solve; the number of youngsters who are not the brightest or the richest and who are being pushed backwards and backwards in the social scale.

It is true that we cannot we idealistic with the desire of having all students, with different averages in the same level of Universities. In fact I wonder that it is fair to give scholarships to those students who have demonstrated their interest and qualifications during their high school years. But, I do not agree with the fact that students who are not qualified, are accepted in recognized, and usually expensive, Universities just because their parents are rich or influential. It is not fair, because their place should be occupied by a more qualified person, with or without scholarship.

To avoid overcrowded universities, with a mixture of different levels of students. Any student who is not bright enough to go to a competitive University, should have the chance of, maybe later, being able to transfer there. The solution to this problem is to create special free centers. These "special centers" would be for those who, in the future, intend to enter into a higher competitive environment. After reaching a certain average, then they would be able to transfer.

The right to study and the right of being proud of oneself, is something that every citizen has the right to have. The "special centers" are the opportunity for those who are interested in a high university level scale, but need a little help.

Essay Score 6

Clearly demonstrates competence in writing on both the rhetorical and syntactic levels, though it may have occasional errors.

A paper in this category

- is well organized and well developed
- effectively addresses the writing task
- uses appropriate details to support a thesis or illustrate ideas
- shows unity, coherence, and progression
- displays consistent facility in the use of language
- demonstrates syntactic variety and appropriate word choice

Example:

Is Higher Education A Right Or A Privilege?

The importance of education cannot be over-emphasised. It has been said that "education makes a man" and rightly so. Without the tools of an education where would man be? While everybody realises that a basic education is a necessity, not everyone feels the same about higher education. To some, getting a college education is just another paper qualification that is pursued by those who can afford the time and the means for it. To them, it is far better to go out to the "real world" and earn a living. Fortunately (it is hoped) the numbers who feel this way are few.

College education should not be viewed as an extravagance to be available to only students who have sufficient money or to students who are considered intelligent. The right to knowledge, at whatever level, should not be denied to anyone seeking it. Of course whether one exercises the option to get a college education in a different matter entirely.

It has become increasingly important in recent years that paper qualifications are very important. A person with a college degree has more opportunities open to him. He will be able to get a job that has a higher salary and thus be able to enjoy a higher standard of living.

Society also stands to gain in the long run. A person with a college education would be able to contribute his knowledge to improve the productivity of his firm. The increased productivity of the firm would in turn generate economic growth. With economic growth, the society and the nation prosper.

Thus it can be seen that college education should not be considered a privilege but a right. It is an important foundation on which the future of a nation lies. With the rapid advancement of knowledge, especially in the fields of science and technology, college education should be considered the minimum qualifications of students.

STRATEGIES FOR THE TWE

1. Practice!
   To be a good reader, you must read, read, read. Similarly, to be a good writer, you must write, write, write. Try to combine your reading practice with your writing practice. After you finish one of the reading passages in this book, you should formulate a question similar to the sample questions in this section and then write a response to your question. For example, what is a similar occurrence in my own country?

2. Budget your time on the TWE.
   This timetable will help you organize your time.

8 minutes	Prepare an outline
5 minutes	Write the introduction
7 minutes	Write the body
5 minutes	Write the conclusion
5 minutes	Review and revise

3. Read and analyze the question carefully.

4. Look for words that signal the type of organization you will use: compare/contrast, support/defend your opinion, predict the outcome, etc.

5. Focus on the topic! Write only on the subject in the question. Do not write on anything else.

6. State your purpose clearly in the first paragraph.

7. Write one paragraph for each main point.

8. Summarize your main points clearly.

9. Be sure to write legibly. Don't forget to indent the first word of each paragraph.

▢ Strategy-Building Activity

Keep practicing!

Practice is found in the essay questions in the Skill Building exercises. You should develop an essay from each of the questions. Use the model outline below for the first essay question. After you have prepared the outline, write the essay and revise it. You can use your own paper for the other practice outlines and essays.

Model Outline

Introduction

_____
_____
_____

Body: (You may have more or less than 3 general statements; you may have more or less than 3 facts.)

General Statement 1: _____

   Fact 1: _____

   Fact 2: _____

   Fact 3: _____

General Statement 2: _____

   Fact 1: _____

   Fact 2: _____

   Fact 3: _____

General Statement 3: _____

   Fact 1: _____

   Fact 2: _____

   Fact 3: _____

Conclusion:

_____
_____
_____

SKILLS TO DEVELOP

1. Organize your content.

The most important part of any essay is to think and plan *before* you begin to write. Before you make any attempt to write the essay itself, you need to decide what you are going to say and what facts will support your arguments.

A good way to plan your organization is to practice outlining. In the reading passages in the Regents/Prentice Hall TOEFL Prep Book, try to find the general statements and the facts that support those statements. After you have outlined them, rewrite them (paraphrase them). This will give you practice in outlining, writing, and paraphrasing.

2. Organize your essay.

It is more important to write an essay that is well organized with paragraphs that are well developed than to try to use complicated grammatical structures and "big" words. You should try to use the structures and the words you know well even if they would seem simple if translated in your own language. Written English is very straightforward. Try to express your ideas as simply as possible.

A typical 250- to 300-word essay is made up of three distinct parts:

1. *Introduction:* Restate the question and tell how you are going to answer the question.
2. *Body:* Provide your opinion or solution to the problem. Use general statements supported by facts.
3. *Conclusion:* Summarize the answer to the question.

Generally, the introduction and conclusion are each one paragraph long. The body of the essay may be several paragraphs long.

3. Organize your paragraph.

A typical paragraph is made up of one **general statement** followed by several **supporting statements (facts)**.

General statement

Inner-city neighborhoods are noisy.

Supporting statements

Trucks and buses run along the streets all day long.

Children play games in their yards until evening.

Radios and TV can be heard from open windows.

Airplanes fly low overhead.

The general statements are often paraphrased and combined in the introduction to prepare (alert) the reader; the introduction states the writer's intentions. The general statements are often paraphrased and combined again in the conclusion of the essay to remind the reader of the author's intentions.

4. Check your work.

   Learn to be your own critic. Allow a few minutes before the end of the 30 minutes to review and revise your work. Look for misspellings, grammatical errors, and errors in organizational style.

5. Be familiar with the type of essay topics.

   You will have no choice of topics in the Essay section. But there are several discourse styles in English that you should be aware of.

   Comparing and contrasting
   Describing a chart or graph
   Stating and supporting a personal opinion
   Stating a case

Below are lists of vocabulary and grammar patterns often associated with these discourse styles. If you become familiar with these styles and the vocabulary associated with these styles, you will be better prepared to develop your essay. The essay question on the TOEFL may combine two or more of these styles.

Comparing and Contrasting

Contrast	Contrast	Compare
but . . . than	and . . . than	and
than	instead of	like
unlike	but . . . as	as . . . as
more	-er	but . . . than
and	-est	more . . . -er

Describing a Chart or Graph

bottom	circle	right-hand side
top	square	left-hand side
data	figure	table
increased	extend	begin
decreased	stop	last until

Stating a Personal Opinion

Personal opinions are not necessarily facts and are often expressed using vocabulary and grammatical structures that suggest supposition.

The passive voice

It is thought that the family is less important as a social unit today than it was fifty years ago.

Personal nouns and pronouns *I, you, he, she, we, they, it*

We support the free-trade movement, but they do not.

Gandhi believed conflicts should be resolved peacefully.

Adverbial qualifiers *probably, likely, maybe, usually,* etc.

The future is likely to be more difficult for me than for the next generation.

Verbs *believe, think, seem, consider, agree, claim, suppose,* etc.

I agree with the main tenets of the proposal.

Prepositional Phrases: *In my view, in my opinion,* etc.

In my opinion, the law should be rescinded.

Stating a Case

In making an argument, you may have to describe a situation at the present time **(description)**; how it might be changed **(process)**; and what effect the change might cause **(cause and effect/prediction)**.

Description

The vocabulary used for this section will depend, of course, on what is being described. You should practice for this section by writing physical descriptions of people, buildings, and cities. In addition, you should practice writing descriptions of ideas (for example, What is the Theory of Relativity?).

Process

first	then	during
second	next	while
third	before	when

Cause and Effect

the consequence	accordingly	that is why
as a result	if	for
therefore	by	cause
for this reason	so	make
thus	because of	provided
because	through	unless
result in	bring about	ensues
hence	when	as

Prediction

predict (that)	in the future	in the foreseeable future
projected	it is likely that	most likely consequences
foresee	inevitable outcome	the future implications
the next step	subsequent move	the end result
probability of	plan to	presume

340 Essay Targets

SKILL-BUILDING EXERCISES

COMPARING AND CONTRASTING

Essay Question 1

There are advantages and disadvantages to living and working in either a small town or a large city. Give one or two advantages and disadvantages of living in either. In which would you prefer to live and why?

Essay Question 2

People choose to have large families for many reasons. What are the advantages and disadvantages of a large family? Of a small family? Which would you prefer and why?

Essay Question 3

At U.S. universities and colleges, students sometimes are obliged to share a room with a stranger or live by themselves. Describe briefly what you think are the negative and positive aspects of sharing a room with a stranger or living by yourself. Which living arrangement would you prefer and why?

Essay Question 4

Obligatory service to one's country is required of the youth of many countries around the world. Other countries have no compulsory military or social service. Do you believe that such service to one's country should be mandatory? What would be the potential ramifications of such service or lack of service?

Essay Question 5

How people spend their time when they are not working is called leisure-time activities. How would you compare the leisure-time activities of rural people as opposed to urban people? Which would you prefer?

Essay Targets 341

DESCRIBING A GRAPH

Essay Question 6

Compare the two graphs and write a few sentences comparing the figures in each.

Is there a correlation between your study habits and your grades? What is your best subject? Why is it your best subject?

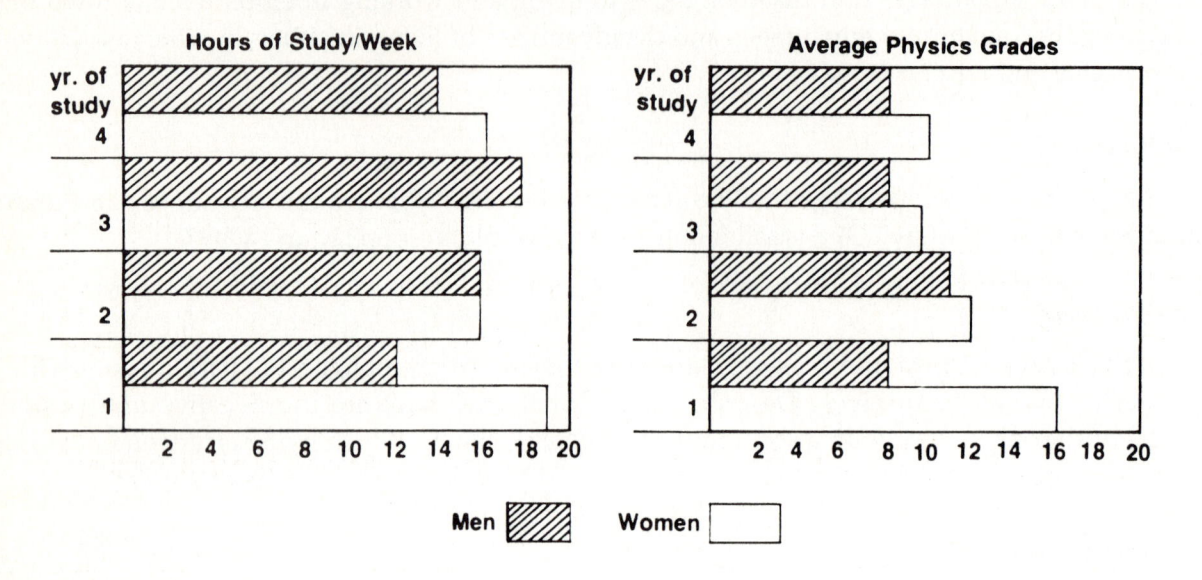

Essay Question 7

Compare the two graphs and write a few sentences comparing the findings of each.

Describe what you know about your country's literacy rate and your government's expenditures on education.

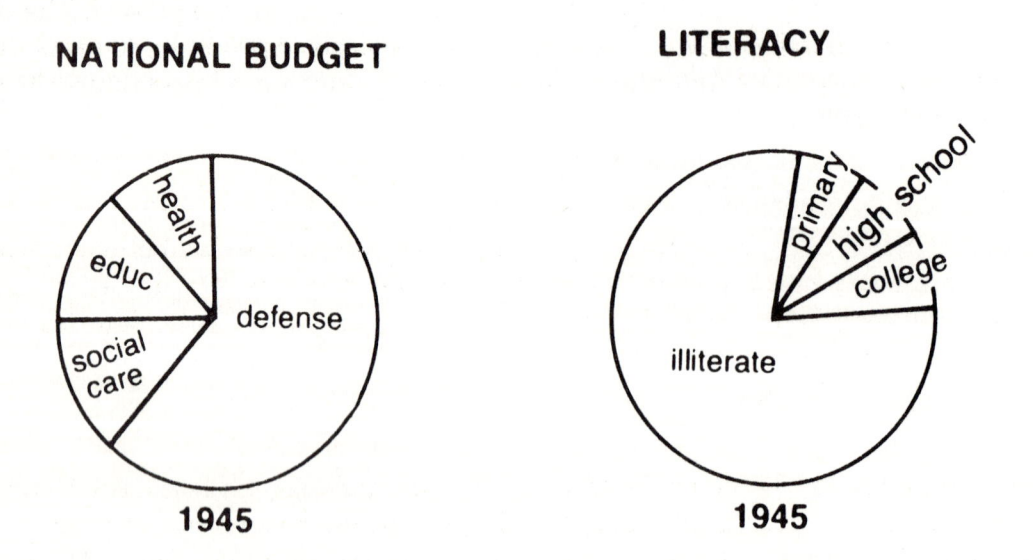

342   Essay Targets

Essay Question 8

Compare the two graphs and write a few sentences comparing the figures in each.

What do you know about the rate of cancer and the number of smokers in your country? What conclusions can you draw from the graph about your health?

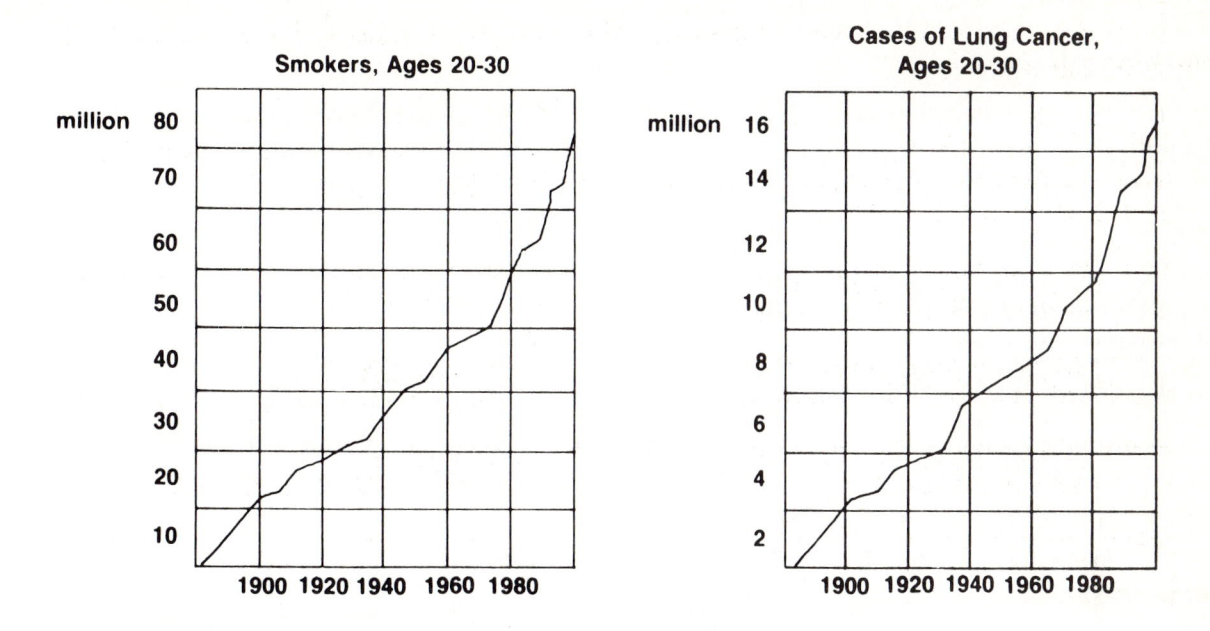

STATING A CASE

Essay Question 9

Zoning regulations in the city prohibit buildings over three stories tall. A developer has applied to the city to build a six-story building. The six-story building would displace many low-income families and would be different from the buildings in the neighborhood. The developer has promised to add a much-needed community center and other public services. As a citizen of the community, you must decide whether or not you support the developer and write your reasons to the city council.

Essay Question 10

Country X has little arable land. Country Z has lush vegetation and borders a sea. A river flows through country X and country Z to the sea. Country X plans to divert the river to provide more water for its arid lands. State the arguments for and against the diversion. Tell which side you support and why.

Essay Question 11

The government has decided to build a new international airport that is much larger than the present one. It will create more jobs and allow bigger and more planes to land, thus increasing trade potential. The airport will be two hours away from the city center and will be built in the middle of a traditional farming community. Give the arguments pro and con for the airport and tell why you favor one side.

Essay Question 12

Schools in wealthy areas generally have access to the most modern equipment, including computers, for education. Schools in less-developed areas are often unable to provide their students with the opportunity to become computer-literate. What will be the effects of this disparity? What steps would you take to deal with this situation?

Essay Question 13

As air travel becomes more popular, the number of new planes being produced cannot keep pace with the demand. Consequently, many airlines are buying and using old planes. What role, if any, must a government take to make air travel safe? What are the responsibilities of the airline? Of the traveller?

STATING A PERSONAL OPINION

Essay Question 14

Continuing your education in a foreign country away from your family may create hardships for you and your family. What are some of the hardships? What are some of the rewards you expect from your education away from home?

Essay Question 15

Radio stations have a variety of programs for a variety of listeners' tastes. Which shows do you enjoy listening to or which do you not like to listen to? Why or why not? What does your choice depend on?

Essay Question 16

Many cultures interpret the word *friendship* differently. How would you define it? What are some of the qualities you expect to find in your close friends?

Essay Question 17

As the world's population gets older, the social structure that kept the family together is changing. What do you think life will be like in the future for the elderly? What recommendations would you make to a commission studying the quality of life of our senior citizens?

FINAL SKILL-BUILDING EXERCISES

After you have written an essay on each question, start again! Write a new essay on each question.

Grade your own essays. Is your grade higher the second time? Why or why not? Maybe you should write a third essay!

APPENDIX

■ PRACTICE TEST TAPESCRIPTS

PRACTICE TEST 1

PART A

1. (Man A) Joan will fly rather than drive.
2. (Man B) Swimming is better exercise than walking.
3. (Woman) Raise your hand if you don't understand.
4. (Man B) The morning weather report follows the local news.
5. (Man B) Margaret's directions are so simple anyone can follow them.
6. (Man A) Mary saw two movies in one afternoon.
7. (Man B) Mark was the last one off the bus.
8. (Woman) Don't work so much.
9. (Man A) Why don't we have lunch one of these days?
10. (Woman) When we moved to this city, we made many new friends.
11. (Man B) Since the weather was warm, we waited outside.
12. (Woman) If you're going past the post office, I need some stamps.
13. (Man B) I'm sorry, but I'll be late tomorrow.
14. (Man A) To get a gym locker, you have to sign up in the Athletic Office.
15. (Woman) Do you prefer classical music to rock?
16. (Man B) If you mail the letter this afternoon, they should receive it next Monday.
17. (Woman) The library is open until six tonight, but it is closed tomorrow.
18. (Man A) Since the light is not very good in this room, could you turn on another light?
19. (Man B) You should read the directions before starting the experiment.
20. (Man A) I must finish this book by the end of the week.

PART B

21. (Man A) I'd like to apply for a loan, please.
    (Woman) Fill out this form and see one of our officers.
    (Man B) Where are they?
22. (Woman) I finally have an appointment with my doctor.
    (Man B) You've had that cold all week, haven't you?
    (Man A) What can we assume about the woman?
23. (Man B) I've been here for 25 minutes. How often do the buses pass here?
    (Woman) They usually come every 15 minutes.
    (Man A) Where does this conversation probably take place?
24. (Man B) I think I'll make some tea. Would you like some?
    (Woman) Yes, please. Is there any cream or sugar?
    (Man A) What will the man probably do?
25. (Woman) The classrooms are usually cleaned twice a week, on Monday and Wednesday.
    (Man A) Well, let's have them done on Friday, too.
    (Man B) How often will the classrooms be cleaned from now on?
26. (Man A) Every time I call the number, I get a busy signal.
    (Woman) Wait an hour and try again.
    (Man B) What does the woman suggest the man do?
27. (Woman) Are we going to eat at 5 or 6?
    (Man B) We'll eat at 4 because the movie starts at 6:30.
    (Man A) What are they going to do first?
28. (Woman) I'm sorry, sir. This section of the restaurant is for nonsmokers.
    (Man B) I thought this WAS the smoking section.
    (Man A) Why is the man upset?
29. (Man A) We'd better hurry. I'm afraid we'll miss the plane.
    (Woman) Relax. We've got plenty of time. Have some more coffee.
    (Man B) How does the man feel?
30. (Man A) Can you read this card for me?
    (Man B) You forgot your glasses again, didn't you?
    (Woman) What does the conversation mean?
31. (Man B) You can't park your car here. This is a school entrance.
    (Woman) I'll only be a minute, officer.
    (Man A) What does the woman want to do?
32. (Woman) How soon until you retire?
    (Man A) Well, I'll be 65 next week, and I'll walk out that door then.
    (Man B) What will the man do next week?
33. (Woman) Fill it up and check the oil, please.
    (Man B) Could you pull a little closer to the pump, please?
    (Man A) Where does this conversation probably take place?

Appendix 345

34. (Man B) I hope you'll be able to join us for lunch tomorrow.
    (Woman) I'd like to, but I'm meeting a friend at the train station.
    (Man A) What does the woman mean?
35. (Man B) I didn't make a reservation. Do you have a room for tonight?
    (Woman) I'm sorry. We're completely booked.
    (Man A) Where does this conversation probably take place?

PART C

(Man A) Questions 36 through 41 refer to the following lecture.

(Woman) Dreams have always interested poets and philosophers, but in the last decade scientists became interested in dreams, too. What is the meaning of dreams? What is their purpose? It seems that our dreams at night affect our mood during the day. Scientists have determined that our feelings of happiness or unhappiness may depend on our dreams.

By observing people sleeping, scientists have concluded that normal sleep is divided into 5 distinct stages: stages 1 through 4 and REM. REM is an acronym for rapid eye movement. Most dreaming takes place during REM and, for most adults, REM occurs four to six times a night.

What we dream at night is not as important as whom we dream about. More precisely, the number of people in our dreams is the important element. The more people in our dreams, the happier we will be. Conversely, the fewer people in our dreams, the less happy we will be.

Psychiatrist Milton Kramer believes that "the bad thing in a dream is to be alone." There is something about interacting with people that produces happiness both in our dreams and when we are awake.

36. (Man B) What has always interested poets and philosophers?
37. (Man B) When did scientists become interested in dreams?
38. (Man B) How many stages of sleep are there?
39. (Man B) What does the "R" in REM stand for?
40. (Man B) What do people usually experience during REM?
41. (Man B) What is the effect of interacting with many people in a dream?

(Man A) Questions 42 through 45 refer to the following dialog.

(Woman) I wish that girl would turn down her music. I can't stand this noise. I think I'm going to go deaf.

(Man B) Well, you might! Noise is a serious health hazard. I read that if we're exposed to over 100 decibels for two hours or more we can suffer hearing loss.

(Woman) How much is that? I'm sure that kid with her stereo must be over 100.

(Man B) Close to it. Amplified music is only about 95 decibels, but a rock concert is about 130. Teenagers and people in their twenties are going to suffer hearing loss without a doubt. Noise is harmful for other reasons, too. If a noise wakes us up in the middle of the night, we experience stress. Stress is a factor in a variety of health problems, from heart disease to high blood pressure.

(Woman) There must be some local ordinances that prohibit excessive noise. I'll check into it, but if people want to hurt their eardrums, it's their business. Still, I want to hear the birds sing when I get older.

42. (Man A) What are the speakers concerned about?
43. (Man A) After how many hours of exposure to high-decibel noise does it become harmful?
44. (Man A) Which group is likely to experience the most impaired hearing?
45. (Man A) About how many decibels is a rock concert?

(Man B) Questions 46 through 50 refer to the following lecture.

(Man A) As part of your first assignment for the introductory course to archaeology, I want you all to collect a bag of garbage from different neighborhoods and analyze it.

You may think this sounds funny, but that's exactly what archaeologists do: study ancient garbage. We look at the bones, the pot shards, and even the refuse around the fire to make guesses about the socioeconomic status of the inhabitants of a given area.

In this class, we will make the same kinds of assumptions, except we will use garbage from our lifetime—"contemporary garbage."

Our students last semester searched through bags of half-empty jars of food, bottles, wrappers, vegetable peels—everything that people would throw away. They discovered that middle-income households buy more lamb, pork, and chicken, and surprisingly, throw bits of it away. This group tended to waste food. On the other hand, both poor and wealthy families bought better-quality food and wasted less of it. Another interesting and unpredictable fact was that lower-income households bought expensive educational toys and kitchen materials.

By studying the garbage patterns of our neighborhoods, we will be able to validate last semester's hypotheses or challenge them. And that's what scientific investigation is about—making a hypothesis, testing it, and revising it. Now go collect that garbage.

46. (Woman) When was this lecture probably given?
47. (Woman) What class was the lecture given in?
48. (Woman) What is said about middle-income families?
49. (Woman) Which item would a lower-income household probably NOT buy?
50. (Woman) Why are the students collecting garbage?

346   Appendix

PRACTICE TEST 2

PART A

1. (Woman) How did you get here?
2. (Man B) I haven't received my newspaper for two days.
3. (Man A) The exam will be on the first four chapters of the book.
4. (Man B) If you are hungry, why don't you have a snack?
5. (Woman) The taxi cost us ten dollars from the airport to the town.
6. (Man B) How about taking a ride this afternoon?
7. (Man A) I have too much homework to go out this weekend.
8. (Woman) The train was supposed to be here ten minutes ago.
9. (Man A) I woke up when the phone rang.
10. (Woman) These parking spaces are reserved for faculty and visitors.
11. (Man B) Did Richard return the books to the library yet?
12. (Man A) When you see the statue, you'll turn right and go two more blocks.
13. (Woman) We can count on over 2,000 people to come to the conference this weekend.
14. (Man A) I always watch the 6 p.m. news on Channel 4.
15. (Man B) My phone's been out of order since last week.
16. (Woman) The fire broke out on the building's third floor.
17. (Man B) Mr. Johnson went to bed at 10, but didn't fall asleep until midnight.
18. (Man A) Let's get something to eat before the movie.
19. (Woman) My grades aren't good enough to get into the best schools.
20. (Man B) The grass on our lawn will die unless we get some rain.

PART B

21. (Woman) Was Mrs. Smith the first to arrive this morning?
    (Man A) Yes, but she forgot to turn on the air conditioning.
    (Man B) What does the man imply?
22. (Man A) For tomorrow's test, can we use a calculator?
    (Man B) No, you should learn basic calculation skills.
    (Woman) What subject are they talking about?
23. (Man B) Do you know where my glasses are? I thought I left them on the bookshelf.
    (Woman) I saw them on top of your briefcase on the hall table.
    (Man A) What did the man lose?
24. (Man B) Do you want to read this book when I'm finished?
    (Woman) I'd like to, but I don't have time.
    (Man A) What does the woman imply?
25. (Man B) Good afternoon. May I help you?
    (Man A) Yes, I want to mail this package and buy some stamps.
    (Woman) Where is this conversation taking place?
26. (Man A) Another rejection letter! I'll never get into a good school.
    (Woman) Maybe you should take a year off and travel.
    (Man B) Why is this man so upset?
27. (Woman) Is this the check-cashing line?
    (Man A) Yes, and also the line for deposits and withdrawals.
    (Man B) Where is this conversation probably taking place?
28. (Woman) How do you take your coffee? Milk? Sugar?
    (Man B) Actually, I would prefer tea, if it's not too much trouble.
    (Man A) What does this man mean?
29. (Man B) We're out of paper. I'll run and get some.
    (Man A) I'll go with you. I can use some air.
    (Woman) Where will they probably go?
30. (Man B) Congratulations. You earned that grade.
    (Woman) I really studied for that exam. Now, I can take it easy for a while.
    (Man A) Why is the woman so happy?
31. (Woman) Have you written your paper yet? It's due tomorrow morning.
    (Man A) No, I plan to stay up all night.
    (Man B) What does the man imply?
32. (Woman) Help me move this desk over by the window, would you?
    (Man B) The last time I helped you move something, my back hurt for a week.
    (Man A) Why does the woman want help?
33. (Man A) Would you like a one-way or round-trip ticket?
    (Woman) I'm coming back by car, so one-way is all I need.
    (Man B) What is the woman about to do?
34. (Woman) I'm going to make my weekly visit to Mary tonight.
    (Man B) She's been in the hospital for a month, hasn't she?
    (Man A) How long has Mary been sick?
35. (Man A) You need exact change or a token for the bus.
    (Woman) Guess I'll have to take a cab.
    (Man B) What does the woman mean?

PART C

(Man B) Questions 36 through 40 refer to the following dialog.
(Man A) This month is the anniversary of the Moon Walk.
(Woman) You're not talking about the dance, I presume.
(Man A) No, in 1969, Neil Armstrong and Buzz Aldrin stepped on the moon.
(Woman) I was just kidding. How could I forget that? I was teaching an introduction to geology class for majors at the University of Colorado. We were glued to the television set. Then, when the astronauts returned, specimens of the lunar surface were sent to certain schools. We were able to keep several moon rocks in our science museum.
(Man A) Did the rocks look different from the average rock you see on the side of the road?
(Woman) In appearance, not particularly, but there are differences in composition. One of the more interesting differences is that moon rocks lack water. Also, the moon rocks contain oxygen, but not the kind of oxygen earth rocks have. For example, the oxygen in moon rocks can be released through heating.
    There are two simple classifications of moon rocks—light rocks and dark rocks. The dark rocks come from what we call the lowland areas of the moon. These areas were impacted by a meteor or meteorite, and consequently the rocks are very dense—fused together like lava.

Appendix 347

		Light rocks, on the other hand, come from highland areas and are less dense.
	(Man A)	Are there any places on earth that have similar rocks?
	(Woman)	Well, a few places. Rocks like the basalts and breccia [note pronunciation brecchia] are found in Iceland, Hawaii, and the western part of the United States.
	(Man A)	I wonder if we'll ever be mining the minerals on the moon.
36.	(Man B)	What distinguishes moon rocks from those on earth?
37.	(Man B)	How does oxygen in moon rocks differ from that in earth rocks?
38.	(Man B)	Where were the darker rocks found?
39.	(Man B)	What caused the impacted lowland areas of the moon?
40.	(Man B)	According to the passage, where on Earth can rocks similar to moon rocks be found?
	(Woman)	Questions 41 through 45 refer to the following lecture.
	(Man A)	In a private-enterprise economy, it is common, ordinary people like you and me that determine what goods are produced and what services are provided. If we are not willing to buy a particular brand of car, or a particular color of a car, that car or that color car will go out of production. If we find that we need someplace to put our children while we work, we create a demand—in this case, a demand for day care centers for children. It is the demand or lack of demand that determines what restaurants will open and stay open, what products will line the shelves and what ones will be taken off. You can notice, when you look at magazines from the forties or fifties, how advertisements have changed. Magazines of the forties glorify train travel as fast, comfortable, and even elegant. No travel ads today can legitimately push elegance, but trains continue to push comfort and convenience. New technology, for example, jet planes, has caused us to change our demand. Our demand can change because our own tastes change. (We may prefer to slow down and take the train; this will cause a demand for improved train service.) Or demand may change because our income changes. (In this case, we purchase our own railroad car.)

		These three factors—our tastes, our income, and new technologies—influence demand. But notice that as demand for one product decreases, demand for another product will increase. If a car is too expensive, we will take the bus, or walk. This increases the demand for good walking shoes.
41.	(Man B)	Who is responsible for the availability of goods and services?
42.	(Man B)	Why would more red cars be produced than white?
43.	(Man B)	Who created a demand for day care centers?
44.	(Man B)	What caused the demise of train travel?
45.	(Man B)	What factor will cause improved train service?
	(Man B)	Questions 46 through 50 refer to the following dialog.
	(Man A)	I'm going to an exhibition of photographs this afternoon. Would you like to come?
	(Woman)	That depends. Who's the photographer?
	(Man A)	It's a group show. No one famous *yet*.
	(Woman)	"Yet" is an important word. Photography is becoming a very popular art form. Gallery owners will really try to promote young photographers to make sure their prices go up and up.
	(Man A)	You know you can buy photographs from the middle of the nineteenth century cheaper than you can buy some contemporary work.
	(Woman)	Well, price doesn't always equal quality. Fads and fashion dictate price, not quality. It's hard to determine what is art, isn't it? Some of the photographs look just like snapshots, others are very stylized. But even the photographs that look as informal as snapshots take a long time to set up and shoot.
	(Man A)	Quality art can be determined by what a museum buys and exhibits. If a museum buys an artist, his work becomes more valuable. I don't like to buy art if I can't resell it at a good price. I have to like the piece, of course, but I want to make sure I can resell it later at a higher price than I bought it.
46.	(Man B)	How was photography defined?
47.	(Man B)	What could be said about contemporary photographs in relation to older photographs?
48.	(Man B)	Which, according to the man, is the determiner of quality?
49.	(Man B)	What word characterizes snapshots?
50.	(Man B)	How does the man determine what to buy?

PRACTICE TEST 3

PART A

1.	(Man A)	The plane flew west over the mountains from Denver to Utah.
2.	(Man B)	We've been trying to call since 11:00, and it's 11:30 now.
3.	(Woman)	The woman tore her dress when she sat down.
4.	(Man A)	The exam would not have been as easy if I hadn't studied.
5.	(Man B)	The flight from Brazil was listed to arrive at 6:10, but by 7:00 it still hadn't arrived.
6.	(Woman)	The magazine was sent to the printer before it was approved by the editor.
7.	(Man A)	We threw a blanket over our shoulders to protect us from the sudden downpour.

8. (Man B) The anger he displayed showed he would not listen to reason.
9. (Woman) I have never heard a story about orphans that didn't make me want to weep.
10. (Man A) Prizes were given to all employees who had been with the company for at least five years.
11. (Man B) The grain embargo was only one of the bills occupying the senator's attention.
12. (Woman) The strong gusts caused the speaker to hold onto his papers.
13. (Man A) I rose at 8:30 to make my 9 o'clock class, but I was still 15 minutes late.
14. (Man B) Unless electric consumption is reduced, the city will have to triple its power generation capacity by next year.
15. (Woman) If there had been greater support, the motion would have been approved.
16. (Man A) The commander gave the enlisted men their awards, promoting two to a higher rank.
17. (Man B) The shuttle mission could have lasted longer had the pump not malfunctioned.
18. (Woman) The display monitor showed that a typing error occurred.
19. (Man A) The gas tank in my new car is larger than the one in my old car, but gas was less expensive for my old car than it is now.
20. (Man B) We went to bed at midnight, but we set the alarm to wake us early at 5:00.

PART B

21. (Woman) I'm going to the doctor. I have something wrong with my contact lenses.
    (Man A) That's too bad.
    (Man B) What does the man mean?
22. (Woman) Do you get up at 5 every morning?
    (Man A) Yes, and I need seven hours of sleep. I should go to bed by 9 or 10, I guess.
    (Man B) How much sleep does the man need?
23. (Woman) The 5:00 bus is more expensive but faster.
    (Man A) To save 80 cents, I'll wait 20 minutes for the 5:20.
    (Man B) What bus will the man take?
24. (Man A) I'm exhausted today. I can't work anymore.
    (Woman) We still have to finish the report for tomorrow's deadline.
    (Man B) What describes the man?
25. (Man A) If you hadn't mentioned their dinner party, I could have gone home.
    (Woman) That would have been the third time you've disappointed them this month.
    (Man B) What's he going to do?
26. (Man A) Mrs. Smith, have you, or your husband, or any members of your family suffered from any form of mental illness?
    (Woman) No, but my father's family has a history of heart problems.
    (Man B) Who suffers from heart disease?
27. (Woman) I could be ready sooner if you'd help me take out the trash.
    (Man A) Sure. Where do I take it?
    (Man B) What does the woman want?
28. (Woman) Be glad you aren't at the other restaurant. They serve even bigger meals.

    (Man A) This is more than I can eat. Even you can't finish it all.
    (Man B) What does the man mean?
29. (Man A) After I take my car to be repaired, I'll go straight to my office.
    (Woman) Please stop for groceries on the way home if you have time.
    (Man B) What will the man do first?
30. (Woman) My shoes are too new. I even wore thick socks and I got blisters.
    (Man A) Perhaps you walked too far. You should wear new shoes only an hour a day.
    (Man B) What caused the blisters?
31. (Man A) My headaches are terrible. Maybe I need more sleep.
    (Woman) Actually, you need less sun and some aspirin. Plus it would help if you wore a hat. The sun is too bright.
    (Man B) What caused his headache?
32. (Woman) Annie invited me to Bill's house for Joe's birthday.
    (Man A) You haven't forgotten my dinner party, have you?
    (Man B) Whose house is the birthday party at?
33. (Man A) You're a good height. Just a little plump.
    (Woman) I wish I were taller. My hair would look longer if I were taller.
    (Man B) What describes this woman?
34. (Man A) I always begin my lectures with a joke. That puts the audience at ease.
    (Woman) Then they laugh to put *you* at ease.
    (Man B) How does the man like to begin?
35. (Woman) This is the silliest book I have ever read. It's plain ridiculous.
    (Man A) I've read duller books, though, but not one so long.
    (Man B) How does the man feel about the book?

PART C

(Man A) Questions 36 through 40 refer to the following lecture.
(Woman) Bats, contrary to popular opinion, are not evil creatures. In fact, bats are extremely valuable because they eat an enormous amount of insects. In addition, they help to pollinate certain plants and spread the seeds of others. Bats, which are the only flying mammals, are divided into two groups according to their eating habits: those that eat insects and those that eat fruits and blossoms. Because bats generally live in caves and come out only at night, their habits were not studied for a long time and they were viewed with suspicion and fear.

Many people are concerned that bats will settle in their hair, but actually a healthy bat will always avoid a collision. A bat emits a high-pitched sound, which echoes from any object the sound hits. By this echo, the bat can tell what the object is and where it is. Unless your hair is full of insects, you never have to worry about a bat landing on your head. Unfortunately, these myths and fears have caused entire bat populations to be exterminated.

Fear is the bat's worst enemy. Farmers have been known to set fires in the caves where bats live and have killed tens of thousands of bats at one time. Today there is an increased interest in bats and an organization has been formed to help conserve the existing bat population of the world. Mass killings are not the only cause of the death of certain bat populations. The people of some cultures love to eat them. There is a big market for bat meat, which is considered a delicacy. Many countries have stopped the import and export of bats.

36. (Man B) How does the speaker describe the bat?
37. (Man B) What is used to classify bats?
38. (Man B) How does a bat locate an object?
39. (Man B) What is the bat's worst enemy?
40. (Man B) Why must bat populations be conserved?

(Man A) Questions 41 through 45 refer to the following dialog.
(Woman) Ships are still a widely used form of transportation.
(Man B) Yes, you tend to forget about them unless you live near water. But passengers and goods are still transported up and down rivers and across lakes, seas, and oceans. The advantage of water routes is that, unlike roads, they were already there; they didn't have to be made or maintained.
(Woman) When you look at water transportation historically, you can see why nations with strong navies were the most powerful. The Phoenicians and Greeks were famous for their shipping expertise. Their routes extended all the way from the Mediterranean to India and along the coasts of Africa.
(Man B) Good harbors had to be found or built, however, and there had to be wood available for ship building.
(Woman) That's why the United States dominated the market in the nineteenth century. The large forests provided ready resources for building swift sailing vessels and cities like New York, Boston, and Baltimore have great harbors.
(Man B) Today, however, the high cost of American labor and ship construction has made it difficult for the United States to compete. Other countries now control the shipping lanes.

41. (Man A) According to the passage, what is a widely used form of transportation?
42. (Man A) What is the disadvantage of roads?
43. (Man A) In ancient times, which countries were the strongest?
44. (Man A) Why did the United States dominate the shipping market in the nineteenth century?
45. (Man B) Why is the United States no longer competitive in commercial shipping?

(Man A) Questions 46 through 50 refer to the following lecture.
(Woman) Some fifty years ago the world of art was elated with the shock of discovery. It was suddenly recognized that within the so-called dark continent a great art tradition had been flourishing for centuries. And it was observed that this African art anticipated in practice many of the most modern theories of artistic creation and technique.
For quite a while occasional African masks, wooden statues, ivories, and bronzes had been filtering back to Europe—the great British expedition to Benin in 1897 alone netted over two thousand bronzes, ivory, and wood carvings. But most of this art had been entombed in museum collections and forgotten by all but ethnologists. Europe and America had to grow in aesthetic theory before they could appreciate and understand African art, even though the technical excellence of African bronze casting was immediately recognized.
Today, however, thanks to the Cubist revolution, resulting in an entirely new aesthetic approach to works of art and our modern trend to cultural syncretism, it is no longer necessary to apologize for African art. It is universally recognized as one of the great artistic heritages of the world.

46. (Man B) What happened about 50 years ago?
47. (Man B) What important influence changed critics' attitudes toward African art?
48. (Man B) How long has Africa participated in artistic creation?
49. (Man B) How is African art considered in the modern world?
50. (Man B) What was historically recognized as an example of technical excellence?

PRACTICE TEST 4

PART A

1. (Man A) I beat the rug to get it clean, but the dust flew in my hair.
2. (Man B) Two boys started the marathon, and both finished.
3. (Woman) I had made reservations for 15, but there were 17 people in our party.
4. (Man A) Martin Luther King, Jr. had no intention of becoming so famous.
5. (Man B) Never in his life had the geologist seen anything like the Grand Canyon.
6. (Woman) The sports equipment that belongs to the school must be returned to the trainer at the end of the session.
7. (Man A) Because the sky was cloudy, no one was able to observe the eclipse.
8. (Man B) If the firemen had been called, they could have put out the fire.
9. (Woman) After I ate, I went to the movie, but Jim had already seen it, so he went to the store instead.
10. (Man A) The insurance coverage of Plan A is not as complete as that of Plan B but is more complete than Plan C.

350 Appendix

11.	(Man B)	The widest part of the river is a few miles from here.
12.	(Woman)	The bus pulled away from the curb before the attendant loaded the bags.
13.	(Man A)	Since the absentee votes were not counted, the election is invalid.
14.	(Man B)	The batteries have been in the camera too long, and now the flash won't work.
15.	(Woman)	Having worked with that technician before, we were reluctant to give him more responsibility.
16.	(Man A)	This error would never have occurred if the rules hadn't been ignored.
17.	(Man B)	The problem wouldn't have become so serious if it had been dealt with sooner.
18.	(Woman)	The committee established 30 recommendations for the Review Board to consider.
19.	(Man A)	Even if we leave within the next half-hour, we'll still be too late for the ceremony.
20.	(Man B)	The grain of the wood was gray, but I polished it anyway till it shone.

PART B

21.	(Man A)	Can't you walk a little faster?
	(Woman)	This is the fastest I can.
	(Man B)	What does the man think about the woman?
22.	(Woman)	Where have you been?
	(Man A)	I went for a walk, then decided to call on some friends.
	(Man B)	What did the man do first?
23.	(Woman)	If you had listened to me, we'd be at the party by now. Move over. I'll drive.
	(Man A)	I was sure I knew how to get there. I'll turn around.
	(Man B)	What's the problem?
24.	(Man A)	I gave the man full payment when he asked for it.
	(Woman)	No wonder he hasn't finished the job yet.
	(Man B)	Whom are they talking about?
25.	(Woman)	Your nose is like your mother's.
	(Man A)	Yours is like your father's. My eyes are like my grandfather's!
	(Man B)	Whose nose does the woman's nose resemble?
26.	(Man A)	Hand me the papers from my briefcase.
	(Woman)	Is that your briefcase there, next to the typewriter?
	(Man B)	What does he want?
27.	(Man A)	How many classes are you taking?
	(Woman)	I've decided to take only one course and try to find a job.
	(Man B)	What will the woman do?
28.	(Woman)	If your dog is eight, that's about 80 in human terms, right?
	(Man A)	No, it's seven human years to each year of a dog's life.
	(Man B)	How old is the dog?
29.	(Man A)	I gave you two dollars. You've given me back 50 cents.
	(Woman)	That's right. The milk cost $1.50.
	(Man B)	How much change was there?
30.	(Man A)	Those shoes you're wearing are a beautiful color.
	(Woman)	I know. It's your favorite. You always choose it, for ties, shirts, suits . . . everything.
	(Man B)	What does the man like?
31.	(Woman)	You never should have gone out in the rain.
	(Man A)	I wouldn't have, but they were expecting me.
	(Man B)	What did the woman want the man to do?
32.	(Man A)	You look much slimmer.
	(Woman)	I stopped eating bread last week.
	(Man B)	What happened to the woman?
33.	(Woman)	If you had more experience, I'd hire you this minute.
	(Man A)	My supervisors will tell you that I learn very quickly!
	(Man B)	Where does this conversation take place?
34.	(Man A)	Should we take out or eat in tonight?
	(Woman)	I'm too tired to cook.
	(Man B)	What does the woman mean?
35.	(Woman)	If these prices get any higher, I'll have to go on a diet.
	(Man A)	You should anyway.
	(Man B)	What does the man mean?

PART C

(Man A)	Questions 36 through 40 refer to the following lecture.
(Man B)	Among the most exciting educational research findings of recent years is that human beings have "multiple intelligences." Prior to this study, people were considered either intelligent or not, based on the results of an IQ test.
	However, we now know that a person's IQ reflects only a part of a person's "multiple intelligence." These are secrets just now being uncovered, and they help to explain how "smart" people can be "stupid," and vice versa. The reality is that we are smart in different ways and are smarter in some situations than in others.
36.	(Woman)	What general opinion preceded this study?
37.	(Woman)	What do the recent findings show?
38.	(Woman)	What does "multiple intelligences" refer to?
39.	(Woman)	What part does an IQ have in these findings?
40.	(Woman)	How does one explain "smart" people doing something "stupid"?
(Man A)	Questions 41 through 45 refer to the following lecture.
(Man B)	Carbohydrates are often considered to be less than nutritious, undesirable, or fattening. In fact, carbohydrates are essential in the diet to provide energy. This in turn permits proteins to be used for growth and maintenance of body cells. Carbohydrates are essential and should never be drastically cut from the diet.
	Carbohydrates are named for their chemical composition: carbon, hydrogen, and oxygen. Through a highly complex mechanism involving the sun, air, and soil, plants store energy in the form of carbohydrates. Carbohydrates make up the supporting tissue of plants and are an important food for all animals, including humans.
	When people eat cereal grains, fruits, and vegetables—rich sources of carbohydrates—they obtain energy directly at the rate of 4 calories per gram; when animals eat plants, humans benefit indirectly by eating meat. Carbohydrates from cereal grains represent the primary source of energy for many nations of the world.
41.	(Woman)	How are carbohydrates presented?
42.	(Woman)	What do carbohydrates provide?

Appendix 351

43.	(Woman)	Which of the following is a rich source of carbohydrates?		(Woman)	The people who really made money were the men who provided the services for the gold seekers. Prospectors always needed tools, food, donkeys, horses, and mules.
44.	(Woman)	What is the primary source of energy internationally?			
45.	(Woman)	What stores energy in the form of carbohydrates?		(Man B)	Yes, the mule herder was probably the most wealthy man in the town. Everyone needed a mule.
	(Man A)	Questions 46 through 50 refer to the following dialog.			
	(Woman)	When most Americans think of the Gold Rush, they think of the discovery of gold in California in 1848. Prospectors, merchants, and adventurers from east of the Mississippi rushed west to California to make their fortunes.		(Woman)	It seems they could get by without a wife or a family, but they had to have a mule.
				(Man B)	A few of the towns where gold was discovered are still inhabited. Most are ghost towns. No one lives there but wild animals.
			46.	(Man A)	Where was the 1848 Gold Rush?
			47.	(Man A)	What was required to work a mine?
	(Man B)	Very few of them became rich, though. It was hard work. City people from New York and Pennsylvania weren't used to working with their hands. It required a great deal of capital even to look for a mine, and if you were lucky enough to find one, then it took a great deal of money to take the gold out of the mine.	48.	(Man A)	According to the speakers, who profited the most from the Gold Rush?
			49.	(Man A)	What did every prospector need?
			50.	(Man A)	What has happened to most of the Gold Rush towns?

PRACTICE TEST 5

PART A

1.	(Man A)	The accountant can't be trusted because he doesn't have much sense.
2.	(Man B)	We hiked a total of thirty miles, but our coach walked only half as far.
3.	(Woman)	Newly designed jets make less noise than the older ones even though the new jets are much larger.
4.	(Man A)	The memorial was dedicated by the widows of the victims.
5.	(Man B)	The landlord couldn't understand why the tenant refused to rent the house from him.
6.	(Woman)	Everyone but the engineer agreed that the building plans should be submitted to the city planner.
7.	(Man A)	The nurse's clock was broken, so she overslept and was late for duty.
8.	(Man B)	If she married a prince, she'd be a princess.
9.	(Woman)	Until clocks were invented, people used constellations to tell time at night.
10.	(Man A)	The 13 students will meet the teacher at 9 o'clock to take the test.
11.	(Man B)	The highway department needed more men to complete the road-widening work by winter.
12.	(Woman)	Before opening the cover to the vat, you must turn off the electricity and put on protective clothing.
13.	(Man A)	If the exchange student had studied, she would have gotten an A.
14.	(Man B)	The door was left open, so the wind blew the vase of flowers off the table.
15.	(Woman)	Concerned citizens' groups keep a close watch on the activities of the mayor and his council.
16.	(Man A)	Despite his crippling disease, Stephen Hawking is considered one of the world's most brilliant and productive scientists.
17.	(Man B)	Since water is an excellent conductor of electricity, it isn't a good idea to swim during an electrical storm.
18.	(Woman)	Thirteen of us tried to go to the concert, but only eight of us could get in.
19.	(Man A)	I woke at 8:30, knowing the appointment was at 9:45, but despite all my plans, I still got there at 10.
20.	(Man B)	The prime minister's speech was not well received.

PART B

21.	(Man A)	Would you mind if I opened the window and the curtains? We need some fresh air.
	(Woman)	We also need to keep it quiet in here.
	(Man B)	What does the woman mean?
22.	(Man A)	Why did you get up at 6? I thought your meeting wasn't until 10.
	(Woman)	I always jog in the park from 7 to 8.
	(Man B)	When was her meeting?
23.	(Woman)	How much did the aerograms cost?
	(Man A)	Oh, 46 cents each. They came stamped.
	(Man B)	How much did the aerograms cost?
24.	(Woman)	These are simply delicious grapes.
	(Man A)	You're certainly eating them heartily enough.
	(Man B)	How is she eating her food?
25.	(Man A)	I don't like the prices on this menu. They always seem too high.
	(Woman)	You never want to eat anywhere else, though.
	(Man B)	What does the man like?
26.	(Man A)	Where is the umbrella that was in the closet? I have to return it to my boss.
	(Woman)	I gave it to your brother.
	(Man B)	Whose umbrella does the brother have?
27.	(Woman)	You rowed hard today and won the race.
	(Man A)	Yes, I practiced a lot all month and didn't eat much yesterday.
	(Man B)	Why did the man win?
28.	(Woman)	If I go to Paris, will you meet me there? We can visit my cousin's new home.
	(Man A)	I have to go to London, but if I have time, I'll meet you there on the weekend.
	(Man B)	What's the man going to do?

29.	(Man A)	Did you go to the store before or after you took a nap this afternoon?	38.	(Man B)	What is necessary for successful reading?
	(Woman)	After. First, I took a nap, and then I took a walk. I did the shopping before I had dinner.	39.	(Man B)	How is reading described?
			40.	(Man B)	What is given as an example of an ineffective program?
	(Man B)	What did the woman do last?			
30.	(Man A)	Could you sign on this line? I'll find a box for your glasses.		(Man B)	Questions 41 through 45 refer to the following dialog.
	(Woman)	Can they be gift-wrapped?		(Woman)	Your resume shows you studied in Perugia, Italy. I've heard of Perugia before.
	(Man B)	Where does this conversation take place?			
31.	(Woman)	I'll never learn this language properly. It's too difficult!		(Man A)	Well, it's known because there's a big chocolate factory there.
	(Man A)	Don't give up!		(Woman)	But I'm thinking of something else . . . in history or art. . . .
	(Man B)	What does the man mean?			
32.	(Man A)	We must have a bad connection. I can hardly hear you.		(Man A)	There is a famous Etruscan arch. In fact, it's located near the university I attended.
	(Woman)	I was only complaining about my job.		(Woman)	Yes, that's it! It must have been quite an experience studying in such surroundings.
	(Man B)	Where is this conversation taking place?			
33.	(Man A)	When does the express train leave? At 8:45?		(Man A)	It was exhilarating. I plan to go back someday.
	(Woman)	No, at 9:30, I believe.	41.	(Man B)	What is the main topic of the conversation?
	(Man B)	When does the express train leave?	42.	(Man B)	What is the relationship between the two speakers?
34.	(Woman)	The boat only holds four people. How did you reserve five seats?	43.	(Man B)	Where does the conversation take place?
			44.	(Man B)	When does the conversation take place?
	(Man A)	They've enlarged it to carry six. I'll reserve the last seat for you.	45.	(Man B)	What will the woman probably do next?
	(Man B)	How many people can go on the boat?		(Man B)	Questions 46 through 50 refer to the following lecture.
35.	(Woman)	Did you hear about the man next door? His car was stolen overnight.		(Man A)	Spanish explorers first came to Texas in 1519, but it took over 160 years before the first Spanish settlers arrived. The native Indian tribes were hostile to the new settlers and many of the settlements were abandoned. The remaining settlements also came under attack from the French colony, which then bordered Texas.
	(Man A)	What? In this neighborhood?			
	(Man B)	What happened?			

PART C

	(Man A)	Questions 36 through 40 refer to the following lecture.			In 1812, Mexico, which controlled Texas, gained its independence from Spain. Mexico encouraged American settlers to move to Texas. The first colony was led by Stephen Austin who is now called the Father of Texas; the state capital, Austin, is named after him.
	(Woman)	Computer-based reading programs must be founded on an understanding of both computers and reading instruction. Programs that ignore either element will be less than fully effective. A computer program with spectacular graphics and sophisticated computer operations is of little value if it fails to teach needed reading skills. Similarly, an electronic page-turner wastes the potential of a powerful instructional tool.			
					The American settlers soon outnumbered the Mexican settlers and they resented Mexican laws restricting immigration and requiring all settlers to be Catholic. In 1835, the Texans temporarily rid the territory of the Mexican military. But it was not until 1836, after several bloody battles, including the defense of the Alamo, that Texas became an independent republic.
		All reading instruction is ultimately based on teachers' beliefs and assumptions about the reading process and the optimal conditions for facilitating reading acquisition. Reading is an active process in which a reader uses a variety of psycholinguistic skills to infer the writer's intended meaning. The cues that assist the reading process are phonic skills, linguistic skills, knowledge about the surrounding world, and problem-solving strategies. This view of reading leads to several assumptions about the optimal instructional approaches for teaching reading to students.			
					This independence lasted nine years, and then in 1845 Texas joined the United States and became the 28th state in the Union. Today it is the second-largest state in the Union.
			46.	(Woman)	Where did the first European settlers in Texas come from?
			47.	(Woman)	What word describes the attitude of the Indians toward the settlers?
			48.	(Woman)	Which country encouraged American settlers to move to Texas?
36.	(Man B)	How are computers described?	49.	(Woman)	What did Mexican laws impose?
37.	(Man B)	What does a sound reading instruction program include?	50.	(Woman)	When did Texas become an independent republic?

PRACTICE TEST 6

PART A

1. (Man A) My daughter has been helping my son with his studies.
2. (Man B) Flight 818 departs at 20 of 8 tonight.
3. (Woman) Prices couldn't fall any lower.
4. (Man A) The lack of rain caused an increase in food prices.
5. (Man B) If we can't raise more money, the project will be cancelled.
6. (Woman) The price tag said $12.00, but there was a 33 1/3% discount on all merchandise.
7. (Man A) It is critical that trainees pay close attention to detail.
8. (Man B) The janitor found the teacher's briefcase and gave it to the principal.
9. (Woman) More books were on display this year even though many publishers did not exhibit at the fair.
10. (Man A) If you see an accident, you should report it to the police immediately.
11. (Man B) Bill sipped his drink slowly.
12. (Woman) Half of us went to the movies and the rest stayed home.
13. (Man A) The participants were seated around an oval table.
14. (Man B) The first payment for $49.14 is due on the 4th of this month.
15. (Woman) Our professor said he would never change his mind.
16. (Man A) The boy missed the ball, which hit the window and broke it.
17. (Man B) My father's brother came to visit last summer by car.
18. (Woman) If it rains, we'll cancel the picnic.
19. (Man A) The conductor signaled the engine, then climbed aboard the train.
20. (Man B) The budget for defense is greater than the budget for education and health combined.

PART B

21. (Man A) Is that a new pair of shoes you're wearing?
    (Woman) Yes, do you like the color?
    (Man B) What did the woman do?
22. (Woman) If George comes to dinner, there'll be 10 for dinner.
    (Man A) Let's invite two more. Then there'll be an even dozen.
    (Man B) If everyone comes, how many will have dinner?
23. (Man A) The fence measures 16 by 6 by 60.
    (Woman) 60 inches! Isn't that an odd length?
    (Man B) How long is the fence?
24. (Man A) I can't find my pen. I need to write a check.
    (Woman) I'll help you look for it later. Right now I need your help fixing this shelf.
    (Man B) What will they do first?
25. (Man A) This isn't the worst hotel that I've been in.
    (Woman) I hate this hotel and I'm checking out.
    (Man B) What is the woman going to do?
26. (Woman) If everyone agrees to come to the reception, what will we do?
    (Man A) Don't worry. Of the 50 we invited, only half indicated they were coming.
    (Man B) How many people are expected?
27. (Woman) Be careful of the ice on the bridge.
    (Man A) I'll slow down when I get there.
    (Man B) What is the potential problem?
28. (Man A) If I pass this test, I can go to the college of my choice.
    (Woman) If not, you can work for your father.
    (Man B) What happens if the man passes the test?
29. (Man A) Come on in! The water's great!
    (Woman) OK. I'll go get my suit on.
    (Man B) What are they talking about?
30. (Man A) Tonight I'm leaving for a ten-day cruise.
    (Woman) I envy your long vacation. Mine is only four days long.
    (Man B) How long is the woman's vacation?
31. (Woman) Is there a dog in the house?
    (Man A) I hope not. I'm allergic to dogs.
    (Man B) Why is the man concerned?
32. (Woman) The fundraising committee raised only half of what it needed.
    (Man A) One-quarter of a million is respectable, however.
    (Man B) How much money did they raise?
33. (Man A) Are you catching the 11:50 train to Washington?
    (Woman) Yes. I thought I'd get a cab in about 15 minutes.
    (Man B) When will the woman catch the cab?
34. (Man A) I used to collect rare books, but now I barely look at them.
    (Woman) That's a pity. I'm always rereading mine.
    (Man B) What does the woman like to do?
35. (Man A) I never want to go to that restaurant again.
    (Woman) Me neither. Both the service and food were bad.
    (Man B) Why are the two upset?

PART C

(Woman) Questions 36 through 40 refer to the following lecture.
(Man B) Frederick W. Taylor, often referred to as the Father of Scientific Management, is the best known of all the scientific managers. Born in Germantown, Pennsylvania, in 1856, he spent many of his early years attending school in Germany and France and traveling on the European continent. In 1872, he enrolled at Phillips Exeter Academy to prepare for Harvard College. Although he passed the Harvard entrance exams with honors, poor eyesight prevented him from attending the college. In late 1874, Taylor entered the pattern-making and machinist trades in a small company owned by family friends. In 1878, employment in the machinist trade was difficult to obtain, so Taylor went to work as a laborer at the Midvale Steel Company. Within

354 Appendix

eight years he rose from ordinary laborer to chief engineer of the works. Meanwhile, continuing his education through correspondence courses and home study, he managed to complete all requirements for a mechanical engineering degree at Stevens Institute.

36. (Man A) What is Frederick Taylor referred to as?
37. (Man A) Where was Frederick Taylor born?
38. (Man A) Why did Taylor fail to go to Harvard after high school?
39. (Man A) How long did it take Taylor to rise from laborer to chief engineer?
40. (Man A) How did Taylor become an engineer?

(Man A) Questions 41 through 45 refer to the following dialog.
(Woman) People believe that dogs were the first domestic animals. Drawings on cave walls indicate that dogs were used for hunting by primitive man. They probably originated in southwest Asia as part of the wolf family. In ancient Egypt, there were only two distinct breeds recorded: a short-legged type and a greyhound type.
(Man B) Today there are about 200 different breeds of dogs, each selectively bred for a different purpose. The sporting dogs, for example, hunt by air scent, whereas the hound group tracks its prey by ground scent.
(Woman) Dogs really have a good sense of smell, don't they? They always seem to find their way home.
(Man B) That's where most dogs are today: home. Few work for their living. The majority of dogs today are just companions, except guard dogs.
(Woman) There was a study done in the United States that showed that dogs make good companions for the sick. Lonely, old people who are sick often feel much better when they are given a dog to pet or hold. The dog gives them a purpose—someone they can take care of.

(Man B) That's why dogs are called man's best friend. They have unquestioning loyalty to their owners. That's one of their most attractive characteristics. Dog and owner become mutually dependent on one another. It's nice to have a friend who will never disappoint you.

41. (Man A) Where did dogs probably originate?
42. (Man A) What were dogs first used for?
43. (Man A) How does a sporting dog find its prey?
44. (Man A) What is the primary function of dogs today?
45. (Man A) What is one of the most attractive features of dogs?

(Man A) Questions 46 through 50 refer to the following lecture.
(Woman) To define an essay precisely is extremely difficult. It is at once apparent that the essay is as distinctively and fundamentally literary, and as demanding of skill and creative power, as poetry, fiction, biography, or drama. Etymologically, the word "essay" indicates something tenuous, tentative, or unfinished, so that the indefiniteness of the thing itself is firmly fixed in its name. Its inherent vagueness has become more vague by the operation of a sort of historical natural law; among the strays of literature, those mavericks whose ownership and bloodlines are uncertain have been usually branded as essays. In effect the frontier between the essay and other literary forms is, as Carl Van Doren said, as imperceptible as a political boundary like the Mason-Dixon line, yet clear to anyone who crosses it.

46. (Man B) What is an essay compared to?
47. (Man B) What did the word essay originally mean?
48. (Man B) What is an essay an example of?
49. (Man B) What is the Mason-Dixon line?
50. (Man B) Who is quoted in the lecture?

LISTENING TARGETS TAPESCRIPTS

STATEMENTS

Similar Sounds

1. He has a habit of going to bed early.
2. Given his health, he cannot work overtime.
3. Keeping close to her, he was able to hear their conversation.
4. The ice on the lake will melt in this heat.
5. The boat sank fairly quickly in the storm.

Number Discrimination

1. Open your books to page 16.
2. Flight 13 to Madrid leaves at 8:30.
3. Eighteen of us expect to graduate on the 8th.
4. John was born on June 30, 1985.
5. At 20 minutes before 9, teams began to appear on the field.

Synonyms

1. She was barely able to lift the package.
2. Practically all bears outside their natural habitat are kept in cages.
3. We lost sight of them in the enveloping mist.
4. The river was too high for the raft trip we'd planned.
5. She'd just recovered from a bout of flu when she was called away on business.

Negation

1. We don't think any of the boys was invited to go.
2. There were not enough chairs for those who did not come on time.
3. I wouldn't blame anyone who couldn't stay awake for this performance.
4. Anytime he calls me, I pretend I am out.
5. Marjorie had no reason to buy the book.

Contextual Reference

1. Claire and Ann found their route was more direct and consequently faster than mine.
2. Although Bill liked his cousin Paul, he was fonder of his brother Jim.
3. I let my mother take George's car to pick up his laundry.
4. My father and his brother visited my sister at camp.
5. Even when I tell John the answers, he still asks Karen for hers.

Cause and Effect

1. Since the taxi was caught in traffic, I missed the plane.
2. Because it rained, the birds stopped singing.
3. She was ill that day and had to miss the exam.
4. I smiled at him, and he began to talk more openly.
5. When she knew of his presence in the program, she changed her plans.

Conditionals

1. If the rain had abated, we could have left sooner.
2. If you close the door, the noise will decrease.
3. If I were younger, I would not make the same mistakes.
4. If more complaints are registered, the product will be recalled.
5. If she arrives before dusk, we'll go for a long walk.

Chronological Order

1. When the diners were finished with their trays, the waitress took them away.
2. After we went skiing, we relaxed by the fire they had ready when we returned.
3. First we went to the store, then we cooked dinner, and at last we went to bed.
4. When he told us he was coming, we began to paint the guest room.
5. She stopped by the party first before going to the concert.

Comparisons

1. The engineer insisted that the bridge be made wider.
2. Cliff does better than Joe on these tests, I think.
3. The growth of the suburbs has made it more difficult for small urban stores.
4. The runway of the new airport is the longest in the Eastern Hemisphere, but not in the world.
5. The days in the winter are shorter than in the summer.

SHORT DIALOGS

Similar Sounds

1. (Woman) Stop me if you've heard this one.
   (Man A) Please, we can't take any more of your humor.
   (Man B) What is the woman going to do?
2. (Man A) I wouldn't take any bets that horse would win.
   (Woman) Really? I was going to say he looks as if he could beat them all.
   (Man B) What does the man think?
3. (Man A) Is it the wind or are you making that noise?
   (Woman) It's the flapping curtain. Close the window.
   (Man B) What causes the sound?
4. (Woman) Don't you like the dark?
   (Man A) I'd prefer the light. Can you find the switch?
   (Man B) What does the man want?
5. (Man A) Is this what you planned? It seems all wrong to me.
   (Woman) This group of plants belongs here. Where would you put them?
   (Man B) What are they discussing?

Number Discrimination

1. (Man A) Are we supposed to leave at 8:13?
   (Woman) I'm not sure. All I remember is that the flight number is 833.
   (Man B) What time does the man think they'll leave?
2. (Man A) There are only 13 chairs for 14 of us.
   (Woman) Why not find another, then?
   (Man B) How many chairs are there?
3. (Woman) The flight leaves on the 8th at 9:15.
   (Man A) That seems a long time from now.
   (Man B) What day does the flight leave?
4. (Woman) One of her grades was 90, and another was 50.
   (Man A) Her work is very uneven.
   (Man B) What was the woman's low grade?
5. (Man A) The temperature is supposed to reach 88 today and go down to 60 this evening.
   (Woman) Isn't that more than 18 degrees difference?
   (Man B) What is the evening temperature forecast?

Synonyms

1. (Man A) There was a great deal of sleet last night. Did you hear the wind?
   (Woman) That's why I couldn't sleep. The wind was so strong.
   (Man B) What did they experience last night?
2. (Woman) I love the beach when the sand is fine and the water is just barely making waves.
   (Man A) I prefer an angry sea. That makes me feel better whenever I'm sad.
   (Man B) What does the man like?
3. (Man A) Will you have dinner with me on the boat?
   (Woman) I thought you might launch the boat at noon, so we could have lunch at sea and dinner in port.
   (Man B) What has the woman planned?
4. (Woman) The predominant factor is my need for relaxation.
   (Man A) There must be other alternatives to early retirement.
   (Man B) What is the woman going to do?
5. (Woman) There are so many children at the school, I wonder how the teacher keeps track of them.
   (Man A) I get cold feet at the thought of teaching. Standing in front of the room frightens me.
   (Man B) What is the man's attitude toward teaching?

Negation

1. (Man A) I'm not prepared for the test. I'm nervous. Aren't you?
   (Woman) No, I'm not. I studied.
   (Man B) What describes the man?
2. (Man A) Isn't that the book I loaned you a while ago?
   (Woman) I'm afraid I'm very bad at returning things.
   (Man B) What describes the woman's emotion?
3. (Man A) I never drink water without ice.
   (Woman) Don't you think that's bad for your stomach?
   (Man B) What would be the woman's advice?
4. (Man A) Wasn't that a good way to see the show?
   (Woman) I think we could have had better seats.
   (Man B) Where did this conversation take place?
5. (Woman) I don't believe we've ever met before, have we?
   (Man A) We've been introduced at other parties. Don't you remember?
   (Man B) What does the man mean?

Contextual Reference

1. (Woman) Please take this package and give it to Kate to give to her brother.
   (Man A) Kate's not here. I'll take care of it.
   (Man B) Whom is the package for?
2. (Woman) Did Louise tell you that John is coming to visit tomorrow?
   (Man A) Yes, she told me yesterday that he'd be here by the weekend.
   (Man B) When does John arrive?
3. (Man A) I bought a scarf for Laura at the store Joan owns.
   (Woman) Is it like the one I have?
   (Man B) To whom is the man giving the scarf?
4. (Woman) George and his family are planning to live in your old family house.
   (Man A) No one's been there since grandfather died.
   (Man B) Who will live in the house?
5. (Man A) My grades are higher than Susan's and lower than Sidney's.
   (Woman) And mine are higher than Sidney's.
   (Man B) Whose grades are the lowest?

Cause and Effect

1. (Man A) Because I was late, they would not let me take the test.
   (Woman) What will you do now? Take a job?
   (Man B) How did being late affect the man?
2. (Man A) Why are you eating that apple?
   (Woman) It's the only food in the house.
   (Man B) Why did the woman choose the apple?
3. (Man A) My feet swell in the heat, and then my shoes get tight.
   (Woman) Have you tried stretching them? I understand it works.
   (Man B) What does the heat affect?
4. (Man A) When I go on a diet, I eat only grapefruit, and that takes off weight quickly.
   (Woman) I prefer to eat whatever I want and then run to lose weight.
   (Man B) What causes the man's weight loss?
5. (Man A) Because I love autumn, I take vacations during that time of year.
   (Woman) Isn't it cold and wet most of the season? I would be bothered by that.
   (Man B) What season is the woman referring to?

Conditionals

1. (Man A) It would be easier to drive if there were no other cars on the road.
   (Woman) Did you bring your license this time?
   (Man B) What would the man prefer?
2. (Woman) If you're going there anyway, would you change my travelers' checks at the bank?
   (Man A) It depends on whether or not they'll accept my passport as identification.
   (Man B) Where is the man going?
3. (Woman) If you spill ink on the tablecloth, what then?
   (Man A) I'll buy you another one.
   (Man B) What word describes the man?
4. (Man A) The doctor said if I kept smoking, I would increase my chances of having a heart attack.
   (Woman) Did he suggest losing some weight, too?
   (Man B) How does the woman perceive the man?
5. (Man A) Next time I see Fred, I'll ask him if he's forgotten he owes me money.
   (Woman) Why not just ask him to repay you?
   (Man B) What will the man do to Fred?

Chronological Order

1. (Man A) When I came home, I saw the fire had gone out.
   (Woman) I must not have used enough kindling when I started it.
   (Man B) When was the fire built?
2. (Woman) When Sally arrives in an hour, we can go shopping.
   (Man A) Let's finish the dishes now, and then we can talk until she comes.
   (Man B) When will they wash the dishes?

3. (Woman) When I travel, I like to get up, tour museums, walk through the town, and rest in the afternoon.
   (Man A) And you never eat until evening?
   (Man B) What does the woman do after she gets up?
4. (Man A) Who would have thought that by the time he arrived, we'd have left?
   (Woman) I feel bad. I said we'd wait for him.
   (Man B) Why is the woman unhappy?
5. (Man A) I'll invite you to our country house as soon as I finish my thesis.
   (Woman) At the rate you write, that may be next year.
   (Man B) When is she invited?

Comparisons

1. (Woman) This light shines more brightly than the one upstairs.
   (Man A) It's the same wattage. It must be the color of the shade, then.
   (Man B) What makes the light seem brighter?
2. (Man A) The mountain seems higher. It makes me dizzy to climb it this year, but it's worth it for the view.
   (Woman) The mountain may not be higher, but we're older.
   (Man B) What has changed since last year?
3. (Woman) The current deficit is the greatest this country's seen.
   (Man A) Next year it will be even bigger.
   (Man B) What are they talking about?
4. (Man A) I think this exercise program has made me stronger.
   (Woman) You look better, and I'm sure you feel better.
   (Man B) What has the man been doing?
5. (Man A) This is the longest play I've ever seen. We've been here three hours, and we have another act to go.
   (Woman) It's shorter than the eight-hour play we saw last year.
   (Man B) How do the plays compare?

MINI-TALKS

(Man A) Questions 1 through 5 refer to the following lecture.
(Woman) The most critical time in the life of a human is the first few hours after birth. Doctors have learned that a newborn infant cannot be treated like a small child. This is especially true of "high-risk babies"—babies who are born prematurely or underweight or with some life-threatening defect. These babies need immediate, imaginative, intensive care, not only for survival but to help avoid physical problems later in life. This specialized care is called neonatology, and it is concerned with the first three months of life.

Dozens of major hospitals have opened newborn intensive care units where specialists are ready to use their skills as the need arises. They are alerted to pregnancies that may develop complications. For example, if a woman who is pregnant enters the hospital and is under the age of 18 or over the age of 40, or has a medical problem, the neonatologists are advised. The neonatologists can then attend the delivery of a baby, rush the newborn infant to the special care unit, examine it, and provide treatment or surgery if needed. In addition to lifesaving equipment, the care units depend on nurses and volunteers who rock, feed, and play with the infant and provide the most essential medicine—love. Doctors have found that lack of love has adverse physical and psychological effects on newborn babies. The most common cause of infant deaths is prematurity. But since the establishment of infant care centers, the survival rate for high-risk babies in the United States has risen from 75 percent to 90 percent.

1. (Man B) When is the most critical time in the life of a human being?
2. (Man B) What are premature babies known as?
3. (Man B) Which group is most likely to have a complicated pregnancy?
4. (Man B) What is neonatology's primary concern?
5. (Man B) What percentage of premature infants survive?

(Man A) Questions 6 through 9 refer to the following lecture.
(Man B) The earliest origins of romance novels are obscure. However, some believe the origins are found in songs of the eleventh-century troubadours. These songs with their accent on love predict the advent of the romantic novel. Indeed, the very term romance, from the French *roman*, or fiction, indicates that romance novels were regarded as a fabulous state not quite based in reality.

While today literary experts may deplore the turning of major publishing houses toward the mass market of romance readers, the publishers are supporting a time-honored tradition. Let us not forget that the novels of Sir Walter Scott, for example, are shameless gothic romances made respectable by means of thin veils of history. The gothic novel of the late eighteenth century inspired a whole host of second- and third-generation romance authors. Both the historical and the gothic romance are alive and well today, thanks to the readership's avid appetite for the fabulous, the supernatural, and the lovelorn.

6. (Woman) What did early readers consider romance novels to be?
7. (Woman) What gives the gothic novel respectability?
8. (Woman) Who publishes romance novels these days?
9. (Woman) When did the gothic novel appear?

(Man A) Questions 10 through 12 refer to the following lecture.
(Woman) The English Romantic poets were distinguished by a naturalness of style hitherto unknown in the classically pure, rigidly formulated work of the Enlightenment authors. Difficult as it is for us to comprehend now, when his language appears stilted, even flowery, to the modern ear, Wordsworth's earliest poems were considered radical inspirations to a whole generation.

In fact, to write a simple poem about seeing daffodils was a thing unheard of in the lofty ranks of England's serious poets of the time. Wordsworth's focus on a common experience, remembered and related without recourse to hyperbole, immediately set him apart from the rest. He was followed of course by Coleridge, then Shelly, and Byron, and finally Keats—the latter three of whom were to make fun of their hero as he became more famous, more respectable, and finally more labored in his verse.

Still Wordsworth's contributions freed his successors forever from the need to create in labored language on subjects of suitable importance. He was a revolutionary, no matter what his sentiments became in later life.

10. (Man B) Who were Wordsworth's colleagues and followers?
11. (Man B) What distinguished his verse?
12. (Man B) What did his poetry do for his colleagues?

(Man A) Questions 13 through 16 refer to the following lecture.
(Man B)   Jackson Pollock and David Smith stand as two giants of the contemporary postwar art world. Indeed, their contributions to painting and sculpture may be said to be responsible for the shift in focus from Europe to the United States—specifically, the New York Abstract Expressionists and their colleagues. This dominance of the international art scene lasted for the next three decades and only recently has reversed, as the European Expressionists have once again captured critical attention.
    Under Pollock, painting became an interior journey, a turning away from the external horrors of war, its false heroics and nationalistic fervor. Like others of his generation, he was disillusioned with the experiences of the last two decades. His art became a way to transcend that anger and dismay.

13. (Woman) What was Pollock's medium?
14. (Woman) What group has held critical attention recently?
15. (Woman) What was the impulse for Pollock's paintings?
16. (Woman) What is Pollock's style?

(Man A) Questions 17 through 19 refer to the following lecture.
(Woman)   The new American cuisine is really an adaptation of European, Eastern, and Latin American recipes to the ingredients occurring naturally in the United States. With a heightened public consciousness about fats, carbohydrates, and food additives, American cuisine of this new type has become synonymous with lower calories, smaller portions beautifully served, unusual treatment of vegetables and fresh fish, and an emphasis on the healthful side of each meal.
    While many maintain that this standard grew up on the West Coast during the late 1960s and early 1970s, a few students of cuisine point out that this consciousness has been with us far longer, and is responsible for several excellent, long-recognized restaurants on the East Coast as well.

17. (Man B) Does the lecturer believe there is an indigenous American cuisine?
18. (Man B) What is associated with American cuisine?
19. (Man B) Where do most believe American cuisine originated?

DIALOGS

(Man A) Questions 1 through 4 refer to the following dialog.
(Woman) Did Johnny start preschool this September?
(Man B) Yes. I enrolled him at the Elm Street Preschool. I looked into a lot of different area preschools, and I liked the philosophy at Elm Street best.
(Woman) A philosophy for a preschool? Really?
(Man B) Oh, yes. It's very important. Some preschools encourage so-called academics, while others concentrate on social skills.
(Woman) What does that mean exactly?
(Man B) Well, the academic preschools teach numbers and letters. The others give the children opportunities for creative play. They believe that children learn best by playing. They also stress how to share, how to take turns, how to solve problems by talking it out.
(Woman) Gee, I never knew choosing a preschool was so complicated. Which philosophy does the Elm Street preschool follow?
(Man B) It believes that three- and four-year-olds aren't ready to form letters or to understand the abstraction of numbers. It gives the kids lots of opportunities to play in groups.

1. (Man A) What is the main topic of this conversation?
2. (Man A) What is the relationship of the two speakers?
3. (Man A) How would you describe the Elm Street Preschool?
4. (Man A) How did the woman describe choosing a preschool?

(Man B) Questions 5 through 9 refer to the following dialog.
(Man A) Well, what did you think of the party?
(Woman) I enjoyed the company and the food. It's too bad the music was so loud.
(Man A) But it was great music—great for dancing!
(Woman) Maybe so, but it sure made it difficult to hold a conversation. Anyway, not many people were dancing!
(Man A) It was a party! Why be so serious? You can always have discussions. . . .
(Woman) I like meeting new people. I don't necessarily discuss serious matters. And back to the music, as a musician, don't you think such a high volume distorts the music?

5. (Man B) What is the main topic of the conversation?
6. (Man B) What did the woman like?
7. (Man B) What is the man like?
8. (Man B) What was the woman's complaint?
9. (Man B) What is the man's occupation?

(Man A) Questions 10 through 14 refer to the following dialog.
(Man B) Excuse me, but have you seen my little gray dog?
(Woman) No, I'm sorry, I haven't. What's his name?
(Man B) Her name, actually. I call her Cinders because she's the color of soot.
(Woman) Why isn't she on a leash?
(Man B) She saw a squirrel and broke away before I could catch her.

10. (Man A) What word best describes the dog?
11. (Man A) Where does the conversation take place?
12. (Man A) Why did the dog run away?
13. (Man A) What would the woman recommend?
14. (Man A) What do soot and the dog have in common?

(Man A) Questions 15 through 17 refer to the following dialog.
(Man B) I can't wait to see the zoo. What time will the bus come?
(Woman) I think it's supposed to arrive around noon.
(Man B) When are we supposed to eat?
(Woman) On the bus. Didn't you remember to bring your lunch?
(Man B) No one told me to.
(Woman) That's not true. The teacher told us Friday.
(Man B) I wasn't here then.

15. (Man A) Where is the class going?
16. (Man A) What did the students need to bring?
17. (Man A) Why didn't the man have food?

Appendix 359

EXPLANATORY ANSWERS

PRACTICE TEST 1

SECTION 1

LISTENING COMPREHENSION

Part A

1. (A) Synonym: (A) is the closest in meaning. (B) similar sounds: *rather* and *father*; (C) similar sounds: *will fly* and *and I*; (D) is a contradiction of the statement.
2. (B) Comparison: (B) means the same, but uses a different vocabulary. (A) is a contradiction; (C) and (D) are true, but ignore the comparison with *walking*.
3. (C) Conditional: (C) is the closest in meaning to the statement. (A) similar sounds: *understand* and *stand*; (B) translates the first part of the statement too literally; (D) cannot be inferred from the information given.
4. (C) Chronological order: (C) means the same, but uses a different vocabulary. (A), (B), and (D) cannot be inferred from the information given.
5. (B) Contextual reference: (B) is a simplified version of the statement. (A) misinterprets the meaning of *follow* in this context; (C) and (D) cannot be inferred from the information given.
6. (B) Number discrimination: (B) is an inference of the statement. (A) similar sounds: *two movies* and *two of us*; (C) similar sounds: *afternoon* and *noon*; (D) similar sounds: *two movies* and *Tuesday*.
7. (C) Chronological order: (C) means the same, but uses a different vocabulary. (A) is a contradiction of the statement; (B) similar sounds: *last one off the bus* and *last bus*; (D) contradicts the statement.
8. (A) Synonym: (A) means the same, but uses a different vocabulary. (B), (C), and (D) cannot be inferred from the information given.
9. (A) Negation and Synonym: (A) means the same, but uses a different vocabulary. (B) confuses the meaning of the statement; (C) and (D) ask different questions.
10. (C) Chronological order: (C) means the same, but uses a different vocabulary. (A) confuses who moved; (B) offers a reason not contained in the statement; (D) cannot be inferred from the information given.
11. (A) Contextual reference: (A) means the same, but uses a different vocabulary. (B) and (D) confuse the meaning of the statement; (C) is a contradiction of the statement.
12. (A) Conditional: (A) means the same, but uses a different vocabulary. (B) misinterprets the conditional for an action in the past; (C) confuses *I need* with *I'll buy*; (D) confuses the adverb *past* and the verb *past*.
13. (B) Contextual reference: (B) means the same, but uses a different vocabulary. (A) contradicts the statement; (C) cannot be inferred from the information given; (D) changes the meaning of the statement.
14. (D) Contextual reference: (D) means the same, but uses a different vocabulary. (A) and (C) focus on *up in the Athletic Office*; (B) confuses the homonyms *gym* and *Jim*.
15. (B) Comparison: (B) means the same, but uses a different vocabulary. (A), (C), and (D) cannot be inferred from the information given.
16. (B) Chronological order: (B) is a simplified version of the statement. (A) cannot be inferred from the information given; (C) confuses the meaning of *this afternoon* in this context; (D) confuses the meaning of *next Monday* in this context.
17. (A) Number discrimination: (A) means the same, but uses a different vocabulary. (B) is true, but it ignores important elements of the statement; (C) and (D) cannot be inferred from the information given.
18. (B) Comparison: (B) is a simplified version of the statement. (A) is a contradiction of the information given; (C) cannot be inferred from the information given; (D) confuses the meaning of *another* for *other*.
19. (D) Synonym: (D) means the same, but uses a different vocabulary. (A), (B), and (C) cannot be inferred from the information given.
20. (C) Synonym: (C) means the same, but uses a different vocabulary. (A) cannot be inferred from the information given; (B) is a contradiction of the statement; (D) similar sounds: *bookcase* for *book*.

Part B

21. (D) Contextual reference: (D) is an inference from the information given. The key words are *loan* and *officers*.
22. (B) Contextual reference: (B) the key words are *you've had that cold*. (D) confuses the noun *cold* (ailment) with the adjective *cold* (temperature).
23. (B) Contextual reference: (B) this dialogue forces the listener to focus on the main subject—*buses*.
24. (B) Chronological order: (B) the key clause is *I'll make some tea*. (A) and (C) cannot be inferred from the information given; (D) confuses the topic.
25. (C) Number discrimination: (C) the key words are *for Friday, too*. (B) ignores what the man says.
26. (A) Cause and effect: (A) is a simplified version of the statement. (B) confuses *try again* with *try harder*; (C) confuses *get a busy signal* with *get busy*; (D) is not mentioned.
27. (C) Chronological order: (C) the key words are *eat at 4* (compared with 5 or 6). (A) is a contradiction; (B) and (D) are not mentioned.
28. (B) Cause and effect: (B) is the logical conclusion. (A), (C), and (D) cannot be inferred from the information given.
29. (B) Synonym: (B) is the logical conclusion. (A) misinterprets *afraid we'll miss* for *afraid of*; (C) and (D) cannot be inferred from the information given.
30. (B) Synonym: (B) is a logical inference based on the information given. (A) and (C) cannot be inferred from the information given; (D) similar sounds: *card* with *car*; *forgot your glasses* with *forgot your car*.
31. (B) Contextual reference: (B) is a logical inference based on the key words. (A) and (C) cannot be inferred from the information given; (D) similar sounds: *officer* with *office*.
32. (A) Chronological order: (A) is another way of saying *retire*. (B) similar sounds: *retires* with *tires*; (C) cannot be inferred from the information given; (D) similar sounds: *walk out the door* with *take a walk*.
33. (C) Contextual reference: (C) is a logical inference based on the key words: *fill it up, oil,* and *pump*. (A), (B), and (D) cannot be inferred from the information given.
34. (A) Synonym: (A) is a logical inference based on the information given. (B) confuses who's traveling; (C) cannot be inferred from the information given; (D) confuses whose friend is arriving.
35. (C) Contextual reference: (C) is the only logical conclusion; key words are *reservations, room*. (A), (B), and (D) cannot be inferred from the information given.

Part C

36. (A) Mini-Talk
37. (D) Mini-Talk
38. (C) Mini-Talk
39. (C) Mini-Talk
40. (A) Mini-Talk
41. (B) Mini-Talk
42. (C) Dialog
43. (B) Dialog
44. (A) Dialog
45. (B) Dialog
46. (A) Mini-Talk
47. (D) Mini-Talk
48. (B) Mini-Talk
49. (C) Mini-Talk
50. (A) Mini-Talk

SECTION 2

STRUCTURE AND WRITTEN EXPRESSION

1. (B) Word families: *Traditionally*
2. (B) Prepositions: *different from*
3. (B) Adjective clauses: *in which participants have*; introduces adjective clause
4. (D) Verb: subject-verb agreement: *there is*; see *a potential*
5. (C) Articles: *the atmosphere*
6. (B) Verb: inappropriate tense: *experiencing*; see *are. . . .*
7. (B) Parallel structures: *not just (not only) . . . but*
8. (D) Active/passive verbs: *composed*; see *were*
9. (A) Pronouns: agreement: *its*
10. (A) Verb: inappropriate tense: *they produced*; see *were losing*
11. (B) Noun clauses: *that* (object of believe)
12. (A) Pronouns: agreement: *their*; agrees with *residents and visitors*
13. (C) Parallel structures: *economically*; see *environmentally and*
14. (D) Active/passive verbs: *was established*
15. (D) Adverb clauses: *While*
16. (B) Verb: subject-verb agreement: *writer is*
17. (C) Verb omitted: *they have little sense*
18. (C) Adjective clauses: omit; *are still*
19. (A) Word families: *unlike*
20. (A) Verb: inappropriate tense: *drink*
21. (C) Verb: subject-verb agreement: *groups . . . check*
22. (B) Gerunds: *by* (preposition) *checking*
23. (B) Verb: inappropriate tense: *known*
24. (D) Pronouns: agreement: *songbirds . . . . their own*
25. (B) Word order: adjective/adverb placement: *growing need*
26. (B) Comparisons: *too thin*
27. (C) Word families: *health care*
28. (B) Adjective clauses: *and are capable*
29. (B) Verb: subject-verb agreement: *Leaves have*
30. (C) Word families: *may live*
31. (C) Verb: inappropriate tense: *exposure* or *exposing animals*
32. (A) Subject repeated: repetition omit *they*
33. (C) Pronouns: agreement: *its way*
34. (A) Adjective clauses: *Consumers spend*
35. (B) Word order: adjective/adverb placement: *electric elevator*
36. (C) Verb omitted: *that does not spoil*
37. (C) Infinitives: *to reduce*
38. (D) Articles: *the ocean*
39. (A) Word families: *Contrary*
40. (A) Comparatives: *the longest*

SECTION 3

READING COMPREHENSION AND VOCABULARY

1.	(C)	31.	(A)	Factual: positive
2.	(B)	32.	(B)	Factual: positive
3.	(D)	33.	(A)	Factual: positive
4.	(A)	34.	(B)	Inference: specific
5.	(B)	35.	(B)	Factual: positive
6.	(B)	36.	(A)	Factual: positive
7.	(D)	37.	(A)	Factual: positive
8.	(B)	38.	(B)	Factual: negative
9.	(C)	39.	(C)	Factual: positive
10.	(B)	40.	(A)	Factual: positive
11.	(D)	41.	(A)	Factual: positive
12.	(A)	42.	(C)	Inference: specific
13.	(B)	43.	(C)	Factual: positive
14.	(C)	44.	(A)	Factual: positive
15.	(A)	45.	(D)	Main idea
16.	(C)	46.	(C)	Inference: general
17.	(B)	47.	(A)	Viewpoint
18.	(A)	48.	(B)	Inference: specific
19.	(B)	49.	(C)	Factual: positive
20.	(D)	50.	(D)	Factual: positive
21.	(D)	51.	(A)	Factual: positive
22.	(C)	52.	(B)	Main idea
23.	(C)	53.	(B)	Main idea
24.	(A)	54.	(B)	Inference: general
25.	(B)	55.	(B)	Factual: positive
26.	(B)	56.	(C)	Factual: positive
27.	(D)	57.	(B)	Factual: positive
28.	(B)	58.	(D)	Factual: positive
29.	(C)	59.	(A)	Factual: positive
30.	(A)	60.	(A)	Inference: general

PRACTICE TEST 2

SECTION 1

LISTENING COMPREHENSION

Part A

1. (B) Synonym: (B) is the closest in meaning. (A) asks *where*; (C) asks *how long*; (D) asks for a reason for the delay.
2. (D) Negation: (D) offers a reason why the man hasn't received his two newspapers. (A) cannot be inferred from the information given; (B) similar sounds: *receive* and *receipt*; (C) confuses *newspapers* with *days*.
3. (D) Number discrimination: (D) means the same, but uses a different vocabulary. (A) cannot be inferred from the information given; (B) confuses the preposition *on* as indicating location; (C) ignores *exam* and confuses the meaning of *first*.
4. (A) Conditional: (A) means the same, but uses a different vocabulary. (B) focuses on the negative *don't*; (C) confuses the condition, *If you are hungry*; (D) focuses on *why don't you* and contradicts the meaning of the original statement.

5. (D) Number discrimination: (D) is a simplified version of the statement. (A) similar sounds: *ten dollars* and *ten people*; (B) similar sounds: *ten dollars* and *ten miles*; (C) misinterprets the direction of the ride.
6. (C) Synonym: (C) means the same, but uses a different vocabulary. (A) and (B) focus on *how*, but misinterpret its meaning; (D) similar sounds: *afternoon* and *noon*.
7. (B) Cause and effect: (C) is a simplified version of the statement. (A) similar sounds: *housework* and *homework*; (C) cannot be inferred from the information given; (D) mixes up the tenses; confuses the meaning of the statement.
8. (A) Synonym: (A) is a simplified version of the statement. (B) similar sounds: *train* and *plane*; confuses the time element; (C) similar sounds: *train* and *rain*; (D) confuses the meaning of the statement; similar sounds: *train* and *grain*.

9. (C) Chronological order: (C) means the same, but uses a different vocabulary. (A) confuses the meaning of the statement; (B) similar sounds: *woke* and *walk*; (D) is a contradiction of the statement.
10. (D) Synonym: (D) means the same, but uses a different vocabulary. (A) similar sounds: *park* and *parking*; *reserved* and *preserved*; (B) confuses the meaning of the statement; (C) focuses on *reserved* and misinterprets its meaning.
11. (C) Synonym: (C) means the same, but uses a different vocabulary. (A) confuses the meaning of the statement; (B) confuses the tenses of the verbs; (D) focuses on the books as opposed to the action of Richard's returning them.
12. (D) Chronological order: (D) is a simplified version of the directions given. (A) is not a direction; (B) and (C) confuse the meaning of the statement.
13. (A) Number discrimination: (A) is the closest in meaning. (B) similar sounds: *counted* and *count on*; (C) and (D) confuse the meaning of the statement.
14. (B) Number discrimination: (B) is the only truthful option. (A), (C), and (D) confuse the numbers.
15. (B) Synonym: (B) means the same, but uses a different vocabulary. (A) misinterprets *out of order*; (C) and (D) similar sounds: *phone* and *loan*.
16. (B) Synonym: (B) means the same, but uses a different vocabulary. (A) confuses the noun and participle form of *building*; (C) and (D) cannot be inferred from the information given.
17. (D) Chronological order: (D) is the only truthful option. (A), (B), and (C) confuse the meaning of the statement.
18. (B) Chronological order: (B) means the same, but uses a different vocabulary. (A) cannot be inferred from the information given; (C) similar sounds: *moving* and *movie*; (D) confuses the meaning of the statement.
19. (B) Negation: (B) is the closest in meaning. (A) is an inference, but too impersonal; (C) and (D) cannot be inferred from the information given.
20. (D) Conditional: (D) is a simplified version of the statement. (A) and (B) are contradictions of the statement. (C) similar sounds: *glass* and *the grass*.

Part B

21. (C) Contextual reference: (C) is an inference from the information given. (A) and (D) cannot be inferred from the information given; (B) is a contradiction.
22. (A) Contextual reference: (A) The key words are *calculator* and *calculation skills*. (B), (C), and (D) are not related to these key words.
23. (B) Contextual reference: (B) This dialog forces the listener to focus on the main subject, the glasses. (A) is not mentioned; (C) is heard as part of *bookcase*; (D) is mentioned as a possible place to find the glasses.
24. (D) Cause and effect: (D) The key clause is *but I don't have time*. (A) and (B) cannot be inferred from the information given; (C) misinterprets *but I don't have time* as referring to chronological time.
25. (B) Contextual reference: (B) The key words are *mail a package and buy some stamps*. (A) and (D) may have picked up *buy*, but not *stamps*; (C) misinterprets *lamps* for *stamps*.

26. (A) Negation: (A) The key phrase is *Another rejection letter!* (B) and (C) cannot be inferred from the information given; (D) confuses the meaning of the statement.
27. (C) Contextual reference: (C) The key words are *check cashing, deposits, withdrawals*. (A) and (B) are possible places where *lines* occur, but do not include the key words; (D) is unrelated to the information given.
28. (D) Contextual reference: (D) is a logical conclusion. (A), (B), and (C) cannot be inferred from the information given.
29. (C) Contextual reference: (C) A stationery store sells paper products. (A) misinterprets *use some air* as for putting air in tires (possibly); (C) picks up on *use some air* as referring to an air conditioner; (D) may interpret *I'll run* as a sport, as in jogging.
30. (A) Synonym: (A) The key words are *Congratulations* and *grade*. (B) is a contradiction; (C) picks up on earned, but interprets it with money; (D) cannot be inferred from the information given.
31. (D) Cause and effect: (D) is a logical inference based on the information given. (A) is a contradiction; (B) cannot be inferred from the information given; (C) picks up on the word *due*, but misinterprets the meaning in the original statement.
32. (A) Contextual reference: (A) is the only logical conclusion. (B) cannot be inferred from the information given; the subjects of (C) and (D) are mentioned, but the meanings cannot be inferred from the information given.
33. (D) Contextual reference: (D) The key words are *one-way or round-trip ticket*. (A), (B), and (C) cannot be inferred from the information given.
34. (C) Contextual reference: (C) The key word is *month*, which equals approximately 4 weeks. (A), (B), and (D) are miscalculations.
35. (C) Contextual reference: (C) is the only logical conclusion. (A) and (D) cannot be inferred from the information given; (B) equates *money* with *change*, which isn't true.

Part C

36. (A) Dialog
37. (C) Dialog
38. (B) Dialog
39. (A) Dialog
40. (A) Dialog
41. (B) Mini-Talk
42. (B) Mini-Talk
43. (D) Mini-Talk
44. (A) Mini-Talk
45. (A) Mini-Talk
46. (C) Dialog
47. (B) Dialog
48. (A) Dialog
49. (A) Dialog
50. (B) Dialog

Explanatory Answers

SECTION 2

STRUCTURE AND WRITTEN EXPRESSION

1. (C) Prepositions: *required of*
2. (B) Verb: inappropriate tense: *happened*; see *ago*
3. (D) Prepositions: *between*
4. (A) Comparisons: *a greater number of*; see *than*
5. (D) Pronouns: form: *one*; see *only*
6. (B) Word order: adjective/adverb placement: *no single food*
7. (C) Infinitives: *to exchange*; see *agreed*
8. (B) Infinitives: *to be*; see *acknowledged*
9. (D) Comparisons: *the smallest*
10. (D) Parallel structures: *begin*; see *will arrive at . . . and*
11. (D) Word families: adjective: *historical*
12. (C) Participle form: *known*
13. (B) Gerunds: *Manufacturing*
14. (B) Parallel structures: *has produced*; see *has consumed*
15. (C) Verb: inappropriate tense: *are caused*
16. (A) Word families: adjective: *high*
17. (B) Verb: unnecessary form: *needs to*
18. (D) Word order: adjective/adverb placement: *citizenship* here is adjective: *citizenship training*
19. (C) Comparisons: *the longest*
20. (A) Word families: *annually*
21. (B) Parallel structures: *percent* is singular: *80 percent fat*
22. (C) Word families: *usually*
23. (A) Word order: adjective/adverb placement: *natural beauty*
24. (C) Verb omitted: *are restricted* or *should be restricted*
25. (C) Gerunds: see *practice of printing . . . and selling*
26. (D) Word families: *second*
27. (A) Subject repeated: *films were first made*
28. (B) Pronouns: agreement: *geologists . . . their predictions*
29. (C) Verb: subject-verb agreement: *The establishment . . . provides*
30. (B) Verb: subject-verb agreement: *The . . . melting . . . is*
31. (A) Word families: noun: *invention*
32. (B) Subject repeated: omit *it*
33. (B) Infinitives: *easy to handle*
34. (D) Pronouns: agreement: *Babies . . . their*
35. (D) Verb tense: inappropriate tense: *did*; see *ago*
36. (C) Word families: adjective: *available*
37. (D) Verb: subject-verb agreement: *the . . . points . . . are*
38. (D) Participle form: past participle in adj. phrase: *known*
39. (C) Participle form: adjective: *established*
40. (B) Verb: subject-verb agreement: *people find*

SECTION 3

READING COMPREHENSION AND VOCABULARY

1. (C)
2. (A)
3. (D)
4. (A)
5. (C)
6. (D)
7. (A)
8. (A)
9. (D)
10. (D)
11. (D)
12. (B)
13. (B)
14. (A)
15. (B)
16. (C)
17. (C)
18. (A)
19. (D)
20. (A)
21. (A)
22. (C)
23. (C)
24. (A)
25. (D)
26. (C)
27. (C)
28. (A)
29. (C)
30. (A)
31. (C) Main idea
32. (A) Inference: general
33. (D) Factual: positive
34. (A) Factual: positive
35. (C) Factual: positive
36. (C) Factual: positive
37. (B) Inference: specific
38. (C) Factual: positive
39. (C) Written expression
40. (B) Main idea
41. (B) Factual: positive
42. (B) Inference: general
43. (C) Organization
44. (D) Inference: general
45. (A) Factual: positive
46. (C) Factual: positive
47. (D) Main idea
48. (B) Factual: positive
49. (B) Factual: positive
50. (A) Written expression
51. (A) Factual: positive
52. (D) Factual: positive
53. (B) Factual: positive
54. (C) Factual: negative
55. (B) Factual: positive
56. (D) Written expression
57. (A) Factual: positive
58. (A) Main idea
59. (B) Viewpoint
60. (D) Follow-on

PRACTICE TEST 3

SECTION 1

LISTENING COMPREHENSION

Part A

1. (C) Contextual reference: (C) is a simplified version of the statement. (A) similar sounds: *plane* and *train*; (B) misinterprets *flew*; (D) is true, but unrelated to the statement.
2. (C) Number discrimination: (C) is a summary of the statement. (A) is a contradiction; (B) and (D) are false implications.
3. (B) Similar sounds: (B) is a simplified version of the statement. (A) similar sounds: *dress* and *distress*; (C) similar sounds: *dress* and *address*; (D) similar sounds: *tore* and *store; down* and *town*.
4. (A) Negation: (A) is a summary of the sentence. (B), (C), and (D) are contradictions of the statement.
5. (A) Negation: (A) is a simplified version of the statement. (B) cannot be inferred from the information given; (C) is unrelated; (D) is a contradiction of the statement.
6. (C) Chronological order: (C) is the only truthful option. (A) and (B) are contradictions to the statement; (D) confuses the meaning of the statement.
7. (D) Cause and effect: (D) is an inference; key words are *protect, downpour*. (A) and (B) incorrectly focus on *blanket*; (C) is a contradiction of the statement.
8. (B) Synonym: (B) means the same, but uses a different vocabulary. (A) similar sounds: *reason* and *raisins*; (C) similar sounds: *display* and *play*; (D) confuses the meaning of the statement.
9. (C) Synonym: (C) means the same, but uses a different vocabulary. (A) and (D) are unrelated to the statement; (B) similar sounds: *weep* and *sweep*.
10. (D) Contextual reference: (D) is the closest in meaning to the statement. (A) and (B) focus only on *five* and not its referent; (C) cannot be inferred from the information given.
11. (D) Contextual reference: (D) is an inference; key words are *only one of the bills*. (A) incorrectly focuses on *grain*; (B) similar sounds: *bills* and *Bill*; (C) is not related to the information in the statement; similar sounds: *grain* and *rain*.
12. (A) Synonym: (A) means the same, but uses a different vocabulary. (B) and (C) cannot be inferred from the information given; (D) is unrelated to the statement.
13. (A) Number discrimination: (A) is a summary of the statement. (B) is a miscalculation; (C) and (D) are contradictions.
14. (C) Conditional: (C) is a simplified version of the statement. (A) incorrectly focuses on *triple*; (B) cannot be inferred from the information given; (D) is unrelated to the statement.
15. (C) Conditional: (C) is a summary of the statement. (A) is a misinterpretation of *support* and possibly *motion*; (B) is unrelated to the statement, and (D) confuses the meaning of *motion*.
16. (B) Contextual reference: (B) is a summary of the statement. (A) and (C) cannot be inferred from the information given; (D) similar sounds: *enlisted* and *list*.
17. (C) Conditional: (C) is a simplified version of the statement. (A) and (B) are unrelated to the statement; (D) cannot be inferred from the information given.
18. (D) Synonym: (D) is a simplified version of the statement. (A) and (B) focus on *error* as a synonym for *mistake*, but are unrelated to the meaning of the statement; (C) is also unrelated.
19. (D) Contextual reference: (D) is the only truthful option. (A) and (C) are contradictions of the statement; (B) cannot be inferred from the information given.
20. (A) Contextual reference: (A) is the only truthful option. (B) and (C) cannot be inferred from the information given; (D) is a contradiction of the statement.

Part B

21. (A) Synonym: (A) means the same as "That's too bad." The other options are incorrect interpretations.
22. (B) Number discrimination: (B) This question forces the listener to focus on a detail—*how many hours*. (A), (C), and (D) are numbers referred to in other parts of the dialog.
23. (C) Number discrimination: (C) The listener must focus on one detail—*which bus*. (A), (B), and (D) are miscalculations or misinterpretations.
24. (C) Synonym: (C) This dialog focuses on the meaning of *exhausted*. (A), (B), and (D) do not explain the vocabulary focus.
25. (D) Contextual reference: (D) is the logical conclusion. (A) and (B) are contradictions; (C) is not mentioned in the dialog.
26. (B) Contextual reference: (B) From the phrase, *my father's family*. (A), (C), and (D) are incorrect.
27. (A) Similar sounds: (A) is the only truthful option. (B) similar sounds: *trash* and *rash*; (C) is unrelated; (D) cannot be inferred from the information given.
28. (C) Comparison: (C) is the logical conclusion. (A) presumes they both have an opinion of the other restaurant; (B) is a contradiction; (D) cannot be inferred from the information given.
29. (A) Chronological order: (A) This question asks the listener to focus on the sequence of events. (B) happened second; (C) will have happened last; (D) is the next to the last event.
30. (C) Cause and effect: (C) is a logical conclusion; key words are *are too new; I even wore*. (A) and (B) would not be the cause of blisters; (D) is not mentioned in the dialog.
31. (D) Cause and effect: (D) The clause, *you need less sun*. (A) indicates a misunderstanding of the dialog; (B) is his suggestion; (C) is offered as a solution.
32. (C) Contextual reference: (C) This question focuses on a detail—*whose house*. The other options are incorrect.
33. (B) Synonym: (B) is the only truthful option. (A) and (D) are contradictions; (C) is not mentioned.
34. (A) Contextual reference: (A) is a paraphrase of a joke. (B) is not mentioned in the dialog; (C) and (D) are misinterpretations.

Explanatory Answers 365

35. (C) Contextual reference: (C) is the logical conclusion; key phrase is *but not one so long*. (A) is a contradiction; (B) is the woman's opinion; (D) incorrectly focuses on the woman's phrase, *plain ridiculous*.

Part C

36. (B) Mini-Talk
37. (D) Mini-Talk
38. (C) Mini-Talk
39. (C) Mini-Talk
40. (B) Mini-Talk
41. (A) Dialog
42. (B) Dialog
43. (A) Dialog
44. (C) Dialog
45. (B) Dialog
46. (D) Mini-Talk
47. (B) Mini-Talk
48. (D) Mini-Talk
49. (B) Mini-Talk
50. (A) Mini-Talk

SECTION 2

STRUCTURE AND WRITTEN EXPRESSION

1. (C) Adjective clauses: *who is (who* takes singular verb)
2. (B) Pronouns: agreement: *their (police* is considered plural)
3. (A) Prepositions: *on the frontier*
4. (D) Conditionals: *Unless there is a snowstorm*
5. (D) Parallel structures: joining two adjectives with correct conjunction: *fast and efficient*
6. (C) Verb: inappropriate tense; present perfect: *(calculators) have proved*
7. (D) Participle form: *rapidly expanding*
8. (A) Word order: subject-verb: *what the priority should be*
9. (D) Comparisons (equality): *as well as*
10. (C) Word families: adjective: *equal*
11. (B) Verb: inappropriate tense: simple present: *believe*
12. (C) Adjective clauses: marker + verb: *who is*
13. (A) Adverb clauses: *Even though many do not want*
14. (B) Adjective clauses: *whose origin remains obscure*
15. (D) Gerunds: *After hearing*
16. (A) Verb: unnecessary form: delete *being*
17. (C) Verb: subject-verb agreement: *believe*
18. (A) Verb omitted: *to be: who are always*
19. (D) Pronouns: agreement: *on her head*
20. (D) Parallel structures: *by inhibiting them*
21. (A) Verb omitted: *was preserved*
22. (D) Verb: inappropriate tense: see *is brought: explodes*
23. (A) Reduced adjective clauses: *substances produced*
24. (B) Word order: adjective/adverb placement: *potters are seldom*
25. (C) Adverb clauses: *because the food*
26. (B) Parallel structures: *and driving/being in traffic jams*
27. (B) Infinitives: *to imagine*
28. (D) Verb omitted: *the Nile was three times*
29. (D) Parallel structures: *as the least*
30. (C) Parallel structures: *than the lion*
31. (B) Pronouns: form: *enabling them to work*
32. (D) Prepositions: *of the school*
33. (C) Gerunds: *out of traveling;* or noun; *travel*
34. (A) Subject repeated: *Since first being performed*
35. (A) Adverb clauses: *Even though the African tsetse*
36. (B) Parallel structures: *the appearance but the sounds*
37. (A) Subject repeated: *which will be torn down*
38. (B) Word order: adjective/adverb placement: *that organized sports*
39. (C) Verb: inappropriate tense: *than is;* see *currently*
40. (B) Subject repeated: *should include*

SECTION 3

READING COMPREHENSION AND VOCABULARY

1. (B)
2. (C)
3. (C)
4. (B)
5. (D)
6. (A)
7. (A)
8. (B)
9. (B)
10. (A)
11. (C)
12. (A)
13. (A)
14. (B)
15. (C)
16. (A)
17. (B)
18. (D)
19. (B)
20. (A)
21. (A)
22. (B)
23. (D)
24. (B)
25. (A)
26. (C)
27. (A)
28. (A)
29. (B)
30. (C)
31. (C) Factual: positive
32. (D) Factual: positive

33. (B) Factual: positive
34. (B) Main idea
35. (B) Organization
36. (A) Main idea
37. (D) Inference: specific
38. (B) Written expression
39. (C) Written expression
40. (A) Factual: positive
41. (C) Factual: positive
42. (C) Viewpoint
43. (C) Factual: positive
44. (B) Inference: general
45. (C) Organization
46. (C) Viewpoint
47. (A) Written expression
48. (B) Main idea
49. (A) Inference: specific
50. (D) Inference: specific
51. (B) Factual: positive
52. (A) Follow-on
53. (C) Written expression
54. (B) Main idea
55. (B) Factual: positive
56. (B) Factual: positive
57. (A) Inference: general
58. (B) Analogy
59. (B) Follow-on
60. (C) Viewpoint

PRACTICE TEST 4

SECTION 1

LISTENING COMPREHENSION

Part A

1. (C) Cause and effect: (C) is a simplified version of the statement. (A) is unrelated to the statement; (B) similar sounds: *rug* and *bug*; (D) is a contradiction of the statement.
2. (A) Number discrimination: (A) is a summary of the statement. (B) and (D) are not mentioned; (C) cannot be inferred from the information given.
3. (B) Number discrimination: (B) is a simplified version of the statement. (A), (C), and (D) confuse the numbers.
4. (A) Synonym: (A) means the same, but uses a different vocabulary. (B) and (C) are contradictions of the statement; (D) cannot be inferred from the information given.
5. (D) Negation: (D) is a summary of the statement. (A) and (C) are contradictions of the statement; (B) cannot be inferred from the information given.
6. (D) Contextual reference: (D) is a simplified version of the statement. (A), (B), and (C) cannot be inferred from the information given.
7. (C) Synonym: (C) means the same, but uses a different vocabulary. (A) and (B) incorrectly focus on *eclipse*; (D) is a contradiction of the statement.
8. (D) Conditional: (D) is the logical conclusion. (A) and (B) are contradictions of the statement; (C) is a confusion of the statement.
9. (A) Chronological order: (A) This question tests the listener's ability to follow a sequence of events. (B) and (C) are contradictions; (D) cannot be inferred from the information given.
10. (B) Contextual reference: (B) is the closest in meaning to the statement. (A), (C), and (D) are contradictions of the statement.
11. (D) Contextual reference: (D) means the same, but uses a different vocabulary. (A) is a contradiction; (B) and (C) similar sounds: *mile* and *smile*.
12. (C) Chronological order: (C) is a summary of the statement. (A) is a contradiction; (B) and (D) are unrelated to the statement.
13. (D) Conditional: (D) is a summary of the statement. All other options are unrelated to the statement.
14. (B) Cause and effect: (B) is a summary of the statement. (A), (C), and (D) incorrectly focus on *too long*.
15. (C) Synonym: (C) is a summary of the statement. (A) and (D) cannot be inferred from the information given; (B) is unrelated to the statement.
16. (B) Conditional: (B) is a summary of the statement. (A) and (C) are contradictions; (D) cannot be inferred from the information given.
17. (C) Conditional: (C) is a simplified version of the statement. (A) cannot be inferred from the information given; (B) is unrelated to the statement; (D) is a contradiction.
18. (B) Number discrimination: (B) is a simplified version of the statement. (A), (C), and (D) confuse the meaning of the statement.
19. (D) Synonym: (D) is the only truthful option. (A) and (C) are contradictions of the statement; (B) cannot be inferred from the information given.
20. (D) Contextual reference: (D) is a summary of the first part of the statement. (A) and (B) are unrelated to the meaning of the statement; (C) cannot be inferred from the information given.

Part B

21. (A) Contextual reference: (A) From the question, *Can't you walk a little faster?* (B) and (D) are contradictions.
22. (C) Chronological order: (C) This question forces the listener to focus on a sequence. (A) happens last; (B) and (D) aren't mentioned.
23. (D) Synonym: (D) is the logical conclusion. (A), (B), and (C) are misinterpretations.
24. (B) Contextual reference: (B) is the logical conclusion; key words are *finished the job*. (A), (C), and (D) do not relate to the dialog.
25. (D) Contextual reference: (D) The listener must focus on a detail—*the woman's nose*. The other options are incorrect.
26. (D) Contextual reference: (D) From the clause, *Hand me my papers.* (A), (B), and (C) are incorrect.

Explanatory Answers 367

27. (A) Chronological order: (A) is the only truthful option. (B) similar sounds: *course* for *cruise*; (C) and (D) are unrelated.
28. (B) Number discrimination: (B) From the clause, *If your dog is eight*. (A) refers to seven human years; (C) and (D) are unrelated to the statement.
29. (A) Number discrimination: (A) From . . . *given me back 50 cents*. (B) is unrelated; (C) was the cost of the milk; (D) is the amount of money given.
30. (B) Contextual reference: (B) Key words are *a beautiful color . . . It's your favorite*. The other options are incorrect.
31. (C) Negation: (C) From the clause, *you never should have gone out*. (A) and (B) are contradictions; (D) is confused and similar sounds: *rain* for *train*.
32. (D) Cause and effect: (D) is the logical conclusion; key words are *You look much slimmer*. The other options are not mentioned.
33. (C) Contextual reference: (C) is the best answer. (A), (B), and (D) are not feasible in this context.
34. (C) Synonym: (C) means the same, but uses a different vocabulary. (A) cannot be inferred from the information given; (B) and (D) are misinterpretations.
35. (D) Cause and effect: (D) is the logical conclusion; key phrase is *you should anyway*. (A) and (B) are unrelated; (C) is a contradiction.

Part C

36. (A) Mini-Talk
37. (D) Mini-Talk
38. (B) Mini-Talk
39. (A) Mini-Talk
40. (A) Mini-Talk
41. (B) Mini-Talk
42. (D) Mini-Talk
43. (B) Mini-Talk
44. (A) Mini-Talk
45. (B) Mini-Talk
46. (A) Dialog
47. (B) Dialog
48. (D) Dialog
49. (C) Dialog
50. (A) Dialog

SECTION 2

STRUCTURE AND WRITTEN EXPRESSION

1. (B) Verb: inappropriate tense: *dissolves*
2. (C) Word order: adjective/adverb placement: *The work of that artist*
3. (A) Comparisons: *faster*
4. (C) Pronouns: agreement: *rats . . . their*
5. (A) Conditionals: present unreal: *would be*
6. (C) Adverb clauses: marker: *because*
7. (D) Parallel structures: see *either . . . or*
8. (B) Gerunds: object of preposition: *After: exploding*
9. (D) Word order: adjective/adverb placement: *are probably more common*
10. (B) Adjective clauses: *is the best time to harvest*
11. (C) Word families: noun: *generator*
12. (D) Noun clauses: marker: *what*
13. (A) Active/passive voice: *was caused by*
14. (B) Participle form: *(which is) accumulating*
15. (D) Verb: inappropriate form: *direct* (see *requests*)
16. (B) Subject repeated: delete *they*
17. (D) Word families: *temporary*
18. (A) Active/passive verbs: *After being given*
19. (B) Pronouns: agreement: *the Spanish . . . their*
20. (D) Verb: inappropriate tense: *who died . . . abandoned*
21. (C) Verb: inappropriate tense: *is expected* or *can be expected*
22. (D) Pronouns: agreement: *themselves*
23. (B) Noun clauses: conjunction: *that the tomb*
24. (B) Parallel structures: *both . . . and*
25. (B) Articles: *horsehair* or *a horsehair*
26. (B) Comparisons: *thinner*
27. (D) Conditionals: *would decrease*
28. (C) Parallel structures: *and security*
29. (B) Verb: unnecessary form: delete *did*
30. (A) Verb: inappropriate form: simple present: *makes*
31. (C) Word order: adjective/adverb placement: *is seldom acclaimed*
32. (D) Prepositions: *belief in individualism*
33. (B) Reduced adjective clauses: *coming*
34. (B) Adjective clauses: marker omissions: *additives which will reduce*
35. (D) Parallel structures: adjective: *aggressive*
36. (C) Verb: subject-verb agreement: *blood cells . . . are stored*
37. (C) Adjective clauses: marker omission: *which/who had been*
38. (D) Infinitives: *to return*
39. (A) Verb omitted: *who had been*
40. (D) Verb omitted: *as the death rate did* or *as did the death rate*

SECTION 3

READING COMPREHENSION AND VOCABULARY

1. (A)
2. (B)
3. (C)
4. (A)
5. (D)
6. (A)
7. (A)
8. (C)
9. (B)
10. (A)
11. (A)
12. (C)

13.	(B)	
14.	(A)	
15.	(B)	
16.	(D)	
17.	(B)	
18.	(B)	
19.	(C)	
20.	(C)	
21.	(D)	
22.	(A)	
23.	(C)	
24.	(A)	
25.	(D)	
26.	(C)	
27.	(B)	
28.	(C)	
29.	(D)	
30.	(D)	
31.	(B)	Main idea
32.	(C)	Factual: positive
33.	(B)	Inference: specific
34.	(C)	Written expression
35.	(B)	Viewpoint
36.	(A)	Organization

37.	(A)	Written expression
38.	(C)	Main idea
39.	(B)	Viewpoint
40.	(D)	Inference: general
41.	(B)	Written expression
42.	(B)	Organization
43.	(C)	Follow-on
44.	(D)	Main idea
45.	(B)	Factual: positive
46.	(A)	Factual: positive
47.	(D)	Factual: negative
48.	(C)	Main idea
49.	(C)	Viewpoint
50.	(D)	Organization
51.	(B)	Main idea
52.	(C)	Factual: positive
53.	(D)	Factual: negative
54.	(B)	Inference: general
55.	(B)	Viewpoint
56.	(D)	Follow-on
57.	(C)	Main idea
58.	(A)	Factual: positive
59.	(C)	Inference: specific
60.	(B)	Written expression

PRACTICE TEST 5

SECTION 1

LISTENING COMPREHENSION

Part A

1. (C) Synonym: (C) is a simplified version of the statement. (A) similar sounds: *sense* and *cents*. (B) and (D) cannot be inferred from the information given.

2. (B) Contextual Reference: (B) is the computational answer to 1/2 of 30 miles. (A) is a contradiction; (C) similar sounds: *30* and *13*; (D) is a contradiction.

3. (A) Contextual reference: (A) is a simplified version of the statement. (B), (C), and (D) are contradictions.

4. (D) Synonym: (D) means the same, but uses a different vocabulary. (A) and (C) are unrelated to the statement; (B) may confuse *widow* with *window*.

5. (C) Contextual reference: (C) is a simplified version of the statement. (A), (B), and (D) are contradictions of the statement.

6. (C) Contextual reference: (C) is the only truthful option. (A) and (D) are unrelated to the statement; (B) is a contradiction.

7. (B) Cause and effect: (B) is a simplified version of the statement. (A) incorrectly focuses on *over*, as in *overslept*; (C) and (D) cannot be inferred from the information given.

8. (D) Conditional: (D) means the same; but uses a different vocabulary. (A) is a contradiction of the statement; (B) presumes the marriage occurred; (C) cannot be inferred from the information given.

9. (C) Synonym: (C) is a simplified version of the statement. (A) and (D) are contradictions of the statement; (B) may be true, but is unrelated to the statement.

10. (D) Number discrimination: (D) is a simplified version of the statement. (A) similar sounds: *9 o'clock* and *5 o'clock;* (B) similar sounds: *thirteen* and *thirty*; (C) similar sounds: *thirteen* and *twelve*.

11. (B) Synonym: (B) is a simplified version of the statement. (A) is a contradiction; (C) cannot be inferred from the information given; (D) ignores *by winter* in the statement.

12. (D) Chronological order: (D) focuses on *when*. (A) and (B) cannot be inferred from the information given; (C) is a contradiction.

13. (B) Conditional: (B) is the only truthful option. The others are confused versions.

14. (D) Cause and effect: (D) is the only truthful option. (A), (B), and (C) are contradictions of the statement.

15. (B) Synonym: (B) is the closest in meaning. (A) similar sounds: *concerned* and *concert*; (C) similar sounds: *concerned* and *consensus*; (D) similar sounds: *a close watch* and *a new watch*.

16. (C) Synonym: (C) is a simplified version of the statement. (A) cannot be inferred from the information given; (B) is a contradiction of the statement; (D) is not related to the information in the statement.

17. (D) Negation: (D) is a simplified version of the statement. (A) confuses *conductor* (electrical) with *conductor* (musical); (B) is not related to the information in the statement; (C) is true, but unrelated to the statement.

18. (D) Contextual Reference: (D) is a simplified version of the statement. (A) and (B) misinterprets the numbers; (C) is a contradiction of the statement.

19. (B) Contextual Reference: (B) is the only truthful option. (A) is a miscalculation; (C) similar sounds: *8:30* and *8:13*; (D) is a contradiction of the statement.

20. (D) Synonym: (D) is a simplified version of the statement. (A) similar sounds: *minister* as *priest*; (B) misinterprets *prime minister*, (C) misinterprets *received* in the context of the statement.

Explanatory Answers 369

Part B

21. (B) Cause and effect: (B) From the sentence, *keep it quiet in here,* it must be concluded that the woman thinks it's too noisy. (A), (C), and (D) are unrelated.
22. (D) Chronological order: (D) This question forces the listener to focus on a detail—*the time of the meeting.* (A), (B), and (C) are times referred to in other parts of the dialog.
23. (A) Number discrimination: (A) The listener must focus on one detail—*the price of the aerograms.* (B), (C), and (D) are miscalculations or misinterpretations.
24. (A) Synonym: (A) This dialog focuses on the meaning of *heartily.* (B), (C), and (D) do not explain the vocabulary focus.
25. (C) Contextual reference: (C) is the logical conclusion. (A) is a contradiction; (B) and (D) are not mentioned in the dialog.
26. (C) Contextual reference: (C) From the statement, *I have to return it to my boss.* (A), (B), and (D) are incorrect.
27. (A) Cause and effect: (A) is the only truthful option. (B) is a contradiction; (C) confuses the time of the action; (D) cannot be inferred from the information given.
28. (C) Contextual reference: (C) is the only truthful option. (A) and (D) are only a possibility; (B) is not mentioned in the dialog.
29. (D) Chronological order: (D) This question asks the listener to focus on the sequence of events. (A) happened first; (B) happened before dinner; (C) happened after the nap.
30. (A) Contextual reference: (A) is a logical conclusion; key words are *sign on this line* and *gift-wrapped.* (B), (C), and (D) are not mentioned in the dialog.
31. (D) Synonym: (D) The expression, *Don't give up!* means *Keep on trying.* (A), (B), and (C) indicate a misunderstanding of the expression.
32. (D) Contextual reference: (D) is the logical conclusion; key words are *bad connection.* The other options are based on misinterpretations.
33. (D) Number discrimination: (D) The question focuses on the time. The other options are based on misinterpretations of the numbers.
34. (B) Number discrimination: (B) is a summary of the dialog. (A) is not mentioned in the dialog; (C) and (D) are misinterpretations of the numbers.
35. (B) Synonym: (B) is a summary of the dialog. (A) confuses what was robbed; (C) and (D) are based on misinterpretations of the facts in the dialog.

Part C

36. (D) Mini-Talk
37. (B) Mini-Talk
38. (A) Mini-Talk
39. (D) Mini-Talk
40. (B) Mini-Talk
41. (B) Dialog
42. (D) Dialog
43. (C) Dialog
44. (D) Dialog
45. (A) Dialog
46. (B) Mini-Talk
47. (D) Mini-Talk
48. (A) Mini-Talk
49. (C) Mini-Talk
50. (C) Mini-Talk

SECTION 2

STRUCTURE AND WRITTEN EXPRESSION

1. (C) Verb: inappropriate tense: present perfect: see time expression *this year*
2. (D) Parallel structures: *beer* and *wine*
3. (A) Verb: inappropriate tense: see time expression *Every fall*
4. (C) Pronouns: form: *theirs* = their opinion
5. (D) Prepositions: to provide with (something)
6. (C) Active/passive voice: DDT cannot be the doer of the action
7. (A) Word order: adjective/adverb placement: *all* (knives and balls) *at the same time*
8. (D) Reduced adjective clauses: (that/which was) *recorded in the tenth century*
9. (D) Adverb clauses: marker: *Before;* see *had organized*
10. (B) Word families: noun form: direct object of *has increased*
11. (C) Noun clauses: *that* introduces the noun clause; object of *think*
12. (A) Pronouns: form: (C) is often confused, but is a contraction for *who is*
13. (C) Comparisons: *Rainfall* is noncount, and so requires *less*
14. (D) Reduced adjective clauses: (who was) *regretting*
15. (C) Participle form: phrase modifies *committee*
16. (C) Noun clauses: *what was used*
17. (A) Verb: subject-verb agreement: *engines use*
18. (A) Verb omitted: *to be: Not being able*
19. (A) Verb: unnecessary form: *had* should be deleted; see *became*
20. (D) Verb: inappropriate tense: *were obliged;* see *eliminated*
21. (C) Verb: subject-verb agreement: *police* requires a plural verb: *who were*
22. (B) Pronouns: agreement: change *his* to *her* to agree with *Dame Judith Anderson*
23. (A) Subject repeated: delete *they*
24. (B) Verb: inappropriate tense: *will improve*
25. (D) Parallel structures: *or;* see *either*
26. (D) Comparisons: omit *more*
27. (B) Articles: *the South Pacific*
28. (C) Word families: noun *damage*
29. (B) Active/passive: *will be inhabited by*
30. (A) Verb: unnecessary form
31. (B) Word order: adjective/adverb placement: *have recently made*
32. (D) Word order: subject-verb: *At no time can . . . be condoned*
33. (C) Comparisons: superlative form: *the most famous* or *the best-known;* see *the* and *in the world*
34. (B) Word families: adjective required to modify *labor: hard physical labor*
35. (A) Word families: stative verb requires adjective form: *smells so sweet*
36. (A) Gerunds: *limits cutting*
37. (C) Adjective clauses: *furniture which was made* or *furniture made*
38. (A) Participle form: irregular verb *fit*
39. (A) Infinitives: *If banks were to increase*
40. (A) Reduced adjective clauses: *before moving to*

370 Explanatory Answers

SECTION 3

READING COMPREHENSION AND VOCABULARY

1.	(B)	31.	(D)	Viewpoint
2.	(D)	32.	(A)	Factual: negative
3.	(A)	33.	(C)	Viewpoint
4.	(A)	34.	(B)	Main idea
5.	(C)	35.	(C)	Written expression
6.	(D)	36.	(B)	Main idea
7.	(C)	37.	(D)	Factual: negative
8.	(A)	38.	(D)	Follow-on
9.	(B)	39.	(B)	Written expression
10.	(B)	40.	(C)	Viewpoint
11.	(C)	41.	(C)	Factual: positive
12.	(A)	42.	(C)	Main idea
13.	(D)	43.	(C)	Written expression
14.	(A)	44.	(A)	Viewpoint
15.	(C)	45.	(C)	Factual: positive
16.	(D)	46.	(C)	Inference: specific
17.	(A)	47.	(C)	Inference: specific
18.	(B)	48.	(B)	Main idea
19.	(D)	49.	(C)	Main idea
20.	(C)	50.	(B)	Factual: positive
21.	(C)	51.	(C)	Factual: negative
22.	(A)	52.	(C)	Factual: positive
23.	(D)	53.	(A)	Factual: positive
24.	(A)	54.	(C)	Main idea
25.	(D)	55.	(B)	Written expression
26.	(A)	56.	(D)	Inference: specific
27.	(B)	57.	(A)	Inference: specific
28.	(B)	58.	(B)	Factual: positive
29.	(A)	59.	(A)	Factual: positive
30.	(C)	60.	(C)	Written expression

PRACTICE TEST 6

SECTION 1

LISTENING COMPREHENSION

Part A

1. (D) Contextual reference: (D) is a simplified version of the statement. (A) similar sounds: *son* and *sun*; (B) and (C) similar sounds: *daughter* and *father*; cannot be inferred from the information given.
2. (A) Number discrimination: (A) states only the time of the flight, and uses a different vocabulary. (B) similar sounds: "*20 of 8*" and *8:20;* (C) misinterprets the date of the departure; (D) misinterprets the time of the departure.
3. (C) Synonym: (C) means the same, but uses a different vocabulary. (A) similar sounds: *price* and *rice*; (B) focuses incorrectly on *fall*; (D) similar sounds: *price* and *surprised*.
4. (C) Cause and effect: (C) means the same, but uses a different vocabulary. (A) is an implication; (B) may be true, but is not related to the statement; (D) similar sounds: *rain* and *train*; cannot be inferred from the information given.
5. (B) Conditional: (B) is a simplified version of the statement. (A), (C), and (D) are contradictions.
6. (A) Contextual Reference: (A) is a simplified version of the statement. (B), (C), and (D) cannot be inferred from the statement.
7. (A) Synonym: (A) means the same, but uses a different vocabulary. (B) similar sounds: *critical* and *critics, pay close attention* and *listen carefully;* (C) similar sounds: *pay attention* and *paid; detail* and *deal;* (D) similar sounds: *critical* and *criticism*.
8. (D) Contextual reference: (D) is a simplified version of the statement. (A) is an inference that cannot be made from this information. (B) is not related to the information in the statement; (C) confuses the meaning of the statement.
9. (D) Contextual reference: (D) is a simplified version of the statement. (A), (B), and (C) are contradictions.
10. (B) Conditional: (B) is a simplified version of the statement. (A) and (D) confuse the meaning of the statement; (C) presupposes incorrectly that there was an accident.
11. (D) Synonym: (D) means the same, but uses a different vocabulary. (A) and (B) are contradictions; (C) is not related to the information in the statement.
12. (D) Contextual reference: (D) means the same, but uses a different vocabulary. (A), (B), and (C) are contradictions.
13. (C) Synonym: (C) means the same, but uses a different vocabulary. (A) similar sounds: *table* and *label*; (B) similar sounds: *oval* and *jovial*; (D) similar sounds: *around* and *round*.

Explanatory Answers 371

14. (D) Number discrimination: (D) is the only truthful option. (A) similar sounds: *forty* with *fourteen*; (B) is not related to the information in the statement; (C) similar sounds: the *4th* with the *14th*.
15. (A) Negation: (A) is a simplified version of the statement. (B) is unrelated to the statement; (C) is a contradiction of the statement; (D) is a conclusion that cannot be made from the information given.
16. (C) Cause and effect: (C) is the only truthful option. (A) is a contradiction of the statement; (B) and (D) are not related to the information in the statement.
17. (D) Contextual reference: (D) is a simplified version of the statement. (A) similar sounds: *father's brother* with *brother*; (B) is not related to the information in the statement, and may also confuse *visit* with *fixed*; (C) similar sounds: *father's brother* and *mother and father*.
18. (D) Conditional: (D) means the same, but uses a different vocabulary. (A) cannot be inferred from the information given; (B) presupposes that the rain already occurred; (C)
19. (C) Chronological order: (C) is the only truthful option. (A) is unrelated to the statement; (B) confuses the meaning of the statement; (D) is a contradiction.
20. (A) Contextual reference: (A) is a simplified version of the statement. (B), (C), and (D) are contradictions.

Part B

21. (B) Contextual reference: (B) From the question referring to shoes, and the positive *yes*, it must be concluded that the woman bought a new pair of shoes. (A) is unrelated to the statement; (C) similar sounds: *pair* and *pear*; (D) contains an incorrect inference from *color* to *blue*.
22. (C) Contextual reference: (C) An even dozen equals 12. (A), (B), and (D) misinterpret numbers.
23. (C) Number discrimination: (C) This dialog focuses on aural discrimination among *six, sixteen, sixty,* and *sixty-six*; (C) offers the biggest number mentioned in the dialog.
24. (C) Chronological order: (C) This dialog checks the sequence of events. The actions in (A), (B), and (D) will happen after the shelf is fixed.
25. (B) Synonym: (B) means the same as *checking out*. (A) is a contradiction; (C) cannot be inferred from the information given; (D) confuses *checking out* with the expression *to check something out* or *to look into something*.
26. (A) Number discrimination: (A) Twenty-five is one-half of fifty. (B), (C), and (D) are miscalculations based on missed aural discrimination of numbers.

27. (C) Cause and effect: (C) The topic is *ice on the bridge*. (A), (B), and (D) are not related to the information in the dialog.
28. (A) Conditional: (A) is the logical conclusion. (B) is a contradiction; (C) and (D) are not mentioned in the dialog and cannot be concluded.
29. (B) Contextual reference: (B) The key words are *come in*; *water* and *suit*. (A) is unrelated; (C) may confuse the idea of *suit* as *clothes*; (D) may confuse *water* with the idea of refreshments.
30. (B) Number discrimination: (B) is a restatement of the dialog. (A) is unrelated; (C) contains the incorrect *more*; (D) contains the length of the man's vacation.
31. (C) Cause and effect: (C) is a restatement of the dialog. (A), (B), and (D) cannot be inferred from the information given.
32. (A) Number discrimination: (A) is a restatement of the dialog. (B), (C), and (D) misinterpret the number.
33. (B) Number discrimination: (B) The question focuses on the time; (B) is a restatement. (A) and (D) misinterpret the number; (C) similar sounds: *50 minutes* and *15 minutes*.
34. (B) Synonym: (B) is a restatement of the dialog. (A) is what the man used to like to do; (C) cannot be inferred from the information given; (D) similar sounds: *mine* and *wine*.
35. (B) Comparison: (B) is the only logical conclusion. (A) is a contradiction; (C) and (D) cannot be inferred from the information given.

Part C

36. (D) Mini-Talk
37. (D) Mini-Talk
38. (B) Mini-Talk
39. (C) Mini-Talk
40. (B) Mini-Talk
41. (D) Dialog
42. (B) Dialog
43. (A) Dialog
44. (D) Dialog
45. (A) Dialog
46. (B) Mini-Talk
47. (C) Mini-Talk
48. (B) Mini-Talk
49. (D) Mini-Talk
50. (A) Mini-Talk

SECTION 2

STRUCTURE AND WRITTEN EXPRESSION

1. (D) Adjective clause: *participants coming*
2. (A) Gerunds: *accustomed to punching*
3. (B) Pronouns: *reprimanded us*
4. (C) Prepositions: *In the lawyer's opinion*
5. (D) Adverb clauses: *even though he was*
6. (B) Parallel structures: *Identifying . . . solving*
7. (A) Articles: *an honor*
8. (C) Verb: inappropriate tense: *when they heard*
9. (A) Word order: adjective/adverb placement: *they are always open to suggestions*
10. (C) Conditionals: *Should it rain now*
11. (D) Comparisons: *the worst city*
12. (C) Word families: *we could hardly hear*
13. (A) Word order: adjective/adverb placement: *never to do that again*
14. (A) Verb tense: *was not*
15. (B) Verb: inappropriate tense: *people often need*
16. (C) Subject repeated: delete *it*
17. (C) Word families: *nonsmokers are*
18. (C) Verb: subject-verb agreement: *have resulted*
19. (D) Verb: unnecessary form: *staff supported him*
20. (D) Parallel structures: *to leave and (to) head*

21. (B) Verb: subject-verb agreement: *experiments were placed*
22. (C) Pronouns: *her;* see *Earhart*
23. (A) Pronouns: *their;* see *anthropologists*
24. (D) Prepositions: *spread around*
25. (B) Parallel structures: *judgment and his ability*
26. (B) Parallel structures: *Welcoming and preparing*
27. (D) Articles: *a thermometer* or *thermometers*
28. (A) Word order: adjective/adverb placement verbs: *the Indian woman*
29. (B) Active/Passive verbs: *have been used*
30. (A) Adjective clauses: *who follow*
31. (B) Comparisons: *less;* see *farther*
32. (B) Word order: subject/verb agreement: *doctors treat*
33. (B) Verb: subject-verb agreement: *letters present*
34. (C) Word order: adjective/adverb placement: *long-neglected rights*
35. (B) Conditionals: *is pumped*
36. (A) Verb: unnecessary form: delete *is;* see *English is common language*
37. (C) Word order: subject/verb agreement: *bee stings can*
38. (B) Adjective clauses: *which are modeled*
39. (C) Parallel structures: *left controls . . . right controls*
40. (A) Subject repeated: delete *immigrants*

SECTION 3

READING COMPREHENSION AND VOCABULARY

1. (A)
2. (B)
3. (A)
4. (B)
5. (A)
6. (A)
7. (C)
8. (C)
9. (D)
10. (B)
11. (D)
12. (A)
13. (D)
14. (C)
15. (A)
16. (D)
17. (B)
18. (D)
19. (A)
20. (A)
21. (B)
22. (D)
23. (B)
24. (A)
25. (C)
26. (A)
27. (C)
28. (A)
29. (B)
30. (A)

31. (C) Main idea
32. (C) Factual: negative
33. (A) Factual: positive
34. (A) Factual: positive
35. (D) Factual: positive
36. (A) Analogy
37. (D) Main idea
38. (A) Organization
39. (C) Viewpoint
40. (B) Factual: positive
41. (A) Viewpoint
42. (C) Inference: specific
43. (A) Main idea
44. (D) Factual: negative
45. (B) Inference: general
46. (C) Factual: positive
47. (D) Inference: specific
48. (B) Analogy
49. (C) Factual: positive
50. (D) Main idea
51. (B) Inference: specific
52. (B) Organization
53. (C) Follow-on
54. (B) Factual: positive
55. (B) Main idea
56. (A) Main idea
57. (D) Analogy
58. (B) Factual: positive
59. (C) Viewpoint
60. (B) Written expression

LISTENING TARGETS ANSWER KEY

Statements

Similar Sounds

1. (A)
2. (B)
3. (D)
4. (B)
5. (D)

Number Discrimination

1. (A)
2. (D)
3. (B)
4. (B)
5. (D)

Synonyms

1. (D)
2. (D)
3. (C)
4. (B)
5. (A)

Negation

1. (A)
2. (A)
3. (D)
4. (C)
5. (D)

Contextual Reference

1. (C)
2. (B)
3. (C)
4. (D)
5. (D)

Cause and Effect

1. (A)
2. (B)
3. (C)
4. (A)
5. (D)

Conditionals

1. (B)
2. (C)
3. (D)
4. (A)
5. (D)

Chronological Order

1. (D)
2. (B)
3. (C)
4. (A)
5. (D)

Comparisons

1. (A)
2. (C)
3. (B)
4. (A)
5. (B)

Short Dialogs

Similar Sounds

1. (D)
2. (D)
3. (B)
4. (B)
5. (A)

Number Discrimination

1. (B)
2. (A)
3. (A)
4. (C)
5. (C)

Synonyms

1. (A)
2. (C)
3. (A)
4. (D)
5. (B)

Negation

1. (A)
2. (D)
3. (A)
4. (D)
5. (C)

Contextual Reference

1. (C)
2. (C)
3. (A)
4. (B)
5. (A)

Cause and Effect

1. (C)
2. (B)
3. (A)
4. (B)
5. (A)

Conditionals

1. (D)
2. (C)
3. (C)
4. (B)
5. (B)

Chronological Order

1. (A)
2. (D)
3. (C)
4. (B)
5. (C)

Comparisons

1. (B)
2. (D)
3. (C)
4. (C)
5. (A)

Mini-Talks

1. (B)
2. (D)
3. (A)
4. (A)
5. (D)
6. (B)
7. (A)
8. (D)
9. (D)
10. (A)
11. (D)
12. (B)
13. (B)
14. (C)
15. (C)
16. (B)
17. (D)
18. (D)
19. (A)

Dialogs

1. (B)
2. (A)
3. (D)
4. (B)
5. (C)
6. (D)
7. (A)
8. (C)
9. (B)
10. (D)
11. (C)
12. (B)
13. (A)
14. (B)
15. (A)
16. (C)
17. (A)

STRUCTURE TARGETS ANSWER KEY

SUBJECT

Subject Omitted

1. (B) The verb *rounded* needs a subject like *he, the robot, the scientist*, etc.
2. (A) The verb *have trekked* needs a subject like *tourists, pilgrims*, etc.
3. (A) The verb *has* needs a subject like *the mayor, the developer, she*, etc.
4. (A) The verb *read* needs a subject like *the teacher, the students, the children*, etc.
5. (C) The verb *sailed* needs a subject like *he*.
6. (A) The verb *moved* needs a subject like *the cat, the burglar, he*, etc.
7. (B) The verb *grows* needs the subject pronoun *it*.
8. (A) The verb *does not seem* needs the subject pronoun *it*.

Subject Repeated

1. (A) The subject of the verb *was kept* is *The book*. The extra *it* is not necessary.
2. (A) The phrase *a twentieth-century invention* is a reduced adjective phrase. It does not need a subject or verb; it refers to *the computer*.
3. (B) The subject of the adjective clause is *which*, referring to *rate*. The *it* is not necessary.
4. (A) The subject of the adjective clause is *which*, referring to *treaties*. The pronoun *they* is not necessary.
5. (D) The subject of the adjective clause is *that*, referring to *precision*. The pronoun *it* is not necessary.
6. (A) The subject of the verb *is* is *dance*. The pronoun *it* is not necessary.
7. (D) The subject of the verb phrase *has been refitted* is *Alexandria*. The pronoun *it* is not necessary.
8. (B) The subject of the adjective clause is *which*, referring to *subject*. The pronoun *it* is not necessary.
9. (D) The subject of the verb *was* is *building*. The pronoun *it* is not necessary.
10. (B) The subject of the adjective clause is *which*, referring to *typewriter*. The pronoun *it* is not necessary.

Explanatory Answers 375

VERBS

Verb Omitted

1. (A) concern *has* grown
2. (C) which *are* driven
3. (D) he won't *be* able to pay
4. (B) Cairo University *was* founded
5. (A) should *adhere/stick* to a routine
6. (D) clerk claimed he *was* too busy
7. (C) even if it *meant* raising fees
8. (B) you must *call/try* early in the morning
9. (B) tenth graders *were* continuing
10. (D) because she *was* so tired

Verb with Unnecessary Form

1. (A) were trampled
2. (B) thoroughly convinced the committee
3. (C) to drive
4. (D) hides which protect them
5. (C) to assimilate
6. (D) disease is increasing
7. (A) like plumbers
8. (D) he collapsed
9. (C) less remains of old Tokyo
10. (A) owners of the building took a look

Inappropriate Verb Tense

1. (A) My book has three torn pages.
2. (B) experiences
3. (A) can best be controlled
4. (B) that erupted first
5. (C) did
6. (D) had been
7. (C) apply immediately
8. (B) have forced a decline
9. (B) had access
10. (A) were clearing

Extra Exercises

1. (B)
2. (A)
3. (A)
4. (C)
5. (B)
6. (D)
7. (B)
8. (A)

SUBJECT-VERB AGREEMENT

Agreement I

1. (A) The *boy* is thought to be one
2. (C) The advent *has* provided
3. (B) water *produces* a negative charge
4. (C) law *safeguards* against
5. (B) we *have* no business
6. (B) banks *have* demonstrated
7. (D) eruptions *are* imminent
8. (C) systems *appear* to communicate
9. (C) all of humankind *lives*
10. (D) they *deserve*

Agreement II

1. (B) My English grade *was sent*
2. (A) Monuments *were* built
3. (D) stories *are considered*
4. (A) The counselors *feel*
5. (D) it *sends*
6. (D) Several authors *have prevailed*
7. (B) The camel *nods*
8. (D) the cover that *protects*
9. (D) measures which *have proved*
10. (B) power *is* small

ARTICLES

Articles I

1. (C)
2. (D)
3. (B)
4. (A)
5. (C)
6. (B)
7. (C)
8. (C)
9. (D)
10. (C)

Articles II

1. (B) on *the* shelf
2. (C) *a* piece of paper
3. (C) most like houses
4. (B) in Tokyo
5. (D) of music
6. (D) of broadcasting
7. (B) *the* class
8. (B) *a* problem
9. (B) *a* change of clothes
10. (D) *a* work station

376 Explanatory Answers

WORD ORDER

Subject and Verb Placement

1. (B)
2. (B)
3. (B)
4. (C)
5. (D)
6. (C)
7. (C)
8. (A)

Adjective and Adverb Placement I

1. (D)
2. (D)
3. (A)
4. (B)
5. (A)
6. (C)
7. (A)
8. (B)
9. (A)
10. (B)

Adjective and Adverb Placement II

1. (C) inexpensive, peripheral products
2. (D) less concentration
3. (C) intelligent guesses
4. (D) made by hand
5. (D) next clear evening
6. (A) The hotel strike greatly
7. (B) arrived late
8. (B) wealthy patrons
9. (A) Cars parked illegally
10. (D) in dangerous areas

PRONOUNS

Agreement

1. (B)
2. (C)
3. (B)
4. (D)
5. (A)
6. (A)
7. (C)
8. (A)
9. (A)
10. (B)

Form

1. (B)
2. (C)
3. (D)
4. (B)
5. (D)
6. (A)
7. (C)
8. (A)
9. (B)
10. (A)

Extra Exercises

1. (B) *its*
2. (B) omit *they*
3. (A) subject omitted: Outdoing himself, *he* (the runner) came
4. (C) and *it*—the instrument could not measure
5. (B) caught sight of *him*
6. (B) on *his* ability
7. (D) to *her*
8. (B) If you thought about *it*, you would see

PREPOSITIONS AND TWO/THREE-WORD VERBS

Prepositions I

1. (B)
2. (A)
3. (C)
4. (D)
5. (D)
6. (C)
7. (B)
8. (C)
9. (D)
10. (A)

Prepositions II

1. (B) placed *on* a flat surface
2. (C) bring *about* the pain
3. (D) places her *ahead of* (or *above*) her rivals
4. (B) met *with* enthusiasm
5. (B) saw the birds
6. (C) to cut *back*
7. (A) All *through* the night
8. (A) student *in* my grammar class
9. (B) spreads *through/across* the sky
10. (D) were put *aside* until

Explanatory Answers 377

SUBORDINATE CLAUSES

Noun Clauses

1. (A)
2. (D)
3. (A)
4. (B)
5. (C)
6. (D)
7. (A)
8. (B)
9. (B)
10. (D)

Adjective Clauses I

1. (C)
2. (D)
3. (C)
4. (A)
5. (C)
6. (A)
7. (D)
8. (B)

Adjective Clauses II

1. (D) which *he* started
2. (C) citizens *who* left
3. (A) The exhibition, *which* toured
4. (A) which *was* introduced
5. (A) A new running shoe *which* monitors
6. (B) that sponsored
7. (D) grass *that* isn't mowed
8. (A) who have maintained the grounds
9. (A) The accountant *who* is known
10. (B) sights *that* attract

Adverb Clauses I

1. (B)
2. (C)
3. (D)
4. (D)
5. (C)
6. (B)
7. (A)
8. (A)

Adverb Clauses II

1. (A) *Since* the burning
2. (D) arguments *before* the motion
3. (D) when *they* arrived
4. (A) before *it* was expected
5. (B) protect
6. (A) Even though *they* maintained
7. (A) *If* the rain had not stopped
8. (A) were changed

Reduced Adjective Clauses I

1. (C)
2. (C)
3. (B)
4. (C)
5. (B)
6. (C)
7. (D)
8. (A)

Reduced Adjective Clauses II

1. (A) Canal, said to be
2. (C) donated by
3. (B) pull strong enough
4. (A) The crowd, anxiously awaiting
5. (B) tower monitoring the changing weather
6. (A) The talks promoting
7. (A) delays caused by
8. (B) being hot and weary
9. (C) dangerous obliging
10. (A) press implying that

Reduced Adverb Clauses I

1. (D)
2. (A)
3. (B)
4. (B)
5. (C)
6. (A)
7. (B)
8. (B)

Reduced Adverb Clauses II

1. (A) Although frequently misinterpreted
2. (A) while providing (omit *it is*)
3. (A) omit *it*
4. (A) Although nutlike (omit *is*)
5. (A) Athletes, when competing (omit *they*)
6. (C) before crossing (omit *they*)
7. (A) Before *designing* the building
8. (B) and reducing heat in the summer
9. (A) When travelling (omit *they*)
10. (A) Since moving (omit *they*)

378 Explanatory Answers

PARALLEL STRUCTURES AND CONJUNCTIONS

Parallel Structures

1. (D) simpler
2. (B) to detect prey and also to stun
3. (B) entering. . .and causing
4. (B) child abuse
5. (B) Catching.. ., but fishing
6. (A) the hour you are leaving and the time you are arriving
7. (B) lying. . . and cheating
8. (C) control

GERUNDS AND INFINITIVES

Gerunds and Infinitives I

1. (B)
2. (C)
3. (C)
4. (A)
5. (B)
6. (D)
7. (B)
8. (C)

Gerunds and Infinitives II

1. (D) smoking
2. (A) Commuting. . .and fighting
3. (D) to succeed
4. (A) appreciated your contributing
5. (D) verbalizing
6. (B) putting
7. (C) mind smoking
8. (C) (to) anticipate

PARTICIPLES

Participle Form

1. (B)
2. (D)
3. (A)
4. (D)
5. (D)
6. (A)
7. (B)
8. (A)

Explanatory Answers 379

CONDITIONALS

Conditionals I

1. (C)
2. (A)
3. (B)
4. (C)
5. (C)
6. (D)
7. (A)
8. (B)
9. (C)
10. (A)

Conditionals II

1. (B) would have accepted
2. (D) has
3. (C) would not have ventured
4. (A) were available
5. (C) veto
6. (C) not be
7. (A) had followed
8. (B) would have enjoyed
9. (C) will be
10. (C) agree

COMPARISONS

Comparisons I

1. (A)
2. (D)
3. (C)
4. (B)
5. (C)
6. (A)
7. (A)
8. (C)
9. (A)
10. (B)

Comparisons II

1. (A) longer
2. (A) the easiest
3. (D) as close as
4. (B) directly
5. (D) than male
6. (A) rapid (or very rapid)
7. (B) fewer
8. (A) close enough
9. (A) more
10. (C) lower

SUBJUNCTIVE

Subjunctive I

1. (B)
2. (A)
3. (D)
4. (C)
5. (D)
6. (A)
7. (D)
8. (B)
9. (A)
10. (C)

Subjunctive II

1. (C) have
2. (A) be cut
3. (B) be emphasized
4. (D) include
5. (A) pay
6. (B) reflect
7. (B) be
8. (D) suggest
9. (A) applicant be a college graduate
10. (B) groups accept

WORD FAMILIES

Word Families I

1. (B)
2. (D)
3. (D)
4. (B)
5. (D)
6. (A)
7. (A)
8. (C)
9. (D)
10. (A)

Word Families II

1. (D) commercial
2. (A) carefully
3. (B) wooden
4. (B) loyally
5. (B) massive
6. (C) abundance
7. (B) warning
8. (D) comment
9. (D) immediately
10. (D) suspended

ACTIVE/PASSIVE VERBS

Active/Passive I

1. (C)
2. (C)
3. (C)
4. (B)
5. (D)
6. (A)
7. (B)
8. (C)
9. (B)
10. (A)

Active/Passive II

1. (C) project was completed
2. (D) stresses caused
3. (B) inserted
4. (A) applied
5. (B) be removed
6. (B) propelled
7. (D) to be emulated
8. (A) detected
9. (A) are taken
10. (C) have not been placed

GRAMMAR REVIEW

Grammar Review I

1. (C) Passive voice: *(to be + past participle form)*
2. (B) Passive voice: The river banks cannot protect themselves.
3. (B) Subject-verb agreement: *Children...earn more money as adults*
4. (A) Comparative form: *...as (adjective) as*
5. (A) Prepositional phrase (idiomatic phrase): *by the hour*
6. (C) Reduced adjective clause: *illnesses (that are) added together*
7. (B) Conjunction: check word meanings
8. (C) Reduced adjective clause: *(which is) believed by many*
9. (B) Noun clause: *(the reason) why the dinosaur became*
10. (B) Conjunction: check word meanings
11. (B) Word order: structure for emphasis
12. (B) Parallelism: *(local), regional, and international*
13. (D) Possessive form: (the roots of the maple tree) = *its roots*
14. (D) Noun clause: *(that) it isn't easy*
15. (B) Word form/subject-verb agreement: *(There is) no difference*
16. (B) Comparative form: *is much (heavier) than*
17. (C) Article: No article is used in a general statement.
18. (D) Word family: *its* (noun)
19. (B) Adjective clause: pronoun + verb
20. (D) Prepositions: see *span*

Grammar Review II

1. (D) Parallelism: adverb forms: change to *instantly*
2. (B) Active voice: *The fences (surrounded) the bases.*
3. (A) Articles: *is (a) well-known architect*
4. (C) Passive voice: *has been greatly affected (by)*
5. (A) Comparative forms: superlative: change to *most*
6. (A) Word form: change to *chewing*
7. (A) Verb omission: *who (is) an inventor*
8. (B) Possessive adjectives: change to *his* or *her*
9. (C) Noun clause: missing marker: *on what caused the Ice Age*
10. (A) Conjunctions: check word meaning
11. (A) Adjective form: change to *hard-working* or *hard working*
12. (C) Parallelism: infinitive forms: change to *give descriptions*
13. (A) Pronouns: the subject is *It*
14. (B) Pronouns: change *it* to *there*
15. (A) Word order: change to *is it*
16. (B) Comparative form: adjectives; delete *as*
17. (B) Subject-verb agreement: *The practice... (is) not*
18. (B) Comparative form: adjectives: *has (more) trees*
19. (B) Verb tense: simple present: change to *was*
20. (C) Word family: adjective form: change to *characterized*

Explanatory Answers 381

VOCABULARY TARGETS

Synonyms

1. (D)	10. (B)	19. (B)	28. (C)
2. (A)	11. (B)	20. (A)	29. (B)
3. (A)	12. (A)	21. (D)	30. (A)
4. (B)	13. (D)	22. (A)	31. (D)
5. (C)	14. (B)	23. (C)	32. (D)
6. (D)	15. (A)	24. (A)	33. (A)
7. (D)	16. (A)	25. (B)	34. (D)
8. (A)	17. (D)	26. (D)	35. (C)
9. (B)	18. (C)	27. (B)	

Prefixes

1. (A)	6. (D)	11. (D)	16. (D)
2. (D)	7. (C)	12. (A)	17. (D)
3. (D)	8. (C)	13. (A)	18. (B)
4. (B)	9. (B)	14. (B)	19. (D)
5. (D)	10. (C)	15. (D)	20. (B)

General Vocabulary

1. (C)	6. (A)	11. (B)	16. (C)
2. (B)	7. (C)	12. (B)	17. (C)
3. (A)	8. (D)	13. (C)	18. (A)
4. (D)	9. (A)	14. (A)	19. (C)
5. (D)	10. (C)	15. (A)	20. (B)

READING TARGETS ANSWER KEY

Strategy-Building Activities

1. (C)
2. (B)
3. (D)
4. (A)
5. (A)
6. (D)
7. (A)
8. (A)
9. (A)
10. (B)

HUMANITIES

1. (C) Main idea
2. (D) Factual: positive
3. (B) Factual: positive
4. (C) Written expression
5. (B) Organization
6. (B) Written expression
7. (C) Main idea
8. (C) Organization
9. (A) Main idea
10. (C) Viewpoint
11. (C) Written expression
12. (A) Follow-on
13. (D) Main idea
14. (A) Factual: negative
15. (B) Factual: positive
16. (B) Factual: positive
17. (C) Inference: specific
18. (C) Factual: positive

HISTORY

1. (D) Main idea
2. (B) Factual: positive
3. (A) Viewpoint
4. (A) Written expression
5. (C) Written expression
6. (D) Factual: positive
7. (C) Analogy
8. (D) Factual: positive
9. (B) Inference: general
10. (B) Inference: specific
11. (C) Factual: positive
12. (A) Inference: specific
13. (D) Factual: positive

EDUCATION

1. (B) Viewpoint
2. (C) Factual: positive
3. (A) Factual: positive
4. (B) Viewpoint
5. (A) Viewpoint
6. (A) Follow-on
7. (C) Factual: positive
8. (B) Main idea
9. (C) Factual: positive
10. (B) Organization
11. (B) Written expression
12. (B) Viewpoint
13. (C) Main idea
14. (B) Factual: positive
15. (C) Analogy
16. (D) Inference: specific
17. (D) Written expression
18. (A) Viewpoint

SCIENCE

1. (C) Main idea
2. (B) Factual: positive
3. (D) Factual: negative
4. (B) Inference: general
5. (D) Factual: positive
6. (C) Factual: positive
7. (C) Main idea
8. (A) Factual: positive
9. (C) Written expression
10. (C) Organization
11. (D) Organization
12. (D) Factual: positive
13. (C) Factual: positive
14. (B) Viewpoint
15. (B) Factual: positive

APPLIED SCIENCE

1. (C) Factual: positive
2. (A) Main idea
3. (D) Viewpoint
4. (C) Factual: negative
5. (C) Analogy
6. (A) Written expression
7. (C) Main idea
8. (A) Inference: general
9. (B) Factual: positive
10. (A) Viewpoint
11. (D) Inference: general
12. (D) Written expression
13. (C) Main idea
14. (B) Factual: positive
15. (A) Written expression
16. (C) Factual: negative

GENERAL READINGS

1. (B) Main idea
2. (B) Main idea
3. (B) Factual: positive
4. (D) Written expression
5. (B) Written expression
6. (C) Inference: specific
7. (C) Factual: positive
8. (C) Factual: positive
9. (B) Inference: general
10. (B) Main idea
11. (D) Main idea
12. (B) Factual: positive
13. (C) Viewpoint
14. (B) Factual: positive
15. (B) Factual: positive

ANSWER SHEETS

ANSWER SHEET FOR PRACTICE TEST 1

Tear this sheet out and use it to mark your answers.

SECTION 1
LISTENING COMPREHENSION

SECTION 2
STRUCTURE AND WRITTEN EXPRESSION

SECTION 3
READING COMPREHENSION AND VOCABULARY

ANSWER SHEET FOR PRACTICE TEST 2

Tear this sheet out and use it to mark your answers.

SECTION 1
LISTENING COMPREHENSION

SECTION 2
STRUCTURE AND WRITTEN EXPRESSION

SECTION 3
READING COMPREHENSION AND VOCABULARY

ANSWER SHEET FOR PRACTICE TEST 3

Tear this sheet out and use it to mark your answers.

SECTION 1
LISTENING COMPREHENSION

SECTION 2
STRUCTURE AND WRITTEN EXPRESSION

SECTION 3
READING COMPREHENSION AND VOCABULARY

ANSWER SHEET FOR PRACTICE TEST 4

Tear this sheet out and use it to mark your answers.

SECTION 1
LISTENING COMPREHENSION

SECTION 2
STRUCTURE AND WRITTEN EXPRESSION

SECTION 3
READING COMPREHENSION AND VOCABULARY

ANSWER SHEET FOR PRACTICE TEST 5

Tear this sheet out and use it to mark your answers.

SECTION 1
LISTENING COMPREHENSION

SECTION 2
STRUCTURE AND WRITTEN EXPRESSION

SECTION 3
READING COMPREHENSION AND VOCABULARY

ANSWER SHEET FOR PRACTICE TEST 6

Tear this sheet out and use it to mark your answers.

SECTION 1
LISTENING COMPREHENSION

SECTION 2
STRUCTURE AND WRITTEN EXPRESSION

SECTION 3
READING COMPREHENSION AND VOCABULARY

ANSWER SHEET FOR LISTENING TARGET EXERCISES

Tear this sheet out and use it to mark your answers.

Statements

Similar Sounds	Number Discrimination	Synonyms	Negation
1. A B C D	1. A B C D	1. A B C D	1. A B C D
2. A B C D	2. A B C D	2. A B C D	2. A B C D
3. A B C D	3. A B C D	3. A B C D	3. A B C D
4. A B C D	4. A B C D	4. A B C D	4. A B C D
5. A B C D	5. A B C D	5. A B C D	5. A B C D

Contextual References	Cause and Effect	Conditionals	Chronological Order	Comparisons
1. A B C D	1. A B C D	1. A B C D	1. A B C D	1. A B C D
2. A B C D	2. A B C D	2. A B C D	2. A B C D	2. A B C D
3. A B C D	3. A B C D	3. A B C D	3. A B C D	3. A B C D
4. A B C D	4. A B C D	4. A B C D	4. A B C D	4. A B C D
5. A B C D	5. A B C D	5. A B C D	5. A B C D	5. A B C D

Short Dialogs

Similar Sounds	Number Discrimination	Synonyms	Negation
1. A B C D	1. A B C D	1. A B C D	1. A B C D
2. A B C D	2. A B C D	2. A B C D	2. A B C D
3. A B C D	3. A B C D	3. A B C D	3. A B C D
4. A B C D	4. A B C D	4. A B C D	4. A B C D
5. A B C D	5. A B C D	5. A B C D	5. A B C D

Contextual References	Cause and Effect	Conditionals	Chronological Order	Comparisons
1. A B C D	1. A B C D	1. A B C D	1. A B C D	1. A B C D
2. A B C D	2. A B C D	2. A B C D	2. A B C D	2. A B C D
3. A B C D	3. A B C D	3. A B C D	3. A B C D	3. A B C D
4. A B C D	4. A B C D	4. A B C D	4. A B C D	4. A B C D
5. A B C D	5. A B C D	5. A B C D	5. A B C D	5. A B C D

Mini-Talks and Dialogs

Mini-Talks

1. A B C D	11. A B C D
2. A B C D	12. A B C D
3. A B C D	13. A B C D
4. A B C D	14. A B C D
5. A B C D	15. A B C D
6. A B C D	16. A B C D
7. A B C D	17. A B C D
8. A B C D	18. A B C D
9. A B C D	19. A B C D
10. A B C D	

Dialogs

1. A B C D	11. A B C D
2. A B C D	12. A B C D
3. A B C D	13. A B C D
4. A B C D	14. A B C D
5. A B C D	15. A B C D
6. A B C D	16. A B C D
7. A B C D	17. A B C D
8. A B C D	
9. A B C D	
10. A B C D	

© 1992 by REGENTS/PRENTICE HALL, A Division of Simon & Schuster, Englewood Cliffs, New Jersey 07632

ANSWER SHEET FOR STRUCTURE TARGET EXERCISES

Tear this sheet out and use it to mark your answers.

Subject

Omitted
Repeated

Verb

Omitted
Unnecessary Form

Verb con't.

Inappropriate Verb Tense
Extra Exercises

Subject-Verb Agreement

Agreement I
Agreement II

Articles

Articles I
Articles II

Word Order

Subject and Verb Placement
Adjective and Adverb Placement I
Adjective and Adverb Placement II

Pronouns

Agreement
Form
Extra Exercises

Prepositions

Prepositions I
Prepositions II

Answer Sheets: Structure Targets   399

Subordinate Clauses

Noun Clauses I — **Adjective Clauses I** — **Adjective Clauses II** — **Adverb Clauses I** — **Adverb Clauses II**

(Answer bubbles 1–10 for Noun Clauses I; 1–8 for Adjective Clauses I; 1–10 for Adjective Clauses II; 1–8 for Adverb Clauses I; 1–8 for Adverb Clauses II, each with options A B C D)

Reduced Adjective Clauses I — **Reduced Adjective Clauses II** — **Reduced Adverb Clauses I** — **Reduced Adverb Clauses II**

Parallel Structures and Conjunctions

Parallel Structures

(Answer bubbles 1–8 for Reduced Adjective Clauses I; 1–10 for Reduced Adjective Clauses II; 1–10 for Reduced Adverb Clauses I; 1–10 for Reduced Adverb Clauses II; 1–8 for Parallel Structures, each with options A B C D)

Gerunds and Infinitives

Gerunds and Infinitives I — **Gerunds and Infinitives II**

Participles

Participle Form

(Answer bubbles 1–8 each with options A B C D)

Conditionals

Conditionals I — **Conditionals II**

Comparisons

Comparisons I — **Comparisons II**

(Answer bubbles 1–10 each with options A B C D)

Answer Sheets: Structure Targets 401

© 1992 by REGENTS/PRENTICE HALL. A Division of Simon & Schuster, Englewood Cliffs, New Jersey 07632

Subjunctive

Subjunctive I

	A	B	C	D
1.	Ⓐ	Ⓑ	Ⓒ	Ⓓ
2.	Ⓐ	Ⓑ	Ⓒ	Ⓓ
3.	Ⓐ	Ⓑ	Ⓒ	Ⓓ
4.	Ⓐ	Ⓑ	Ⓒ	Ⓓ
5.	Ⓐ	Ⓑ	Ⓒ	Ⓓ
6.	Ⓐ	Ⓑ	Ⓒ	Ⓓ
7.	Ⓐ	Ⓑ	Ⓒ	Ⓓ
8.	Ⓐ	Ⓑ	Ⓒ	Ⓓ
9.	Ⓐ	Ⓑ	Ⓒ	Ⓓ
10.	Ⓐ	Ⓑ	Ⓒ	Ⓓ

Subjunctive II

	A	B	C	D
1.	Ⓐ	Ⓑ	Ⓒ	Ⓓ
2.	Ⓐ	Ⓑ	Ⓒ	Ⓓ
3.	Ⓐ	Ⓑ	Ⓒ	Ⓓ
4.	Ⓐ	Ⓑ	Ⓒ	Ⓓ
5.	Ⓐ	Ⓑ	Ⓒ	Ⓓ
6.	Ⓐ	Ⓑ	Ⓒ	Ⓓ
7.	Ⓐ	Ⓑ	Ⓒ	Ⓓ
8.	Ⓐ	Ⓑ	Ⓒ	Ⓓ
9.	Ⓐ	Ⓑ	Ⓒ	Ⓓ
10.	Ⓐ	Ⓑ	Ⓒ	Ⓓ

Word Families

Word Families I — items 1–10, options A B C D

Word Families II — items 1–10, options A B C D

Active/Passive Verbs

Active/Passive I — items 1–10, options A B C D

Active/Passive II — items 1–10, options A B C D

Grammar Review

Grammar Review I — items 1–20, options A B C D

Grammar Review II — items 1–20, options A B C D

© 1992 by REGENTS/PRENTICE HALL. A Division of Simon & Schuster, Englewood Cliffs, New Jersey 07632

ANSWER SHEET FOR VOCABULARY TARGET EXERCISES

Tear this sheet out and use it to mark your answers.

Synonyms and **Prefixes** and **General Vocabulary** bubble answer sheets (A B C D) for numbered items.

ANSWER SHEET FOR READING TARGET EXERCISES
Tear this sheet out and use it to mark your answers.

Strategy-Building Activities, **Humanities**, **History**, **Education**, **Science**, **Applied Science**, **General Readings**

Personal Study Plan

Listening Targets   Practice Tests

STATEMENTS	1	2	3	4	5	6
Similar Sounds						
Number Discrimination						
Synonyms						
Negation						
Contextual Reference						
Cause and Effect						
Conditionals						
Chronological Order						
Comparisons						
SHORT DIALOGS						
Similar Sounds						
Number Discrimination						
Synonyms						
Negation						
Contextual Reference						
Cause and Effect						
Conditionals						
Chronological Order						
Comparisons						
MINI-TALKS						
Mini-Talks						
Dialogs						

Structure Targets   Practice Tests

Structure	1	2	3	4	5	6
Subject Omitted						
Subject Repeated						
Verb Omitted						
Verb: Unnecessary Form						
Verb: Inappropriate Tense						
Verb: Subject-Verb Agreement						
Articles						
Word Order: Subject-Verb						
W/O: Adjective/Adverb Placement						
Pronouns: Agreement						
Pronouns: Form						
Prepositions						
Noun Clauses						
Adjective Clauses						
Adverb Clauses						
Reduced Adjective Clauses						
Reduced Adverb Clauses						
Parallel Structures						
Gerunds and Infinitives						
Participle Form						
Conditionals						
Comparisons						
Subjunctive						
Word Families						
Active/Passive Verbs						